Software Design
for Microprocessors

John G. Wester

Texas Instruments Learning Center

William D. Simpson

Staff Consultant, Texas Instruments
Learning Center

This book has been prepared by the staff of the Texas Instruments Learning Center. Special acknowledgement is made to staff members of other organizations within Texas Instruments that made invaluable contributions in the form of example problems, specifications and applications data.

Digital Circuits Division — SBP0400

Dick Horton
Robert Bergeler
Gerald McGee

MOS Division — TMS 1000

Charles Brixey

Digital Systems Division — TMS 8080, TMS 9900

Lynn King
Steve Flannigan
Henry Armus

PREFACE

At the time of this writing, the term "Microprocessor" has become the new buzzword in the electronics industry. The manufacturers of digital integrated circuits have made the transition to large scale integration (LSI) in which the number of gates per square unit of silicon continues to increase almost logarithmically with time. The first major impact of LSI was in memories. As semiconductor memories became competitive with core memories and their use expanded, prices continued to drop and a new opportunity for the use of digital technology appeared. Advances in LSI (especially MOS technology) made it possible for the arithmetic and logic functions as well as the control functions of a computer to be implemented in a single LSI chip (now generally called a microprocessor). By combining these two fundamental units of a computer with semiconductor memories, LSI computing became a technological reality. The market expanded and as more and more semiconductor manufacturers introduced microprocessors, prices began to follow the traditional semiconductor learning curve downward, making microprocessors and LSI computing an economic reality. The outlook is for this trend to continue making the microprocessor the most cost effective solution to an ever increasing number of applications.

Opportunities for applications of microprocessors and LSI computing lie all around us . . . . from process control, to automotive control, to data processing, and even to games. The market for microprocessors and their end products are inestimable at the dawning of this new era. To understand this, we need only be reminded that the markets for computers and copiers were likewise inestimable at the time of their introduction.

Because microprocessor applications will be so numerous, and because the applications are *computer like*, there must be a change in the thought processes on the part of designers to take full advantage of these new computing elements. A substantial part of the design cycle will be the generation of programs (software). One set of microprocessor and memory devices can be used in a variety of applications, the only change being the program or the sequence of instructions the unit will execute.

This book was written to assist technical and non-technical people in taking their first steps toward designing with microprocessors and related software. Topics range from the basics of binary numbers to complex examples of microprocessor applications. Although this book was written primarily for those with little or no programming experience, even seasoned programmers will find the applications examples challenging as well as educational. It is hoped that a significant number of the readers of this book will accept the challenge to learn more about microprocessors and software design, and ultimately will benefit from their participation in this new and exciting era.

CONTENTS

Chapter		*Title*	*Page*

INTRODUCTION . . . . *xi*

1.   BASIC CONCEPTS 1-1

    1.1   General 1-1

    1.2   Definition 1-1

    1.3   Machine Architecture 1-2

        1.3.1   Control Unit 1-3

        1.3.2   Arithmetic and Logic Unit 1-5

        1.3.3   Memory Unit 1-6

        1.3.4   Input/Output Unit 1-8

        1.3.5   Special Architectural Features 1-8

    1.4   Software 1-13

        1.4.1   Notation Methods 1-14

        1.4.2   Instructions 1-16

        1.4.3   Instruction Classification 1-16

        1.4.4   Formats 1-17

        1.4.5   Multifunction Instructions 1-18

        1.4.6   Timing 1-18

        1.4.7   Summary 1-18

    1.5   Addressing 1-19

        1.5.1   Immediate Addressing 1-19

        1.5.2   Direct Addressing 1-19

        1.5.3   Indirect Addressing 1-21

        1.5.4   Relative Addressing 1-21

2.   HOW TO BUILD SOFTWARE 2-1

    2.1   Software Design 2-1

    2.2   Concept Definition 2-1

    2.3   Flowcharting 2-1

        2.3.1   Concept-Level Flow Chart 2-2

        2.3.2   Algorithm-Level Flow Chart 2-2

    2.4   Algorithm Development 2-6

        2.4.1   Simple Algorithm Development 2-6

        2.4.2   Complex Algorithm Partitioning . . . 2-10

    2.5   Coding Techniques 2-12

        2.5.1   Machine Code Programming 2-12

        2.5.2   Assembler Programming 2-15

        2.5.3   Versatile Programming Aids 2-17

    2.6   Software Utility Routines 2-21

    2.7   Timing Concepts 2-21

    2.8   Summary 2-22

3.   SUPPORT AND DOCUMENTATION FOR SOFTWARE 3-1

    3.1   General 3-1

    3.2   Microprocessor Logistics Selection Factors 3-4

    3.3   Host Computer Software Development System 3-5

CONTENTS (Continued)

Chapter				*Title*	*Page*
3.	3.3	3.3.1	Advantages		3-7
		3.3.2	Disadvantages		3-7
	3.4		Microprocessor-Based Software Development System		3-7
		3.4.1	Advantages		3-8
		3.4.2	Disadvantages		3-8
	3.5		Input/Output Techniques		3-9
		3.5.1	Input		3-9
		3.5.2	Output		3-9
	3.6		Documentation		3-9
	3.7		Summary		3-10
4.			MECHANICS OF PROGRAMMING		4-1
	4.1		A Sample Microprocessor Software Design		4-1
	4.2		System Definition		4-1
		4.2.1	Problem Statement		4-1
		4.2.2	Algorithm Development		4-2
		4.2.3	Timing Concepts		4-4
	4.3		Flowcharting		4-7
		4.3.1	Concept Flow Chart		4-7
		4.3.2	Algorithm Flow Chart		4-7
	4.4		Hardware Definition		4-13
		4.4.1	Figment 4 Architecture		4-13
		4.4.2	Figment 4 Instructions		4-15
		4.4.3	Figment 4 Addressing		4-16
		4.4.4	Figment 4 Timing		4-16
		4.4.5	Figment 4 Instruction Decode and Control		4-16
	4.5		Instruction-Level Flow Chart		4-16
		4.5.1	Timing Flow Chart		4-23
	4.6		Coding		4-24
	4.7		Assembly Process		4-31
	4.8		Object Code – Program Loading/Storage		4-33
	4.9		Summary		4-33
5.			MICROPROCESSOR SAMPLE DESIGN PROBLEMS		5-1
	5.1		TMS 1000 Problem		5-1
		5.1.1	Problem Statement – Electronic Taxi Meter		5-1
		5.1.2	Hardware Definition		5-1
		5.1.3	Software Definition and Flow Charts		5-3
		5.1.4	Example Problem Flow Chart		5-5
		5.1.5	Example Problem Coding		5-10
		5.1.6	Software Assembly Listing		5-11
		5.1.7	TTL Implementation of TMS 1000 Problem		5-11
	5.2		TMS 8080 Problem		5-18
		5.2.1	Problem Statement – Badge Reading System		5-18
		5.2.2	Hardware Definition		5-18
		5.2.3	Understanding the TMS 8080 Microprocessor		5-20
		5.2.4	Understanding the TMS 5501 Interface Chip		5-32
		5.2.5	Software Development		5-32
		5.2.6	Software System Concept		5-34
		5.2.7	Example Problem Flow Chart		5-36

CONTENTS (Concluded)

Chapter			*Title*	*Page*
5.	5.2	5.2.8	Example Problem Coding	5-37
		5.2.9	Detailed Software Flow Charts	5-37
		5.2.10	Interrupt Details	5-42
		5.2.11	Assembly Listing of Software	5-57
	5.3		TMS 9900 Problem	5-71
		5.3.1	Problem Statement	5-71
		5.3.2	Hardware Definition	5-71
		5.3.3	Software Definition	5-73
		5.3.4	Flow Chart	5-77
		5.3.5	Problem Coding	5-77
	5.4		SBP0400 Problem	5-85
		5.4.1	Problem Statement	5-85
		5.4.2	Problem Description	5-85
		5.4.3	Example Problem Flow Chart	5-85
		5.4.4	Example Problem	5-89
		5.4.5	Microinstruction Flow Description	5-89
		5.4.6	Coding	5-97
	5.5		Summary	5-99

APPENDICES

	A.	NUMBER SYSTEMS AND BINARY ARITHMETIC	A-1
	B.	BOOLEAN ALGEBRA	B-1
	C.	TABLES AND DATA	C-1
	D.	FLOW CHART SYMBOLS	D-1
	E.	VARIOUS TEXAS INSTRUMENTS PUBLICATIONS	E-1

GLOSSARY G-1

ILLUSTRATIONS

Figure	Title	Page
1.1	Basic Boolean Concepts	1-2
1.2	Basic Architectural Element Interconnections	1-4
1.3	Typical Register	1-5
1.4	Special Registers	1-9
1.5	Special Register Information Flow	1-10
1.6	Expanded Information Flow	1-11
1.7	Microprogram Concept	1-12
1.8	Stack Concept	1-12
1.9	Stack and Stack Pointer	1-13
1.10	Binary-Hexadecimal Representation	1-15
1.11	Addressing Modes — Immediate and Direct	1-20
1.12	Addressing Modes — Indirect and Relative	1-22
1.13	Addressing Example	1-23
2.1	Concept-Level Flow Chart — Polled I/O	2-3
2.2	Concept-Level Flow Chart — Interrupt I/O	2-4
2.3	Algorithm-Level Flow Chart (for Step 4 of Figure 2.1)	2-5
2.4	Instruction-Level Flow Chart (for Steps 2-6 of Figure 2.3)	2-7
2.5	Simple Feedback Control System	2-8
2.6	Algorithm for Control System of Figure 2.5	2-9
2.7	Wait Loop Algorithm	2-10
2.8	Generalized Microprocessor System	2-11
2.9	Flow Chart for Coding Examples	2-13
2.10	Subroutine Use	2-18
2.11	Use of Index Register	2-20
3.1	Software Programming Steps	3-2
3.2	Software Development	3-3
3.3	Processing Steps Using Large-Scale Computers	3-6
4.1	Microprocessor Message Switcher	4-2
4.2	Character Timing	4-3
4.3	Character Timing Concept	4-5
4.4	Instruction Timing and Time Delay	4-6
4.5	Concept Level Flow Chart	4-8
4.6	Algorithm Flow Chart	4-9
4.7	Figment 4 Architecture	4-14
4.8	Figment 4 Instruction Format	4-17
4.9	Instruction Level Flow Chart	4-18
5.1	System Diagram	5-2
5.2	RAM Data Map	5-4
5.3	Initialization Flow Chart	5-5
5.4	Executive Flow Chart	5-6
5.5	Count Flow Chart	5-7
5.6	Example Problem Flow Chart (Blank)	5-8
5.7	Example Problem Flow Chart (Completed)	5-9
5.8	Example Coding Sheet (Blank)	5-10

ILLUSTRATIONS (Continued)

Figure	*Title*	*Page*
5.9	TTL Implementation Block Diagram	5-15
5.10	Timing Diagram	5-16
5.11	Access Control System Block Diagram	5-19
5.12	Address Decode	5-21
5.13	Central Processing Unit	5-22
5.14	ROM and RAM Chips	5-23
5.15	Interrupt Circuit	5-24
5.16	I/O Badge Reader Interface	5-25
5.17	Location Identification Switches	5-26
5.18	Sensor Selector	5-27
5.19	Clock Circuit	5-28
5.20	Example Problem Flow Chart (Blank)	5-38
5.21	Coding Form (Blank)	5-39
5.22	System Setup	5-40
5.23	Badge Read	5-41
5.24	End Sequence	5-42
5.25	Example of Interrupt Processing	5-43
5.26	System Setup and Interrupts	5-44
5.27	Timer Interrupt	5-45
5.28	Interrupts	5-46
5.29	System Setup	5-47
5.30	Badge Read	5-51
5.31	End Sequence	5-54
5.32	733 ASR Line Assignments	5-72
5.33	Program Flow Chart	5-78
5.34	SBP0400-Based Security Access System	5-86
5.35	I/O Control Block Diagram	5-87
5.36	Macroinstruction Flow Chart	5-88
5.37	Microinstruction Flow Chart	5-90
5.38	Example Problem Flow Chart (Blank)	5-92
5.39	Coding Sheet (Partial)	5-93

TABLES

Table	Title	Page
1.1	Sequence of Operations	1-10
1.2	Common High-Level Languages (Circa, 1975)	1-14
1.3	Typical Instruction Groups	1-17
1.4	Addressing Modes	1-19
2.1	BCD-to-Binary Conversion	2-12
2.2	Absolute Address Coding — Input Test Routine	2-14
2.3	Use of Index Register	2-15
2.4	Instructions for Clearing the Five Tables of Figure 2.11	2-21
4.1	Time Delays for Various Values of a and b	4-23
4.2	Valid Numbers for Time Units	4-24
4.3	Figment 4 Instruction Set	4-25
4.4	Complete Program Listing	4-26
4.5	Counting by Four in Hexadecimal	4-31
5.1	Instruction Subset	5-11
5.2	Power Up Initialization Routine	5-12
5.3	Executive Routine	5-13
5.4	Count Routine	5-14
5.5	TTL Devices and Quantities	5-17
5.6	Program Control Instructions	5-31
5.7	Instructions Used in the Design Example	5-33
5.8	Memory Map	5-35
5.9	Coding Instructions	5-37
5.10	Program Counter Interrupt Instructions	5-55
5.11	Stack Content for Program Counter Trace	5-56
5.12	TMS 8080 Design Example Listing	5-58
5.13	Command Lines (733 ASR Inputs)	5-73
5.14	TTY/EIA Module Status Lines (733 ASR Outputs)	5-73
5.15	TMS 9900 IDT Sample Program	5-80
5.16	Machine Level Code	5-98

INTRODUCTION

From the beginning of time, man has sought ways to make routine jobs easier. Indeed, the whole world of invention finds its motivation in the desire of man to rise above routine, menial, time-consuming, inefficient, dull, and boring work. In order to help him in counting and calculating, man devised systems of sticks and stones and beads. The abacus, dating back to around 450 B.C., uses beads on sticks to represent numbers and it is still in use today in some parts of the world.

The first true calculating machine was designed by Pascal and completed in 1642. This unit performed calculations in base ten using a system of gears and wheels. In about 1671, Leibniz invented a more versatile machine including multiplication and division capabilities. One of the more outstanding features of this particular early machine was that it used binary arithmetic, that is the number system of base two. (Refer to Appendix A.)

In more recent times (since 1800), historians mark the inventions of Charles Babbage not only for achievement in the development of mechanical calculating equipment, but also as the point in time when the word "computer" could first be used. In fact his analytical engine is architecturally the forerunner of the modern digital computer.

The next step forward in modern computing machines was the Mark I developed by a team at Harvard University in 1944. This machine was a room-sized, electromechanical sequence-controlled, calculating machine. It was architecturally similar to the analytical engine of Babbage in that it employed binary arithmetic, and it contained the same basic computing machine elements, but in addition it was equipped with more versatile input/output capability.

Shortly after the Mark I came the invention of the ENIAC. In this system, the electromechanical logic elements of the previous machine were replaced by vacuum tubes which substantially increased the speed of calculation. Also, along about this time, in the late 1940s, additional breakthroughs were made in the development of digital systems. The first of these was the development of the stored program concept by Jon von Neumann. The second was the development of the transistor in 1948 at Bell Labs. Von Newmann's development of the stored program is extremely significant in light of the difficulty with which early calculating-type machines were changed from one program to another.

To distinguish between the material components of the computer (the hardware) and the stored program or the instruction content of the memory, the term **software** came into being. Software represents the **stored program** information, the ones and zeros that reside in a memory that instruct the machine as to its sequence of operations.

The basic concept of stored programs should be further explained in order that its importance be fully understood. The fundamental concept of storing instructions in the form of a string of ones and zeros much like binary numbers used as data are stored, means that the steps the machine will take in the execution of a particular program can easily be changed by loading new instructions into the memory. In effect, the memory is used to store both instructions and data words without any difference in content as far as the memory is concerned. Thus the control unit of the computer executes a function or "program" by reading a sequence of instructions directly from the memory. The obvious advantages are speed and completely autonomous computer control.

The stored program concept brought on the development of large memories since it was now apparent that a single-purpose memory could be employed for data and machine instructions. One of the first machines to use a stored program was the EDVAC. It was similar to preceding machines in that it contained the four basic units of the computer (memory, arithmetic unit, control unit, and I/O) and it employed binary arithmetic. The EDVAC class of machine gave birth to an industry characterized by the new philosophies of accomplishing system capabilities with hardware *and* software.

Along with the technological advances in machines, the importance of semiconductor technology cannot be overstated in its impact on computers and computing machinery. Over a hundred years had elapsed between the invention of Babbage's analytical engine and the development of the first electronic digital computer (1946). Tracking close on this event was the invention of the transistor in 1948, which was a significant achievement in electronic technology. The transistor made it economically feasible to construct large digital machines. However, only a short ten years elapsed from the invention of the transistor until the first integrated circuit was developed. Introduction of integrated circuits in 1958 was coincident with the first commercially available computers built with transistors. In other words, it took ten years for transistor technology to be fully utilized in computers. In the middle 1960s, a short five years later, computers were being introduced using integrated circuits. Table I lists the major electronic development milestones which contributed to the digital hardware evolution.

Table I. Milestones in Electronics and Computers

1883	Semiconductor diode — selenium rectification
1904	Vacuum diode
1906	Vacuum triode — electronic amplification
1946	ENIAC — first electronic calculating machine
1948	EDVAC — first stored program computer
1948	Transistor — semiconductor amplification
1951	*Univac* — first commercially produced computer
1958	Transistor computer
1958	Integrated circuit
1964	Integrated circuit computer
1964	Large scale integration
1965	Minicomputer
1970	LSI semiconductor memories
1971	Microprocessor

When systems were first designed to use integrated circuit technology, they had to be simulated in other technologies first in order to completely test or debug them before implementation. This design difficulty was expensive and time consuming. However, as semiconductor technology advanced and higher circuit integration was possible, the circuit components became less expensive and the digital computer explosion occurred. Further advances in density of circuit integration, commonly termed large-scale integration or LSI, have continued. LSI development combined with the stored program concept which launched the computer era, are giving birth to the microprocessor and microcomputer era.

This microprocessor era, characterized by the invasion of digital technology into all facets of modern life, has just begun. The economic springboard of LSI technology, as evidenced by microprocessors, will provide digital hardware at lower and lower costs and will create a literal explosion of applications. For this step function of applications to occur, a broad range of managers, designers, students, and users will have to learn more about this high circuit density technology and the concept of how the resultant components can accomplish so many diverse things through software. It is through programs stored in the modern digital machine that the machine comes to life and accomplishes a function. It is through an understanding of how these programs operate and how to create them that people will participate in this exciting revolution.

This book addresses the "how to" of learning in a "learn by doing" mode. The first chapter covers definition of terms, a study of basic machine architecture, and the fundamentals of machine instructions. The next two chapters cover the techniques of writing programs and the logistics and support required to develop software. Chapter 4 leads one through the invention of a simple computing machine and its application to a communications problem. Four sample microprocessor applications in Chapter 5 contrast the architectural capabilities and limitations of different classes of microprocessors. Comprehensive appendices contain additional basic material and useful reference data.

The treatment of software in this book is confined to machine-level and assembly-level programming. The topic of higher level language programming is left to existing texts on this subject.

CHAPTER 1

BASIC CONCEPTS

1.1 GENERAL

We may think of the world of software as a map. First of all, we must understand how to read the symbology pictured on the map. This requires that we learn the language and special terms. Second, we must understand what to expect as we go from one point to the next on the map. We must understand the route we plan to take to achieve the required functions from the many routes available. And, finally, we must achieve a proficiency with a basic map to fully understand the benefits to be gained by specialized maps, such as those portraying topography. So it is with software, that by learning the language and special terms and by studying basic programming techniques, we will gain insight into the more complex facets of the complete subject of software.

1.2 DEFINITION

We will begin by defining some terms. They are:

Bit	A contraction of "binary digit" identifying a single position in a binary number. As a binary bit, it may only be a "1" or a "0". (Also, the basic unit of information.)
Word	A string of bits, usually specified as the number of parallel bits that a computer's ALU, registers, memory, or data paths can handle.
Byte	A string of bits, usually the smallest number that can be operated on within the computer (e.g., a 16-bit word may contain two 8-bit bytes).
Character	A letter, digit, or symbol that is a representation of data. It is common to find 8-bit character codes in computer work. (Eight bits can specify $2^8 = 256$ characters or with a check bit $2^7 = 128$ characters.)

In defining the first term above, the terms "1" and "0" were used. What in themselves do these terms mean? Because we will specify a binary bit, what this "1" and "0" are really saying is, "it is easier to construct an electronic circuit that recognizes two levels, and "on" or an "off" state, rather than a circuit that recognizes ten levels such as in a decimal-counting scheme. When identifying the binary levels in electronic circuitry, there are two accepted definitions:

Positive Logic

"1" = voltage high
"0" = voltage low

Negative Logic

"1" = voltage low
"0" = voltage high

By far the more common is the positive logic convention.

How then is this world of binary arithmetic coupled to useful work? It is through the medium of Boolean algebra. Boolean algebra states the rules of accomplishing functions with just ones and zeros. Shown in Figure 1.1 are some sample Boolean functions, the AND, OR, and complement function along with truth tables for input/output relationship. For a more complete definition, refer to Appendix B. When these functions are implemented with electronic circuitry (hardware) and are coupled together into an overall solution to a complex problem, this circuit combination is called a "hardwired" solution. If the circuit implementation includes the ability to change the way these functions interact with each other by a control word, then we have software control of hardware. Put together a string of these control words and we have the same circuitry being modified by software at each step to accomplish an overall complex function. This produces a "program."

1.3 MACHINE ARCHITECTURE

In understanding how to build software programs, it is important to have a basic knowledge of the hardware. What are the basic parts? What are their features? How do they work together? What are the features of the complete system? This may be accomplished by a study of machine architecture. We will introduce only the fundamental concepts of architecture. If further detail is desired, appropriate system texts should be consulted.

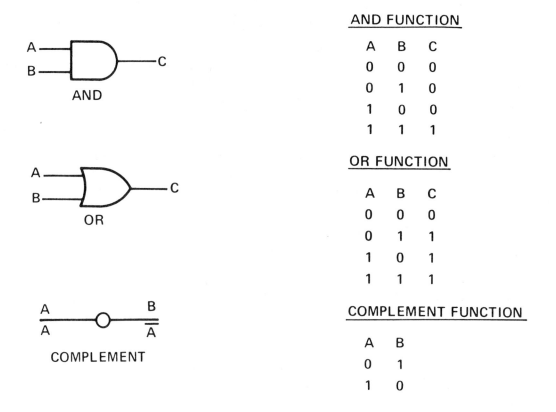

AND FUNCTION

A	B	C
0	0	0
0	1	0
1	0	0
1	1	1

OR FUNCTION

A	B	C
0	0	0
0	1	1
1	0	1
1	1	1

COMPLEMENT FUNCTION

A	B
0	1
1	0

Figure 1.1. Basic Boolean Concepts

At the concept level — what is a microprocessor/microcomputer? It is an assemblage of hardware that performs tasks in a particular programmed sequence on given inputs to obtain required outputs. In any microprocessor or minicomputer, the four fundamental architectural elements are some form of control unit, the arithmetic and logic unit (ALU), a memory, and input/output (I/O) units.

Input/output	Provides a method of communicating with exterior or peripheral units, be it another computer, a terminal, another storage device, a printer, etc., (data flow in and out).
Memory	Stores data and programs as binary words. (The memory does not know which is data and which is program.)
Control	Decodes the instruction and generates the signals necessary to make the ALU or the total assembly (microcomputer or computer) accomplish the function.
ALU	Performs the arithmetic and logic functions directed by the controller on data presented to it by memory or input/output.

Figure 1.2 shows two types of interconnections of these four basic building blocks. In Figure 1.2(a), the input/output unit is able to store information in the memory. From there it may be operated on by the arithmetic unit and results stored in the memory, and subsequently, the memory data may be sent to the output unit for interfacing to the other equipment. The second configuration in Figure 1.2(b) shows a more common architectural organization in which the memory and I/O circuits are on a common bus structure. A unidirectional (one-way) address bus enables the control unit to select any word of memory or any I/O position with a unique combination of ones and zeros on this bus. The data bus is bidirectional (two-way) and allows transfer of information from the I/O into the memory or into the arithmetic and logic unit, as well as transfers of information between the memory and the ALU or the input/output unit. The significance of this architecture is that it enables the system designer to consider the input/output circuits in exactly the same manner as he considers memory. That is, the input/output storage registers of the I/O unit are given addresses in exactly the same way as each unique word in the memory is given an address.

1.3.1 Control Unit

In early calculating machines, the control unit included not only the driving, timing, and synchronizing elements, but also the program, or the sequential steps that were to be undertaken for a given problem. In modern digital computers, the program is stored in the memory so the control unit must include instruction addressing and decoding logic. At startup time, the control unit supplies to the memory the address of the first instruction to be executed. The memory responds by sending a word of data along the data bus to the control unit. This is an instruction fetch cycle. This information is interpreted by the instruction decode logic and the appropriate action is taken. One example would be an instruction to "load the accumulator with a given word from memory." In this case, the control unit would send the address of that data word to the memory, the memory would respond by putting that word of information on the data bus and the control unit would effect the storing of that information in the accumulator register of the ALU. This is the instruction execute cycle. At the completion of each instruction, the control unit must have developed the address of the next instruction to be executed and sent that address to the memory. Thus, the instruction fetch and execute cycles normally alternate one after another.

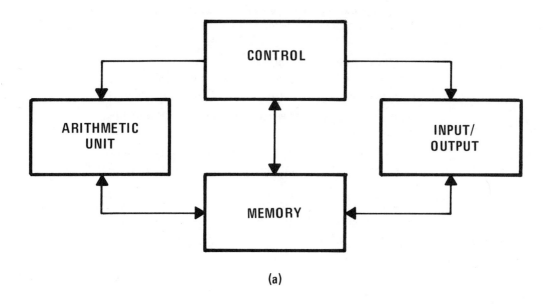

(a)

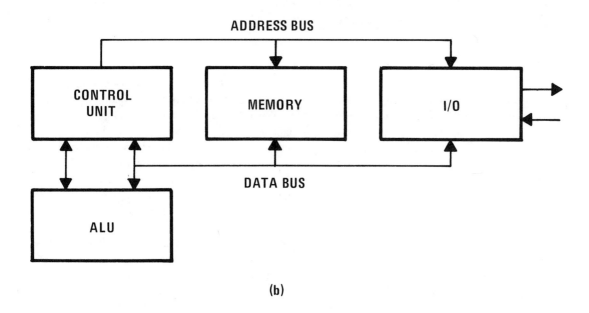

(b)

Figure 1.2. Basic Architectural Element Interconnections

1.3.2 Arithmetic and Logic Unit

The arithmetic and logic unit (ALU) contains the logic circuits to implement the fundamental arithmetic and logic functions such as adding, shifting, complementing, etc. Thus, this is the unit that accomplishes the previously discussed Boolean functions on the data of interest.

Frequently discussions refer to various circuits called registers. For purposes of this discussion, think of a register as a circuit having the ability to store a binary word. Typically a register may have features that allow information to be transferred to the input or output in parallel or in serial format from either end as shown in Figure 1.3. An accumulator is a register that holds current data or receives the results of an arithmetic operation on data. The ALU may contain one or more accumulators which typically have at least as many bits as the memory words. However, some designs provide double-length accumulators to facilitate double-precision arithmetic required in such operations as multiplication. (Refer to Appendix B.) The ALU may also include one or more working registers in which intermediate results are stored temporarily.

From a programming standpoint, the arithmetic unit is the focal point of most of the instructions in a digital machine. Fundamentally, these instructions may be loading and storing data (called operands); arithmetic instructions, such as add and subtract; logic instructions, such as AND, OR, and COMPARE (refer to Appendix B); and conditional branching instructions which test one or more bits of the accumulator as the basis for a branching decision. Sufficient logic is ordinarily included to test the content of the accumulator either bit-by-bit or for the condition of all zeros.

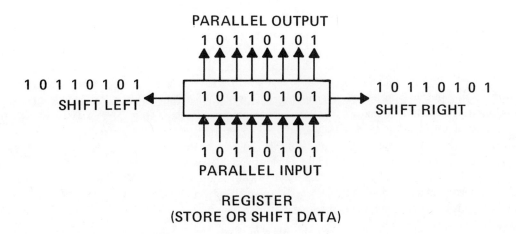

Figure 1.3. Typical Register

Although the control unit contains the basic clock and timing circuits for the internal operation of the system, frequently the system designer sees the arithmetic unit as the effective source of special timing signals. This is true because the designer can cause the ALU to consume a unit of time in an interactive program loop and then control the number of passes through the loop to gain synchronization with an element outside the machine. It is important to note also that the system designer is not as concerned about the way the arithmetic unit performs its logical function internally as about the length of time it takes to implement each instruction, the logical result of each instruction, and the impact on the control of elements outside the computer. This may be more easily understood if the two basic operating modes of digital systems, polling and interrupt, are defined. In a polling system, the control unit simply addresses through the input/output devices to determine if a transaction is required. Thus no random timing problems occur. However, in an interrupt system, events outside the control unit may need to interrupt normal operation. In this type of system, lengths of time to execute instructions and "software" timing loops (executed by the ALU as described above) take on additional importance.

In microprocessor architecture, it is common to find the control unit and the arithmetic and logic units combined in a single integrated circuit.

1.3.3 Memory Unit

The memory is the computer's general storage unit for binary information. Memories are organized into words of various lengths, such as four, eight, twelve, or sixteen bits. Both instructions and data may be stored in any sequence since there is no difference in these bits as far as the memory is concerned. General categories of information in a memory are as follows:

      Fixed instructions

      Variable instructions

      Data

      Fixed messages — characters

      Variable messages

Various technologies have been used for general-purpose random access memories (RAMs) in computers. Until the early 1970s, the primary technology for main memories was magnetic core. However, at this point in time, semiconductor memories became economically competitive with core memories despite the fact that storage in semiconductor RAMs is volatile, that is, the information is lost when the power is turned off. Techniques for overcoming memory volatility include the use of nonvolatile Read-Only Memories (ROMs), or programmable Read-Only Memories (PROMs), for storing fixed information. A read-only memory can be used to store the instructions of a program once the program has been tested thoroughly. However, a read/write memory would be required to store those instructions in which the address field is variable, as well as data for input and output. The system designer must configure his memory map with unique addresses for the read-only memory, random access memory, and I/O sections. In considering this kind of requirement, the designer is setting up his memory partitioning or memory map.

In architectures such as that shown in Figure 1.2(b), the I/O system is configured to look like memory from a programming standpoint. Thus, a unique block of addresses is set aside for the input/output unit. This is useful to facilitate transfer of bulk information between the computer and the outside world. When large or bulk memories are required for a system, such as magnetic tapes or discs, they are connected to the computer via the input/output. In this way information is transferred in large blocks from these large bulk memories to the main memory. The control unit ordinarily does not have direct control over this bulk transfer between memories. Rather a technique for control of this transfer called DMA (Direct Memory Access) is used. DMA hardware is included in the control unit to facilitate block data transfers without tieing up the rest of the machine's assets while the control unit is entirely consumed by data transfer. Thus DMA may be thought of as a specialized controller that keeps the main controller free.

It is important to have a good understanding of the terms that apply to the memory or memories of a computer. First of all, a memory is *organized* into a number of *words* of a fixed length e.g., eight or sixteen bits. A *word* is the smallest number of bits that may be *written* into, or *read* from a memory in one *cycle*. The *address* is the binary number which specifies the location of each *word* within the memory. Since the address is a string of ones and zeros and must be decoded within the memory to specify the exact word, memories are organized in such a way that the number of words within the memory is a power of two, (e.g., 1024, 2048, 4096, etc.).

In memory *cycles*, the address input lines must be set with the appropriate ones and zeros representing the specific word in the memory to be accessed. A control line for either *reading* from, or *writing* into the memory must be set, and a timing pulse must be given to start the memory cycle. The *cycle time* of a memory is the minimum amount of time between two of these start pulses. In other words, *cycle time* for a read cycle is the length of time that a memory must have to perform its entire sequence of steps from decoding the address, to presenting the data on the data lines, and being prepared for the next memory cycle. In addition, the memory will also have a write cycle time that may be different from the read cycle time. Memory *access time* is the time between a timing pulse and the arrival of data on the data lines and is generally shorter than the *cycle time*. If the *cycle time* · is one microsecond, for example, the *access time* may be 500 nanoseconds. *Access time* is applicable only to read cycles, since it refers to data being established on the data lines by the memory.

There are a number of abbreviations that refer to the memory organization concepts such as ROM, RAM, and PROM. A ROM is a read-only memory, that is, one in which data is normally not altered or modified once it is written into the memory. There will be no write cycles for a ROM. RAM (Random Access Memory) generally refers to the type of memory, the contents of which are alterable, or one in which both read and write cycles may be used. The term *random access* means that addresses may be supplied to the memory in a random fashion as opposed to sequential addressing. (It is important to recognize that ROMs are generally *random access*; however, they are not referred to as RAMs.)

The term PROM means Programmable Read-Only Memory and refers to a specific variety of ROM in which data are stored after fabrication. Generally, ROMs are programmed as a part of the manufacturing process by establishing the ones and zeros at a mask level at the time of fabrication. A PROM, on the other hand, requires special programming apparatus which allows the system designer to establish the ones or zeros in the memory cells after the memory is fabricated. One type of PROM programmer is designed to apply a pulse of sufficient voltage at certain pins to burn or fuse small strips of metal in the memory, thereby changing the content of specific memory cells from ones to zeros (or vice versa).

Aside from the terms which describe the organization of a memory, some terms apply to the fabrication technology. These are *semiconductor* memory, *core* memory, *magnetic-tape* memory, *disk* memory or *drum* memory. A nonvolatile memory is one in which the data is not lost if the power is turned off. Magnetic technologies are nonvolatile. With the exception of *read-only* memories, or programmable read-only memories, *semiconductor* memories are *volatile*, that is, the memory data is lost whenever power is removed. Battery power is often used for volatile semiconductor memories to enable the memory cells to maintain data even though the main power is interrupted.

Another group of terms refer to the way a memory is applied. These are *main* memory, *bulk* memory, *scratch-pad* memory and perhaps *bootstrap* memory. The *main* memory is the one normally accessed by the control unit to provide instructions and data for the computing process. A *scratch-pad* memory may contain a series of instructions or data to be implemented at a very high speed. A *scratch-pad* memory is normally a small, very high-speed memory for this special application. *Bulk* memory is one such as *magnetic tape, disk*, or *drum* and is not always directly accessible to the control unit. Data is transferred in fairly large blocks from *bulk* memory to *main* memory for use in the computing process. A *bootstrap* memory is generally a ROM which holds a basic instruction loading program for cold startup.

1.3.4 Input/Output Unit

The input/output (I/O) section of a digital computer performs the fundamental function of interfacing the computer to peripheral devices, such as bulk memories, paper-tape devices, teletypes, etc., and a virtually limitless number of measurement and control systems. The I/O unit normally performs parallel to serial, or serial to parallel conversions and data buffering so that data transfers into and out of the computer may be performed on a group of bits at one time. The number of bits in a single transfer is normally the number of bits in a memory word. Input and output instructions facilitate the transfer of data between the arithmetic unit or the memory and the buffers in the I/O unit. The I/O unit also performs synchronization with devices outside the computer which must transfer information at substantially different rates than that of the computer data bus. Level shifting and amplification as well as code conversion are sometimes required in the I/O unit.

In systems where the I/O unit is configured to be operated upon in the same manner as the memory, the system designer views the I/O section as an extension of memory and is able to use memory reference instructions to transfer data to and from this special block of memory addresses.

1.3.5 Special Architectural Features

A full explanation of all the ramifications of architectural features is beyond the scope of this book. However, there is a specific set of features that must be understood at a more detailed level than the generalized treatment of the previous four units. This detailed investigation may at first seem to be a group of unrelated features. However, in progressing through the book, the need for understanding these features will become clear.

1.3.5.1 Special Registers

Distributed throughout most digital machines are several special-purpose registers. Shown in Figure 1.4 are three of these registers that are of particular interest. Notice that two of the registers reside inside the domain of the control section. The first of these is the instruction register or the IR. Its purpose is to store the binary word or instruction from which the machine is currently operating. The binary word stored here is known as the present instruction. The second register is identified as the program counter (PC). The function of the program counter is to hold the binary word that represents the address of the next instruction. Typically the program counter has incrementing circuitry associated with it. The purpose of the additional circuitry is to make it easy to add one to

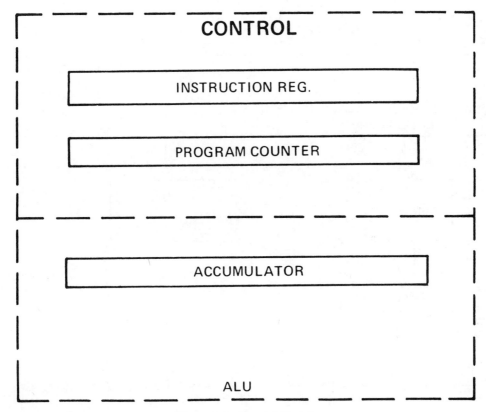

Figure 1.4. Special Registers

the present address to get the "next" address or next instruction. In some machines, additional circuitry recognizes changes of one, two, or four to the present address if the need exists. This need can be visualized by thinking of a memory organized in 8-bit words, yet the machine requires 16 or 32-bit instructions. These instructions, then, must be formulated in a serial fashion. Thus these instructions will consist of multiples of two or four memory words.

The third special register, shown in Figure 1.4, is housed in the ALU section of the machine and is called the accumulator. As mentioned previously, its purpose is to hold the current data being operated on. In addition, generally the accumulator also operates as a depository for data just operated on in the ALU. In various machines, there may be more than one accumulator and a "double-the-normal-length register" to accommodate special operations. This double-length requirement can easily be visualized by thinking of the 8-bit answer produced by multiplying two 4-bit numbers together (refer to Appendix A).

Visualize these three registers operating together by studying Figure 1.5. On startup, the machine could have circuitry that would clear the three registers. This would cause the first register, the PC to call up the instruction in memory location 0000, the first location in memory. This instruction would then be called into the IR and the machine would begin operation. From this point on the machine would execute a version of the operations shown in Table 1.1. Notice that after progressing through the sequence of four steps, the machine would return to step 1 and repeat the process.

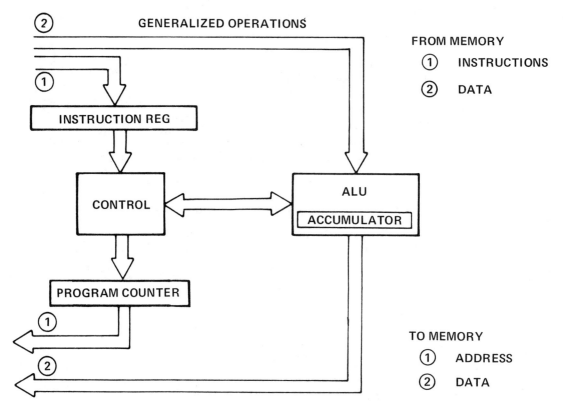

Figure 1.5. Special Register Information Flow

Table 1.1. Sequence of Operations

1. Fetch Instruction

    Generate Address
    Obtain Data

2. Decode

3. Fetch Operand

    Generate Address
    Obtain Data

4. Execute

An expanded version of Figure 1.5 is shown in Figure 1.6, notice the main memory function, a second instruction register, and a control memory have been added. If a machine has user-defined instructions or microprogramming, then the user has access to the control memory and can define what is contained in it. If, on the other hand, a machine operates from fixed instructions at the macro level, there is no access to the control memory. Therefore, we have classified one instruction register for macroinstructions and another for microinstructions. Why two levels of instruction? Simply to allow the machine to operate from higher level instructions. At the micro level, each time a clock pulse arrives, a new microinstruction must be available to tell the machine what to do. If on the other hand, a multi-clock-phase "machine cycle" that contains strings of microinstructions is the level of programming, the effort is much less tedious. Thus, machines are, in fact, programmed at two levels, the micro level and the strings of micro level known as the macro level.

This is an important concept and bears repeating in an alternate way. Refer to Figure 1.7 to see the concept of microprogramming. In this figure, a macroinstruction is called from main memory and stored in the macroinstruction register. This word essentially is a starting address for the control memory. Then the machine sequences through the microinstructions housed in the control memory. As each instruction is called, the machine decodes it, executes that operation, and alters the address to call the next microinstruction. When the present macro is completed, the machine then fetches the next macroinstruction from main memory and the process repeats.

Another important special register concept is that of a stack shown in Figure 1.8. The purpose of the stack is to provide a means for storing the contents of critical registers when an interrupt to the normal program occurs. If a machine is operating on a string of instructions and it is desired to change due to some outside influence, the machine would have to store the IR, PC, and data registers, as required, and then fetch the new instructions to begin operation on the new program. These interrupts can be handled in a variety of ways but typically the machine will be of the following type:

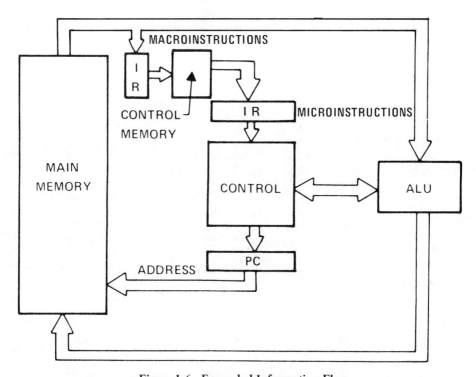

Figure 1.6. Expanded Information Flow

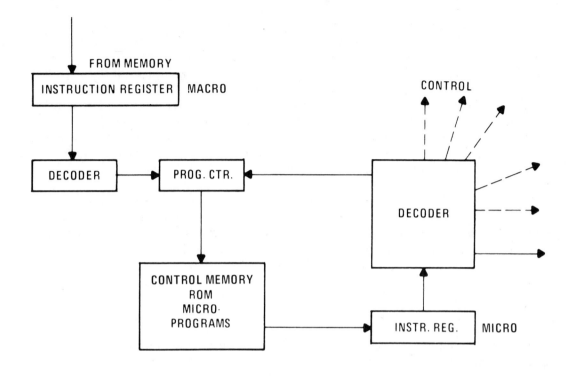

Figure 1.7. Microprogram Concept

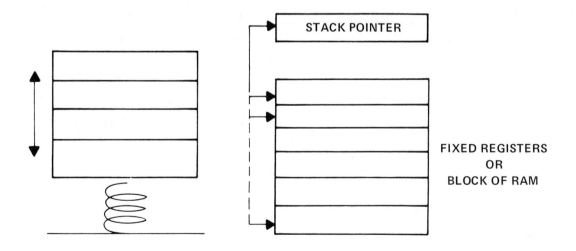

Figure 1.8. Stack Concept

Single level — Recognizes only a single interrupt line and must perform a search to find where in memory to go.

Priority — Recognizes multiple interrupt lines but must search to find where in memory to go.

Vectored Priority — Recognizes multiple interrupt lines and knows where to go immediately from the active interrupt.

Returning to the concept of a stack, when an interrupt occurs, the current data from the various registers, data, PC, IR, is inserted in sequence into a stack of registers reserved for this purpose. This is called "pushing down" the stack. The stack may be a true stack of registers or a series of locations in memory. When the interrupt operation is completed, the program then returns to the top of the stack and takes the data off the top of the stack. Each "pushed down" data then moves up. The next data in the stack is taken until all data is returned as it was before the interrupt and the program can return to resume the previous operation. Bookkeeping chores are handled by a stack pointer that contains the address of the current stack register of interest. The stack pointer operates as a program counter and is shown in concept form in Figure 1.9. It keeps track of the data of interest in the stack.

1.4 SOFTWARE

Early programs for digital machines were written in machine language, that is, each instruction was a unique string of ones and zeros. They were written in order of implementation using the binary word representing each instruction so that a string of instructions was a string of binary numbers. As computer programs began to be more complicated, it became apparent that a numerical or mnemonic language would assist the programmer in writing his program and that there was a need for a special

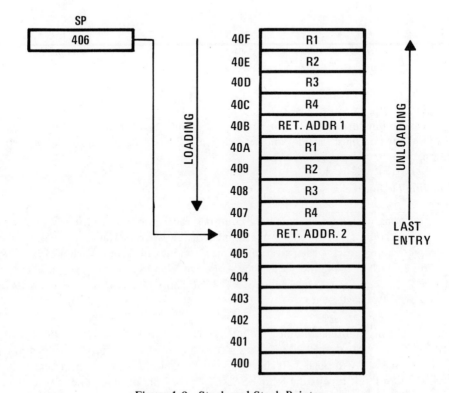

Figure 1.9. Stack and Stack Pointer

program to translate mnemonics into the appropriate machine language instruction codes. This technique became known as using an assembly language. As programming began to develop, programmers became aware of the need for fairly standard programs to allow the computer to accomplish common functions. This need gave rise to the development of what is known as executive or operating systems. As progress was made in the hardware evolution and digital machines became able to handle more complex problems, higher level languages began to appear which were problem or procedure oriented and utilized digital machines themselves for language conversion from high levels down to the ones and zeros of the machine language.

Or, stating it a different way, the most fundamental language is **machine** language in which the programmer writes instructions in the form of ones and zeros. In the **assembly** language, the programmer writes instructions typically using alphabetic characters or mnemonics to label the lines of code and to identify the particular instruction. In addition, plain language is often also used with assembly languages to write comments describing the particular instruction as it applies to the overall program. With assembly language, an assisting program called an assembler was developed to couple a computer into the chore of bookkeeping for the programmer.

In order to further simplify programming, **high-level languages** as previously mentioned, have been developed which are similar to assembly languages except they are problem or procedure oriented. Again, the programmer can use the computer to help translate the high-level language into assembly-level or machine-level code. Thus, the programmer can operate at a much higher efficiency by writing instructions in the high-level language code. Refer to Table 1.2 for a listing of some of the more popular high-level programming languages of today.

Table 1.2. Common High-Level Languages (Circa, 1975)

FORTRAN
COBOL
BASIC
PL/I
PL/M (Subset of PL/I)

In order to communicate ideas concerning programming of digital computers, some terms associated with software must be fully understood. These concepts center on notation, instructions, and addressing.

1.4.1 Notation Methods

In the customary base ten technique of counting, each number is called a *digit*. A three-digit number will allow counting up to 999 for example. In the *binary* system only ones and zeros are allowed to represent quantities — each position in this system is called a *bit*. Each bit has a place value of a power of 2. A three-bit number will allow counting from 000 to 111 eight discrete numbers. (The 111 is a decimal seven, refer to Appendix A for the theory behind number systems.) A string of *binary bits* is normally called a word.

Sometimes binary information not only represents numbers but also alphabetic characters. For such cases, codes have been developed in which some number of binary bits is encoded to represent one character of the set A through Z, 0 through 9, punctuation, or special characters. One specific example of a code of this type is the 8-bit USASCII, United States of America Standard Code for

Information Interchange (refer to Appendix C). Another is EBCDIC, Extended Binary Coded Decimal Interchange Code. Each of these codes represents a technique whereby a character can be coded as a string of ones and zeros so that a computer can operate from and on these data.

Since a long string of ones and zeros is a cumbersome representation of numbers for humans to handle, notations known as octal and hexadecimal have been developed to simplify the steps required in dealing with such numbers. Octal notation means that binary numbers are grouped in 3-bit groups for each octal or number to the base eight. In hexadecimal, four binary bits are combined for each character giving a number system with a base of 16. (Refer to Appendix A for a detailed discussion of the relationships between numbering systems.)

For these discussions, consider the plight of the designer dealing with strings of instructions which represent a program. The designer frequently will do so in octal or hexadecimal notation rather than an endless stream of ones and zeros. Consider a string of binary bits, 16 bits long or four hexadecimal characters as shown in Figure 1.10. It is obvious that the eye can grasp the intelligence contained in four characters faster than 16 binary bits. The problem for beginners is learning the language. With increasing experience octal and hexadecimal can be read as readily as digital. There is a significant advantage in writing or reading four binary bits as a single character. Later in this book, Chapter 5, practice will be gained in using hexadecimal notation (hex) for addresses and instructions. With notation techniques in mind, the next major topic is instructions, what are they, and what do they look like.

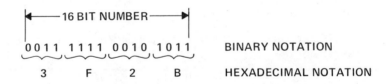

Figure 1.10. Binary-Hexadecimal Representation

1.4.2 Instructions

The stored program concept of digital systems enables a designer to implement a virtually limitless variety of combinational and sequential logic functions. The ease with which this can be done is a function of the architecture and the instruction set of the specific microprocessor to be used.

The fundamental architectural elements of a processing unit are:

1. Program Counter
2. Memory Address Register
3. Memory Data Register
4. Instruction Register with Decode Circuitry
5. Accumulator

The instruction set must enable the application of these functional elements in an orderly manner for achieving any desired program solution. Normally these elements perform sequentially as follows:

1. An address is established (as the result of a previous cycle or power being applied) in the program counter or the memory address register (MAR). The data (ones and zeros) in the memory location thus specified are the next instructions to be implemented. Control signals are sent out to the memory and the word of information may be transferred to the memory data register (MDR).
2. The MDR data may be transferred to the instruction register for decoding.
3. Based on the instruction, which might be, "load the accumulator," a new address is established in the MAR to address the designated data memory word (the operand).
4. Finally, data arrives at the MDR and is transferred to the accumulator (or other destination).

Steps 1 and 2 above, usually called the "fetch" cycle, alternate (generally) with steps 3 and 4, the "execute" cycle.

1.4.3 Instruction Classification

Instructions may be classified into one of the following functional groupings:

1. Data movement
2. Arithmetic and logic
3. Program control
4. Special

Data movement instructions direct the transfer of information to or from the memory, control unit, or I/O unit. Data is transferred one or more words per instruction depending upon the design of the microprocessor. Transfers may also be made between the various registers in the control and arithmetic unit.

Arithmetic and logic instructions are used to perform basic arithmetic (e.g., add, subtract, and sometimes multiply and divide), and logic (e.g., AND, OR, EXCLUSIVE OR) functions. The data upon which these operations are preformed (typically two words) may be in two registers, the accumulator and the memory, or sometimes a register and an input port. The result of the operation is usually placed in the accumulator. In addition to the functions listed above, it is this group of instructions that sets up the conditions tested in the program control conditional branch instructions.

Program control instructions change the content of the program counter which is the address of the instruction to be implemented next. In general, these instructions deal with a jump or branch to a new location in memory and would thus represent the method of implementing discontinuous program functions. These instructions may be unconditionally or conditionally executed. If conditional, they are accomplished by investigating status or flag bits, carry, overflow, sign, or perhaps an "all zeros in the accumulator" test.

The special category comprises instructions which do not directly perform any of the above functions (e.g., enable interrupts, disable interrupts).

Table 1.3 lists a few of the more common instructions found in each of the four categories described above.

Table 1.3. Typical Instruction Groups

I Data Movement	II Arithmetic and Logic	III Problem Control	IV Special
Move MEM. to REG.	ADD	JUMP	Enable Interrupts
Move REG. to REG.	SUBTRACT	BRANCH IF (Condition)	
Move ACC. to OUTPUT	CLEAR	LOAD PROGRAM COUNTER	Disable Interrupts
Move INPUT to ACC. Load ACC.	AND OR	INCREMENT REGISTER AND SKIP NEXT INSTRUCTION IF THE RESULT IS	Load Stack Pointer
Store ACC.	EXCLUSIVE OR	ZERO	
	COMPARE	SKIP NEXT IF (CONDITION)	
	SHIFT		

1.4.4 Formats

Depending upon the architecture of a particular microprocessor, instructions may be fixed length (e.g., one word) or variable length (e.g., one, two, or three words) depending upon the addressing of the operand. Instruction formats vary widely but generally consist of an operation code and an operand address. That is, the instruction word contains a code for what is to be done and a code to locate the object of the action, the operand. For purposes of instruction formats, the instruction set may be divided into two categories:

Data reference instructions

Nondata reference instructions

In the first case, the instruction word must be long enough to specify a data address (or a partial address), whereas the second group contains only an operation code.

Most instruction sets have between 50 and 100 instructions, which means that at least six or seven bits must be available in an instruction word to specify the operation. The range of addressable memory locations, and in fact the addressing technique designed into a microprocessor's architecture, determines the length of the operand field of an instruction. Typically 12 to 16 bits are needed in the address field if the full range of memory is to be addressed directly (4K to 65K words).

In order to minimize instruction word length and to take advantage of the fact that most memory reference instructions in a program specify operands in the "neighborhood" of the instruction, various forms of *relative addressing* have been devised. An operand address of six or seven bits can address a "neighborhood" of 64 or 128 words respectively. (In some architectures, this group of words is called a page.) Addressing details will be discussed later in this chapter.

1.4.5 Multifunction Instructions

Most instructions perform one operation of the types described in Table 1.3 (data movement, arithmetic/logic, program control). However, it is common to find program control instructions combined with arithmetic/logic functions. In these instructions, a register is incremented, decremented, or compared (with another register) and a "jump" is taken based on the result (e.g., zero, greater than).

1.4.6 Timing

In real-time applications of microprocessors, it is necessary to consider the length of time required to execute a string of instructions. Variable length instructions require one, two, or three memory cycles in the fetch phase, and possibly several more in the execute phase depending on the specific instruction. Very few microprocessors execute all instructions in the same amount of time. A careful check of the manufacturer's specification sheet is required for actual timing analysis. Specifically, if an interval between two events is determined external to the digital machine, then the time available to execute a function must be carefully analyzed. In later discussions of simulation in Chapter 3, this can be seen to be a critical function and one of the most difficult to implement.

1.4.7 Summary

In general, instruction sets have the following basic characteristics:

1. Instructions are binary numbers stored in the main memory in the same manner as data. Instruction words may consist of one or more memory words depending upon the architecture of the computer. Some microprocessors use fixed-length instructions, others use variable-length instructions.

2. Instructions may be categorized into data reference and nondata reference instructions. All bits of an instruction word are available to encode a nondata reference instruction, whereas data reference instructions must contain an operation portion and an operand address portion.

3. One instruction cycle may consume one or more memory cycles (one to five memory cycles in most systems). From a timing point of view, it is important to recognize that not all instructions consume the same amount of time, and that nonmemory reference instructions may consume less time than memory reference instructions.

4. From an academic point of view, it is possible to devise an instruction set of fewer than ten instructions which will be capable of implementing any digital computer program. However, the total number of instructions in a program using such an abbreviated instruction set can be very large and, therefore, costly in terms of memory storage and programming time. Efficient, cost-effective programming depends upon a versatile instruction set and the ability of the system designer to utilize these instructions.

It is unnecessary for the system designer to understand fully all of the intricacies of data transfer during the implementation of any instruction. He needs only to comprehend the specification of the instruction in order to utilize that instruction effectively in the design of digital systems.

1.5 ADDRESSING

Probably the single most confusing and the least well-defined element in all of software is the concept of addressing a memory. Instructions specify what is to be done (the operation), and what word receives the action (the operand). But the technique for locating the information, called addressing, can involve several memory cycles and arithmetic operations. Addresses must be determined for both data and *next instructions*.

All memory locations (words) are given numerical "names" or addresses so that the system designer can properly specify the location of instructions and data for a program. The ways that addresses may be generated during program operation are called addressing modes. Table 1.4 lists the fundamental modes and explanations are as follows.

Table 1.4. Addressing Modes

Immediate
Direct
Indirect
Relative

Figures 1.11 and 1.12 are pictorial representations of the four basic addressing modes specified.

1.5.1 Immediate Addressing

If an instruction word contains the *operand*, there is no operand address, and the mode is called *immediate* addressing. Examples of this are: "AND Immediate" — perform a logical AND between the accumulator and the operand portion of the instruction word; and "ADD Immediate" — add the contents of the operand portion of the instruction word to the contents of the accumulator.

Immediate operands are limited to numerical values within the range of bits in the operand field. If an eight-bit field is used, for example, the decimal integer range is from -128 to $+127$.

1.5.2 Direct Addressing

If the operand portion of an instruction contains the *address* of the operand, it is called a *direct* address (Figure 1.11). Examples are MOVE instructions and JUMP instructions. The limitation of direct addressing is the number of memory locations addressable by the operand portion of the

Immediate

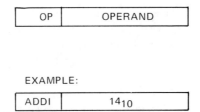

EXAMPLE:

ADDI	14_{10}

"Add (IMMEDIATE) the content of the operand portion of the instruction word".

Direct

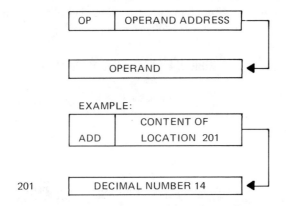

"Add the content of the memory location addressed by the operand portion of the instruction word".

Figure 1.11. Addressing Modes — Immediate and Direct

instruction. If a 4K range is needed, 12 bits would be required for operand field alone. (Since six to eight bits are normally needed for the OP code, this makes instructions 18 to 20 bits long for wide-range direct addressing.)

1.5.3   Indirect Addressing

If the operand address portion of an instruction contains the address of a *pointer* which in turn contains the address of the actual operand, *indirect addressing* has been specified (Figure 1.12). Pointers, or indirect addresses, are useful in implementing operations on each element in a table. The pointer is initially set to the address of the first number in the table. Then as the operation is completed, the pointer is incremented to address the next value in the table, and the program loops through the same string of instructions again. The operand portion of an indirect address instruction *remains constant* and yet is capable of reaching a large number of data words. Only the *pointer* varies.

1.5.4   Relative Addressing

Addresses are often developed by calculation. If the content of the operand field of an instruction is added to the content of a register to produce the desired address, it is called *relative* addressing. The instruction word contains a relative address, and the register contains the base address. This general definition applies to a wide variety of common addressing techniques. A few common examples are: page addressing, indexed addressing, program relative addressing, and register relative addressing.

1. In paging, the relative address range is usually 64 to 128 words (one page). A page buffer contains the high-order address bit (the page address) and the instruction word contains the low-order address which specifies the word on the page.

2. Indexed addressing is another method for generating sequential addresses for program loops. An index register is incremented or decremented in each pass.

3. Program relative addressing means that the PC (program counter) is used as the base register. The range of this relative address is generally ±64 or ±128 words from the location address by the PC.

4. Register relative addressing allows a general register to serve as a base address register. And the instruction operand address (relative address) is added to the base address to obtain the actual operand address (Figure 1.13).

An address computed via one of the above techniques is called the *effective* address of the operand or the *absolute* address.

Many microprocessors use a combination of relative, indexed, and direct or indirect addressing to enhance versatility in programming. The use of this advanced software technique, when the instruction set allows, can dramatically reduce the number of instructions required to perform a given task, and, hence, reduce the execution time of a program.

Architecturally several elements are directly involved in addressing. They are the program counter (PC), index register, general registers, page buffer, and stack pointer (SP).

1. The program counter supplies the address of the next instruction to the memory. As each instruction is accessed, the PC is incremented (sometimes by two or three for multiword instructions) to be ready to call the next instruction. Most microprocessors include instructions to directly load the PC such as JUMP, JUMP-on-condition, and transfer register contents to PC.

Indirect

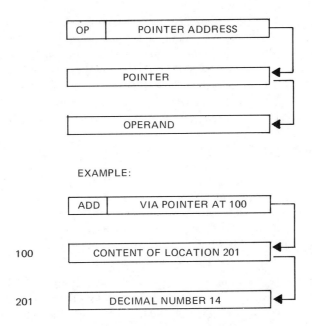

EXAMPLE:

"Add the content of the memory location addressed by the Pointer Word; the Operand portion of the instruction addresses the Pointer".

Relative

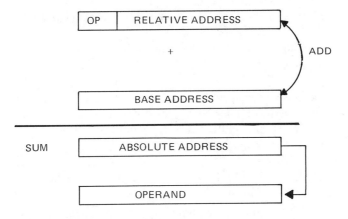

Figure 1.12. Addressing Modes — Indirect and Relative

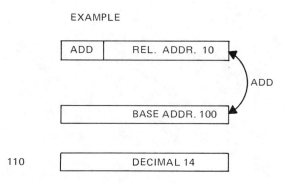

EXAMPLE

"ADD the contents of the memory word addressed by the sum of the operand portion of the instruction word and the base address register".

Figure 1.13. Addressing Example

2. An index register may be directly loaded, then incremented or decremented for purposes of creating a sequential pointer or an iteration counter.

3. A stack pointer is a register containing the address of one word in a block of registers or memory locations designated as a stack. As register data and return addresses are saved, the SP is decremented to point to sequential locations. Unloading the stack means incrementing the pointer as each word of the stack is accessed. Recall, Figure 1.9 illustrates the stack and SP. As an example of the operation, a RETurn instruction causes the SP to call the last entry (e.g., location 406) into the control unit, and place the data in the PC. The SP would then automatically be incremented to 407. Thus, the SP points to the last entry, and is decremented or incremented as data is added to or retrieved from the stack.

General registers, index register, and a page buffer may or may not be included in the architecture. But if they are used, address computation is available in which a portion of the instruction word is added to the register to determine the operand address.

In this chapter, a lot of seemingly disassociated facts have been detailed. At this point, an attempt to tie them together should not be made, rather an individual understanding of each should be the goal.

With a clear understanding of these basic concepts of Chapter 1, a discussion of how software is generated may be undertaken.

CHAPTER 2

HOW TO BUILD SOFTWARE

2.1   SOFTWARE DESIGN

As with most design problems, it is best to start with a framework to define the overall problem and the approach to the solution, and then progressively to fill in the details until the design is complete. Software design falls into this same pattern. In this chapter, a suggested structure for developing the software to accomplish the functions required will be outlined. In the next chapter the logistics required to support the effort described in this chapter will be investigated.

There are three basic ingredients in the structure of the generation of programs for microprocessors. First, the definition of the concepts, complete with algorithm; second, flowcharting; and third, coding.

2.2   CONCEPT DEFINITION

The first step in a system design cycle is to define the objectives the system is to accomplish. The three areas of interest are the inputs to the system, the outputs from the system, and the logical and/or arithmetic steps to be performed. A detailed specification of each area should be made including only those logical and timing constraints that are truly required, leaving as much latitude as possible for design flexibility. The next step is to determine how these specifications can be realized in a sequential manner. A concept-level flow chart can then be written to establish the basic framework for applying a microprocessor as the primary hardware element.

A list of statements should be made detailing conceptually the tasks to be performed by the microprocessor. The designer must lay out detailed sequences of events that are to be measured, monitored, or controlled by the microprocessor. Define as explicitly as possible the logic rules for cause and effect. This could be such things as, "If relay 'A' is on and button 'B' is pushed, turn on motor 'C'". With such statements in hand, alternates should be pursued. Decide whether there are events that will require interrupt processing and how they should be handled. Are there events that must occur in a given time, or is time important at all? When a complete set of conceptual statements exist and alternates have been thoroughly investigated, begin flowcharting.

2.3   FLOWCHARTING

The development of a comprehensive detailed flow chart for a microprocessor system is not normally achieved in a single step. Generally, three levels of flowcharting should be used.

1.   Concept level

2.   Algorithm level

3.   Instruction level

The first two flow charts can be generated without a specific microprocessor in mind. The third, the instruction-level flow chart, must be written for a specific microprocessor because the architecture and instruction set must be known.

The concept-level flow chart contains broad statements defining **what** is to be done. The algorithm flow chart details **how** these things are to be done. Finally, the instruction-level flow chart is the detailed flow chart that provides the road map for software coding.

2.3.1 Concept-Level Flow Chart

Figure 2.1 is a concept-level flow chart for a control system application with polled I/O. (Refer to Appendix D for flow chart symbols.) The statements are written in boxes with arrows to show the sequence of events in the program. Relatively few decision blocks are needed at this step because the statements simply define the major software blocks. Figure 2.2 shows a concept-level flow chart for a system using interrupt I/O techniques. Here the important decision is the branch to the specific interrupt service routine. Notice that there is no preset time delay in this diagram as there was in Figure 2.1. This is true since an interrupt system does not generally require software controlled timing. The system simply waits for an interrupt signal from an I/O device to start processing.

2.3.2 Algorithm-Level Flow Chart

In the second level of flowcharting, the algorithm level, each block of the concept-level flow chart is expanded to show individual steps that are required to achieve the desired result. What is an algorithm? An algorithm is a set of procedures by which a given result is obtained. (Various algorithms may state alternate ways of solving the same problem.) It might be a calculating technique for a time delay, or it could be a technique for summing the terms of an infinite series. It is the set of operations that when implemented by a program, accomplish a specified task.

To illustrate how to work with flow charts, expand step 4 of Figure 2.1 as shown in Figure 2.3. The objective is to read a string of input words, which of course are strings of binary bits, and compare with the readings on the last sampling. If there is a difference, certain action must be taken and this is indicated. Notice that the blocks now describe how a particular job is to be done, yet without the details required by an instruction-level flow chart. Look at the steps in detail.

After initialization of an input word counter, an input word is read and then compared with a previous reading. This obviously indicates the need for a string of words in memory to store the latest reading of each input word. The comparison step, step 3 of Figure 2.3, assumes that an entire word may be compared with a memory word and the result stored as a status test bit. If there is no difference, the word counter is incremented and checked to see if all words have been tested. If not, the routine returns to the starting point to read another input word. If there is a difference between an input word and the previous sampling (step 4), each bit must be tested individually one at a time to determine which bit or bits are different, then the appropriate action must be taken.

The algorithm-level flow chart should be as detailed as possible. In fact, note that the concept flow chart steps are now expanded significantly by the algorithm flow chart. Thus, while the algorithm-level flow chart may expand the concept-level flow chart by a factor of 20 or more, the instruction-level flow chart will expand the algorithm-level flow chart by a factor typically less than three.

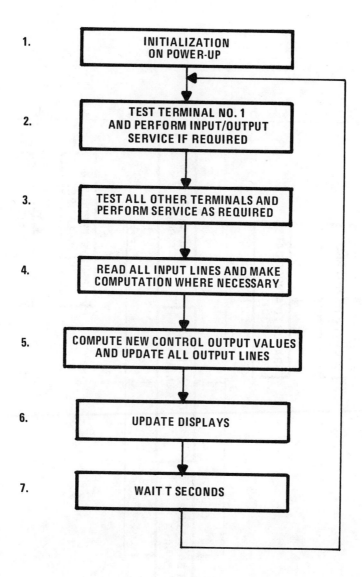

Figure 2.1. Concept-Level Flow Chart – Polled I/O

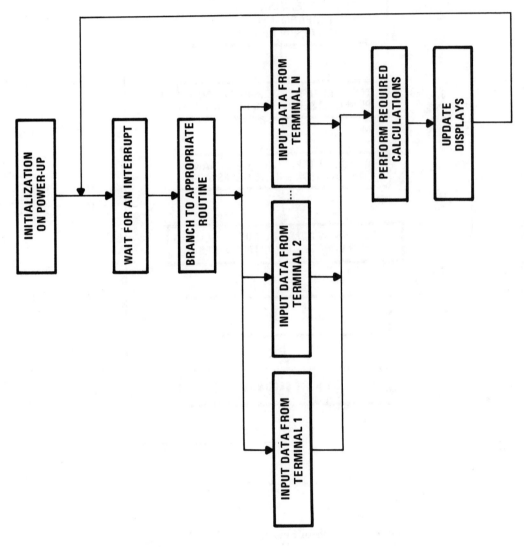

Figure 2.2. Concept-Level Flow Chart – Interrupt I/O

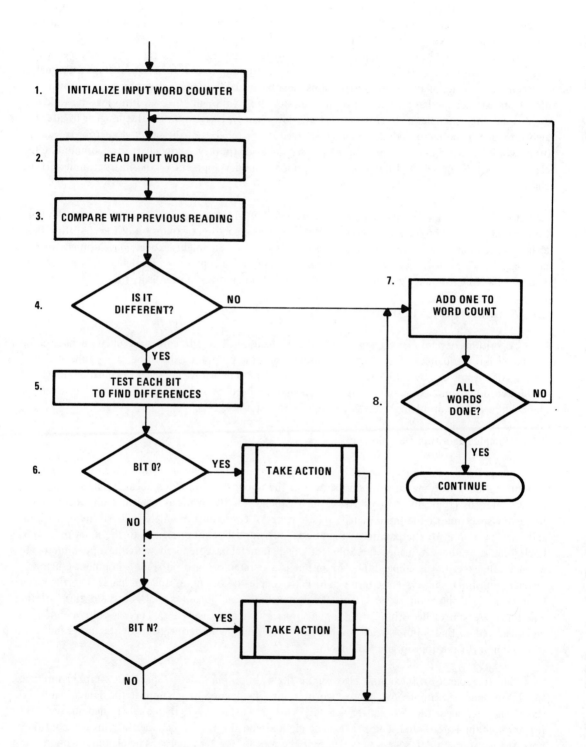

Figure 2.3. Algorithm-Level Flow Chart (for Step 4 of Figure 2.1)

Following the completion of the algorithm-level flow chart, the specific characteristics of a microprocessor required to fulfill the design objectives may be determined and the microprocessor selected. The instruction set and the architecture of the selected microprocessor are the foundation for the instruction-level flow chart. This is the most detailed flow chart and precedes software coding. Sufficient detail should be included in this flow chart such that each block can be represented by one or no more than three instructions. Figure 2.4 is an instruction-level flow chart for steps 2 through 6 of Figure 2.3. Notice that specific instructions must be available in the instruction set for moving the data from the accumulator to the specified register, etc. Although the algorithm may be followed directly for this example of the instruction-level flow chart, it is common for the designer to alter the algorithm at this point to take advantage of special characteristics of the selected microprocessor. In other words, it may be desirable to develop a second algorithm-level flow chart to accommodate the characteristics of the selected microprocessor prior to the development of the instruction-level flow chart.

Concept-level flow charts and instruction-level flow charts are generally the easiest to develop. Conceptual steps are broad and general. Instruction steps are a direct expansion of the algorithm flow chart in accordance with the selected microprocessor. As you might expect, development of the necessary algorithm is the key to easy implementation of a concept with a particular microprocessor. The process of developing algorithms is complex so additional investigation is in order.

2.4   ALGORITHM DEVELOPMENT

Algorithm development begins with the realization that all real-world phenomena can be translated into sequences of steps that eventually become programs consisting of a string of digital words. Algorithms can be rather simple or extremely complex. However, even the most complex can be broken down into component parts which in turn become simple. As an example of a simple algorithm, extract a problem from the control field.

2.4.1   Simple Algorithm Development

Figure 2.5 describes a simple feedback control system in which some parameter such as pressure or temperature is varying with time as shown in the upper diagram. This linear input is sampled at regular intervals (typically at least twice the frequency of the highest relevant component in the frequency spectrum of the input signal). The settings of two controls which establish the upper limit and the lower limit of the parameter might also be sampled as input signals to the microprocessor. Each time a reading is made, the value of the parameter is compared with the upper limit and whenever it exceeds the upper limit, an output is generated to turn on some equipment (such as a refrigeration unit). The system continues to take samples of the input and compares it to the lower limit. Whenever the input is less than the lower limit, an output signal is sent to turn off the equipment. A control algorithm for this application is shown in Figure 2.6. There is only one input to be considered so that input is read and tested to determine whether it is outside the limits and if so, to turn on or off the appropriate equipment.

The final part of this example algorithm is the wait loop in order to space out sampling intervals to "T" seconds per sample. A separate algorithm must be devised to accomplish the delay. Figure 2.7 shows one such algorithm. A register is loaded with a constant "N", then a test is made to see if the register content is zero, and if not, it is decremented and the test is made again. This test continues until the register content is zero, at which time the wait loop is terminated. The maximum amount of time for this wait loop is determined by the number of bits in the register used for a countdown, and the execution time of the instruction in the loop (i.e., test and decrement). If more time is desired, a

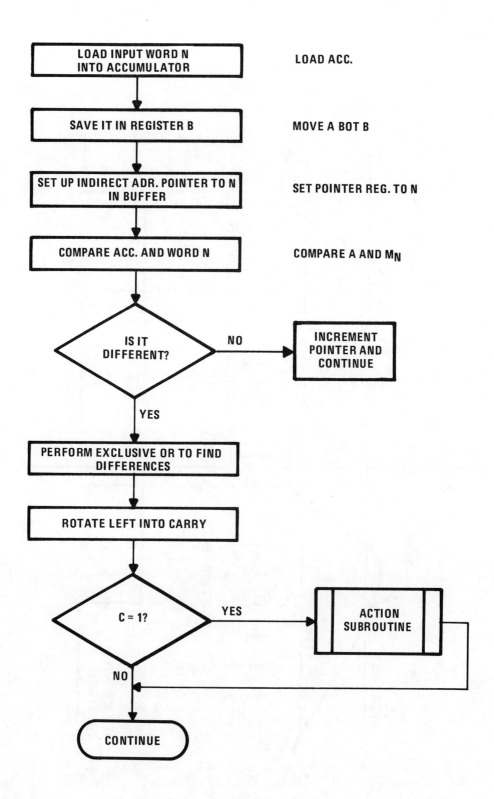

Figure 2.4. Instruction-Level Flow Chart (for Steps 2-6 of Figure 2.3)

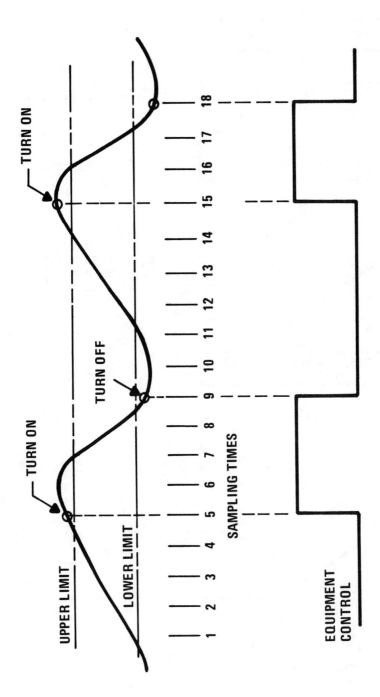

Figure 2.5. Simple Feedback Control System

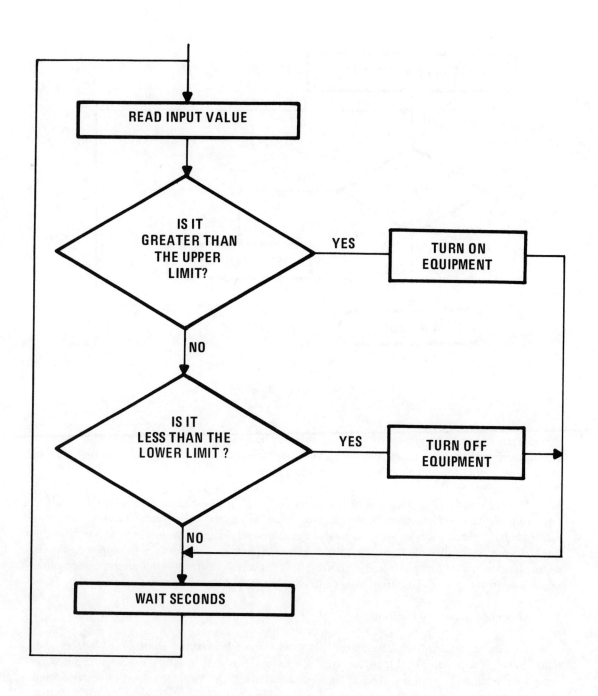

Figure 2.6. Algorithm for Control System of Figure 2.5

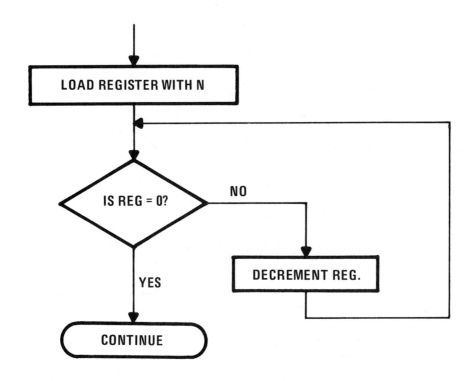

Figure 2.7. Wait Loop Algorithm

second register would be employed and two counting loops used. The first loop would count as shown, then each time it reaches zero the second loop would count one, reload of the first register would be accomplished, and counting down resumed.

Another way to establish sampling (or timing) intervals, is to use an external hardware clock or timer to generate interrupt signals to the microprocessor at regular time intervals (such as every ten milliseconds). If such a device were used, this system could wait for an interrupt signal from the timer, then sample all inputs, perform the required calculations, establish new output signals as required, and then return to a halt condition waiting for a new interrupt. Multiple timers are often valuable in providing several different timing intervals as required by an individual algorithm.

2.4.2 Complex Algorithm Partitioning

To expand on algorithm development, look at a more generalized control-type system with more complex requirements. Figure 2.8 is a generalized hardware diagram for a microprocessor system involving both linear and discrete input and output signals. Assume that a complex algorithm must be developed to process each input signal and establish and update each output signal. Note that it has been assumed that each output signal is the result of calculations made on the input information. Partitioning of the overall complex algorithm into simpler partial algorithms can be demonstrated.

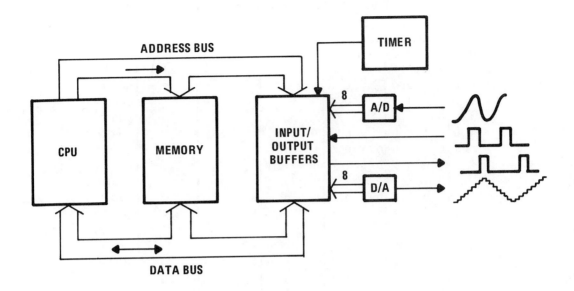

Figure 2.8. Generalized Microprocessor System

Four input lines, for example, could represent a BCD digit (refer to Appendix A for BCD number theory) which must be converted to binary for mathematical operations in a microprocessor which uses only binary arithmetic. Assume further that an algorithm for converting BCD to binary is required for three digits. Table 2.1 shows the BCD digits with values representing 999. By observing that the units digit contains bits that are valid as binary data, the algorithm properly begins with the value of the first bit of the tens digit. A technique must be divised to sense the fact that this bit is set, then appropriately modify the remaining data to extract the total numerical units digit data. One idea is to shift the data to the right one place. This, in binary arithmetic, is equivalent to dividing the binary number by two. A one in the least significant bit of the four bits representing tens information represents 10 in BCD. When this bit is shifted to the right one position, it represents 8 in binary. If the number (10) had been properly divided by two the result should be 5. So, in order to correct for the difference, an algorithm must include a "subtract three" step if the bit shifted into the 8 position is a one. This type of problem exists also for a shift from the hundreds digit into the tens digit.

This technique for BCD to binary conversion is shown in Table 2.1 for the BCD number 999. After the first shift, the value 0011 must be subtracted from both the units and tens digit as indicated by the circled ones. This process continues until the BCD number is wholly converted to binary. The final binary number is actually only 10 bits long. (Notice that the most significant two bits are zero and therefore should be ignored.)

Recognize from the preceding example that algorithm development can become somewhat unorthodox since the goal is to achieve a given result with relatively few instructions and with minimized storage of constants and intermediate data. Obviously, the actual instructions used to implement a given algorithm such as the one illustrated, will be different for each microprocessor. But the algorithm will nevertheless be valid for all microprocessors. Ordinarily, a fairly complex algorithm such as this would be revised somewhat when written for a specific microprocessor.

Table 2.1. BCD-to-Binary Conversion

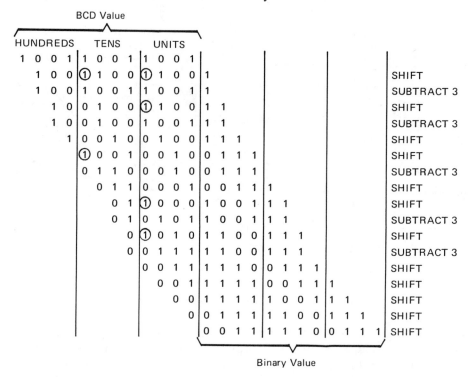

$$999_{10} = 1001\ 1001\ 1001 = 11\ 1110\ 0111_2$$

Circled ones identify points where the 8 bit position of a BCD digit is a 1 after a shift.

Concepts and three levels of flowcharting have been developed. The next step required is to generate a software program for microprocessors through coding.

2.5 CODING TECHNIQUES

Programs for microprocessors may be written in machine code, assembly code, or high-level language code depending upon the microprocessor manufacturer and his support software. Programming in machine code (don't confuse machine code with microprogramming) means that the designer must write each instruction in binary numbers, and typically addressing must be done directly by making absolute address assignments during the writing of the program. That is to say, the programmer must write his program in 1's and 0's and do all his own bookkeeping. A slightly simpler form of coding may be accomplished by using mnemonics instead of binary numbers for the instructions themselves and using decimal and hexadecimal numbers for the addresses.

2.5.1 Machine Code Programming

As an example of this type of machine code programming, the flow chart of a simple routine for reading two values and performing mathematical operations on the two values is shown in Figure 2.9. The absolute address coding technique for this program is shown in Table 2.2. Note that mnemonics are used while explaining absolute addressing requirements. Here the programmer has

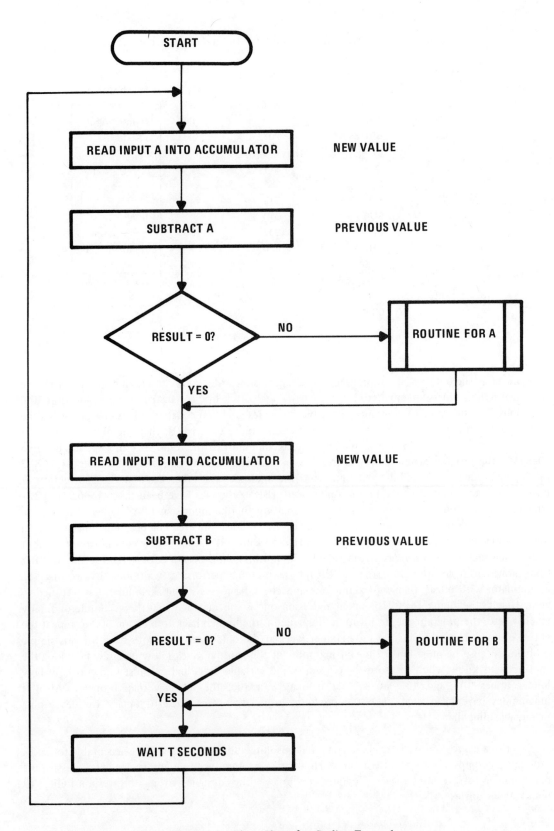

Figure 2.9. Flow Chart for Coding Examples

Table 2.2. Absolute Address Coding — Input Test Routine

	Location	Instruction	Address		Memory Map		
1.	300	LDA	801				
2.	301	SUB	310	802	Input/Output		
3.	302	BRNZ	201	801	Addresses		
4.	303	LDA	802				
5.	304	SUB	311				
6.	305	BRNZ	251				
7.	306	LDA	312				
8.	307	SUB	313		Input		
9.	308	BRNZ	307	300	Test Routine		
10.	309	BR	300		Routine for B		
11.	310	A VALUE		251			
12.	311	B VALUE			Routine for A		
13.	312	00FF		201			
14.	313	0001					

determined at the outset that the program was going to start at location 300; then proceeded to write the instructions in sequential order down through the branch instruction at location 309. Locations 310 through 313 contained data, two variables, and two constants. This program loads the accumulator with the data word from the input circuit addressed by 801, then the previous value for "A" stored in location 310 is subtracted from the accumulator. If the result is zero, there has been no change so the program would continue to location 303 and the new value of "B" from location 802 in the input circuits would be read into the accumulator. Had the result of the subtraction at location 301 not been zero, the branch-on-not-zero (BRNZ) would have been taken to location 201 which is the subroutine for processing new information for the input signal "A". One of the steps in the subroutine would be to store the new value of "A" in location 310. The program continues from location 303 to perform the same type of operation on value "B", reading new data in from the input circuit, subtracting the previously read value "B", and branching-on-not-zero to the routine for "B". Continuing from location 306, the next four instructions perform a wait loop by loading the accumulator with 00FF, then subtracting one and checking to see if the accumulator is returned to zero. If not, the branch to 307 is taken and again one is subtracted. When the accumulator finally reaches zero, the program goes to location 309 which is the branch back to location 300 to repeat the entire process. The problems the programmer faces at the outset are enormous even for this simple problem because he must know the starting point of the routine, must know precisely how long the routine is to know where to store the constants and variable data, and he must know exactly how long routines "A" and "B" are so that he may construct the memory map properly. Also, if mnemonics have been used, then the programmer must convert back to binary for developing memory loading data.

Writing a program with machine code and absolute address coding may be acceptable for short programs, perhaps up to 50 instructions. However, a computer program is needed to assist the programming effort for longer programs to relieve the designer from the responsibility of bookkeeping duties.

2.5.2 Assembler Programming

A program that is used to assist the designer in this way is called an assembler, and the coding technique typically used is called "symbolic address coding". Table 2.3 shows the same program of Table 2.2 written in symbolic address coding. Notice that instructions are written in mnemonics and that addresses are no longer written in numerical fashion but in terms of symbols. The first or starting

Table 2.3. Use of Index Register

	Label	Operation	Operand	Relative Location	Absolute Location
1.	START	LDA	AIN	0	300
2.		SUB	A	1	301
3.		BRNZ	ARTN	2	302
4.		LDA	BIN	3	303
5.		SUB	B	4	304
6.		BRNZ	BRTN	5	305
7.		LDA	HEXFF	6	306
8.		SUB	HEXO1	7	307
9.		BRNZ	*−1	8	308
10.		BR	START	9	309
11.	A	DATA	0	10	310
12.	B	DATA	0	11	311
13.	HEXFF	DATA	HFF	12	312
14.	HEX01	DATA	H01	13	313
15.	AIN	EQU	801		
16.	BIN	EQU	802		
17.	ARTN	Code for Routine A . . .		14	314 . . .
18.	BRTN	Code for Routine B . . .		64	364

address is now labeled "Start" and without any other information, the assembler would interpret this address as zero. Each instruction is assigned a binary number in sequence by the assembler. A location counter in the assembler accomplishes this as it counts each instruction in order. These locations in the sequence become the addresses for the symbolic mnemonics in the label field. When the symbols used in the label field are used in the operand field, the address assigned to the operand bits is the location number assigned by the location counter. Lines 1 through 8 of the symbolic address coding example (Table 2.3) perform exactly the same things as lines 1 through 8 of Table 2.2. However, in this case, the operand field contains strings of letters to form symbolic addresses. Each symbolic address is assigned a value corresponding to its location in the label field. Line 9 of Table 2.3 includes an expression in the operand field. Assume for this assembler that the "asterisk minus one" directs the assembler to assign as the address the value that is one less than the location counter content. That is, the location counter contains a number such as 008 for the BRNZ instruction of line 9. The address to be branched to should be the instruction on line 8 which would be 8 minus 1 or 7. The code shown in lines 11 through 14 directs the assembler to reserve four locations for data. The first two should contain 0 initially and the other two should contain HEX FF and HEX 1 (refer to Appendix A for number theory). Lines 15 and 16 are assembler directives to equate the label to the actual address of the input line. These two instructions do not result in machine-level instructions because they are simply information used by the assembler. After all instructions data and directives have been written, two subroutines must be added to accommodate operands of lines 3 and 6. They are ARTN and BRTN respectively which process the new information from inputs "A" or "B".

It is important to note that in absolute address coding, the designer will have substantial difficulty adding or deleting instructions from the program because of the influence on locations of other instructions, data, and constants. In symbolic address coding, each time instructions are to be added, the designer simply adds those instructions with appropriate symbolic addresses. In the computer, the assembler performs the required calculations to assign new absolute address locations. Notice that in Table 2.3 absolute locations have been listed for the instructions, but in fact only become valid locations upon loading. That is, the object program, the output data from the assembler, may be loaded into the microprocessor with a bias of 300 which then establishes the absolute location assignments listed.

It should be clear by now that an assembler is a fairly complex program and performs a number of very useful functions. A list of the actual activities of a typical assembler follows. An assembler must:

1. Assign addresses to each instruction and maintain a location counter.

2. Allow symbolic addressing and build a symbol table relating symbols to instruction locations.

3. Accept expressions in the operand field and compute addresses as directed. These expressions may include standard arithmetic operations such as plus and minus.

4. Provide directives to reserve locations for data and constants and for equating symbols to absolute memory locations.

5. Allow for comments and descriptive statements.

6. Output to paper tape or other suitable media a string of binary words converted from the mnemonics and symbols which establish the content of each memory location for loading the program.

7. Perform certain tests to aid in programming. These tests are:
   a. Flag all illegal mnemonics.
   b. Check for improper syntax in operands.
   c. Test labels to see if they are all used in some operand.
   d. Flag any undefined symbol.
   e. Flag any multidefined symbol.

8. List all instructions and relative locations (starting at 0000) and error messages, if any.

2.5.3 Versatile Programming Aids

2.5.3.1 Power-On Concepts

One important characteristic of microprocessor programming that must be considered is power-up and initialization. When a microprocessor receives power, there is normally some reset condition to start the program counter at a specified location. The first instruction stored in this location should begin an initialization routine which should clear the necessary architectural elements and make provisions for program and data loading as well.

2.5.3.2 Subroutines

Almost all programs involve the use of subroutines to some extent. This is because certain small common tasks are called frequently during a particular program. Such a task might be the conversion from binary to BCD or the conversion from BCD to binary previously discussed. If these two operations were written as subroutines, the code could be stored in the memory only once and branched to as needed. Whereas, if the code for these subroutines were written each time they were used in a program, there would certainly be redundancy and inefficient use of memory. Figure 2.10 illustrates the location of three routines labeled A, B, and C, and two subroutines which might be called by any of the three. The first subroutine converts binary data to BCD and is called BINB. The second subroutine converts BCD to binary and is called BCDB. These symbolic names are simply the addresses of the first instruction of each subroutine. When a microprocessor implements a subroutine call instruction, some provision is made to preserve the content of the program counter (PC) for use when the steps in the subroutine have been completed. For example, in routine "A" a jump subroutine call (JSB) has been made to the BCD to binary routine. When this instruction is encountered, the control unit automatically stores the content of the PC in some register and then loads the PC with the address of the first instruction of the subroutine. These instructions are then implemented in sequence until the final instruction of the subroutine returns the program counter to the number previously saved.

2.5.3.3 Use of a Stack in Programming

While all microprocessors have different techniques for handling subroutines, there are certain similarities. It is common to find a technique for handling return addresses called a stack discussed in Chapter 1. When a JSB instruction is encountered, the control unit saves the address of the next instruction in that string on the stack, and loads the PC with the starting address of the subroutine. The last instruction of the subroutine is a RETURN instruction which loads the PC with the address saved on the stack. Thus, processing resumes in the calling routine immediately following the JSB instruction.

The technique whereby data is transferred to a subroutine and results of subroutine computations are transferred back to the main routine are called "Calling Sequence" and "Exit Sequence". The main routine has a calling sequence which stores information in registers or specific memory locations just before the jump to subroutine instruction. At the end of the subroutine, data must be stored in registers or specified memory locations prior to a return to the calling routine. In this way, data transfers between main routines and subroutines are standardized.

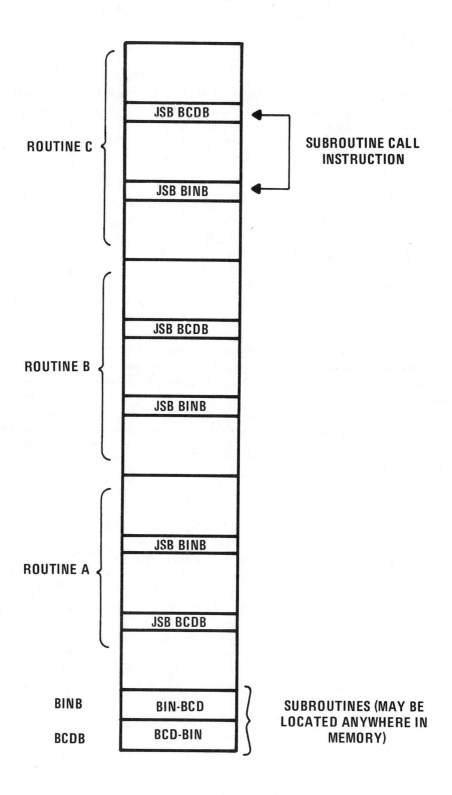

Figure 2.10. Subroutine Use

2.5.3.4 Index Register Use

Efficient programming is accomplished when a designer takes full advantage of an instruction set and architectural elements of a microprocessor. The previous example for a one input-one output control application can easily be expanded via the appropriate programming techniques. Figure 2.11 shows a technique in which data tables could be built for a system with ten stations. In this example, all ten data values for one variable are put into one single table (such as all ten measurements of temperature reside in Table 1; all the values for pressure are in Table 2; the valve position data is in Table 3; and Table 4 contains the number of boxes, etc.). These same pieces of information could have been arranged in ten tables of five entries each where each table would represent one station. However, five tables of ten variables each were chosen to demonstrate the use of an index register.

When a microprocessor is called upon to service different stations, the program could be written for one station and then an index register used to allow it to service all ten stations. In this case, an index register can be used to point to successive entries in the previously described tables so that a single program could load data into these tables or read data from them for any given station depending on the content of the index register.

Assume that a microprocessor allows index addressing. As shown in Figure 2.11, the single index register setting could allow addressing of all five corresponding elements. Note also that it might be necessary to initialize data tables by clearing them. Table 2.4 shows a sequence of instructions which uses the index register to sequentially clear all the locations in these tables. The first instruction clears the accumulator. The second instruction loads the index register labeled "D" with a 10. The next five instructions direct the microprocessor to store the content of the accumulator into the location addressed by the sum of symbolic address TAB 1 and the content of the index register "D". Initially, this is the tenth entry of each table. A DSZ (Decrement and Skip on Zero) instruction has been added for this example to demonstrate the use of a double-function instruction, one that subtracts one from the index register and tests the result to see if it is zero. If it is not zero, the next instruction will be implemented which is a jump back to the location labeled "LOOP". At this point, the index register contains the quantity nine and the ninth entry of each of the tables will be cleared during the next five instructions. Again, the DSZ instruction decrements or subtracts one from the index register, and the loop is continued. At the end of the final pass, the index register contains one and the DSZ instruction subtracting one will cause the index register to go to zero. When this condition happens, the DSZ instruction directs the microprocessor to skip the next instruction (JMP LOOP) and to continue.

When using this technique, the index register is set to the required station number, then input data is read, calculations are made, and output data is stored in output data buffers, all based on entries in the tables defined by the value in the index register. As Figure 2.11 shows, the index register provides the add-on value to allow addressing of corresponding entries in all tables simultaneously.

2.5.3.5 Indirect Addressing

The technique for use of index registers illustrated here is one of many techniques described as "address modification". In microprocessors without index registers, indirect addressing is often used to accomplish the same effect. Five indirect address pointers would be required to select individual elements of the tables. Note that at the end of each pass of a routine in which this technique is used, it would be necessary to increment each of the indirect address words to progress to the next applicable station. The importance of indirect addressing in this concept is that address modification

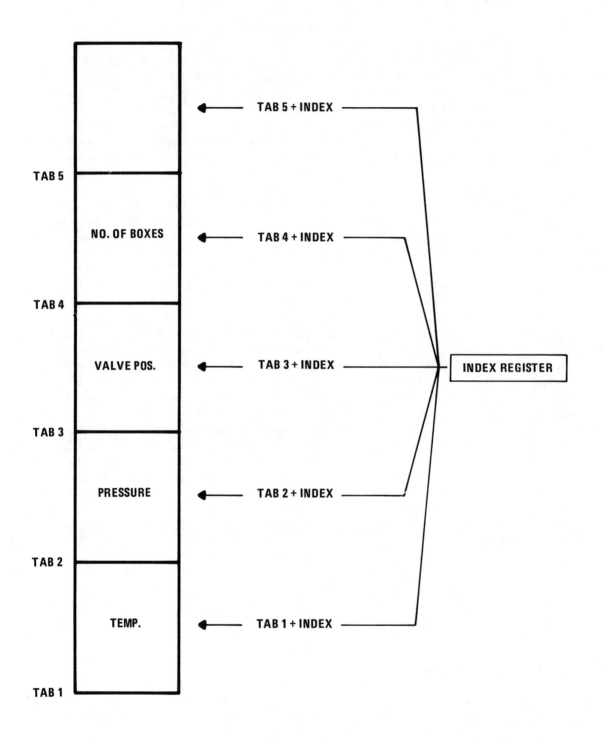

Figure 2.11. Use of Index Register

Table 2.4. Instructions for Clearing the
Five Tables of Figure 2.11

```
CLA                        Clear accumulator
LXI       D    10          Set up index register
STA       TAB1, D          Store ACC in each entry of each table
STA       TAB2, D
STA       TAB3, D
STA       TAB4, D
STA       TAB5, D
DSZ       D                Decrement and test I.R.
JMP       LOOP             If not zero, repeat
(next instruction)         If zero, go on
```

may be applied to indirect address pointers without modifying the address fields of the instructions. Notice also that with indirect addressing there is no single instruction for testing to determine the end of the required number of passes through a program loop. With an index register, a decrement-skip-on-zero instruction provided this feature; with indirect addressing, a separate counter must be set up to count the number of times the program has cycled through the loop.

2.5.3.6   Other Addressing Aids

From the two examples given, it is easy to visualize the effectiveness of the many addressing modes discussed in Chapter 1. It is beyond the scope of this book to discuss each one in detail. A little time spent with a specific microprocessor's specifications should yield expansion of understanding from the basics just discussed.

2.6   SOFTWARE UTILITY ROUTINES

In writing programs for microprocessors, the designer may ask himself, "Must I write everything?". Generally, manufacturers of microprocessors provide the designers with short routines that find common usage in many applications. These can be conversion routines such as BCD to binary, trigonometric functions, exponential functions, and certain I/O service routines such as for a teletype. These routines are called utility routines and some vendors encourage customer interchange of common problems/programs by publishing a low-cost newsletter listing these routines.

You should not however, confuse these routines with the program development aids and diagnostic programs discussed in the next chapter.

2.7   TIMING CONCEPTS

In order to fully understand the requirements on software, the programmer must establish the length of time a microprocessor will require to accomplish a given task. Thus, it is necessary for the designer to make an estimate of the number of instructions required to accomplish a given program or routine. He then must refer to the data supplied by the microprocessor manufacturer in order to establish the actual length of time required by the processor to perform the full set or a subroutine set of instructions. In some microprocessors, the instruction cycle may be determined by the number of memory cycles required to implement that instruction. In others, however, substantial numbers of steps are included beyond memory access steps, and thus, instruction execution time can be substantially longer. In most microprocessor applications, the actual instruction execution time is substantially less than the total time available between successive input data samplings and output data updates. However, since it is difficult at the outset to establish accurately the length of time required by a string of instructions and the effective dead time or idle time of the microprocessor, it is wise to use an external clock to establish uniform time increments and to assist in synchronization with real-world events. On the other hand, it is generally not a good technique to write long time delays into the software because they would have to be changed whenever instructions were added or deleted from the total program.

2.8 SUMMARY

Software for microprocessors is written in a series of steps. Three levels of flowcharting preceding actual coding will make program development very straightforward. The key to efficient programming is the development of algorithms which represent solutions of the processes required with the best resources. Standard packages of software are available from most microprocessor manufacturers to perform assembly tasks for program development, as well as special subroutines (utility library) such as code translators and peripheral device drivers which can be included with the user's special programs.

In the next chapter, software and programming tasks from a logistics viewpoint are investigated. The questions answered in Chapter 3 are: "what type of support is typically available", and "how do I document what is accomplished".

CHAPTER 3

SUPPORT AND DOCUMENTATION FOR SOFTWARE

3.1 GENERAL

Designing with microprocessors means problem solving through software. Software development typically requires the use of computing equipment to process original program code called "source" code. The source program is the data to be input to a computer, and the object code or output from the computer, is the result of a translation made most often by a program called an assembler. Exactly what computer is needed for programming, and where does the assembler come from? How does the designer enter the source code? What does he get back? What buttons does he push to make it all happen? The answers to these questions lie in the logistics of programming.

Refer to Figure 3.1 to see the steps which must be accomplished in generation of a program. The support of logistics goes from definition of the flow chart to loading of the final program ones and zeros into memory.

Recall from earlier discussions that one of three paths may be taken in generation of software programs. These three paths may be seen in Figure 3.2. Regardless of the path taken, good support programs or programming logistics will be key to the success of a system. Referring to Figure 3.1 and 3.2, it can be easily visualized that if the machine code route is chosen, about the only help received will be data sheets from the manufacturer. A good supply of pencils and paper will be required if anything over 50 to 100 lines of code is attempted. However, if an assembler or compiler is used, a great deal of support may be at hand. The example problems of Chapter 5 will illustrate the specifics of individual assemblers but typically a printout as shown below will result.

Statement Number	Address	Object Code	Label	Operation	Operand	Comments
0027	0000	0360	START	RSET		Clear Mask
0028	0002	02F0		LWPI	WSP	Set Register

The statement number will simply be a reference number to allow identification of a specific line of code.

The address denotes the location of a particular instruction in memory assigned by the assembler. They generally are listed in hexadecimal form.

The object code is the primary result of the assembly process. It is the binary representation of the operation and operand and is normally written in hexadecimal form. For machines with multiple byte instructions, multiple columns of object code will be given.

The remainder of the printout is a listing of the program statement as written by the programmer.

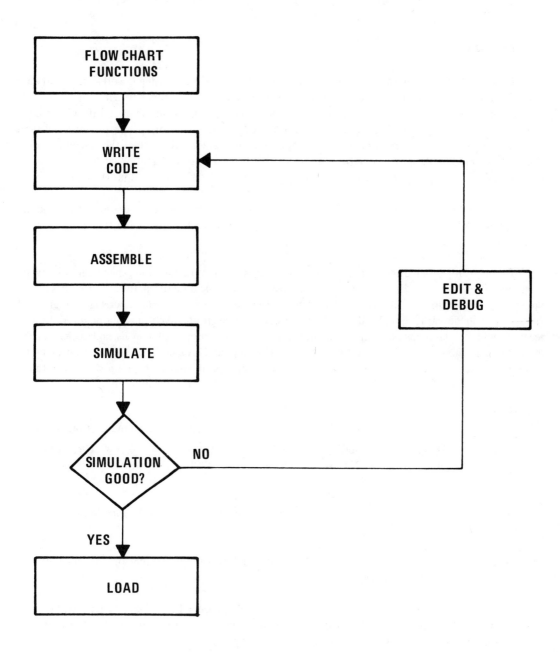

Figure 3.1. Software Programming Steps

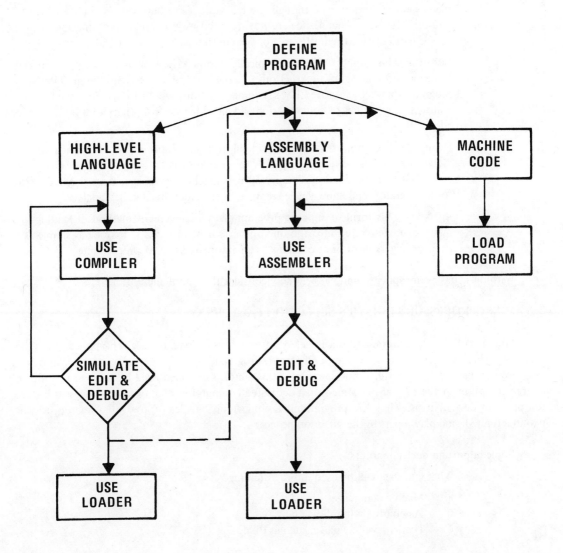

Figure 3.2. Software Development

The remarks column is free space for the programmer. He should utilize this space for reminders and notes on what it is he is trying to accomplish.

The other support programs will be addressed throughout this chapter; however, their functions can be defined.

1. Assembly or Compiler — As discussed above, and typically yields program listings, error conditions, program size, and possibly run time estimates.

2. Simulator — Allows execution of the program on some computers which simulates the system operation even though the microprocessor hardware is not available. As a result, system characteristics are not matched exactly and approximations result. This is particularly true in the area of system timing.

3. Editor — This support program typically allows easy viewing of the program and insertion of change of instructions. If the change code is in the middle of a program, then all associated bookkeeping functions would be accomplished by the editor, i.e., two lines of code inserted and all addresses from that point on have two added.

4. Debug — This support program will allow test conditions to be applied to the system to investigate faults. Typically if an area of code is suspect, a breakpoint is called out and the debug program will halt machine operation there, yield control to the operator, and allow single stepping of the clock for detailed analysis.

5. Loader — This form of support program gives a convenient method of loading the binary data generated into the microprocessor of interest. It may be as simple as a paper-tape generator or as complex as an automated PROM programmer.

With these basic concepts in mind, we will now consider their implementation.

3.2 MICROPROCESSOR LOGISTICS SELECTION FACTORS

One of the most important criteria in selecting a microprocessor for a given application is the ease with which programs can be written and tested. Programming costs are likewise important. Not only are the man-hours important, but sometimes this factor is overshadowed by the cost of time on a large computer or the capital investment in a dedicated computer system or microprocessor system for program development. Thus the programming support or logistics offered by a microprocessor manufacturer should play a part in the selection process.

Some important decision points:

1. What language will be used in programming?

    a. Machine language
    b. Assembly (symbolic) code.
    c. Higher level language, such as PLM

2. What computing equipment is needed to support programming?

    a. Microprocessor-based system
    b. Minicomputer prototyping system
    c. Large-scale computer
    d. Timeshare

3. How is program loaded into the microprocessor memory?

    a. Mask for ROM
    b. Programming a PROM or EROM
    c. Bootstrap and paper tape reader
    d. Bootstrap and mag tape cassette reader
    e. Bootstrap and disk

4. How is testing performed?

    a. Prototyping system
    b. Simulation on a relatively large-scale computer

There are two common approaches to software development for microprocessors: large-scale computer systems and prototyping small-scale microprocessor-based systems.

3.3 HOST COMPUTER SOFTWARE DEVELOPMENT SYSTEM

Use of a large-scale computer (includes minicomputers) for software development means that programming support software from the microprocessor manufacturer must include:

1. Cross-assembler (Cross means assembler is run on machine other than the one programming is being done for)

2. Compiler (if high-level language is to be used)

3. Simulator

4. Debug and Editor

5. Loader

The cross-assembler (assembler for source code in a microprocessor assembly language which is running on some other computer) is the first vital software package. Programs written in the assembly language of the microprocessor are processed by the assembler program to produce machine code usable by the microprocessor. In addition, listings of the assembly language code and the detailed ones and zeros of machine code are made to assist the system designer in testing and debugging phases. Figure 3.3 shows the basic steps in processing programs through the large-scale computer.

After object code has been produced, a testing technique is needed. Since many microprocessors, especially single-chip microcomputers, store instructions in read-only memory (ROM), it is impractical to test the programs on the microprocessor hardware. Initial testing can therefore be carried out in a host computer by using a simulator program. This program executes the microprocessor instruction set as though the host computer were the microprocessor system and provides data for tracing the program operation. Inputs and outputs are simulated not only with logic values but also with timing sequences. Microprocessor execution times will be a critical part of the output listings from a simulation run and should be given careful attention.

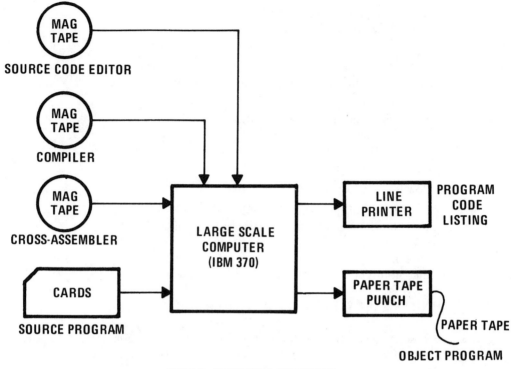

STEP 1. PROGRAM ASSEMBLY

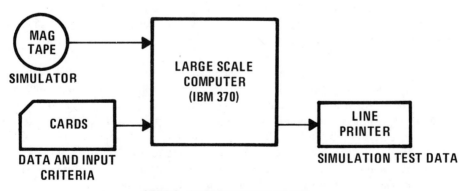

STEP 2. SYSTEM SIMULATION

Figure 3.3. Processing Steps Using Large-Scale Computers

When a specific area of the program development in a host machine requires special attention during testing, a debug or edit program is useful. Here the system designer instructs the computer to trace the status of certain memory words and all the registers during execution of a certain string of instructions. By observing a listing of such step-by-step transactions, the designer can spot difficulties and make appropriate changes in the program. An alternate form of control common in debugging a program would be the technique of inserting breakpoints. When one of the breakpoints is reached, the control would enable the machine to be single-stepped by the operator for detailed analysis of the program.

The use of a large-scale computer for microprocessor software development has several advantages and disadvantages.

3.3.1 Advantages

1. No dedicated software development system is required.

2. Tests can be made to compare various microprocessors for a given application.

3. Simulation provides software testing without hardware.

3.3.2 Disadvantages

1. Complete testing is possible only with hardware in the final configuration.

2. This can be an expensive approach if many passes must be made through the test cycle.

3. Depending upon the particular application, the simulation routine may be inadequate. If this is so, special simulation programs must be written by the designer.

3.4 MICROPROCESSOR-BASED SOFTWARE DEVELOPMENT SYSTEM

Microprocessors that are sufficiently versatile to allow easy interfacing of standard computer peripherals such as magnetic tape, disks, and line printers can be configured into satisfactory software development systems. Support software for this type of system generally consists of:

1. Assembler

2. Compiler (if available)

3. Debug and Editor

4. Loader

The primary advantage of this technique is obvious when a comparison between this list and that of paragraph 3.3 is made. The difference is that program testing may be carried out on the microprocessor immediately following the assembly process, the object code may be entered directly via keyboard or by paper tape into the microprocessor-based software development system. If the memory is large enough, object code may be retained in RAM for access by the microprocessor in a test run. Otherwise, it must be written onto some bulk storage memory such as a cassette or punched into paper tape, and then loaded back into the RAM for testing.

A minimum set of peripherals for this type of system might be a teletype and perhaps high-speed paper-tape punch and reader. By comparison, host computer assemblers would typically be faster. However, the microprocessor-based system allows testing of the software directly.

If the memory is large enough (32K generally), the assembler, editor, and debug programs may be resident simultaneously with the program under development. The advantage in this technique is the minimizing of the loading of programs into the memory via relatively slow peripherals (e.g., teletype or paper-tape reader).

Key questions for microprocessor manufacturers offering microprocessor-based software development systems are:

1. How much memory space is required to hold the assembler program, the editor, the debug program, and any other program development software which the user may require?

2. How does the assembler function? That is, what are the source code media, object code media, listing format, error messages, and the estimated assembly time for typical programs?

3. Is there an operating system or executive program or monitor to oversee the interplay between the assembler, the editor, debug, and development programs?

4. What do the debug and editor programs do? How do they function?

Regarding the last two questions, it is important to identify the software available from the microprocessor manufacturer, and to learn how it works, what it does, how it does it, etc., before selecting the microprocessor. Key to the operation is the monitor or operating system, does it allow a convenient conversational mode between the operator and the microprocessor? The debug program must allow insertion of breakpoints in the test sequence at various points to check the status of all registers before continuing. In general, the use of any support software in a host or resident system must be simple if it is to be effective.

Development of software on a prototyping system has several advantages and disadvantages.

3.4.1 Advantages

1. A closer coupling and better familiarity with the microprocessor exists.

2. Testing does not require the risk of simulation since the program can be checked out in actual operation in the microprocessor.

3. The development system is generally dedicated to software development of the particular microprocessor.

3.4.2 Disadvantages

1. The system is dedicated and therefore is not applicable to other microprocessors.

2. When program development is not required, the system is generally idle which means low utilization of assets.

3.5 INPUT/OUTPUT TECHNIQUES

In each of the foregoing paragraphs, the media for source and object code were discussed as being defined by the particular system. But what are the advantages of one medium over another?

3.5.1 Input

Generally, programming or writing the source code is done in a way that will make editing the simplest. Punched cards are a popular medium since cards can easily be added or replaced. However, with the advent of key-to-disk systems, the physical handling of large decks of cards is becoming less popular.

In fact, for source code, the important factors are:

1. To have some permanent storage medium (cards, cassette, disk)
2. To have a simple editing technique (replacement of cards, update source code on line via an editing program).

Cards are the most likely format for large-scale computers and minicomputers. Paper tape and direct keyboard entry are common in microprocessor-based systems.

3.5.2 Output

Object code output must also be produced in a permanent form (paper tape, cassette, mag-tape) not only for loading into the microprocessor system RAM but also for use in programming PROMs or making masks for ROMs.

One of the most important outputs from the program development process is the program listing, since it frequently takes the most machine time for generation. Often the assembly time is limited by the speed of the printout device. If a line printer or other high-speed printout device can be used, assembly time will be substantially shorter than for the teletype or serial printout device.

Of course, the most versatile systems utilize interactive CRT or visual display during program development, especially debug and edit functions.

3.6 DOCUMENTATION

Programming logistics cannot be complete without appropriate attention to documentation. The most important elements of software documentation are:

1. The specification of the problem
2. The explanation of the problem solution or the overall plan of the algorithms and the software flow charts for routine/subroutine breakdown
3. The line-by-line comments for each instruction that is listed in the assembler printouts.

Explanations of the program in the remarks column of assemblers are vital to adequate documentation not only for systems manuals but also for testing and debugging efforts.

Appropriate comments and explanatory notes are generally entered along with the source code so that they may be included with the first program listings. It should be considered mandatory that the designer write them in detail at the time the program code is first written. Otherwise, it will be virtually impossible to reconstruct the logic and reasoning of the designer by looking only at the strings of instructions.

When two or more persons write programs for a single system, documentation guidelines must be firmly established at the start so that comments and explanations are written with the same basic terminology and so that overall documentation will have continuity.

Documentation, more than any other phase of software generation, will be the primary factor in the success of a program. A poor program with good documentation can be fixed. A good program with poor documentation cannot be used.

3.7 SUMMARY

Programming for microprocessors may typically be accomplished on a relatively large-scale host computer or a microprocessor-based software development system, depending upon the software support of the microprocessor manufacturer.

It is clear that the choices of microprocessor, programming language, and computing hardware to assist in program development, are highly interrelated. In fact, the selection of the microprocessor will generally fix the language and programming computer requirements. It is very important to note that the assembler, as well as other programming support software for a microprocessor, is typically unique and cannot be used for other microprocessors. Similarly, the computer hardware configuration for which a particular assembler was written cannot be changed.

Sophisticated users may be able to develop their own assemblers and other program development software to run on their own computing equipment. However, most designers must rely on the microprocessor manufacturer for software support. The choices of peripherals and input/output media for software support and program development hardware requirements must be obtained from the manufacturer and reviewed during the selection process.

More than any other factor, good documentation will determine the success of a programming effort.

CHAPTER 4

MECHANICS OF PROGRAMMING

4.1   A SAMPLE MICROPROCESSOR SOFTWARE DESIGN

Before programming or coding for a specific microprocessor application can begin, the fundamental groundwork must be laid by defining the basic concepts, structuring algorithms which fit the concept, and detailing the input/output (I/O) specification. In this chapter, a simple message switching system is conceived, and the development of a simple program to implement the functions of the system is explained. As each step in the software program development is achieved, it is demonstrated by a simple example detailing the architecture, instruction set, and software program of an example microprocessor. After the concepts are understood in this simplified example, microprocessor example problems will be discussed in the next chapter.

A complete and thorough description of the problem to be solved must be established. Conceptually, at a general level, a digital system must do three basic things:

1.   Accept input information

2.   Perform logical and arithmetic operations

3.   Provide output information

In effect, the system senses events or accepts data, then using some logic of cause and effect — what happens and why — it provides outputs as required. The timing of events can also be a very important function in making use of digital systems via software.

4.2   SYSTEM DEFINITION

After a system is defined, follow the mechanics of programming from concept to final testing.

4.2.1   Problem Statement

A message switching system is needed in which a single coaxial transmission line brings data in to a point where it must be connected or switched to one of 16 output lines. The input data will contain the information required to operate the switch as follows:

1.   Data will be received as character strings in a standard code.

2.   The first character received will specify the output channel.

3.   The second character will state the number of subsequent characters to be transferred to that output channel.

4.   Character numbers 3 through N will comprise the actual data to be transmitted through the switch.

5.   After all characters in the message are passed through the switch, the output channel is deactivated.

6.   The system then waits for a new message.

Obviously, the problem definition at this point is incomplete, but it is possible to lay out the conceptual planning and as a result find out what additional information is required.

Concept planning — what happens, when and why — can begin with formulation of basic logic ideas and a rough idea of the physical problems. In the message switcher, the first two control characters are the "cause" of the transmission of a character string or message to one of several output channels (the "effect"). If the input is a standard digital signal (e.g., TTL), the switch can be conceived as in Figure 4.1. A microprocessor accepts the single input line and sets one (and only one) output line high selecting one of 16 two-input AND gates.

It is clear that the specification of logic levels, driving capability, and signal timing must be made. In this example, TTL levels will be assumed, the input will drive no more than four TTL loads, and timing will be 300 baud, or 300 bits per second in binary transmission.

4.2.2 Algorithm Development

A conceptual algorithm may be developed at this point, that is, what logic must the digital processor implement to achieve the desired result. A character will be seen by the system as a string of high and low logic-levels with bit times of 3.33 ms. Figure 4.2 shows a technique for timing bits within one character. Using this idea along with the foregoing specifications, the conceptual algorithm may be developed as follows:

1. One input is required.

2. Sixteen outputs are required.

3. The unit must switch the input to one of the outputs.

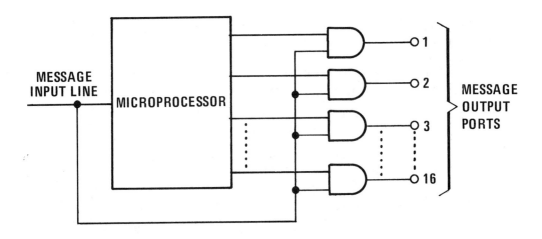

Figure 4.1. Microprocessor Message Switcher

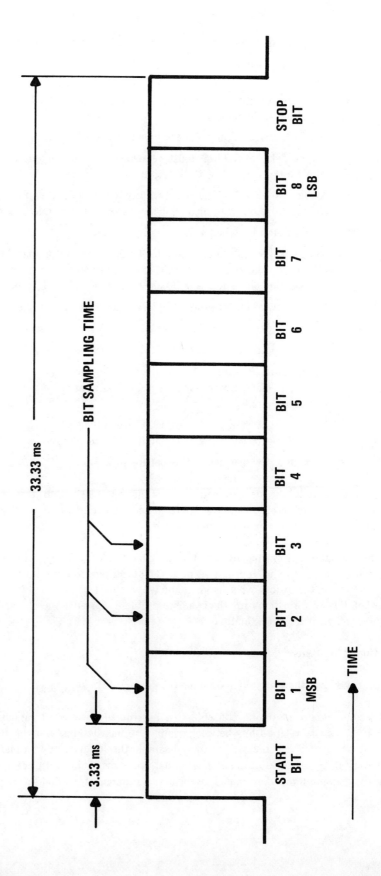

Figure 4.2. Character Timing

4. The first character (eight data bits) specifies the output channel number (1-16).

5. The second character (eight data bits) specifies the message length or number of characters (1-256).

6. Detection of the beginning of a character is achieved by recognition of a high logic-level at the input.

7. Data is received in the most significant bit (MSB) first.

8. A time delay of 3.33 ms must be achieved, preferably via software, to synchronize detection of data bits with the input transmission.

9. A delay of 1.5 x 3.33 ms or 5 ms is needed to define the point in time after the first transition from low to high logic-level when input should be sampled.

10. Skip the start bit when a character is detected.

11. Read the next four bits; each must be 0 before continuing. If they are not 0, return to the starting point and wait for a character. The expected range of channel specification characters is 0000 0000 to 0000 1111 (0 to F HEX).

12. Use the low-order four bits to address one of 16 output lines.

13. Read the next eight-bit character and store as the character count.

14. Set up procedures to decrement the character counter as each character is received.

15. After character count is stored, activate the output line so that subsequent characters may flow through the appropriate gate. Control characters (numbers one and two) do not pass through the switch.

16. When the last character has passed through the gate (character counter equals zero), return the gate select (output) line to a logical zero or low level.

17. Wait for a new message and repeat the process.

The next step is the development of a functional algorithm from the information just developed. This is more detailed and leads to the actual hardware requirements and gives some insight into instruction requirements of the microprocessor.

A functional algorithm means that the designer can completely define the input and output lines as to logic levels, timing, translation, need for buffering, synchronization, etc. In addition, the exact steps taken in the logic — what happens and why — must be specified in detail. To complete the input/output line specifications for the example problem, consider the character rate: is it fixed or may it vary, and what is the maximum rate.

4.2.3 Timing Concepts

Figure 4.3 gives the first step in defining the character timing concept.

A second important timing concept must be studied. How are time delays to be developed? Figure 4.4 shows the relationship between timing of instructions and the time delays. When no character is being received, the system should sample the input at approximately ten times the bit time, or every 0.333 ms. If it does not cause other problems to do so, this sampling could be allowed to run at the maximum rate determined by the actual number of instructions required in the sampling loop.

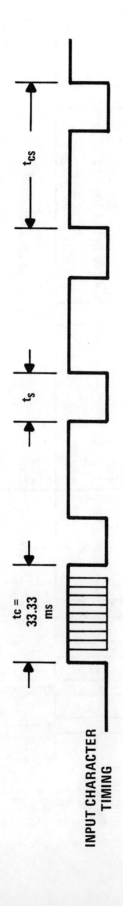

CHARACTER TIME t_c = 33.33 ms

SPACE TIME t_s $\geq$ 3.33 ms

TOTAL TIME t_{cs} $\geq$ 36.67 ms

MAXIMUM CHARACTER RATE = $\dfrac{1}{36.67 \text{ ms}}$ = 27.27 CHARACTERS/SECOND

Figure 4.3. Character Timing Concept

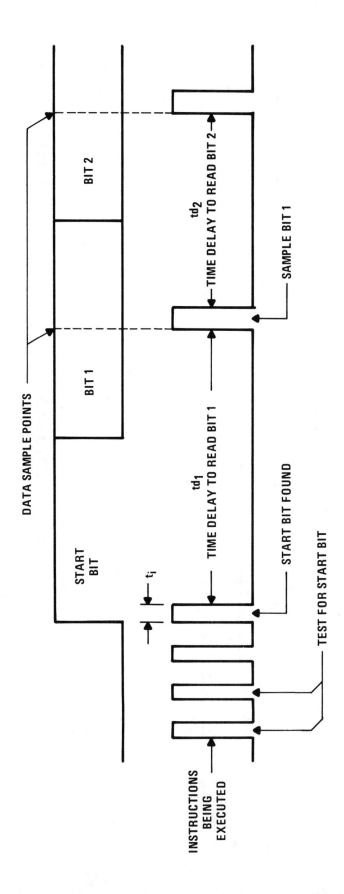

Figure 4.4. Instruction Timing and Time Delay

At this point in functional algorithm development, the I/O techniques of interrupts and polling should be considered to see which can give the best overall system results. In this simple example, the input line is to be continuously polled (sampled), thereby avoiding additional hardware to detect the character.

Referring to Figure 4.4, the instruction execution time, t_i, plus the time delay, td_1, determine the data sampling point for bit 1. Bit 2 is sampled at t_i plus td_2 later. Since the instruction execution speed and the number of instructions are unknown at this time, the time delays cannot be established. Rough figures can be obtained, however, by estimating at least within an order of magnitude what the numbers are.

1. Assume 20 instructions in a data sample loop.

2. Assume 15 μs per instruction.

$$t_i = 20\,(15)\,\mu s = 300\,\mu s$$
$$t_i = 0.300\ ms$$

3. One tenth of a bit time is 0.333 ms

Therefore: $t_i < \dfrac{1}{10}$ bit time

With this rough idea of timing established, flowcharting can begin.

4.3 FLOWCHARTING

As previously discussed, flow charts can be made for three levels of design.

1. Concept level

2. Algorithm level

3. Instruction level

Remember that only when the instruction set of the selected microprocessor is obtained, can the third level flow chart be accomplished.

4.3.1 Concept Flow Chart

Figure 4.5 gives the basic concept-level flow chart for the example problem. The idea is to list in logical order the major events in the program. The designer must make this flow chart sufficiently detailed so that the functional flow chart expansion will be straightforward.

4.3.2 Algorithm Flow Chart

Algorithm flowcharting is the most detailed chart that can be developed without specific reference to a particular microprocessor. This flow chart must state all steps insofar as possible in performing the logic of the system — what happens and why.

Figure 4.6 is the algorithm flow chart for the message switching example. Note the time delays are t_b, 1.5 t_b, and 10 t_b. The value of the t_b can be a design variable, established during actual system testing. This is because t_b is actually a function of the total instruction execution time of the processor. Referring to Figure 4.4 and the instruction timing estimate, the timing criteria can be refined. Note that the flow chart (Figure 4.6) shows only four blocks plus a time delay in the sample loop.

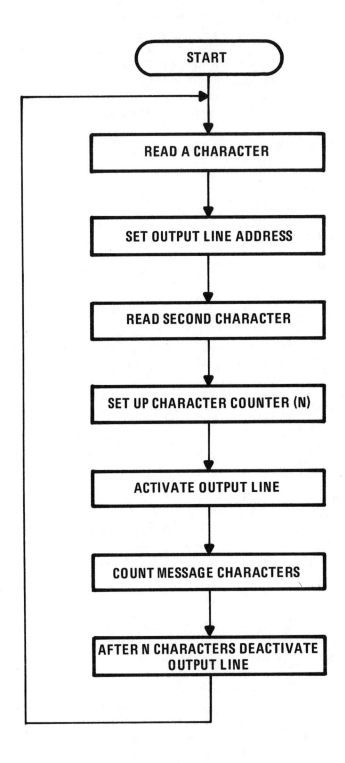

Figure 4.5. Concept Level Flow Chart

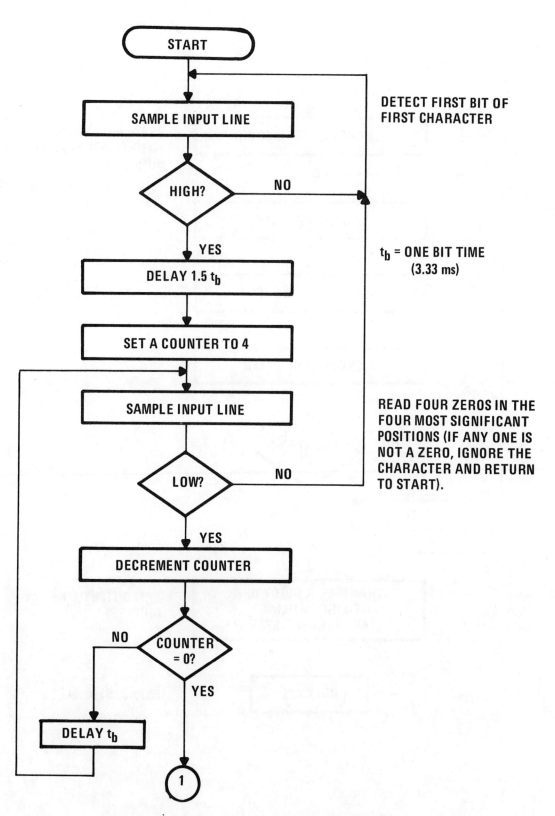

Figure 4.6. Algorithm Flow Chart (Sheet 1 of 4)

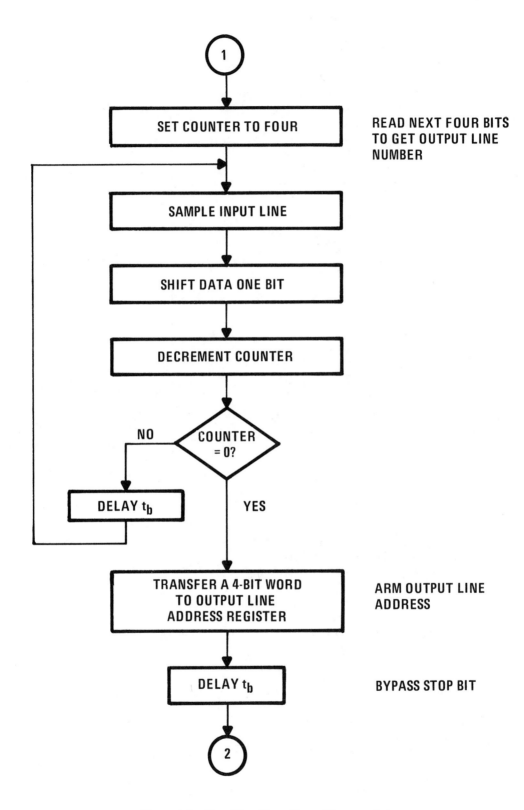

Figure 4.6. Algorithm Flow Chart (Sheet 2 of 4)

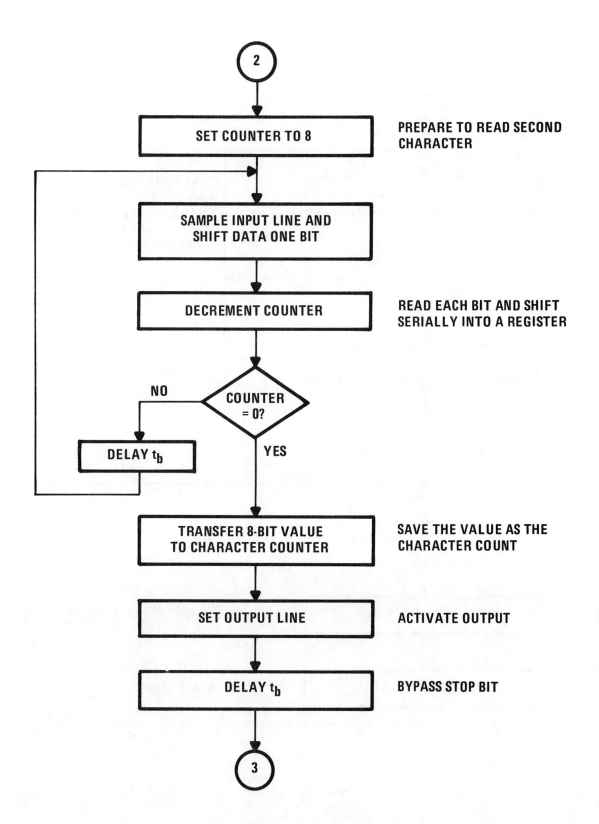

Figure 4.6. Algorithm Flow Chart (Sheet 3 of 4)

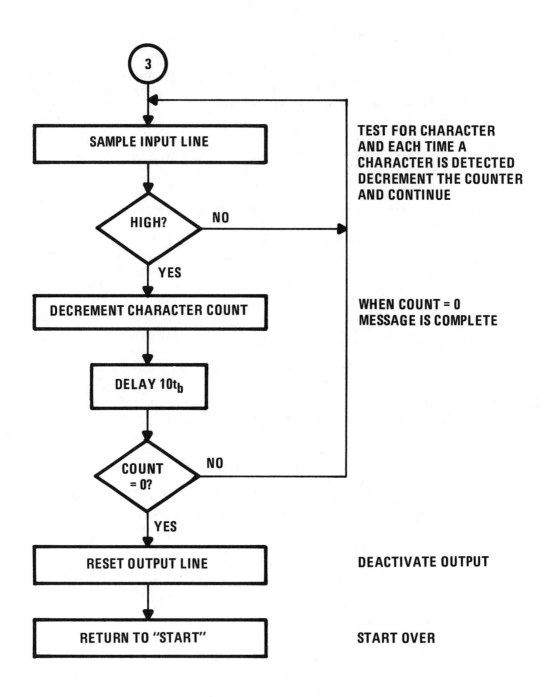

Figure 4.6. Algorithm Flow Chart (Sheet 4 of 4)

1. Input
2. Shift
3. Decrement
4. Test and Branch

If each block of the flow chart were one instruction, an estimate of 20 instructions would be quite high. (Refer back to paragraph 4.2.3.) Thus a second calculation of t_i can be made:

$$t_i = 4 \, (15 \, \mu s) = 60 \, \mu s$$

4.4 HARDWARE DEFINITION

The basic set of four instructions listed above (Input, Shift, Increment, and Branch) can be the nucleus of the microprocessor selection criteria. Actually, the smallest microprocessor (perhaps a microcomputer with external memory for prototyping) might be used. A hypothetical, ultrasimple microprocessor is conceived to satisfy the needs of this example problem. Figure 4.7 outlines the salient features of the "Figment 4" four-bit microcomputer. This hypothetical microcomputer has a very basic instruction set to show the simplest form of programming, and to demonstrate the need for more powerful instructions.

4.4.1 Figment 4 Architecture

As shown in Figure 4.7, the Figment 4 microcomputer has a limited yet versatile set of registers. First, a 12-bit program counter (PC) allows addressing of up to 4K of memory, some of which could be RAM. In the example, 1K words of ROM are combined with 64 words of RAM. The memories share address buses and data buses and therefore are functionally a single memory. The programmer must be careful not to use "store" instructions with operands in the ROM area. Memories are "on-chip" for the monolithic version, and are external in the design and prototyping version.

A memory address register (MAR) receives addresses from the PC when instructions are accessed, and in three stages from the data register (DR) at the data bus when operand addresses are received from the memory. An address buffer is provided to save a return address when a subroutine is called.

Arithmetic and logic instructions apply to the accumulator (with the exception of the register shift). Also, the accumulator is the focal point for data into and out of the memory and the input and output lines.

Input lines are unbuffered and gated into the accumulator. Data from the accumulator may be supplied to the decode/buffer circuit on the output to select one of 16 lines. The four data bits are stored in latch circuits, the outputs of which feed the decode tree. While it is not required for the example, the latch outputs are brought out for parallel data output.

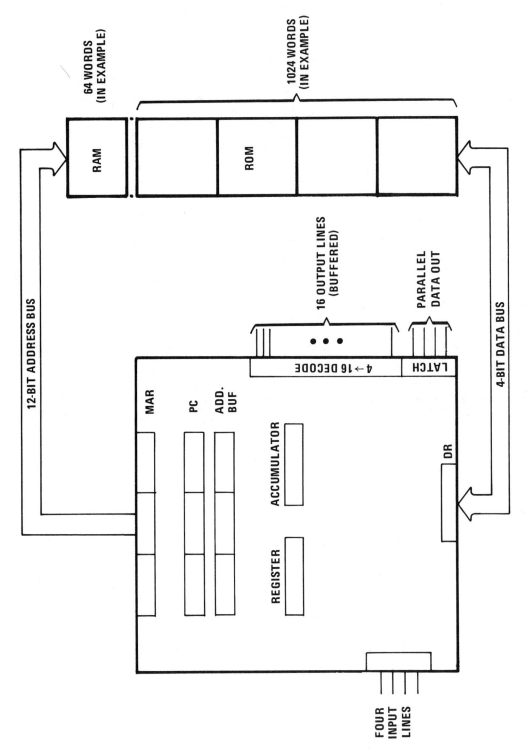

Figure 4.7. Figment 4 Architecture

4.4.2 Figment 4 Instructions

The instruction set of the Figment 4 is limited for instructional purposes to 14 instructions. They are grouped into Input/Output, Data Movement, Logic and Arithmetic, and Program Control as listed below:

1. Input/Output

    IN — Transfer input line logic levels to accumulator

    OUT — Transfer accumulator data to output latch/decode circuit

2. Data Movement

    TAM — Transfer accumulator data to memory

    TMA — Transfer memory data to accumulator

    TAR — Transfer accumulator data to register

    TRA — Transfer register data to accumulator

3. Logic and Arithmetic

    ADD — Sum accumulator with a memory word; result in accumulator

    SUB — Subtract memory word data from accumulator; results in accumulator

    INCR — Increment accumulator

    RSR — Right shift register one bit; zeros fill in high-order bit

    ORR — Accumulator and register ORed; result in register

4. Program Control

    BR — Branch if status bit equals one

    CALL — Branch unconditionally to a subroutine; return address is saved

    RTN — Return from a subroutine (put return address in PC)

All instructions except ADD, SUB, and INCR leave status = 1 **always**. This means that the BR (branch) instruction is an unconditional jump when it follows any instruction other than ADD, SUB, or INCR.

Six of the instructions are memory reference instructions requiring an address for an operand. These are:

- TAM
- TMA
- ADD
- SUB
- BR
- CALL

In each case, four sequential locations (words) in the memory store the 16 bits required. The first four bits (first word) store the instruction code, and the next 12 bits contain the operand address. Figure 4.8 shows the memory reference and register reference instruction formats.

4.4.3 Figment 4 Addressing

Addressing in this microcomputer is in one mode only – direct. The address portion of the memory reference instruction locates the data to be used in transfer or arithmetic instructions. BRanch and CALL instructions contain the "jump-to" address in the address field – words two, three, and four. By using 12 bits for the address, an entire 4K words of memory can be addressed without resorting to paging or indirect addressing. (The Figment 4 allows external memory to be used in addition to the on-chip memories.)

4.4.4 Figment 4 Timing

For purposes of this example, it will be assumed that all instructions consume equal amounts of time. Furthermore, the on-chip clock allows for external rate control via two pins of the package. The highest speed could safely be assumed at approximately 15 μs per instruction. Control of the clock speed is especially useful in synchronizing the microcomputer to other devices in real-time control applications.

4.4.5 Figment 4 Instruction Decode and Control

Although it is not shown on the block diagram of Figure 4.7, the Figment 4 contains instruction decode and control circuits which determine the need for additional words of memory for memory reference instructions, as well as to handle the details of data manipulation and transfer.

4.5 INSTRUCTION-LEVEL FLOW CHART

Now that a microcomputer, the Figment 4, has been selected and the instruction set and architecture studied, the instruction-level flow chart can be completed. The first attempt to write instructions to implement the blanks of the algorithm flow chart usually reveals insight into the architectural elements of the microcomputer and suggests ideas for improved algorithms. Such is the case with the example problem. First, since there is a subroutine technique available via CALL and RTN (return), it will be possible to set up time delays as subroutines. When a delay is needed, the subroutine is called, program control shifts to that block of instructions, and via the return instruction the PC will return control to the calling routine after time-out. A second subroutine is suggested for reading eight-bit characters. Two sequential characters are to be read, one for line number and one for message length. So why not structure a subroutine to read a character? Then the main routine can focus on the data manipulation functions. Figure 4.9 is the complete instruction-level flow chart. A comparison of the first major portions of this chart (down to 2) with the functional flow chart of Figure 4.6 reveals that data manipulation is isolated from character data collection.

When instruction-level flowcharting is done, the designer is constantly aware that the next step, coding, will involve naming certain memory locations where data is to be stored, and labeling instructions for looping. Thus the flow chart includes special mnemonics or names such as TIME1, TIME2 for two different time delay subroutines, HIDAT and LODAT for the names of the two memory bytes used to store the eight-bit character, and KA, KB, etc., for special constants.

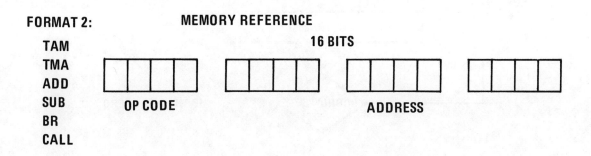

REGISTER REFERENCE

FORMAT 1:

IN
OUT
TAR
TRA
INCR
RSR
ORR
RTN

4 BITS

OP CODE

MEMORY REFERENCE

FORMAT 2:

TAM
TMA
ADD
SUB
BR
CALL

16 BITS

OP CODE

ADDRESS

Figure 4.8. Figment 4 Instruction Format

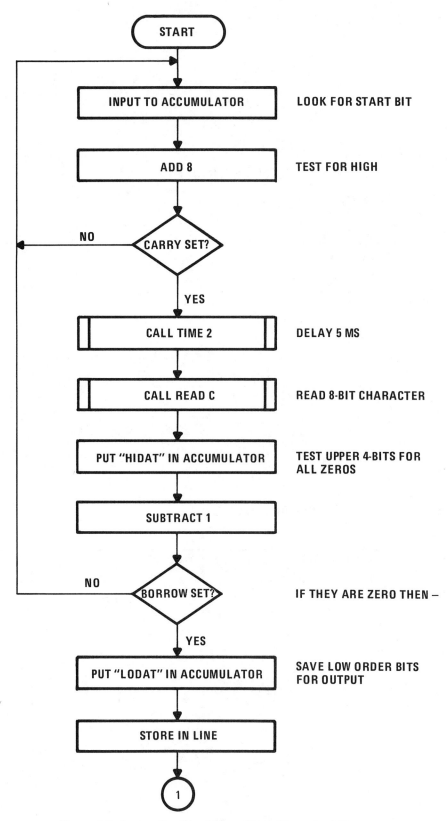

Figure 4.9. Instruction Level Flow Chart (Sheet 1 of 5)

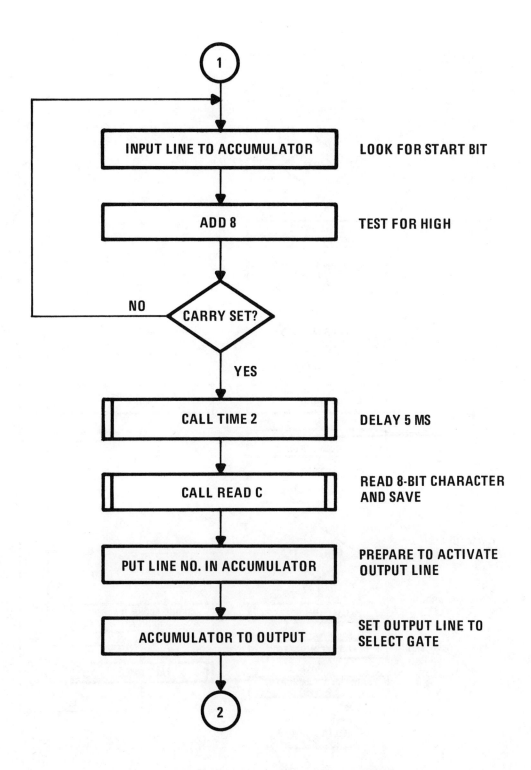

Figure 4.9. Instruction Level Flow Chart (Sheet 2 of 5)

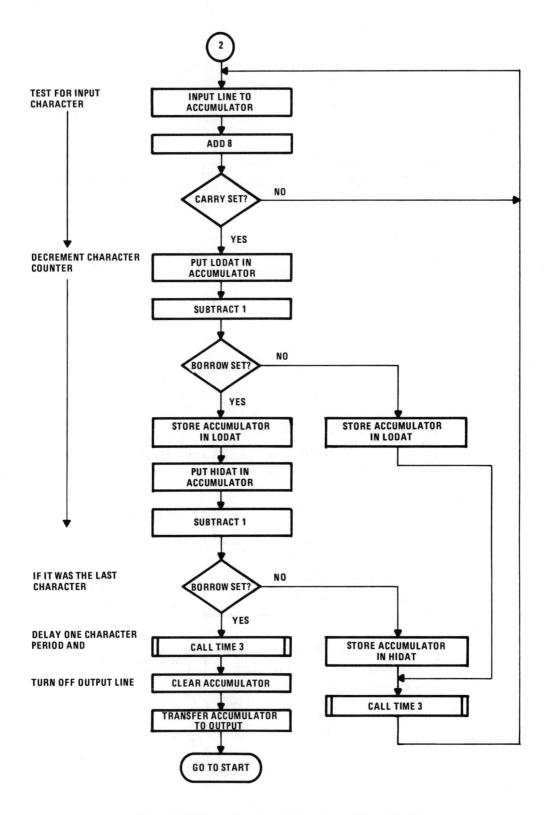

Figure 4.9. Instruction Level Flow Chart (Sheet 3 of 5)

4-20

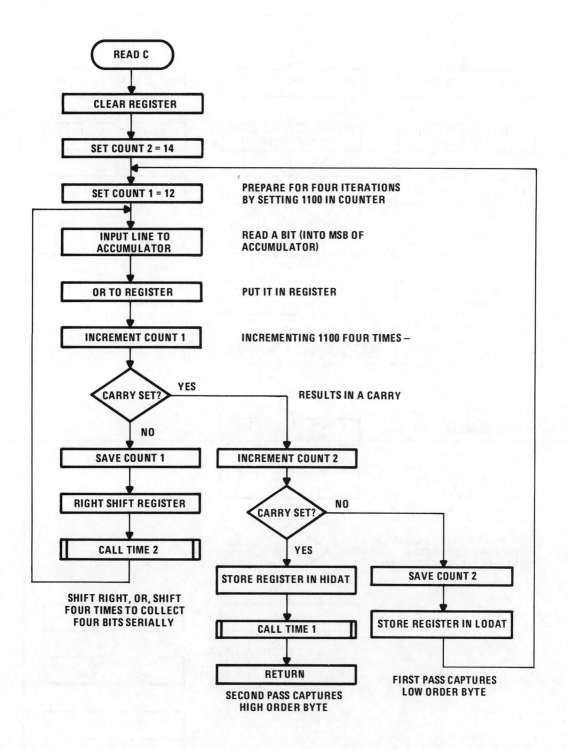

Figure 4.9. Instruction Level Flow Chart (Sheet 4 of 5)

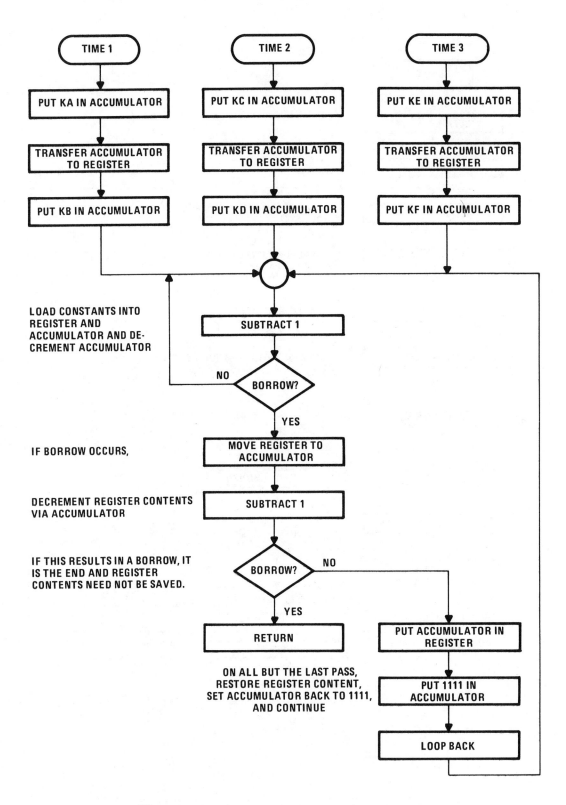

Figure 4.9. Instruction Level Flow Chart (Sheet 5 of 5)

4.5.1 Timing Flow Chart

Time delays via software in real-time systems are desirable from a manufacturing standpoint, but are not necessarily simple for coding. In this case, the number of instructions in a loop and the instruction times are yet to be established. An algorithm for decrementing a two-digit HEX number (eight binary bits) can accomplish the desired delays (see the instruction-level flow chart, Figure 4.9). Assuming values for the two HEX digits "a" and "b" from 00 to FF, and determining the number of instruction cycles is the first step. Table 4.1 gives values for each HEX number in instruction time units. If an instruction time is 15 μs the minimum time delay (00) is 9 x 15 or 135 μseconds.

A second input criteria is that the time unit be related by the following ratio:

$$T_1:T_2:T_3 = 1:1.5:10$$

Three numbers must be selected from all the possible values which will satisfy the ratio. Five sets are shown in Table 4.2, and one is chosen arbitrarily.

Table 4.1. Time Delays for Various Values of a and b

ab (Hexadecimal)	Time Unit (Decimal)	ab (Hexadecimal)	Time Unit (Decimal)
00	9	19	60
01	11	1A	62
02	13	1B	64
03	15	1C	66
04	17	1D	68
05	19	1E	70
06	21	1F	72
07	23	20	74
08	25	30	106
09	27	40	138
0A	29	50	170
0B	31	60	202
0C	33	70	234
0D	35	80	266
0E	37	90	298
0F	39	A0	330
10	42	B0	362
11	44	C0	394
12	46	D0	426
13	48	E0	458
14	50	F0	490
15	52	.	
16	54	.	
17	56	.	
18	58	FF	520 (max)

Table 4.2. Valid Numbers for Time Units

Time Unit	ab (Hexadecimal)	
42	10	
63 (64)	1B	
420	CD	
44	11	
66	1C	
440	D7	
48	13	
72	1F	Chosen Arbitrarily
480	EB	
50	14	
75 (76)	21	
500	F5	
52	15	
78	22	
520	FF	

At 300 baud, the bit time is:

$$\frac{1}{300} \text{ second or 3.333 ms}$$

One-bit time corresponds to 48 time units. The desired instruction time is given by:

$$t_i = \left(\frac{1}{300}\right)\left(\frac{1}{48}\right) \times 10^6 \text{ microseconds}$$

$$t_i = 69.44 \text{ microseconds}$$

This is more than four times the 15-μs specification speed. However, like most microcomputers with an on-chip clock, the Figment 4 provides for an external timing capacitor to establish the clock rate. Obviously this can be adjusted to establish the best absolute timing. Relative timing per the ratio is accomplished via software.

4.6   CODING

The instructions for the Figment 4 microcomputer are given in Table 4.3. Before programming can begin, a thorough understanding of these instructions is required. Refer back to paragraph 4.4.2 for the explanation of each instruction.

Table 4.3. Figment 4 Instruction Set

Group	Code	Mnemonic	No. Bytes	Status Effect
Input/Output	1	IN	1	
	2	OUT	1	
Data Movement	3	TAM	4	
	4	TMA	4	
	5	TAR	1	
	6	TRA	1	
Arithmetic and Logic	7	ADD	4	√
	8	SUB	4	√
	9	INCR	1	√
	A	RSR	1	
	B	ORR	1	
Program Control	C	BR	4	
	D	CALL	4	
	E	RTN	1	

Since the Figment 4 microcomputer always starts with the PC at zero when power is applied, this will be the location of the first instruction. Following the instruction-level flow chart, the designer may write the instructions sequentially filling in the OP and Operand columns primarily. Comments are very useful for reference during debugging.

The first instruction needs no operand. The second instruction operand addresses the location of a constant (an 8). How do you know where that 8 is? Through the use of a pseudo instruction (sometimes called an assembler directive or dummy instruction), the designer allocates storage cells with names for constants. Table 4.4 (pages 005 and 006) demonstrates the OP code of DATA to relate labels such as D8 to the actual decimal number 8, and to reserve memory words for these constants.

Note that constants may be stored in ROM while words reserved for variable data must be in the RAM. Page 006 of Table 4.4 lists the variable data reservation pseudo instructions.

OP and Operand columns are filled in first with labels added as the loop points are defined (such as START, MSGNO, MSSG, etc.). Each BRANCH instruction, for instance, has an operand that must be defined as a label of some other instruction.

Pages 000 through 007 (Table 4.4) give the complete program listing as it might emerge from a computer printout device. Refer to page 001 as the starting point for coding.

Table 4.4. Complete Program Listing

Symbol Table

Symbol	Location	Symbol	Location
D0	110	WAIT 3	079
D1	111	TIME 3	0FC
D8	112	COUNT 1	403
D12	113	COUNT 2	404
D14	114	SAVE 1	0B4
START	000	SAVE 2	0C1
TIME 1	0CF	INPUT	096
TIME 2	0EF	IN2	08E
READ 6	081	KA	115
HIDAT	401	KB	116
LODAT	400	KC	117
LINE	402	KD	118
MSGNO	025	KE	119
MSSG	03B	KF	11A
WAIT 1	06D	LOOP	0D8
WAIT 2	071	CONT	0EA

Table 4.4. Complete Program Listing (Continued)

Location	Content	Label	OP	Operand	Comments
00	1	START	IN		Test input line for
01	7112		ADD	D8	high level.
05	C000		BR	START	Keep trying until
09	D0EF		CALL	TIME 2	high is found. Wait 5 ms
0D	D081		CALL	READC	and load 8 bits.
11	4401		TMA	HIDAT	Test high order four bits
15	8111		SUB	D1	for all zeros.
19	C000		BR	START	If not, start over.
1D	4400		TMA	LODAT	If so, interpret the low
21	3402		TAM	LINE	order four bits as output.
25	1	MSGNO	IN		Look for next character
26	7112		ADD	D8	by detecting high level.
2A	C025		BR	MSGNO	Keep testing until
2E	D0CF		CALL	TIME 2	high is found. Wait 5 ms
32	D081		CALL	READL	and load 8 bits.
36	4402		TMA	LINE	Now transfer line No. to
3A	2		OUT		output. Activate selected gate.
3B	1	MSSG	IN		Detect each character
3C	7112		ADD	D8	of a message at input.
40	C03B		BR	MSSG	Continue test for high.
44	4400		TMA	LODAT	When a character is detected,
48	8111		SUB	D1	subtract one from count
4C	C06D		BR	WAIT 1	and wait one character
50	3400		TAM	LODAT	period before
54	4401		TMA	HIDAT	continuing.
58	8111		SUB	D1	
5C	C079		BR	WAIT 3	

Location	Content	Label	OP	Operand	Comments
60	D0FC		CALL	TIME 3	If this was the last character,
64	4110		TMA	D0	clear accumulator and
68	2		OUT		output to deactivate gate
69	C000		BR	START	and return to start.
6D	3400	WAIT 1	TAM	LODAT	When decrementing counter, if
71	D0FC	WAIT 2	CALL	TIME 3	no borrow, save low byte, wait
75	C03B		BR	MSSG	one character period, and
					return.
79	3079	WAIT 3	TAM	HIDAT	If no borrow from decrement,
7D	C071		BR	WAIT 2	save high byte and wait as
					before.

Table 4.4. Complete Program Listing (Continued)   Page 003

Location	Content	Label	OP	Operand	Comments
81	4110	READC	TMA	D0	Clear accumulator and
85	5		TAR		register and initialize
86	4114		TMA	D14	a count-of-2 in memory.
8A	3404		TAM	COUNT 2	Set up count-of-4 the
8E	4113	IN2	TMA	D12	same way.
92	3403		TAM	COUNT 1	
96	1	INPUT	IN		Read one bit into accumulator
97	B		ORR		and transfer to register.
98	4403		TMA	COUNT 1	Bring in count-of-4 word
9C	9		INCR		and increment it. Status set.
9D	COB4		BR	SAVE 1	No; Go to save 1
A1	4404		TMA	COUNT 2	Yes; bring in count-of-2
A5	9		INCR		and increment it, Status set?
A6	COC1		BR	SAVE 2	No; Go to save 2
AA	6		TRA		Yes; transfer register
AB	3401		TAM	HIDAT	data to acc. and to memory.
AF	DOCF		CALL	TIME 1	Wait one-half bit time
B3	E		RTN		and return.
B4	3403	SAVE 1	TAM	COUNT 1	Store the count-by-4 value.
B8	A		RSR		Shift register data right.
B9	DOEF		CALL	TIME 2	Wait for one bit time and
BD	C096		BR	INPUT	go back for another bit.
C1	3404	SAVE 2	TAM	COUNT 2	Save the count-of-2 number
C5	6		TRA		and put the input
C6	3400		TAM	LODAT	data into acc. and store.
CA	C08E		BR	IN2	Go get another four bits.
CE	E		RTN		

Table 4.4. Complete Program Listing (Continued)

Location	Content	Label	OP	Operand	Comments
CF	4115	TIME 1	TMA	KA	Put HEX 13 in register and
D3	5		TAR		accumulator.
D4	4116		TMA	KB	
D8	8111	LOOP	SUB	D1	Decrement accumulator and
DC	C0D8		BR	LOOP	check for borrow.
E0	6		TRA		If so, decrement
E1	8111		SUB	D1	register content.
E5	C0EA		BR	CONT	Again check for borrow.
E9	E		RTN		If so, END/return.
EA	5	CONT	TAR		If not, return high word to
EB	4118		TMA	KD	register, set accumulator to
EF	C0D8		BR	LOOP	F, and loop back.
F3	4117	TIME 2	TMA	KC	Put HEX 1F in register and
F4	5		TAR		accumulator.
F8	4118		TMA	KD	
FC	C0D8		BR	LOOP	Decrement via main loop.
100	4119	TIME 3	TMA	KE	Put HEX EB in register and
101	5		TAR		accumulator.
105	411A		TMA	KF	
109	C0D8		BR	LOOP	Decrement via main loop.
10D					Unused
10E					↓
10F					

Table of Constants

Location	Content	Label	OP	Operand	Comments
110	0	D0	DATA	0	Decimal 0
111	1	D1	DATA	1	Decimal 1
112	8	D8	DATA	8	Decimal 8
113	C	D12	DATA	12	Decimal 12
114	E	D14	DATA	14	Decimal 14
115	1	KA	DATA	1	Decimal 1
116	3	KB	DATA	3	Decimal 3
117	1	KC	DATA	1	Decimal 1
118	F	KD	DATA	F (H)	Decimal 15
119	E	KE	DATA	E (H)	Decimal 14
11A	B	KF	DATA	B (H)	Decimal 11

Table 4.4. Complete Program Listing (Continued)   Page 006

RAM Layout

Location	Content	Label	OP	Operand	Comments
400	0	LODAT	DATA	0	Low order 8 bits
401	0	HIDAT	DATA	0	High order 8 bits
402	0	LINE	DATA	0	Output line number
403	0	COUNT1	DATA	0	Dynamic counter (4)
404	0	COUNT2	DATA	0	Dynamic counter (2)

Note: RAM data is random when power is first applied. Values are stored in the locations above during operation.

Instruction Code	Mnemonic	No. Times Used
1	IN	4
2	OUT	1
3	TAM	10
4	TMA	18
5	TAR	5
6	TRA	2
7	ADD	3
8	SUB	5
9	INCR	2
A	RSR	1
B	ORR	1
C	BR	18
D	CALL	7
E	RTN	2
	DATA	16

83 Instructions Total
11B Locations Used (283_{10})

4.7 ASSEMBLY PROCESS

In a simple program such as our example, the assembly process can be performed manually. The steps are as follows:

1. Starting with 0000, write the location numbers, counting by four for all memory reference instructions. Table 4.5 will assist in determining number sequences such as 1, 5, 9, D, etc. These numbers should be written in HEX to simplify conversion to binary.

Table 4.5. Counting by Four in Hexadecimal

0	1	2	3
4	5	6	7
8	9	A	B
C	D	E	F

2. Generate the symbol table, Table 4.4 (page 000), in order of occurrence, alphabetical order, or in whatever order makes sense. This table gives the location number for each label. Notice the number corresponds to that place in the code where the symbol (such as START) appears in the *label* column.

3. Fill in the content of each location by first listing the instruction codes (1, 7, C, D, etc.) Then fill in the three operand bytes of the memory reference instructions from the symbol table.

Follow this procedure for the first few instructions. The IN instruction is a one-byte instruction whereas the next nine instructions are all four-byte instructions. This means that the sequence of memory words containing this are:

Location	Instruction	
0	START	
1	ADD	08
2		
3		
4		
5	BR	START
6		
7		
8		
9	CALL	TIME2
10		
11		
12		

To simplify the listing, only the first location for each four-byte instruction need be written, hence, the sequence of location numbers:

$$0$$
$$1$$
$$5$$
$$9$$
$$D$$
$$11$$
$$15$$
etc.

Referring to Table 4.3, each instruction code may be determined. The first number in the content column is the operation code:

1	IN
7	ADD
C	BR
D	CALL
D	CALL
4	TMA
etc.	

Symbol table data is determined by listing all the labels used in the program, and then filling in the correct number for each location. Decimal constants D0, D1, D8, etc., were arbitrarily placed in sequential locations starting with 110. This was done by noting the last instruction was at 109 and the next round number was 110. (Note: typically an assembler would not leave three spare words as was arbitrarily done here.) Symbols START, TIME1, TIME2 are found in the label field of the code on pages 001 and 004. From page 004:

Location	Symbol (In Label Field)
CF	TIME 1
D8	LOOP
EA	CONT
F3	TIME 2
etc.	

Typically, there are a number of checks made by most assemblers and error messages are printed out when errors are encountered. Some error checks might be as follows:

1. Check for illegal OP code

2. Check for a symbol used more than once as a label, thereby creating two or more locations with the same name, an obviously unacceptable ambiguity.

3. Check for an undefined symbol. This is a symbol such as MSSG which appears as an operand but through error was not entered in the label field, or perhaps the symbol was misspelled when entered in the label field (e.g., MSGG instead of MSSG).

4. Check for a symbol that is unreferenced. This is the symbol in the label field which never appears in the operand field. While this is not a fatal error, it is often a useful warning to the designer (and can assist in solving misspelled label errors).

5. Check for proper syntax — there are rules for entering constants (decimal or hexadecimal?), the maximum number of characters in a label, the need for spaces between label, OP, and operand, etc., all of which must be followed. Otherwise, error messages flag ambiguities.

6. Sometimes the assembler will collect statistical data such as shown on page 007 of Table 4.4.

4.8 OBJECT CODE – PROGRAM LOADING/STORAGE

In the example application of the Figment 4 microcomputer, it is conceivable that the actual object code (memory address and content) can be manually entered into PROMs, especially during the development phase. An assembly process as just described in paragraph 4.7 will, however, output this code in some auto load form such as paper tape, cassette, or other storage media. Then a PROM programmer could be driven automatically.

If a mask programmed ROM is to be used for program storage in a microprocessor system, then the program or object code is sent to the semiconductor manufacturer for processing.

If it is desired to put the program in RAM, no changes are necessary in the procedures outlined thus far. However, a small ROM with a "bootstrap" program must be added to enable start-up from power interrupt or power-up conditions when contents of a RAM are lost. The idea is to provide a means for reading data from a paper-tape reader (or other input device) into RAM, storing it in the proper locations, and then transferring control to the RAM program.

4.9 SUMMARY

The Figment 4 example is simplified beyond typical real-world problems. It does, however, yield good insight into how to tackle a software design problem and gives experience in going through the steps. The next chapter is a selection of problems with varying complexity to assist in gaining experience and insight into the design and use of microprocessors.

CHAPTER 5

MICROPROCESSOR SAMPLE DESIGN PROBLEMS

5.1 TMS 1000 PROBLEM

5.1.1 Problem Statement – Electronic Taxi Meter

This example program illustrates the use of a TMS 1000 microcomputer in an electronic taxi meter system. It is clearly a cost-effective replacement for present mechanical systems.

The advantages of using the TMS 1000 in this system are low component cost, low assembly cost (one-chip processing), high reliability, high accuracy, and low power consumption.

The requirements for a taxi meter are demanding. Besides keeping a running total of the fare calculated on a particular fare rate, the meter must also charge a minimum fare based on a variable fare rate. It must be able to multiply fare rates by a factor determined by a time of day and/or a day of the week (higher rates during the evening and/or weekends), compute fares for multiple passengers, etc.

Only a subset of these requirements will be included in this example so that TMS 1000 programming techniques can be demonstrated while keeping extraneous details to a minimum.

The taxi meter in this example keeps a running total of the taxi fare based on both a minimum fare and a fare rate which goes into effect after the distance for a minimum fare is reached. A passenger will be charged the additional fare before the distance is actually traveled. For example, if the minimum fare for the first mile traveled is $0.75, and the fare rate is $0.15 per ¼ mile, then the fare is $0.75 until the taxi has traveled one mile. At that point, $0.15 is added to the fare. When the taxi has traveled 1 ¼ miles, $0.15 is again added to the fare, etc. The system has a start switch that resets the fare display and starts the fare calculation.

5.1.2 Hardware Definition

This electronic taxi meter system can be implemented with the TMS 1000 using the schematic shown in Figure 5.1. To monitor the distance traveled, a magnet and pickup are attached to the axle. This pickup supplies a pulse every tire rotation ($\approx$6.534 feet). This is a noisy pulse which must be amplified and shaped up externally. This may also be a very narrow pulse ($\approx$800 ns) which the TMS 1000 cannot recognize. An external pulse stretcher solves this problem.

To facilitate changes in the fare and distance increments, a diode matrix will be used. A keyboard or thumbwheel switches could be used, but government standards dictate that the system to supply these rates must be secured so that all changes are properly supervised.

The distance on the diode matrix is based on the number of tire rotations and is in binary format. For example, if the distance for a minimum fare is one mile, or 808 rotations [5280/(6.534 ft/rotation)], then 328 in HEX (hexadecimal) must be the input at this position.

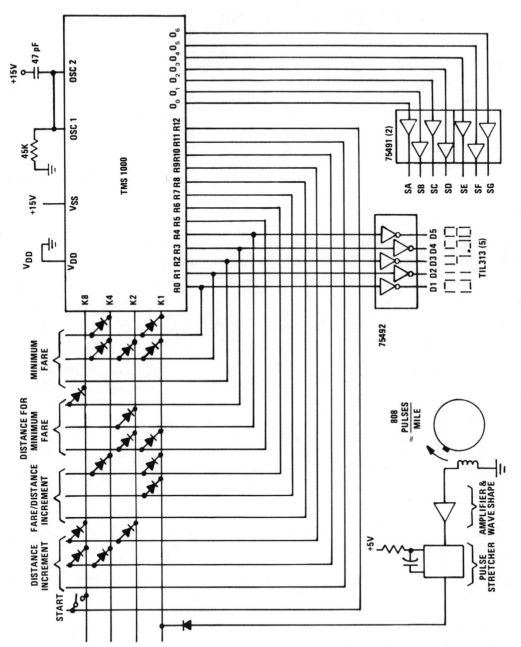

Figure 5.1. System Diagram

The fares are input in binary coded decimal (BCD) format. For instance, a minimum fare of $0.75 is read in as 075.

The start switch contacts will bounce, causing a string of pulses at turn-on; but the software can include appropriate compensation.

To display the fare, five 7-segment, 0.3-inch LED displays are used. These large displays require external buffering.

5.1.3 Software Definition and Flow Charts

The system flow charts are divided into an INITIALIZATION routine (Figure 5.3), an EXECUTIVE routine (Figure 5.4), and a COUNT routine (Figure 5.5). Refer to the example problem in paragraphs 5.1.4 and 5.1.5 to study the detail presented in these flow charts, the system block diagram, and the full system coding of paragraph 5.1.6.

Before actual TMS 1000 flowcharting begins on any problem, data storage areas in the RAM must be allocated. By carefully selecting these areas, the number of ROM words to implement an algorithm and the speed of execution of an algorithm can be minimized. Figure 5.2 is a RAM data map for this problem. Both the minimum fare and fare/distance increment registers are logically adjacent to the display registers. The distance registers are logically adjacent to the distance counter. This optimizes the routines which perform comparisons between these registers. The control flags are located in the same file as the display register. This minimizes X addressing the EXEC routine, where X is set to 00 to address the display register.

As the system is initially powered up, the diode matrix is scanned and their states stored in their respective registers in the TMS 1000 RAM. The diodes are scanned by sequentially setting R output lines and then transferring the K input values to the accumulator. When all the diode states are transferred in, then the contents of the minimum fare register are transferred to the display register. Control then passes to the EXEC routine. The power-up flow chart is shown in Figure 5.3.

EXEC routines (Figure 5.4) refresh the display, test the status of the start switch, and test the pulse input on K1. The refresh routine refreshes the display using a digit scanning technique. Each digit is displayed for about 1 ms. The start switch is tested by setting R12 and testing K8. Closing the start switch sets K8 = 1. When first closed, the minimum fare is transferred to the display register and the distance counter cleared. The TMS 1000 then begins making fare calculations by counting pulses from the axle. A flag bit, labeled STRTFL, will be used to indicate the previous state of the start switch. This is essential since the transition from an open to closed switch initiates the minimum fare transfer and the clearing of the distance counter. When it is determined that the start switch is closed, the pulse input is tested. If the pulse input is high, the COUNT routine is entered. Since the pulse may stay high longer than 5 ms (refresh time), then it is possible to double count one pulse. To prevent this, a flag bit labeled PLSFL is used to indicate the status of the pulse input when last tested. Bit manipulations are simplified in the TMS 1000 because of the availability of the instructions SBIT, RBIT, and TBIT1.

The COUNT routine (Figure 5.5) increments the distance counter until the distance for a minimum fare is reached. At that point, the fare for a distance increment (cents/¼ mile) is added to the display register. After the distance for a minimum fare is reached, the fare for a distance increment is added to the display register whenever the distance counter is equal to the distance increment. A flag, labeled MFFL, will be set when the distance for a minimum fare is reached. The fare for a distance increment is always added to the display register before the distance is traveled.

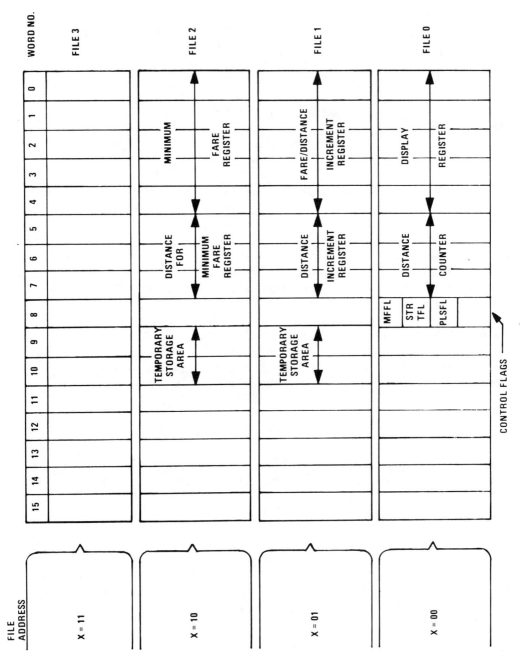

Figure 5.2. RAM Data Map

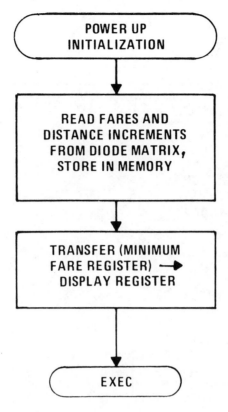

Figure 5.3. Initialization Flow Chart

5.1.4 Example Problem Flow Chart

As an example problem in flowcharting and coding, the first block of the COUNT routine of Figure 5.5 is expanded. The steps required to increment the distance counter are identified. This is to be done by the reader as an exercise using the blank chart, Figure 5.6. Try to fill in the blanks before looking at the completed chart (Figure 5.7), which fits in as the first step of Figure 5.5.

Refer to the system block diagram, Figure 5.1, the RAM layout, Figure 5.2, and the TMS 1000 data book (Appendix E) before you begin your flowcharting.

The steps to be accomplished are:

1. Set up pointer to the distance counter words of RAM

2. Increment this group of words (checking for carry bits)

3. Store results and branch to continuation point.

In Figure 5.2, the RAM layout, note the location of the distance counter in file 0, words 5-7.

Additional information regarding previous and subsequent routines is needed to complete the example.

1. The COUNT routine is entered from the EXEC in which X has been set to 0, thus addressing file 0.

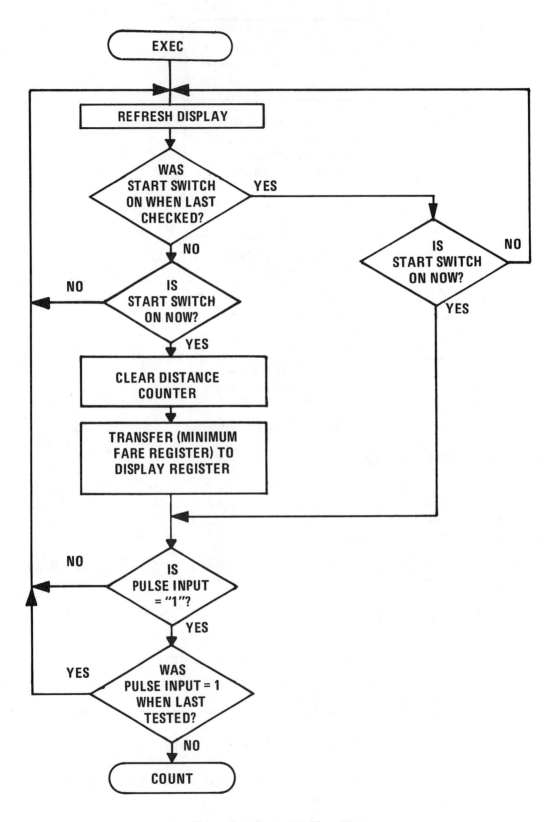

Figure 5.4. Executive Flow Chart

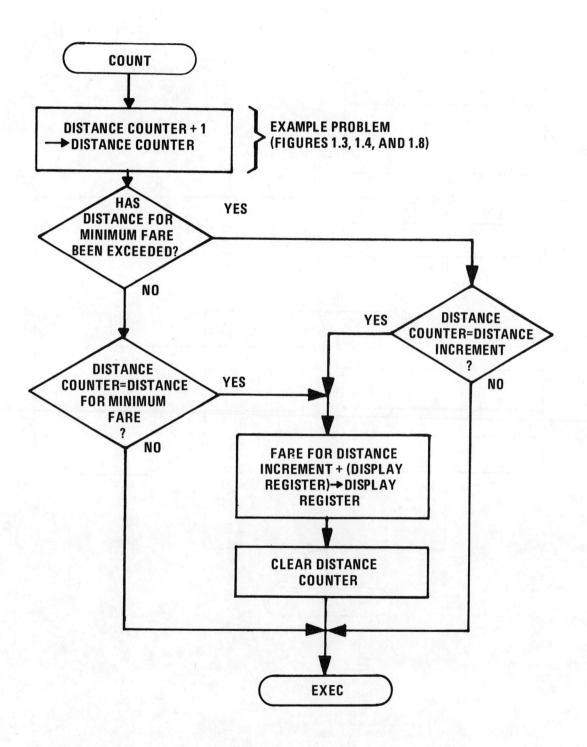

Figure 5.5. Count Flow Chart

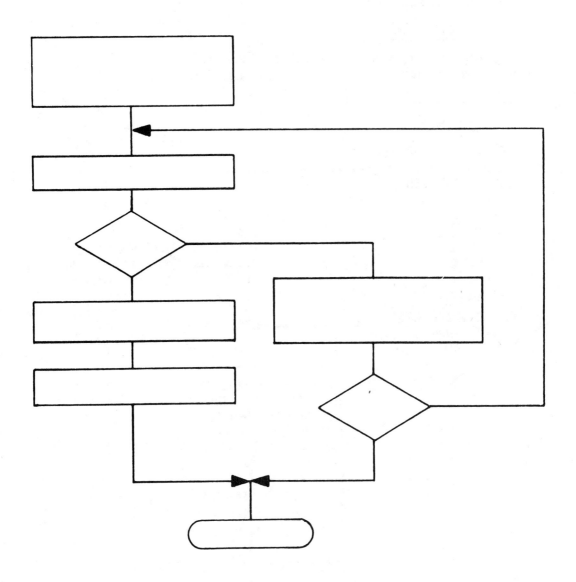

Figure 5.6. Example Problem Flow Chart (Blank)

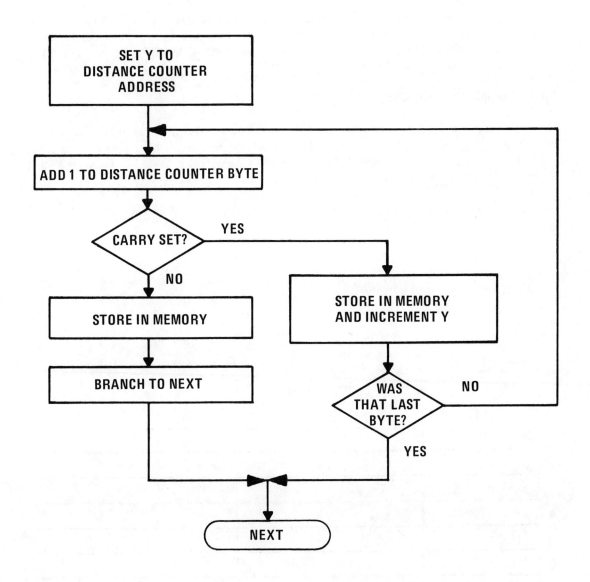

Figure 5.7. Example Problem Flow Chart (Completed)

2. The next portion of the COUNT routine starts with the assumption that X = 0 and Y = 8. Be sure to set Y to 8 as a part of the routine in this example.

3. Note paragraph 2.8, page E-11, of the TMS 1000 data book in Appendix E. (This paragraph explains that following any instruction which does not conditionally set the status bit, the status will always be *one*. Therefore, the branch (BR) instruction following such a nonstatus-setting instruction becomes an unconditional branch. Page E-12 of the TMS 1000 data book lists the instructions and includes a Y in the status effect columns for status-setting instructions. All others set the status bit to one automatically.)

5.1.5   Example Problem Coding

As an exercise in coding for the TMS 1000, the code for the preceding flow chart may be written. A coding sheet (Figure 5.8) is provided and you are encouraged to complete this without referring to paragraph 5.2.11. A subset of the instructions is provided in Table 5.1. These are all that are required for the nine instructions implementing this software section.

The complete listing of the program is shown in paragraph 5.1.6.

CODING FORM

LABEL	INSTRUCTION	OPERAND
1		
2		
3		
4		
5		
6		
7		
8		
9		

Figure 5.8. Example Coding Sheet (Blank)

Table 5.1. Instruction Subset

TCY	Transfer constant to Y register
IMAC	Increment memory and load into acc. if carry, one to status
BR	Branch on status = 1
TAM	Transfer acc. to memory
TAMIY	Transfer acc. to memory and increment Y
YNEC	If Y ≠ constant, one to status

5.1.6 Software Assembly Listing

Tables 5.2, 5.3, and 5.4 give the complete listing of the software written for this example problem. The TMS 1000 data book is required for an understanding of the instruction. However, two instructions are used which are not in the TMS 1000 data book: BRL and CALLL. These are actually assembler directives, and result in two instructions: LDP and BR, or LDP and CALL. These instructions are in the TMS 1000 data book.

5.1.7 TTL Implementation of TMS 1000 Problem

As a comparison to the electronic taxi meter designed with the TMS 1000 microcomputer, an estimate can be made of the relative complexity of such a task using standard TTL networks. Figure 5.9 is a block diagram of the elements of the system. Figure 5.10 is a basic timing diagram for the different elements. The four semivariable pieces of data, minimum fare, distance for minimum fare, fare/distance increment, and distance increment are assumed wired into a circuit board with jumpers.

The functions are in two sections. The distance traveled must be monitored and compared against one of two numbers — the distance for the minimum fare, or the distance increment for a fare increment. When the comparator indicates a match between the preset and actual distance, it signals action for the second portion of the circuit. Here an accumulator must be updated and displayed to show cumulative fare calculations.

5.1.7.1 Distance Measuring Section

Initially, the start switch selects one of two distance values, the minimum fare distance input, via a multiplexer. The input jumper wires are arranged in three BCD digits for ease of setting specific numbers without converting to a binary code. The comparator must compare the set value with the value of a counter which is counting distance increments. Because the preset value is in BCD, the counter must also count in BCD; thus the comparison of 12 preset BCD bits and 12 BCD counter bits signals the end of a distance increment.

After this minimum distance is traveled, the multiplexer must switch to the standard distance increment for further comparisons, and the counter must be reset.

Table 5.2. Power Up Initialization Routine

PAD	LOC	OBJECT CODE	STMT	SOURCE STATEMENT

```
                                    0231      ***●●●●●●●●●●●●●●●●●●●●●●●●●●●●●●●●●●●●●●●●●●●●●●●●●●●●●●●●●●●●●●●●●●●●●●●●●●●●●
                                    0232      *                                              POWER UP INITIALIZATION ROUTINE.           *
                                    0233      *                                              TO INPUT THE STATES OF THE DIODE MATRIX, A  *
                                    0234      *                                              SUBROUTINE, LABELED IN, WILL BE USED.       *
                                    0235      *                                              TO TRANSFER THE CONTENTS OF THE MINIMUM     *
                                    0236      *                                              FARE REGISTER TO THE DISPLAY REGISTER, ANOTHER *
                                    0237      *                                              SUBROUTINE, LABELED TRMFD, WILL BE USED.    *
                                    0238      ***●●●●●●●●●●●●●●●●●●●●●●●●●●●●●●●●●●●●●●●●●●●●●●●●●●●●●●●●●●●●●●●●●●●●●●●●●●●●●


000    3C3   0011 11 01             0240               LDX    2              START BY INITIALIZING M(2,9) AND M(2,10) TO
001    3C4   0100 1001              0241               TCY    9              ZERO, SO THAT THE MINIMUM FARE AND DISTANCE FOR
003    3CC   0110 0000              0242               TCMIY  0              MINIMUM FARE DIODES CAN BE READ AND DATA STORED
007    3DC   0110 0000              0243               TCMIY  0              IN THE CORRECT REGISTERS.

                                    0245      *                             IN UTILIZES STORAGE LOCATIONS M(X,9) AND M(X,10).
                                    0246      *                             M(X,9) IS USED AS THE ADDRESS OF THE CURRENT
                                    0247      *                             R LINE, M(X,10) IS USED AS THE MEMORY Y ADDRESS
                                    0248      *                             WHERE THE DIODE STATES, ADDRESSED BY THAT R
                                    0249      *                             LINE, ARE STORED.

00F    3FC   0100 1001              0251      IN       TCY    9
01F    3FF   0010 0010              0252               TMY                   SET Y = (M(X,9)).
03F    3FF   0000 1101              0253               SETR                  SET THE R LINE ADDRESSED BY Y.
03E    3F9   0010 1111              0254               CLA                   THIS INSTRUCTION ALLOWS THE R LINE TIME TO GO HI.
03D    3F6   000C 100C              0255               TKA                   TRANSFER THE DIODE LINE, ADDRESSED BY R, TO A.
03B    3FF   0000 1100              0256               RSTR                  RESET THE R LINE.
037    3DE   0100 0101              0257               TCY    10
02E    3FD   0010 0010              0258               TMY                   SET Y = (M(X,10)).
01E    3F8   0000 0011              0259               TAM                   STORE A IN THIS MEMORY LOCATION.
03C    4F1   0100 1001              0260               TCY    9              M(X,9) + 1 TO M(X,9).
039    3E6   0010 100C              0261               IMAC                  *
033    3CF   0010 0000              0262               TAMIY                 *
027    3DD   0010 1000              0263               IMAC                  M(X,10) + 1 TO M(X,10).
00E    3FB   0000 0011              0264               TAM                   *
01D    3F7   0111 0100              0265               ALEC   2              IF M(X,10) IS LESS THAN OR EQUAL TO 2, THE DATA
03A    3E9   10 001111              0266               BR     IN             IS BEING TRANSFERRED TO A FARE REGISTER.
035    3D6   0111 0010              0267               ALEC   4              IF INCREMENTING M(X,10) SETS IT EQUAL TO 3, SET
02B    3ED   10 010010              0268               BR     IN5            M(X,10) = 5 SINCE NO DATA IS STORED IN M(X,3 OR 4).
016    3D8   0111 1110              0269               ALEC   7              IF M(X,10) IS LESS THAN OR EQUAL TO 7, THE DATA
02C    3F2   10 001111              0270               BR     IN             IS BEING TRANSFERRED TO A DISTANCE REGISTER.
018    3E0   0000 1111              0271               RETN                  IF M(X,10) IS = TO 8, THEN THE SUBROUTINE IS OVER.

030    3C1   0011 11 10             0273               LDX    1              NOW INITIALIZE M(1,9) AND M(1,10) SO THAT THE
021    3C5   0100 1001              0274               TCY    9              FARE/DISTANCE INCREMENT AND DISTANCE INCREMENT
002    3C8   0110 0110              0275               TCMIY  6              DIODES CAN BE READ AND DATA STORED IN THE CORRECT
005    3D4   0110 0000              0276               TCMIY  0              REGISTERS.
008    3EC   11 001111              0277               CALL   IN             *

017    3DF   0100 0000              0279      TRMFD    TCY    0              THIS SUBROUTINE TRANSFERS THE MINIMUM FARE
02E    3FA   0011 11 01             0280      TR1      LDX    2              TO THE DISPLAY REGISTER AND CLEARS ALL
01C    3F0   0010 0001              0281               TMA                   CONTROL FLAGS.
038    3E1   0011 11 00             0282               LDX    0              *
031    3C6   0010 0000              0283               TAMIY                 *
023    3CD   0101 1010              0284               YNEC   5              *
006    3D8   10 101110              0285               BR     TR1            *
00D    3F4   0100 0001              0286               TCY    8              *
01B    3FF   C11C 0000              0287               TCMIY  0              *
036    3D9   0000 1111              0288               RETN                  THIS SUBROUTINE IS ALSO USED IN THE COUNT ROUTINE.

020    3F5   0100 0011              0290               TCY    12             SET K(12) SO THAT THE START SWITCH STATUS IS
01A    3E8   0000 1101              0291               SETR                  CONTINUOUSLY ON K8. IF THE SWITCH IS OPEN, K8 = 0,
                                    0292                                     IF THE SWITCH IS CLOSED, K8 = 1.
034    3D1   0001 0000              0293               BFL    EXEC           BRANCH TO THE EXEC ROUTINE.
029    3F5   10 000000              0294

012    3C8   0110 1010              0296      IN5      TCMIY  5
024    3D2   0100 1100              0297               TCY    3              SET M(X,3 AND 4) = 0.
008    3E3   0110 0000              0298               TCMIY  0              *
011    3C7   0110 0000              0299               TCMIY  0              *
022    3FA   10 001111              0300               BR     IN

   *●●●●●●●●●●●●●●●●●●●●●●●●●●●●●●●●●●●●●●●●●●●●●●●●●●●●●●●●●●●●●●●●●●●●●●●●●●●●●●●●●●●●●●●●●●●●●●●●●
```

PAGE NUMBER 15 CONTAINS 49 ROM INSTRUCTIONS.

Table 5.3. Executive Routine

ROM PROGRAM ASSEMBLER -- LEVEL D
        RD4 SOURCE PROGRAM   'SAMPLE'   4/11/75

PAGE NO. 0

PAD   LOC OBJECT CODE   STAT   SOURCE STATEMENT

```
                          0063      OPTION XREF
                          0064      OPTION STAT
                          0065      OPTION ROM


      000                   0067      MFEL    EQU   0
      001                   0068      STRTFL  EQU   1
      002                   0069      PLSFL   EQU   2


                          0071      *************************************************************
                          0072      *                                                           *
                          0073      *       THE EXEC ROUTINE IS RESPONSIBLE FOR ALL I/O          *
                          0074      *       OPERATIONS. IN EXEC ARE ROUTINES TO REFRESH THE      *
                          0075      *       DISPLAY, TEST FOR THE PULSE INPUT, AND TEST          *
                          0076      *       THE STATE OF THE START SWITCH AND DEBOUNCE           *
                          0077      *       THIS INPUT WHEN A CHANGE OCCURS.                     *
                                    *************************************************************


0C0   003   0100 1010      0079      EXEC    TCY   5         INITIALIZE Y = 5 FOR THE REFRS ROUTINE ( LEFT
                           0080      *                       TO RIGHT SCAN).
001   004   0010 1100      0081      REFRS   DYN             SET A = (M(0,Y)) TO THE RIGHT OF THE CURRENT DIGIT
0C3   00C   0010 0001      0082              TMA             DISPLAYED. THEN SET Y = TO THE CURRENT DIGIT
007   01C   0010 1011      0083              IYC             AND RESET ITS R LINE.
00F   03C   0000 1100      0084              RSTR            TRANSFER THE NEW DATA TO THE O PLA.
01F   04F   0000 1010      0085              TDO
03F   03F   0010 1100      0086              DYN             SET THE NEW R LINE.
03E   049   0000 1101      0087              SETR            IF Y IS NOT = 15, THEN MORE DIGITS MUST BE
03D   036   0101 1111      0088              YNEC  15        REFRESHED. IF Y = 15, THEN THE REFRESH IS COMPLETE.
03B   02E   10 000001      0089              BR    REFRS

037   01F   0100 0001      0091              TCY   8         ADDRESS M(0,8) WHERE CONTROL FLAGS ARE STORED.
02F   030   0000 1000      0092              TKA             TRANSFER K INPUTS TO A.
01E   038   0011 10 10     0093              TMITI STRTFL    IF THE START FLAG IS SET, BRANCH TO STRTF1. THIS
03C   031   10 100011      0094              BR    STRTF1    INDICATES THAT START WAS CLOSED WHEN LAST TESTED.
039   026   0111 1111      0095              ALEC  7         IF NOT, TEST A FOR A START INPUT (A GTE 8)
00F   00F   10 000100      0096              BR    EXEC      IF NO START, RETURN TO EXEC.
027   01D   11 011011      0097              CALL  DEBNC     IF START, CALL THE DEBNC SUBROUTINE WHICH DELAYS
00E   033   0111 1111      0098              ALEC  7         ABOUT 5 MSEC. NOW RETEST THE START SWITCH.
01D   037   10 000100      0099              BR    EXEC      IF NOW 0, RETURN TO EXEC. IF 1, THEN VALID START.
03A   029   11 010111      0100              CALLL TMFD      ON A VALID START, TRANSFER THE MINIMUM FARE TO THE
035   01A   11 010111      0101
028   020   0100 1010      0102              TCY   5         DISPLAY REGISTER, CLEAR THE CONTROL FLAGS,
016   018   0110 0000      0103              TCMIY 0         AND CLEAR THE DISTANCE COUNTER.
02C   032   0110 0000      0104              TCMIY 0         *
018   020   0110 0000      0105              TCMIY 0         *
030   001   0011 00 10     0106              SMIT  STRTFL    SET THE START FLAG TO INDICATE THAT THE START
                           0107      *                       SWITCH HAS BEEN ACTIVATED.
021   005   0000 1000      0108              TKA             THE ACCUMULATOR HAS BEEN ALTERED SO REINPUT K.
002   00B   0000 0001      0109      CHKPLS  AAAAC           RESET BIT 3 OF THE ACCUMULATOR (THE KB START
                           0110      *                       SWITCH INPUT)
005   014   0111 0000      0111              ALEC  0         IF NO PULSE INPUT, BIT 0 WILL = 0.
00B   02C   10 100010      0112              BR    PLS0
017   01F   0011 10 01     0113              TMITI PLSFL     IF PULSE IS INPUT, TEST THE PULSE FLAG WHICH
02E   03A   10 000000      0114              BR    EXEC      INSURES THAT THE PULSE IS NOT DOUBLE COUNTED.
01C   030   0011 00 01     0115              SMIT  PLSFL     IF NOT SET, SET AND BRANCH TO THE COUNT ROUTINE.
038   021   0101 1100      0116              BRL   COUNT
031   006   10 000100      0117

023   000   0111 1110      0119      STRTF1  ALEC  7         BRANCH HERE IF THE START FLAG = 1. CHECK THE
006   010   10 011011      0120              BR    DEBNC     START SWITCH. IF 0, BRANCH TO DEBOUNCE.
00D   034   10 000010      0121              BR    CHKPLS    IF STILL = 1, BRANCH TO CHKPLS.

01B   025   0100 1111      0123      DEBNC   TCY   15        THIS ROUTINE PROVIDES AN APPROXIMATE 5 MSEC DELAY.
036   019   0010 0011      0124              TYA             *
02D   035   0010 1100      0125      D1      DYN             *
01A   028   10 101101      0126              BR    D1        *
034   011   0000 0111      0127              DAN             *
029   025   10 101101      0128              BR    D1        *
012   004   0000 1000      0129              TKA             *
024   012   0000 1111      0130              RSTI            *

008   023   0111 1110      0132              ALEC  7         IF START IS STILL 0, THEN VALID 0 LEVEL.
011   007   10 000100      0133              BR    STRT0     IF 1, THEN NOISE CAUSED THE INITIAL ZERO.
022   00A   10 000010      0134              BR    CHKPLS

004   013   0100 0001      0136      STRT0   TCY   8         VALID 0 ON START INPUT SO SET START FLAG = 0.
009   024   0011 01 10     0137              RMIT  STRTFL
013   00F   10 000000      0138              BR    EXEC

026   01A   0011 01 01     0140      PLS0    RMIT  PLSFL     BRANCH HERE IF PULSE INPUT = 0 TO SET THE
00C   033   10 000000      0141              BR    EXEC      PULSE FLAG = 0.
                           0142              PAGE
```

****

PAGE NUMBER 0 CONTAINS 54 ROM INSTRUCTIONS.

Table 5.4. Count Routine

PAD	LOC	OBJECT CODE	STMT	SOURCE STATEMENT			
			0143	* ***		
			0144	*			THE COUNT ROUTINE COUNTS THE DISTANCE PULSES AND *
			0145	*			ADDS THE FARE TO THE DISPLAY REGISTER. WHEN THE *
			0146	*			DISTANCE FOR A MINIMUM FARE IS REACHED, THE FARE *
			0147	*			FOR A DISTANCE INCREMENT IS ADDED TO THE DISPLAY. *
			0148	*			REGISTER. FROM THAT POINT ON, THE DISTANCE *
			0149	*			COUNTER IS COMPARED WITH THE DISTANCE INCREMENT. *
			0150	*			WHEN EQUAL, THE ADDITION IS REPEATED. A FLAG, *
			0151	*			LABELED MFFL, WILL BE SET WHEN THE DISTANCE FOR A *
			0152	*			MINIMUM FARE IS REACHED. *
			0153	* ***		
000	043	0100 1010	0155	COUNT	TCY	5	DISTANCE COUNTER + 1 TO DISTANCE COUNTER.
001	044	0010 1000	0156	CNTUP	IMAC		*
003	04C	10 111111	0157		BR	CARY	*
007	C5C	0000 0011	0158		TAM		*
00F	070	0100 0001	0159		TCY	8	*
01F	07F	10 111011	0160		BR	TMFFL	*
03F	07E	0010 0000	0161	CARY	TAMIY		*
03E	079	0101 0001	0162		YNEC	8	*
03D	076	10 000001	0163		BR	CNTUP	*
038	06E	0011 10 00	0165	TMFFL	TBIT1	MFFL	IF THE MINIMUM FARE FLAG IS SET, THE DISTANCE
037	05E	10 110000	0166		BR	MFFL1	COUNTER IS COMPARED TO THE DISTANCE INCREMENT.
02F	070	0010 1010	0167		TCY	5	IF NOT, COMPARE THE DISTANCE COUNTER WITH THE
01F	073	0011 11 01	0168	CMPDMF	LDX	2	DISTANCE FOR A MINIMUM FARE.
03C	071	0010 0001	0169		TMA		*
C39	066	0011 11 00	0170		LDX	0	*
033	04E	0010 0111	0171		SAMAN		*
027	050	0111 0000	0172		ALEC	0	*
00E	079	10 110101	0173		BR	=1	*
010	377	0001 0000	0174	TOEXEC	BFL	EXEC	IF NOT =, RETURN TO EXEC.
03A	069	10 000000	0175				
035	056	0010 1011	0176	=1	IYC		*
02B	060	0101 0001	0177		YNEC	8	*
016	058	10 011110	0178		BR	CMPDMF	*
02C	072	0011 00 00	0179		SBIT	MFFL	IF =, SET THE MINIMUM FARE FLAG AND ADD THE FARE/
018	060	10 000110	0180		BR	ADD	DISTANCE INCREMENT TO THE DISPLAY REGISTER.
030	041	0100 1010	0182	MFFL1	TCY	5	BRANCH HERE IF THE MINIMUM FARE FLAG IS SET AND
021	045	0011 11 10	0183	CMPDI	LDX	1	COMPARE THE DISTANCE COUNTER WITH THE DISTANCE
002	048	0010 0001	0184		TMA		INCREMENT.
005	054	0011 11 00	0185		LDX	0	*
008	06C	0010 0111	0186		SAMAN		*
017	05F	0111 0000	0187		ALEC	0	*
02E	07A	10 111000	0188		BR	=2	*
01C	070	10 011101	0189		BR	TOEXEC	IF NOT =, RETURN TO EXEC.
038	061	0010 1011	0191	=2	IYC		*
031	046	0101 0001	0192		YNEC	8	*
023	04D	10 100001	0193		BR	CMPDI	*
006	05B	0100 0000	0195	ADD	TCY	0	IF EQUAL, ADD THE FARE/DISTANCE INCREMENT TO THE
00D	074	0011 11 10	0196	LOOP	LDX	1	DISPLAY REGISTER.
01B	06F	0010 0101	0197		AMAAC		*
036	059	0011 11 00	0198		LDX	0	*
02D	075	0010 0101	0199		AMAAC		*
01A	068	10 010010	0200		BR	GT9	*
034	051	0111 1001	0201		ALEC	9	*
029	065	10 011001	0202		BR	LT10	*
012	048	0000 0110	0203	GT9	A6AAC		*
024	052	0000 0100	0204		TAMZA		*
008	063	0000 1110	0205		IA		*
011	047	0010 1011	0206	INCY	IYC		*
022	04A	0101 1010	0207		YNEC	5	*
004	053	10 001101	0208		BR	LOOP	*
009	064	0110 0000	0210		TCMIY	0	CLEAR THE DISTANCE COUNTER
013	04F	0110 0000	0211		TCMIY	0	*
026	05A	0110 0000	0212		TCMIY	0	*
00C	073	10 011101	0213		BR	TOEXEC	AND RETURN TO EXEC.
019	067	0000 0100	0215	LT10	TAMZA		
032	049	10 010001	0216		BR	INCY	
			0217		PAGE		

PAGE NUMBER 1 CONTAINS 56 SOM INSTRUCTIONS.

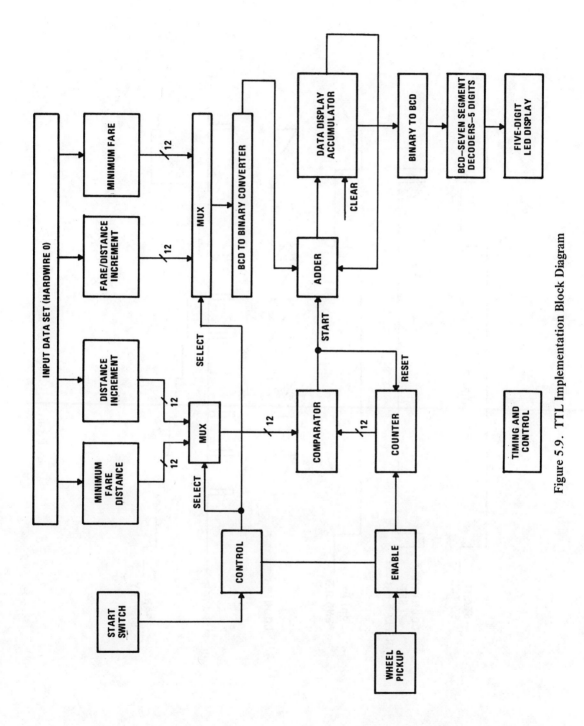

Figure 5.9. TTL Implementation Block Diagram

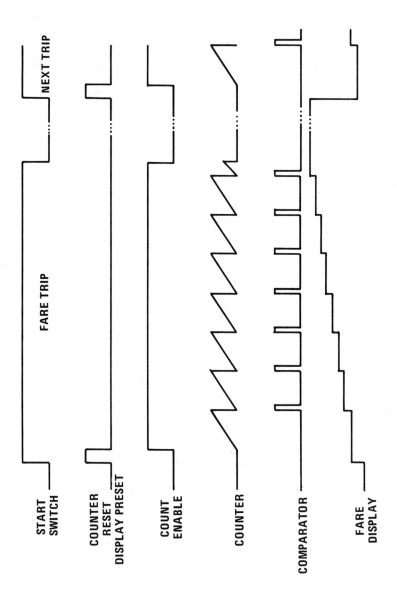

Figure 5.10. Timing Diagram

5.1.7.2 Fare Calculation

On the fare calculation side of the diagram of Figure 5.9, a multiplexer is used to achieve results similar to the preceding section. A minimum fare must first be placed in the fare accumulator, and thereafter another fare increment (for the standard distance) must be added each time the comparator signals a match.

A choice must be made between BCD calculations and binary calculations. In BCD addition, a test must be made on each decade to see if the result is greater than $9(1001_2)$. If it is greater then 6 must be added to generate a carry and achieve a legal code for that decade. This can be fairly complex, so for this example a BCD to binary conversion is made to simplify the adder/accumulator circuits. Because of the size of the accumulator (15 bits), the conversion back to BCD (5 digits) requires 16 packages.

Table 5.5 summarizes the package count for each element of the diagram of Figure 5.9. Notice the tradeoff for conversion to and from binary is at least 22 packages. The TMS 1000 example accomplishes the fare additions in BCD with appropriate "add-six" correction in only 14 instructions (see statements 195-208 in the COUNT routine). This dramatizes the simplicity with which software controlled microprocessors and microcomputers substantially simplify not only the design process, but also the manufacturing and test operations.

The foregoing example is simply an estimate of the straight logic approach to the design of a taxi meter. There are certainly many ways to achieve the desired result, perhaps with fewer networks. But even after simplification and the total tradeoffs are weighed, the TMS 1000 approach will be more cost-effective for large quantity production, to say nothing of improved reliability, lower power consumption, etc.

Table 5.5. TTL Devices and Quantities

Function	Network	Quantity
Minimum Fare Distance	SN74L157	3
Distance Increment	SN74L157	3
Counter (BCD decade)	SN74L90	3
Comparator	SN74L85	4
Fare/Distance Increment	SN74L157	3
Minimum Fare	SN74L157	3
BCD — Binary Converter	SN74184	6
and Shift Register	SN7494	3
Adder	SN7480	1
Binary — BCD Converter	SN74185A	16
Data Accumulator (15 bit)	SN74L91	2
BCD — Seven-Segment (5 digit)	SN7447A	5
Timing & Control		≈ 6
Total		58

5.2 TMS 8080 PROBLEM

5.2.1 Problem Statement — Badge Reading System

The problem is to design a badge reading system to control access to certain areas within a plant or building complex. A central computer (such as a 360) will be used to preset certain numbers into each remote badge reading station to specify the acceptance criteria for entry. Each reader will read data from a badge when inserted, compare with acceptance criteria, and open the door if accepted. Further, the badge number will be transmitted to the central computer for record keeping.

The following basic design criteria are established:

1.   Badges will be constructed with 16 locations of holes for coding (16-bit binary number)

2.   Badge numbers to be accepted are to be loaded from the Central Computer

3.   Badges are to be read with light sensors

4.   Output from reader control circuits are:

    a.   Communication transmission line to Central Computer
    b.   Door lock solenoid
    c.   Lights for:
           Ready
           Wait
           Enter
           Reject
           Read error

5.   Input to reader control circuits are:

    a.   Communication transmission line from Central Computer
    b.   16 Lines from the array of light sensors
    c.   Single line from badge inserted switch

6.   Communications with the Central Computer will be over twisted-pair lines at 300 baud.

7.   Switches must be included for eac t reader station to give it a unique identification number (8 bits).

5.2.2 Hardware Definition

Hardware components selected to perform the task outlined in the problem statement are based on the TMS 8080 microprocessor and related chips. The special devices are as follows:

TMS 8080	Microprocessor
TMS 4700	1024 x 8 ROM
TMS 4036	64 x 8 RAM
TMS 5501	I/O Network

These devices, along with the required standard TTL support chips are shown in Figure 5.11.

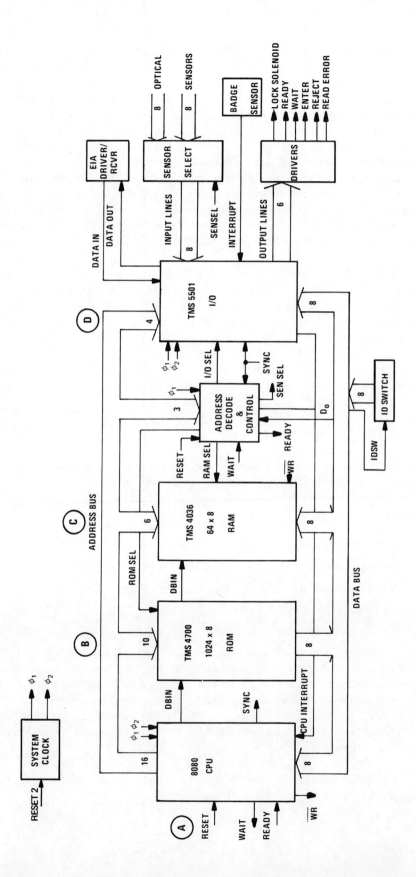

Figure 5.11. Access Control System Block Diagram

5-19

Upon power-up, RESET 1 (A) starts the 8080 microprocessor cycle by causing the program counter (PC) to reset and send 0000 (a 16-bit hex address) out to the ROM (B). (See Figure 5.12 for the timing of Reset 1 and Reset 2 signals.) The first instruction and all fixed instructions for the operation of the badge reader must be contained in the ROM. Storage for badge numbers, the STACK, and indirect address pointers is provided in read/write memory, the RAM (C).

Address bits A_0 through A_9 along with the ROM SELect line activate the ROM, while A_0 through A_5 and the RAM SELect line address the RAM. Figures 5.12, 5.13, and 5.14 detail the signal connections for the address and data for the 8080 microprocessor, and the ROM and RAM. Address bits A_{10}, A_{11}, and A_{12} are input to a multiplexer to select the different elements of the block diagram. Figure 5.15 develops the INTA (interrupt acknowledge) signal from data bit 0 (see 8080 data sheet for explanation of the timing) to disable the memories and ID switch circuit during operation of the I/O circuit as it communicates with the 8080.

The TMS 5501 I/O chip is shown in Figure 5.16, with signatures to identify signals, clocks, and power supplies. The identification switches and their corresponding signatures are shown in Figure 5.17. Note that the 74125 device is a three-state output device to allow isolation from the data bus. Figure 5.18 expands the sensor input signal block of Figure 5.11, and shows the 74157 multiplexer configuration.

Figures 5.15 and 5.19 show the external devices for clock and interrupt control functions. Figure 5.19 also includes logic for the READY signal: the logic level used to indicate to the 8080 that valid data is "ready" on the data lines.

5.2.3   Understanding the TMS 8080 Microprocessor

In addition to the data sheet for the TMS 8080 microprocessor (see Appendix E), the following general observations explain salient features pertinent to the design example.

5.2.3.1   Architecture

Architecturally the 8080 is comprised of the following elements:

- Seven 8-bit general registers A, B, C, D, E, H, and L
- Program counter — 16 bits
- Stack pointer — 16 bits
- Five flag bits — carry, zero, sign, parity, and auxiliary carry

Register A is the accumulator. The other registers are arranged in pairs B and C, D and E, H and L, so that they may be used not only as 8-bit general-purpose registers, but also to provide 16-bit operations such as address calculations. A 16-bit address bus is used to specify up to 65,536 words of memory. The memory address buffer obtains addresses from the program counter (PC), the stack pointer (SP) via the PC, or from register pairs BC, DE, or HL, depending upon the instruction implemented. Addresses are also obtained from memory word pairs (two sequential locations) in memory reference instructions.

A bidirectional 8-bit data bus allows transfer of data into and out of the 8080 microprocessor chip. The memory and I/O unit share both the address and data buses.

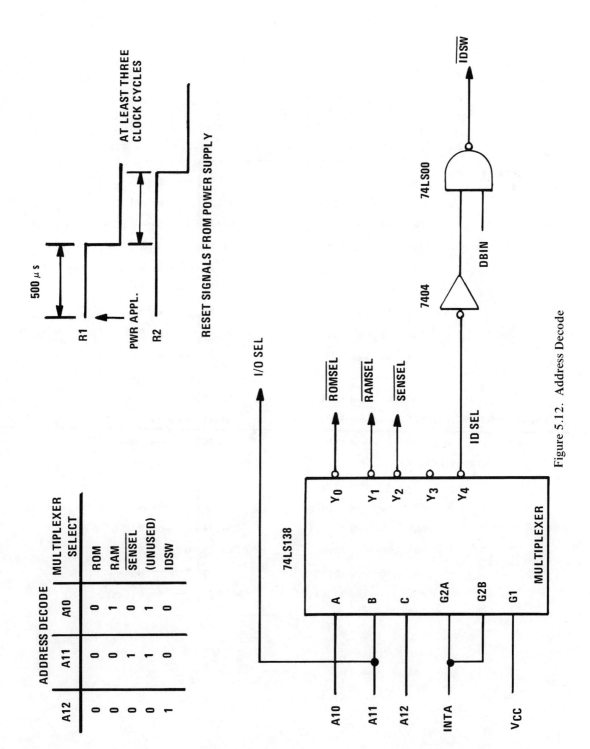

Figure 5.12. Address Decode

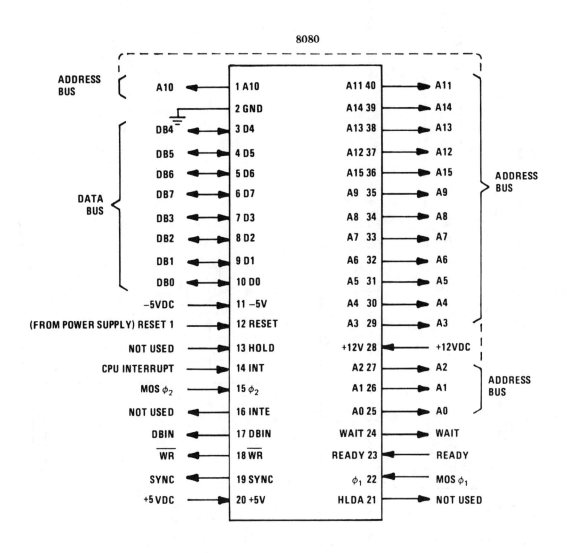

Figure 5.13. Central Processing Unit

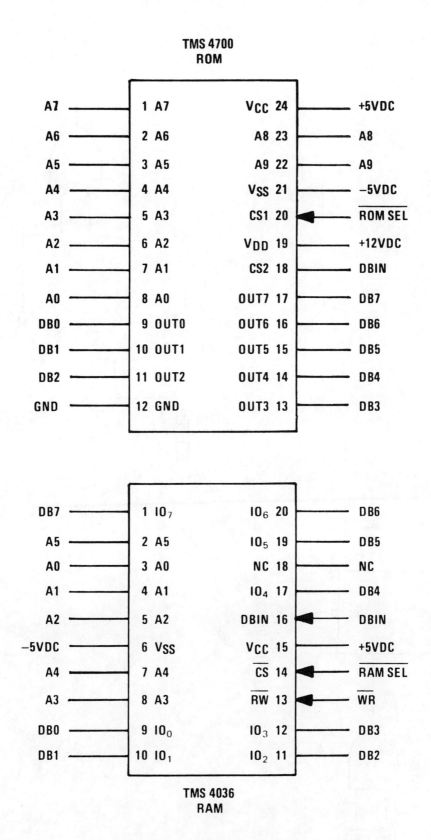

Figure 5.14. ROM and RAM Chips

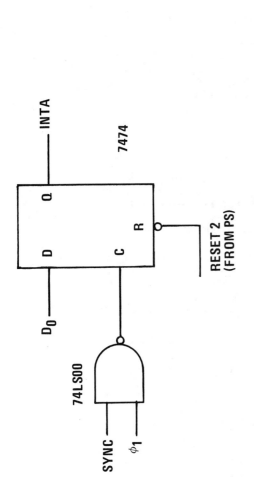

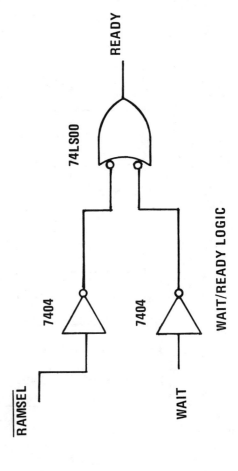

Figure 5.15. Interrupt Circuit

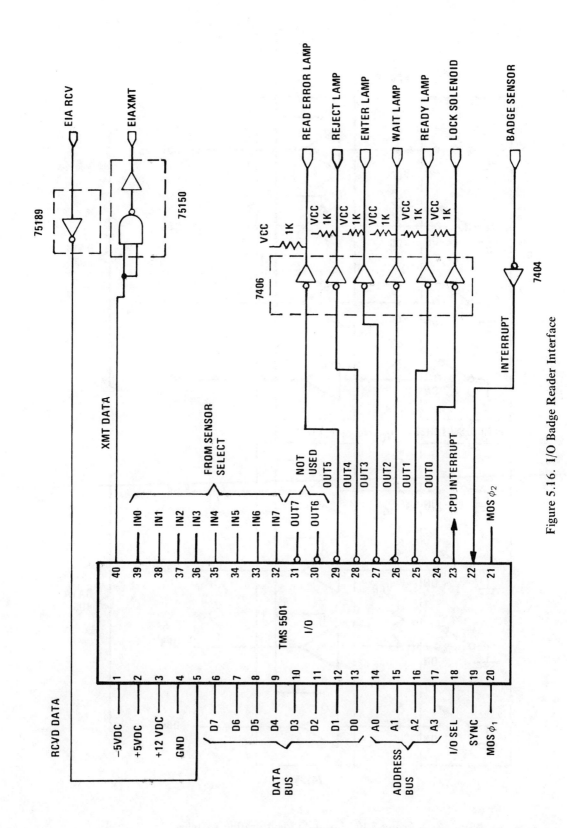

Figure 5.16. I/O Badge Reader Interface

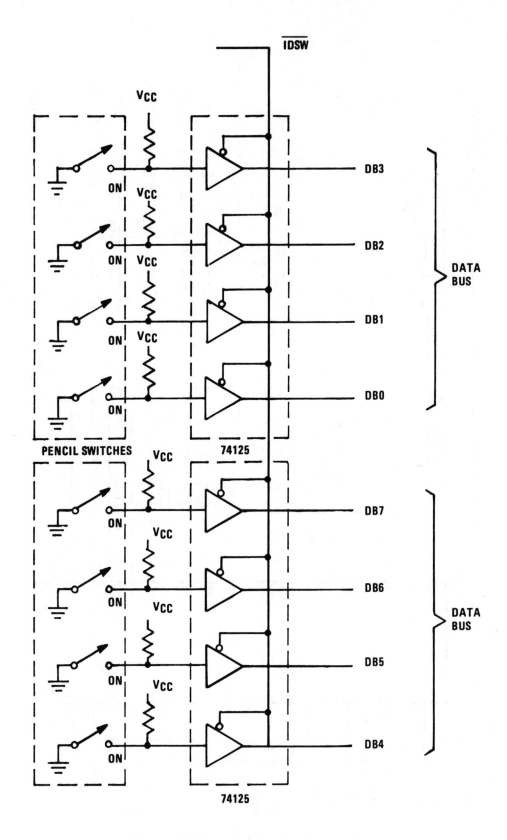

Figure 5.17. Location Identification Switches

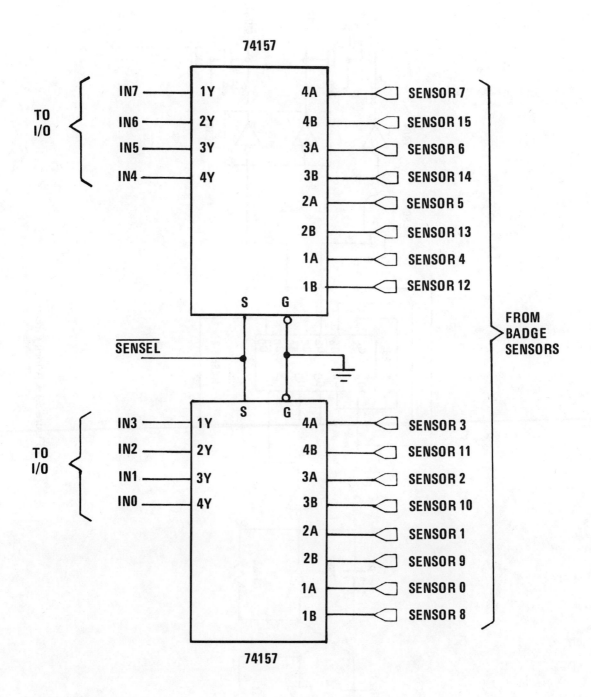

Figure 5.18. Sensor Selector

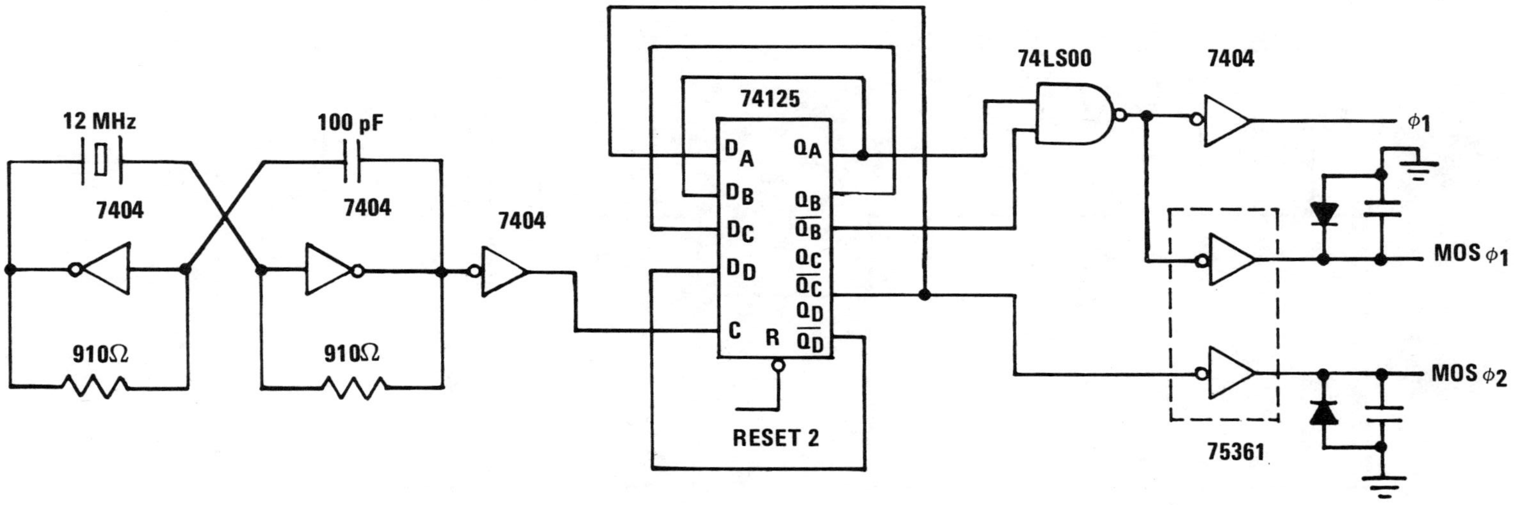

Figure 5.19. Clock Circuit

5.2.3.2 Stack Concept

Any portion of the Read/Write (RAM) memory used with the TMS 8080 microprocessor can be assigned as a STACK. These words are used to store sequentially return addresses and register contents when subroutine and interrupt processing routines are initiated. The technique is that of a "push-down" "pop-up" stack, or last in/first out memory. When a subroutine is called (e.g., CALL instruction), the PC is incremented to the next instruction after the call, and this number (the return address) is stored in the stack. The address of the first instruction of the subroutine is placed in the PC, and processing resumes from there. If the contents of the registers are to be saved, they are stored on the stack via the PUSH instructions at the beginning of the subroutine. At the end of the subroutine, the POP (register restoration) instruction restores the registers to their original contents by transferring data from the STACK to the registers. After this, an RET (return) instruction loads the PC with the address of the instruction where processing of the original routine is to be resumed.

Although the memory is organized into 8-bit words, the stack may be generally visualized as a block of 16-bit words because all transfers into and out of the stack are two bytes (16 bits). Instructions for stack use are:

PUSH	PSW	Saves the accumulator and flags
PUSH	B	Saves registers B and C
PUSH	D	Saves registers D and E
PUSH	H	Saves registers H and L
POP	PSW	Restores the accumulator and flags
POP	B	Restores registers B and C
POP	D	Restores registers D and E
POP	H	Restores registers H and L

To make the push-down/pop-up concept work, a 16-bit stack pointer (SP) is incremented or decremented for each POP or PUSH instruction respectively. The SP must be initialized at the beginning of the program to the highest word *plus 1* in the memory allocation of the stack. This must be done because when the first value is placed in the stack, the SP is decremented before the address is sent out to the memory. Thus, the SP counts *down* to fill the stack, and *up* as the stack empties.

One additional stack pointer control instruction, SPHL, allows transfer of the contents of register pair HL into the SP. Thus the SP may be set to any value.

5.2.3.3 Interrupt Techniques

At power-up, the interrupt control flip-flop is reset and interrupts are disabled. If interrupts are to be processed, the EI (enable interrupt) instruction must be present in the power-up initialization routine prior to the first HLT (halt) instruction. It should be noted that the only way for the TMS 8080 microprocessor to terminate the halt condition is to process an interrupt. The interrupt control flip-flop is reset whenever an interrupt is processed. The EI instruction is required to re-enable interrupts after an interrupt is acknowledged and processing has begun.

When an interrupt signal is received by the TMS 8080, the instruction in process is completed, and the address of the next instruction in that sequence (the return point for the PC) is saved on the stack. At the completion of the storage, an interrupt acknowledge signal is sent to the I/O circuit which must respond with an RST (restart) instruction on the data bus. The eight bits of the restart instruction are:

RST   11 AAA 111

where AAA indicates three variable bits used by the I/O system to signal which of eight elements of the I/O requires service. This does not limit the number of I/O channels to eight; it limits the interrupt vectors to eight. The interrupt vectors, AAA, specify that the contents of the PC be set to one of the eight interrupt trap locations in the first 64 words of memory. These are:

Trap	Starting Address
0	0000
1	0008
2	0010
3	0018
4	0020
5	0028
6	0030
7	0038

There are eight words in each trap for initial processing instructions and a JMP (jump) instruction specifying the location of the remainder of the interrupt processing routine if required.

When an interrupt is processed by the microprocessor, the PC is loaded with the starting address of the interrupt trap, and processing continues to the end of the interrupt service routine. Here, register restoration (POP) and return (RET) instructions send the PC back to the original routine being processed at the time of the interrupt.

Upon power-up, the PC goes to 0000, the beginning address of trap 0. The initialization (or power failure) routine for the system should be stored in the first words of memory (trap 0) to facilitate an automatic power fail/restart operation.

5.2.3.4 Instruction Summary

TMS 8080 instructions consume one, two, or three bytes. Register reference instructions (MOV, INR, ADD) require one byte, immediate address instructions (MVI, ADI, CPI) require two bytes, and memory reference instructions (JMP, CALL, LXI) require three bytes (recall, two bytes, 16 bits, are needed for the memory address). Some of the more important instructions relating to this problem and its solution are explained next. Refer to the TMS 8080 data book in Appendix E for a description of all TMS 8080 instructions.

1. RET — Return (one byte). This instruction causes the last entry in the stack to be transferred to the PC (program counter). It is used at the end of each subroutine in an interrupt type of program structure. The use of a stack for saving return addresses allows unlimited nesting of subroutines and interrupt routines.

2. HLT — Halt (one byte). The PC is incremented but no further processor cycles occur until an interrupt occurs. The return point will be the instruction following the HLT.

3. RST — Restart (one byte). The PC is loaded with one of eight trap locations depending on the three variable bits (11AAA111). This instruction may be implemented by writing it into the instruction sequence (in which case it is equivalent to JMP to one of the eight traps), or by the I/O unit supplying the appropriate eight bits on the data lines after interrupt acknowledge has been sent out from the TMS 8080.

4. LHLD — Load H and L direct (three bytes). The content of two sequential memory locations, the first of which is specified by bytes 2 and 3 of the instruction, is loaded into the H and L register.

5. SHLD — Store H and L direct (three bytes). Same as LHLD except data is transferred from the H and L to two sequential memory locations.

6. PCHL — Transfer H and L data to the PC (one byte). Following LHLD, this instruction effects an indirect address.

7. XRA — Exclusive OR between the accumulator and a register memory location. (one byte). XRA A is used to clear the accumulator (and carry bit). (There is no "clear A" instruction.)

8. EI — Enables interrupt (one byte).

9. JMP, CALL, RET — Program control instructions. Conditional and unconditional transfer of program control to different routines is summarized in Table 5.6. Thirty-one instructions (over 40% of the instruction set) are shown. Each conditional branch instruction tests the status of one of the flag bits. The flags will be set or reset as a result of an instruction such as add or compare.

Table 5.6. Program Control Instructions

Branching

Flag Bit		Jump	Call	Return
Carry	= 1	JC	CC	RC
Carry	= 0	JNC	CNC	RNC
Zero	= 1	JZ	CZ	RZ
Zero	= 0	JNZ	CNZ	RNZ
Sign	= 1	JM	CM	RM
Sign	= 0	JP	CP	RP
Parity	= 1	JPE	CPE	RPE
Parity	= 0	JPD	CPO	RPO
Unconditional		JMP	CALL	RET

EXAMPLE: JC means JUMP IF CARRY BIT = 1

RC means "RETURN" IF CARRY BIT = 1

Other Program Control Instructions

HLT	Halt
RST	Restart (After Interrupt)
SPHL	Load Stack Pointer with content of HL
PCHL	Load Program Counter with content of HL

Table 5.7 lists the instructions used in the design example, the number of bytes required to store each, and the number of bytes affected. It is clear that over half the instructions are 16-bit (two byte) instructions because they establish the content of the PC, SP, or one of the three register pairs, BC, DE, or HL. It is this group of instructions that facilitate the powerful addressing modes of the TMS 8080 microprocessor.

5.2.4 Understanding The TMS 5501 Interface Chip

A fairly complex I/O chip, the TMS 5501 is used in the design example to illustrate the power and importance of interface chips in a microprocessor system. Several key features pertinent to the example are described. (See the data book in Appendix E for full details.)

Architecturally the unit is comprised of:

- Four address lines into a control unit (to select one of 14 functions)
- Data bus buffer (8 bit)
- Five interval timers
- Interrupt vectoring logic
- 8-Bit buffered input port
- 8-Bit buffered output port
- UART with programmable BAUD rate
- Status word buffer
- Discrete command word buffer

In this example, all of the elements are used, of particular significance are the interval timers. The STA instruction may be used with the appropriate address to load an interval timer with a certain number of time elements (64 μs each). (For example, 156 units of time is 9.984 ms.) When the time period has elapsed, the timer generates an interrupt to the microprocessor. The timers count down from a separate clock within the TMS 5501; they are used for time delays in which precise timing is not required.

5.2.5 Software Development

5.2.5.1 Assembler

Paragraph 5.2.11 gives the complete software listing for the program written in assembly language. The features of the assembler (the program that processed the assembly language source code) requiring explanation are:

1. Listing format
2. Location counter
3. Symbol (label) table
4. Directives
5. Number base (10 or 16)

Table 5.7. Instructions Used in the Design Example

Instruction	No. Bytes	No. Bytes Affected	Elements Affected
MOV	1	1	Register/Memory
MVI	2	1	Register/Memory
INR	1	1	Register
DCR	1	1	Register
ADD	1	1	Register/Memory
XRA	1	1	Accum/Reg or Mem
ORA	1	1	Accum/Reg or Mem
CMP	1	1	Accum/Reg or Mem
ANI	2	1	Accum/Memory
CPI	2	1	Accum/Memory
RRC	1	1	Accum.
JMP	3	2	PC
JNZ	3	2	PC
JE	3	2	PC
JM	3	2	PC
HLT	1	2	PC
CALL	3	2	PC
RET	1	2	PC
RC	1	2	PC
RNZ	1	2	PC
RST	1	2	PC
LXI	3	2	SP, BC, DE, HL
PUSH	1	2	PSW, BC, DE, HL
POP	1	2	PSW, BC, DE, HL
STA	3	1	ACC
LDA	3	1	ACC
PCHL	1	2	PC
DAD	1	2	SP, BC, DE, HL
STAX	1	1	BC, DE
LDAX	1	1	BC, DE
INX	1	2	BC, DE, HL
DCX	1	2	BC, DE, HL
SHLD	3	2	HL
LHLD	3	2	HL
EI	1	0	

5.2.5.1.1 Listing Format and Location Counter

During the assembly run, a location counter (a word in memory) keeps track of the number of bytes (8 bit) of memory consumed by the program. As each instruction is listed, the address of the first byte is given as the location in memory and this number is printed in the first column of the printout. The next three columns (0B1, 0B2, 0B3) contain the binary code for the instruction and the operand (two-byte instruction) or operand address (three-byte instruction). Bytes 2 and 3 always specify a memory or I/O address. It is important to note that byte 3 is the more significant byte or high-order byte. Hexadecimal numbers are used in the first four columns. The fifth column in the listing is the label field, where symbols may be written to identify certain memory locations for ease of programming. Each symbol must appear in the program once in the label field and at least once in the operand field of an instruction. The assembler builds a symbol table to equate labels to locations. Instruction mnemonics are printed in column six, and column seven is the operand field. Comments follow the operand field.

5.2.5.1.2 Symbol Table

The assembler uses the symbols from the label field and the location counter to build a symbol table. In this way each symbol may be translated to its numerical location value.

5.2.5.1.3 Directives

When a symbol is used in the operand field but has not appeared in the label field, and EQU directive may be used. In this way, symbols are directly related to numerical values.

5.2.5.1.4 Number Base

In the operand field, numbers are assumed by the assembler to be base 10. If a number is followed by H, the assembler interprets the characters as a hexadecimal number.

5.2.5.2 Memory Map

In the example, memory addresses are divided into ROM, RAM, and I/O sections, As shown in Table 5.8, a little more than half of the 1024-word ROM is consumed. The RAM contains data (read in), indirect address pointers and certain other variables. Also 32 words (eight bits each) are reserved for the stack. This allows the stack to store up to sixteen 16-bit entries.

5.2.6 Software System Concept

1. Communications to the Central CPU will be by 300 baud serial EIA transmission (no parity).

2. Upon power-up, the TMS 8080 will transmit an ENQ character followed by an 8-bit unit ID code. This is field changeable and identifies the system to the Central CPU.

3. The TMS 8080 will wait 15 seconds for download of badge categories. If download is not complete within that time, system will reexecute step 2 indefinitely until a download has occurred. The wait light will be on at all badge stations during this sequence.

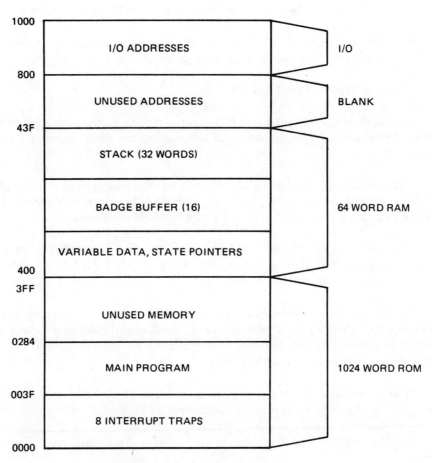

Table 5.8. Memory Map

1000	I/O ADDRESSES	I/O
800	UNUSED ADDRESSES	BLANK
43F	STACK (32 WORDS)	
	BADGE BUFFER (16)	64 WORD RAM
400	VARIABLE DATA, STATE POINTERS	
3FF	UNUSED MEMORY	
0284	MAIN PROGRAM	1024 WORD ROM
003F	8 INTERRUPT TRAPS	
0000		

NOTE: Addresses in hexadecimal

4. The Central CPU will send an STX, system ID, up to 16 4-bit badge categories, delete, and a checksum character. The system will verify the ID code with its own, place the badge categories in RAM, form an 8-bit sum of the badge categories, and compare it with the checksum character. If an error occurs, the system will allow the 15-s time-out feature to trigger and rerequest a Badge Category Download. If no errors are detected, the system will transmit an ACK character to the Central CPU and go to the ready mode.

5. In the ready mode, an interrupt will be generated when a badge is inserted into a reader. The system will delay 200 ms before scanning. The system will then read the badge and save the number in RAM. If the badge reads all ones (no badge in reader), the system will ignore the false badge interrupt. After the first read, a 100-ms delay will occur and a second read of the badge will occur.

6. If the readings of the badge mismatch, the read error light will be turned on and the end sequence entered. After a stable badge read, the ID category will be isolated and a search through the previously downloaded data will be made. If no match is found, the reject light will be lit, and the end sequence entered.

7. If a match is found, the system will transmit an STX, first 8 bits of badge ID, second 8 bits of badge ID, and checksum (sum of both 8-bit badge ID characters) to the Central CPU. The enter light and door unlock solenoid will be turned on for 4 seconds.

8. The end sequence will extinguish all lights and release the door unlock solenoid. The system will then wait for next badge interrupt.

5.2.7 Example Problem Flow Chart

A small portion of the total system design has been extracted as a simple problem example to further the understanding of the details of flowcharting and program coding for a microprocessor system.

The complete system flow charts and program listing are provided for a full solution to the problem. Extensive study is required of the system block diagram, the TMS 8080 data sheet, and the individual part block diagrams to fully understand the problem solution.

A subset from the "badge read" section of the flow chart and coding for this example application of the TMS 8080 microprocessor are provided. Table 5.9 describes the instructions needed to implement the code for the flow chart.

All the necessary elements are present for an exercise in flowcharting and coding for this microprocessor. The reader is encouraged to try developing the software for this small part of the problem to enhance his understanding of programming for microprocessors, and to enable him to follow the complete listings much more easily.

A small portion of the flow chart has been drawn in Figure 5.20 for the purpose of an exercise. See if you can fill it in from the software concepts stated earlier.

For this subflow chart (referring to the software definitions), the following steps must be taken:

1. When a badge is inserted, as signaled by an interrupt, the system must start the *first read step*.

2. *The first step* is to ignore any other interrupt from the reader switch (to prevent contact bounce from causing multiple interrupts).

3. Next the system must wait 200 ms to let input signals settle to quiescent levels.

4. After this time, the *second read operation* must occur: Read the data (16 bits).

5. If the data is all ones, set up for acceptance of a new interrupt and read cycle.

6. If data is not all ones, wait 100 ms before making a second data read operation.

7. Set up for the next read operation.

Try to work this for yourself before looking at the completed flow chart (Figure 5.30).

Table 5.9. Coding Instructions

Instruction	No. Bytes	Description
LDA	3	Load the accumulator with the content of the memory location addressed by bytes 2 and 3.
STA	3	Store the accumulator content in the memory lacation addressed by bytes 2 and 3.
MOV x, y	1	Load x with the content of y (and leave the content of y unchanged). Note: x and y may be registers or memory (but **both** cannot be memory) locations.
CPI	2	Compare Accumulator with register or memory content specified by byte 2.
JNZ	3	Jump, if result of previous instruction (e.g., compare) is **not zero**, to the location addressed by bytes 2 and 3.
JZ	3	Jump if **zero** to the location addressed by bytes 2 and 3.
LXI B	3	Load byte 3 into B, byte 2 into C.
LXI D	3	Load byte 3 into D, byte 2 into E.
LXI H	3	Load byte 3 into H, byte 2 into L.
LXI SP	3	Load byte 3 into SP HIGH, byte 2 into SP LOW.
CALL	3	Save the PC in the stack and jump unconditionally to the instruction addressed by bytes 2 and 3.
SHLD	3	Store content of H and L Registers in the location addressed by bytes 2 and 3.
RET	1	Return PC to the instruction address specified by the last entries in the push-down stack (as addressed by the stack pointer).

5.2.8 Example Problem Coding

Using the blank flow chart (Figure 5.20) and the instructions given in Table 5.9 (these are only a small number of the instructions available), see if you can write the code for the steps. The coding form is given in Figure 5.21.

The actual code included for this portion of the job is accomplished in 25 lines or instruction steps. Your code may use other instructions if you wish, and could be longer or shorter than the target of 25 lines. (See Table 5.12 for the assembly listing of READ1 and READ2 routines.)

5.2.9 Detailed Software Flow Charts

The system flow charts begin with a set of charts that provide an overview of the system. These are divided into System Setup, Figure 5.22; Badge Read, Figure 5.23; and End Sequence, Figure 5.24. The detailed flow charts are keyed to the names on the overview charts as the flow charts are related to the actual code by these names.

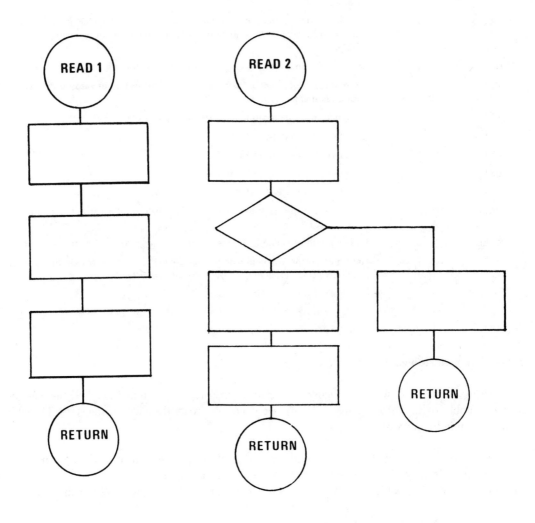

Figure 5.20. Example Problem Flow Chart (Blank)

	LABEL	OP. CODE	OPERAND(S)	COMMENTS
1				
2				
3				
4				
5				
6				
7				
8				
9				
10				
11				
12				
13				
14				
15				
16				
17				
18				
19				
20				
21				
22				
23				
24				
25				
26				
27				
28				
29				
30				

Figure 5.21. Coding Form (Blank)

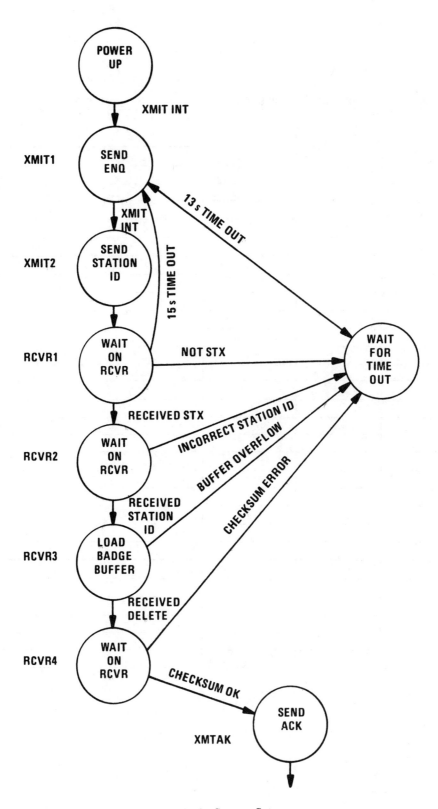

Figure 5.22. System Setup

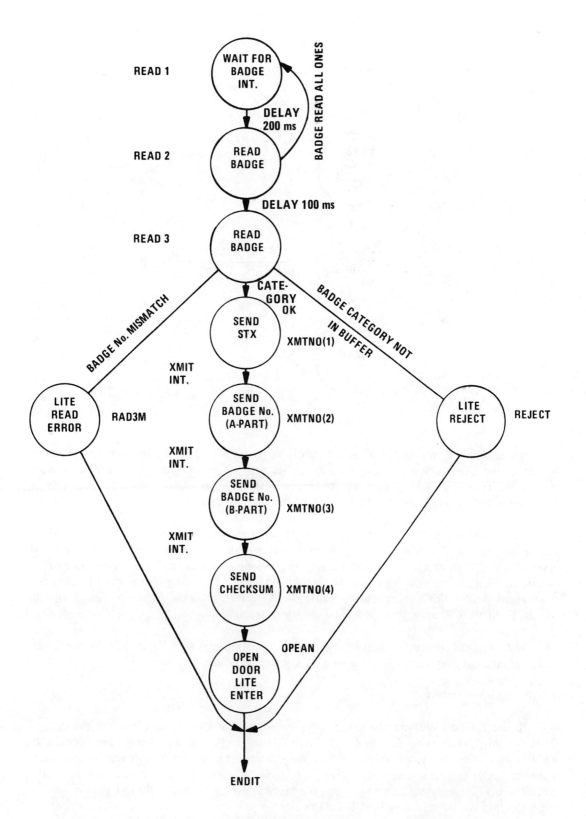

Figure 5.23. Badge Read

5-41

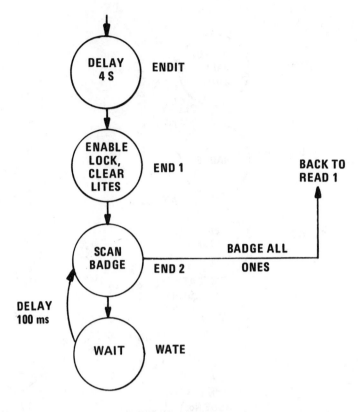

Figure 5.24. End Sequence

An example of interrupt processing is provided in Figure 5.25. This technique of interrupt processing has been chosen because it minimizes interrupt overhead and results in less program storage and thus less memory capacity. Note also that this type of software organization takes advantage of the indirect branch (PCHL) feature of the TMS 8080.

The following detailed flow charts are used to define the software steps. The charts are divided into specific tasks to be accomplished by the microprocessor. In relating the flow charts to the actual code contained in paragraph 5.2.11, note that at the beginning of each small chart is the name which is used in coding. Generally, these are the subroutine names. The ending statement of most of the small charts is RETURN, which returns control to the calling program. Other endings are HALT, BRANCH INDIRECT, and a direct jump to a specific instruction.

The individual subroutines that describe system operation start with Figure 5.26, System Setup and Interrupts and continue through Figure 5.31, the End Sequence.

5.2.10 Interrupt Details

In order to demonstrate the interrupt processing of the TMS 8080, a trace of the PC and STACK is provided in Tables 5.10 and 5.11. Steps 1-31 of the PC sequence are for initialization. In addition to clearing the RAM, there are four state pointers or indirect branch vectors (first eight words of RAM) to be initialized. These are 16-bit *variable* addresses used to steer the PC to the correct instruction sequence depending upon the previous events. To begin, the INT pointer is set to 00BB (see instructions in locations 005F and 0062).

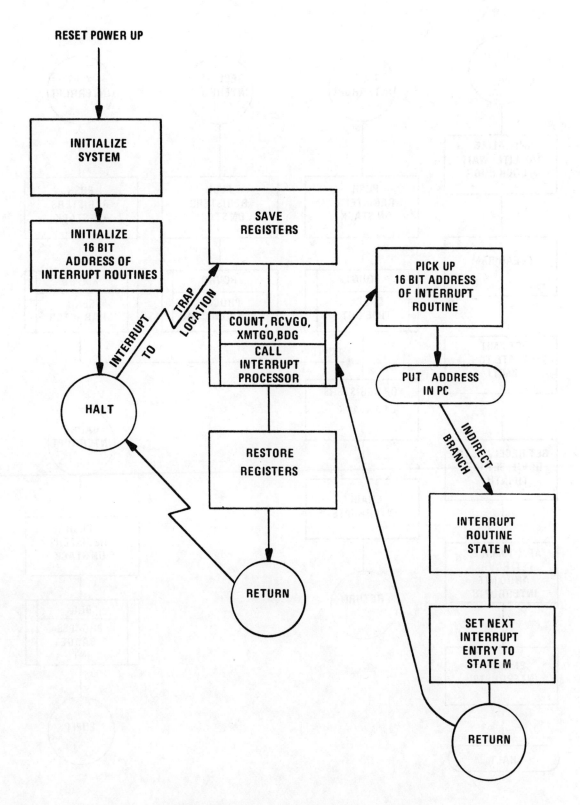

Figure 5.25. Example of Interrupt Processing

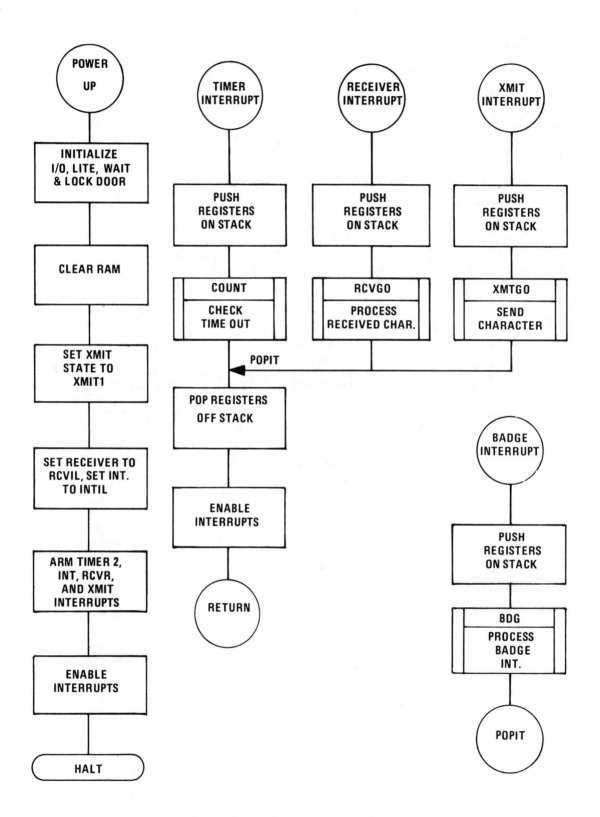

Figure 5.26. System Setup and Interrupts

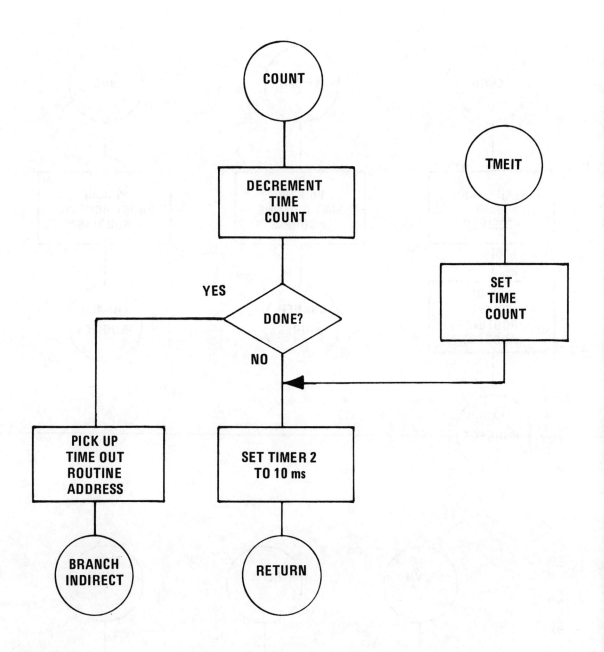

Figure 5.27. Timer Interrupt

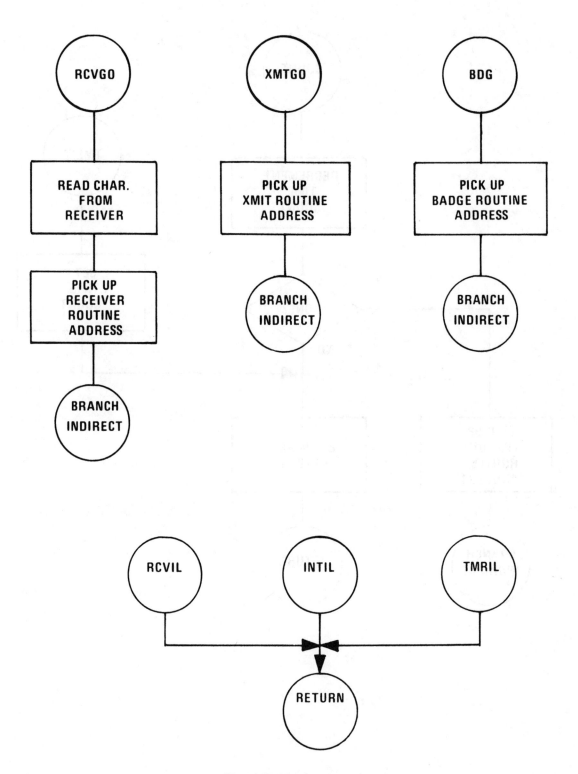

Figure 5.28. Interrupts

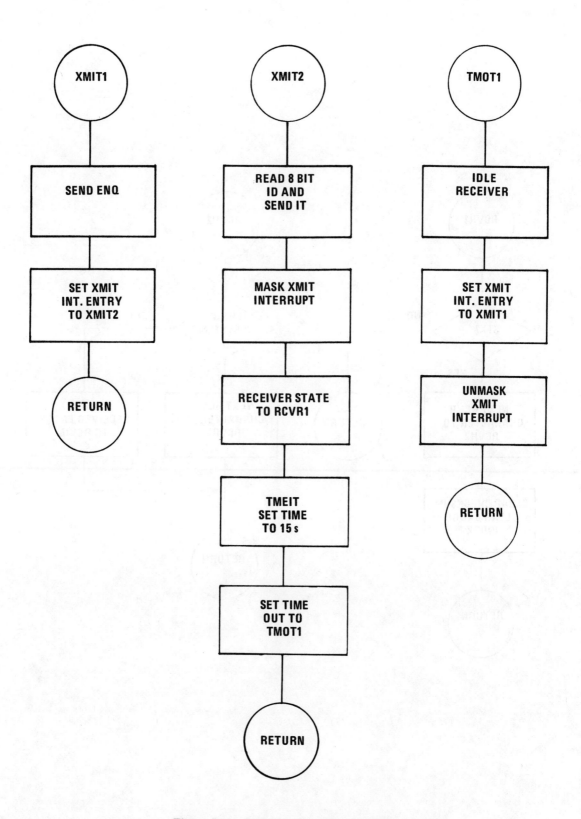

Figure 5.29. System Setup (Sheet 1 of 4)

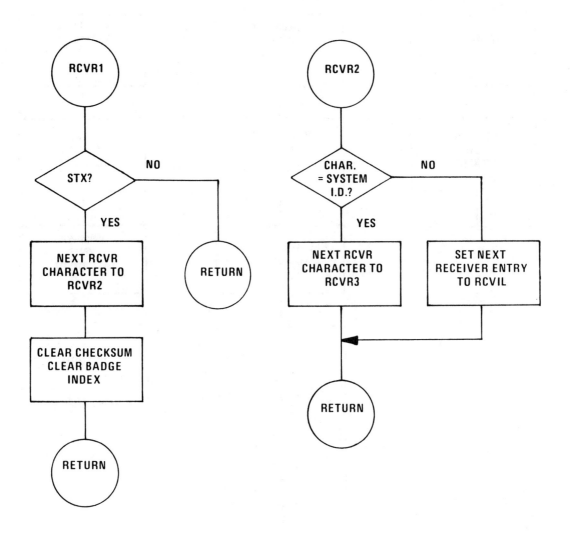

Figure 5.29. System Setup (Sheet 2 of 4)

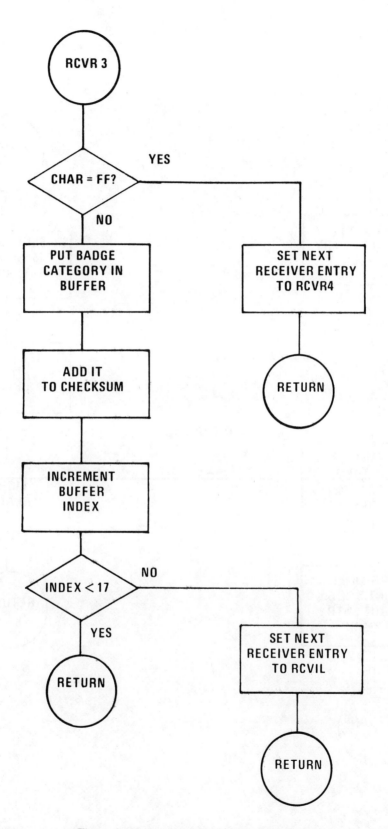

Figure 5.29. System Setup (Sheet 3 of 4)

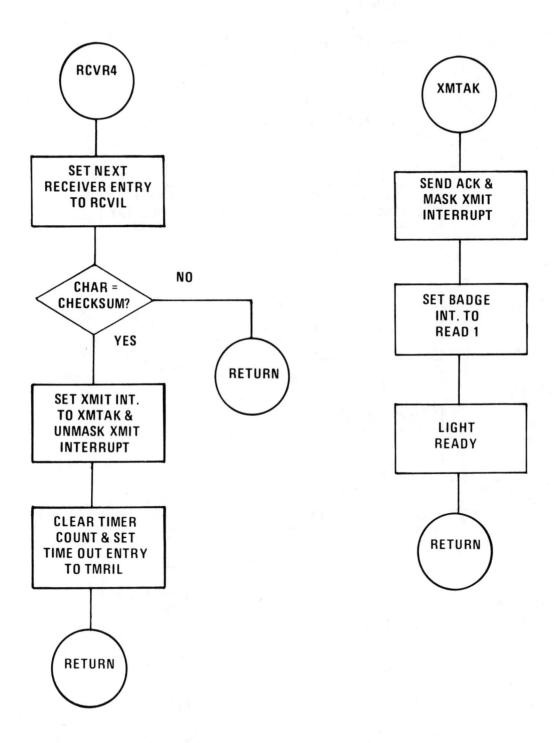

Figure 5.29. System Setup (Sheet 4 of 4)

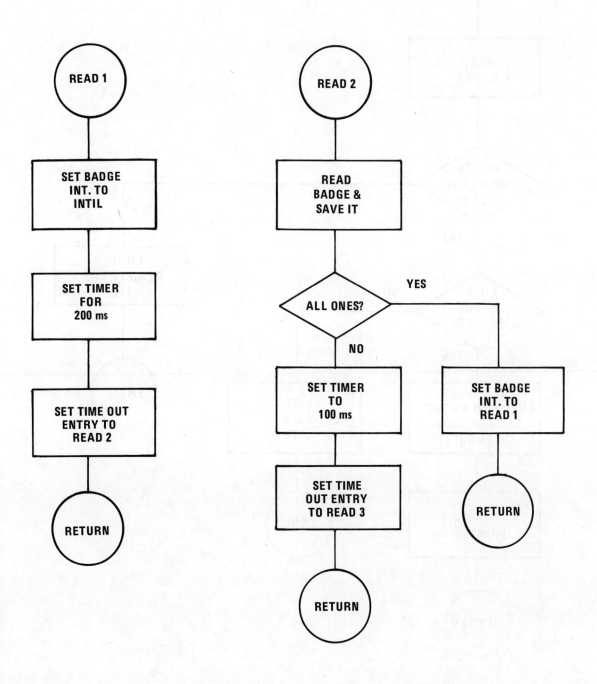

Figure 5.30. Badge Read (Sheet 1 of 3)

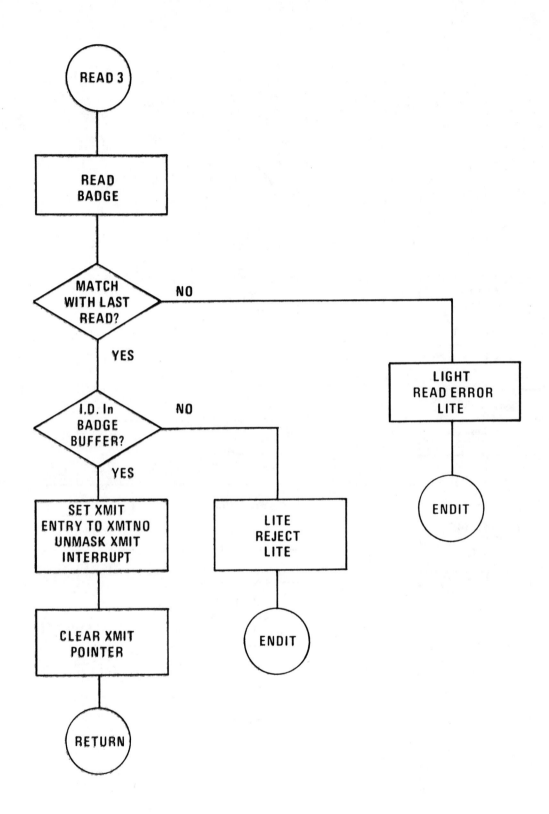

Figure 5.30. Badge Read (Sheet 2 of 3)

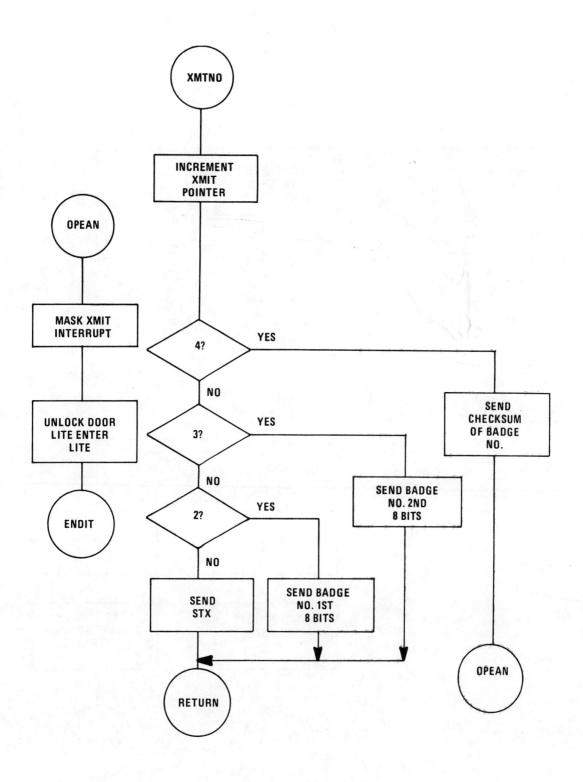

Figure 5.30. Badge Read (Sheet 3 of 3)

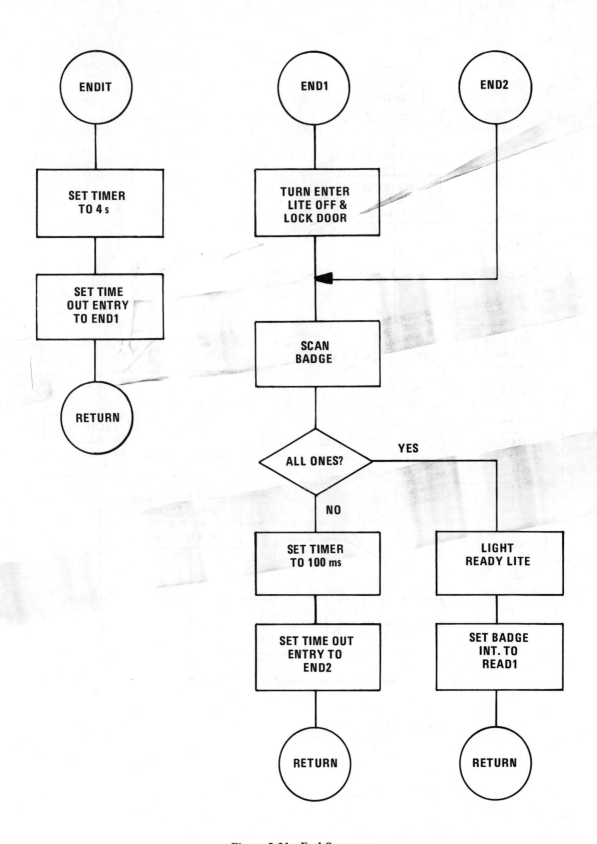

Figure 5.31. End Sequence

Table 5.10. Program Counter Interrupt Instructions

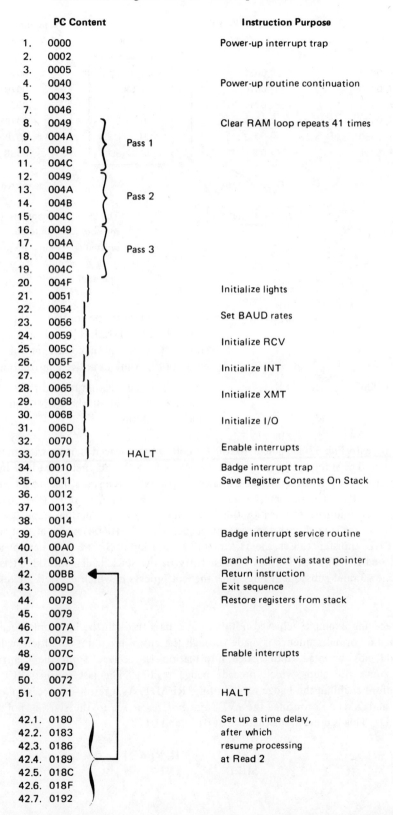

	PC Content	Instruction Purpose
1.	0000	Power-up interrupt trap
2.	0002	
3.	0005	
4.	0040	Power-up routine continuation
5.	0043	
7.	0046	
8.	0049	Clear RAM loop repeats 41 times
9.	004A	Pass 1
10.	004B	
11.	004C	
12.	0049	Pass 2
13.	004A	
14.	004B	
15.	004C	
16.	0049	Pass 3
17.	004A	
18.	004B	
19.	004C	
20.	004F	Initialize lights
21.	0051	
22.	0054	Set BAUD rates
23.	0056	
24.	0059	Initialize RCV
25.	005C	
26.	005F	Initialize INT
27.	0062	
28.	0065	Initialize XMT
29.	0068	
30.	006B	Initialize I/O
31.	006D	
32.	0070	Enable interrupts
33.	0071	HALT
34.	0010	Badge interrupt trap
35.	0011	Save Register Contents On Stack
36.	0012	
37.	0013	
38.	0014	
39.	009A	Badge interrupt service routine
40.	00A0	
41.	00A3	Branch indirect via state pointer
42.	00BB	Return instruction
43.	009D	Exit sequence
44.	0078	Restore registers from stack
45.	0079	
46.	007A	
47.	007B	
48.	007C	Enable interrupts
49.	007D	
50.	0072	
51.	0071	HALT
42.1.	0180	Set up a time delay,
42.2.	0183	after which
42.3.	0186	resume processing
42.4.	0189	at Read 2
42.5.	018C	
42.6.	018F	
42.7.	0192	

Table 5.11. Stack Content for Program Counter Trace

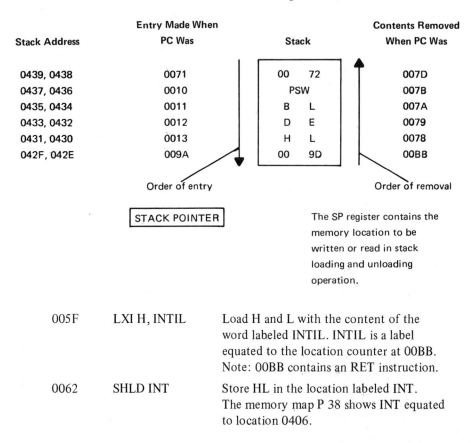

Stack Address	Entry Made When PC Was	Stack		Contents Removed When PC Was
0439, 0438	0071	00	72	007D
0437, 0436	0010	PSW		007B
0435, 0434	0011	B	L	007A
0433, 0432	0012	D	E	0079
0431, 0430	0013	H	L	0078
042F, 042E	009A	00	9D	00BB

Order of entry

Order of removal

STACK POINTER

The SP register contains the memory location to be written or read in stack loading and unloading operation.

005F	LXI H, INTIL	Load H and L with the content of the word labeled INTIL. INTIL is a label equated to the location counter at 00BB. Note: 00BB contains an RET instruction.
0062	SHLD INT	Store HL in the location labeled INT. The memory map P 38 shows INT equated to location 0406.

Beginning with line 33 in Table 5.10, the PC contents are traced starting with an interrupt from the badge reader. The interrupts were previously enabled, so the PC first goes to the badge interrupt trap instruction, 0010. Processing begins by saving registers on the stack. Table 5.11 shows the stack and the PC content at the time entries are made. The instruction at 0014 (line 38) is a JUMP to "BDGIT" a label referring to location 009A. Then a CALL instruction steps the PC to 00A0. Registers H and L are loaded with the content of location INT (0604) which at first contains 00BB. Thus, the PCHL transfer causes the PC to go to location 00BB for the next instruction. The instruction stored is RET. The PC gets the last entry of the stack which was 0090 (see Table 5.11). Table 5.10, line 43, and subsequent lines trace the exit process in which registers are restored and the system halts.

The preceding example achieved nothing but a pass through the interrupt processing routine. However, when a normal sequence is made through the entire program, conditions will be different. Badges should not be read until badge information is received from the Central Computer. Figure 5.22 shows the steps which precede badge reading. The last routine, RCVR4, must be completed before enabling the badge read routine, READ1. As a result of successful completion of the RCVR4 and XMTAK routine, the *INT state pointer* is set to the starting point of the read routine, READ1. This is done in instructions at 0174 and 0177:

```
LXI     H, READ1
SHLD    INT
```

At the end of Table 5.10, there is a list of instructions 42.1 through 42.7 which would replace the instruction at 42 (00BB) when the state pointer contains 0180. Notice that another state pointer, TMR, is used to steer the PC to READ2 routine when the timer interrupt occurs.

5.2.11 Assembly Listing of Software

Table 5.12 is the complete software listing for the project. The format is that of the assembler used to convert assembly language instruction mnemonics to machine code.

ROM addresses are listed in the first column. Instruction operation codes and operands are listed in the next three columns. Notice all numbers are in HEXADECIMAL; 16 bits for the ROM address, and 8 bits for each of the next three fields. Notice that instructions may consume one, two, or three words of memory. The next three columns show the label, instruction, and operand fields of the assembly language code. Finally, comments follow the semicolon.

The column headings OB1, OB2, and OB3 refer to "Operand Byte" 1, 2, and 3. LOC stands for "location" in memory.

This is a problem with a complex software execution. If you have devoted enough time to the material contained herein your confidence level should be increased by a step function now.

Table 5.12. TMS 8080 Design Example Listing

```
                        ; ****************************************************
                        ;
                        ;           RAM LAYOUT
                        ;
                        ; ****************************************************
0000                    RMBGN:  EQU   400H      ;  START OF RAM
0000                    TMR:    EQU   400H      ;  TIMER STATE POINTER
0000                    RCV:    EQU   402H      ;  RCEIVER STATE POINTER
0000                    XMT:    EQU   404H      ;  TRANSMITTER STATE POINTER
0000                    INT:    EQU   406H      ;  BADGE INTERRUPT POINTER
0000                    TMCNT:  EQU   408H      ;  TIMER COUNT
0000                    CKSUM:  EQU   40AH      ;  CHECKSUM
0000                    BDGIX:  EQU   40BH      ;  INDEX TO BADGE ID BUFFER
0000                    BDGNA:  EQU   40CH      ;  BADGE NUM. A
0000                    BDGNB:  EQU   40DH      ;  BADGE NUM. B
0000                    XMTPT:  EQU   40EH      ;  XMITER POINTER
0000                    BDGBF:  EQU   410H      ;  BADGE BUFFER - 16 LOCATIONS
0000                    RMEND:  EQU   43FH      ;  RAM END
0000                    STACK:  EQU   440H      ;  STACK START
                        ; ****************************************************
                        ;
                        ;           COMMUNICATION CHARACTERS
                        ;
                        ; ****************************************************
0000                    STX     EQU   2         ;  START OF TEXT
0000                    ENQ     EQU   5         ;  ENQUIRY
0000                    ACK     EQU   6         ;  ACKNOWLEDGE
                        ; ****************************************************
                        ;
                        ;           I/O  ADDRESSES
                        ;
                        ; ****************************************************
0000                    IDCDE   EQU   1000H     ;  READ ID CODE
0000                    RCVBF:  EQU   800H      ;  RECEIVER BUFFER
0000                    DISCM:  EQU   804H      ;  DISCREAT COMMAND
0000                    RATCM:  EQU   805H      ;  RATE COMMAND
0000                    XMITR:  EQU   806H      ;  TRANSMITTER BUFFER
0000                    OUT:    EQU   807H      ;  I/O OUTPUT BUFFER
0000                    IOMSK:  EQU   808H      ;  I/O INTERRUPT MASK REGISTER
0000                    TIMR:   EQU   80AH      ;  I/O TIMER 2
0000                    SCANA:  EQU   801H      ;  SCAN A INPUT
0000                    SCANB:  EQU   0C01H     ;  SCAN B INPUT
                        ; ****************************************************
                        ;
                        ;           OUTPUT LABELES
                        ;
                        ; ****************************************************
0000                    WAIT:   EQU   04H       ;  WAIT LITE
0000                    ENTER:  EQU   08H       ;  ENTER LITE
0000                    UNLCK:  EQU   01H       ;  UNLOCK DOOR
0000                    REDER:  EQU   20H       ;  READ ERROR LITE
0000                    RJCT:   EQU   10H       ;  REJECT LITE
0000                    RDY:    EQU   02H       ;  READY LITE
```

Table 5.12. TMS 8080 Design Example Listing (Continued)

```
V3L1 LOC   OB1 OB2 OB3 SOURCE LINES     08:25 AM MON  APR 14, 1975   PAGE  0002
     0000                      EJECT
                      ; ****************************************************
                      ;
                      ;         INTERRUPT TRAP LOCATIONS
                      ;
                      ; ****************************************************
                      ;
                      ;         POWER UP TRAP
                      ;
     0000  3E  09         PWRUP: MVI  A,9      ; RESET I/O AND SELECT TIMER 5
     0002  32  04  08            STA  DISCM
     0005  C3  40  00            JMP  PWRON
                      ;
                      ;         TIMER 2 INTERRUPT
                      ;
     0008  F5             TRAP1: PUSH PSW      ; SAVE REGISTERS
     0009  C5                    PUSH B
     000A  D5                    PUSH D
     000B  E5                    PUSH H
     000C  C3  75  00            JMP  TIMER    ; GO TO TIMER ROUTINE
     000F  76                    HLT           ; USE SPARE ROM
                      ;
                      ;         BADGE INTERRUPT
                      ;
     0010  F5             TRAP2: PUSH PSW      ; SAVE REGISTERS
     0011  C5                    PUSH B
     0012  D5                    PUSH D
     0013  E5                    PUSH H
     0014  C3  9A  00            JMP  BDGIT    ; GO TO BADGE INTERRUPT ROUTINE
     0017  76                    HLT           ; USE SPARE ROM
                      ;
                      ;         TIMER 3 NOT USED
                      ;
     0018  76             TRAP3: HLT           ; FILL INTERRUPT TRAP ROUTINE
     0019  76                    HLT
     001A  76                    HLT
     001B  76                    HLT
     001C  76                    HLT
     001D  76                    HLT
     001E  76                    HLT
     001F  76                    HLT
                      ;
                      ;         RECEIVER INTERRUPT
                      ;
     0020  F5             TRAP4: PUSH PSW      ; SAVE REGISTERS
     0021  C5                    PUSH B
     0022  D5                    PUSH D
     0023  E5                    PUSH H
     0024  C3  A4  00            JMP  RCVR     ; GO TO RECEIVER ROUTINE
     0027  76                    HLT           ; USE SPARE ROM
                      ;
                      ;         TRANSMITTER INTERRUPT
                      ;
```

Table 5.12. TMS 8080 Design Example Listing (Continued)

```
V3L1 LOC   OB1 OB2 OB3 SOURCE LINES    08:25 AM MON  APR 14, 1975  PAGE  0003
     0028  F5              TRAP5: PUSH PSW      ; SAVE REGISTERS
     0029  C5                     PUSH B
     002A  D5                     PUSH D
     002B  E5                     PUSH H
     002C  C3  B1  00             JMP  XMIT     ; GO TO TRANSMIT ROUTINE
     002F  76                     HLT           ; USE SPARE ROM
                          ;
                          ;      TIMER 4 NOT US'
                          ;
     0030  76              TRAP6: HLT           ; FILL INTL RUPT TRAP
     0031  76                     HLT
     0032  76                     HLT
     0033  76                     HLT
     0034  76                     HLT
     0035  76                     HLT
     0036  76                     HLT
     0037  76                     HLT
                          ;
                          ;      TIMER 5 NOT USED
                          ;
     0038  76              TRAP7: HLT           ; FILL SPARE ROM
     0039  76                     HLT
     003A  76                     HLT
     003B  76                     HLT
     003C  76                     HLT
     003D  76                     HLT
     003E  76                     HLT
     003F  76                     HLT
```

Table 5.12. TMS 8080 Design Example Listing (Continued)

```
V3L1 LOC   OB1 OB2 OB3 SOURCE LINES      08:25 AM MON  APR 14, 1975  PAGE  0004
    0040                      EJECT
                      ; ********************************************************
                      ;
                      ;       POWER UP ROUTINE
                      ;
                      ; ********************************************************
    0040   31  40  04  PWRON: LXI   SP,STACK ; SET STACK POINTER
    0043   06  40             MVI   B,RMEND-RMBGN+1 ;   CLEAR RAM
    0045   AF                 XRA   A
    0046   21  00  04         LXI   H,RMBGN
    0049   77          PWR1:  MOV   M,A
    004A   23                 INX   H
    004B   05                 DCR   B
    004C   C2  49  00         JNZ   PWR1
                      ;
                      ;
    004F   3E  04             MVI   A,WAIT  ; LITE WAIT LIGHT, CLEAR REST
    0051   32  07  08         STA   OUT
                      ;
                      ;
    0054   3E  84             MVI   A,84H    ; SET COMMUNICATION TO 300 BAUD
    0056   32  05  08         STA   RATCM
                      ;
                      ;
    0059   21  BB  00         LXI   H,RCVIL ; IDLE RECEIVER
    005C   22  02  04         SHLD  RCV
    005F   21  BB  00         LXI   H,INTIL ; IDLE BADGE INTERRUPT
    0062   22  06  04         SHLD  INT
    0065   21  BC  00         LXI   H,XMIT1 ; SET XMIT STATE TO XMIT1
    0068   22  04  04         SHLD  XMT
    006B   3E  36             MVI   A,36H    ; ARM TMR2,INT,RCVR,& XMITTER
    006D   32  08  08         STA   IOMSK
                      ;
                      ;
    0070   FB                 EI            ; ENABLE INTERRUPTS
    0071   76          HLT    HLT           ; WAIT FOR INTERRUPTS
    0072   C3  71  00         JMP   HLT
```

Table 5.12. TMS 8080 Design Example Listing (Continued)

```
V3L1 LOC   OB1 OB2 OB3 SOURCE LINES    08:25 AM MON  APR 14, 1975  PAGE  0005
     0075                  EJECT
                      ; ********************************************************
                      ;
                      ;         TIMER INTERRUPT ROUTINE
                      ;
                      ; ********************************************************
     0075   CD  7E  00  TIMER:  CALL  COUNT     ; GO DECREMENT COUNT
     0078   E1          POPIT:  POP   H         ; RESTORE REGISTERS
     0079   D1                  POP   D
     007A   C1                  POP   B
     007B   F1                  POP   PSW
     007C   FB                  EI
     007D   C9                  RET
                      ;
                      ;
     007E   2A  08  04  COUNT:  LHLD  TMCNT     ; DECREMENT TIMER COUNT
     0081   2B                  DCX   H
     0082   22  08  04          SHLD  TMCNT
     0085   7C                  MOV   A, H
     0086   B5                  ORA   L
     0087   CA  96  00          JZ    TMEDN     ; CHECK IF COUNT DONE DONE
     008A   3E  9C      STRTM:  MVI   A, 156    ; SET TIMER TO 10 MSEC
     008C   32  0A  08          STA   TIMR
     008F   C9                  RET
                      ;
     0090   22  08  04  TMEIT:  SHLD  TMCNT     ; SET COUNT
     0093   C3  8A  00          JMP   STRTM     ; START TIMER
     0096   2A  00  04  TMEDN:  LHLD  TMR       ; BRANC INDIRECT TO NXT TMR STATE
     0099   E9                  PCHL
                      ; ********************************************************
                      ;
                      ;         BADGE INTERRUPT ROUTINE
                      ;
                      ; ********************************************************
     009A   CD  A0  00  BDGIT:  CALL  BDG       ; PROCESS BADGE INTERRUPT
     009D   C3  78  00          JMP   POPIT
                      ;
     00A0   2A  06  04  BDG:    LHLD  INT       ; BRANCH INDIRECT TO INT ROUTINE
     00A3   E9                  PCHL
                      ; ********************************************************
                      ;
                      ;         RECEIVER INTERRUPT ROUTINE
                      ;
                      ; ********************************************************
     00A4   CD  AA  00  RCVR:   CALL  RCVGO     ; PROCESS RECEIVER CHARACTER
     00A7   C3  78  00          JMP   POPIT
                      ;
     00AA   3A  00  08  RCVGO:  LDA   RCVBF     ; READ CHARACTER
     00AD   2A  02  04          LHLD  RCV       ; BRANCH INDIRECT TO RECEIVER STATE
     00B0   E9                  PCHL
                      ; ********************************************************
                      ;
                      ;         TRANSMITTER INTERRUPT ROUTINE
```

Table 5.12. TMS 8080 Design Example Listing (Continued)

```
V3L1 LOC  OB1 OB2 OB3 SOURCE LINES   08:25 AM MON  APR 14, 1975  PAGE  0006
                        ;
                        ;****************************************************
      00B1  CD  B7  00  XMIT:  CALL  XMTGO  ; PROCESS XMITTER INTERRUPT
      00B4  C3  78  00         JMP   POPIT
                        ;
      00B7  2A  04  04  XMTGO: LHLD  XMT    ; BRANCH INDIRECT TO XMIT ROUTINE
      00BA  E9                 PCHL
                        ;****************************************************
                        ;
                        ;       IDLE ROUTINE RETURN ( IGNORES INTERRUPT )
                        ;
                        ;****************************************************
      00BB            RCVIL: EQU   $
      00BB            INTIL: EQU   $
      00BB            TMRIL: EQU   $
      00BB  C9               RET




V3L1 LOC  OB1 OB2 OB3 SOURCE LINES   08:25 AM MON  APR 14, 1975  PAGE  0007
      00BC                      EJECT
                        ;****************************************************
                        ;
                        ;       SEND ENQ-ID TO CENTRAL CPU
                        ;
                        ;       WAIT 15 SEC FOR RESPONSE, IF NO RESPONSE
                        ;                         REPEAT SEQUENCE
                        ;
                        ;****************************************************
      00BC  3E  05  XMIT1: MVI   A, ENQ   ; SEND ENQ
      00BE  32  06  08        STA   XMITR
      00C1  21  C8  00        LXI   H, XMIT2 ; NEXT XMIT STATE - XMIT2
      00C4  22  04  04        SHLD  XMT
      00C7  C9               RET
                        ;
                        ;       SEND ID CHARACTER
                        ;
      00C8  3A  00  10  XMIT2: LDA   IDCDE    ; READ ID CODE
      00CB  32  06  08         STA   XMITR    ; XMIT ID CODE
      00CE  3E  16            MVI   A, 16H    ; MASK XMITER
      00D0  32  08  08        STA   IOMSK
      00D3  21  F8  00        LXI   H, RCVR1 ; RECEIVER STATE TO RCVR1
      00D6  22  02  04        SHLD  RCV
      00D9  21  DC  05        LXI   H, 1500  ; TIME OUT 15 SEC
      00DC  CD  90  00        CALL  TMEIT
      00DF  21  E6  00        LXI   H, TMOT1 ; TIME OUT STATE TO TMOT1
      00E2  22  00  04        SHLD  TMR
      00E5  C9               RET
                        ;
                        ;       FAILED TO RECEIVE RESPONSE FROM
                        ;       CENTRAL CPU WILL CAUSE 15 SEC TIME OUT
                        ;       TO ENTER HERE
                        ;
      00E6  21  BC  00  TMOT1: LXI   H, XMIT1 ; RESEND ID SEQUENCE
      00E9  22  04  04        SHLD  XMT
      00EC  3E  36            MVI   A, 36H    ; UNMASK XMITER
      00EE  32  08  08        STA   IOMSK
      00F1  21  BB  00        LXI   H, RCVIL ; IDLE RECEIVER
      00F4  22  02  04        SHLD  RCV
      00F7  C9               RET
```

Table 5.12. TMS 8080 Design Example Listing (Continued)

```
V3L1 LOC   OB1 OB2 OB3 SOURCE LINES      08:25 AM MON  APR 14, 1975   PAGE  0008
     00F8                     EJECT
                 ;*********************************************************
                 ;
                 ;        RECEIVER/XMITTER PROTOCAL FOR CENTRAL
                 ;        CPU DOWN LOAD OF BADGE ID GROUPS
                 ;
                 ;*********************************************************
     00F8   FE  02      RCVR1:  CPI   STX      ; STX CHARACTER
     00FA   CO                  RNZ            ; IGNORE ALL CHARACTERS BUT ST
     00FB   21  09  01          LXI   H,RCVR2  ; NEXT RECEIVED CHARACTER TO RCVR2
     00FE   22  02  04          SHLD  RCV
     0101   AF                  XRA   A        ; CLEAR CHECKSUM AND BADGE BUF IDX
     0102   32  0A  04          STA   CKSUM
     0105   32  0B  04          STA   BDGIX
     0108   C9                  RET
                 ;
                 ;        GET ID AND CHECK IF OURS
                 ;
     0109   47          RCVR2:  MOV   B,A      ; SAVE RCVD ID IN B
     010A   3A  00  10          LDA   IDCDE    ; READ ID CODE
     010D   21  1B  01          LXI   H,RCVR3  ; NXT CHAR. TO RCVR3 IF
     0110   B8                  CMP   B
     0111   CA  17  01          JZ    RCV2A
     0114   21  BB  00          LXI   H,RCVIL  ;  IF NOT IDLE RCVR
     0117   22  02  04  RCV2A:  SHLD  RCV
     011A   C9                  RET
                 ;
                 ;        PUT ID CODE INTO BADGE ID BUFFER.  FORM CHECKSUM
                 ;        OFFH  CHAR.  TERMINATES SEQUENCE
                 ;
                 ;        ERROR IF MORE THAN 16 ID CODES
                 ;
     011B   FE  FF      RCVR3:  CPI   OFFH     ; END OF SEQUENCE
     011D   CA  40  01          JZ    RCV3E    ; GO TO RCV3E
     0120   21  0B  04          LXI   H,BDGIX
     0123   4E                  MOV   C,M      ; PICK UP BADGE ID TABLE INDEX
     0124   06  00              MVI   B,0
     0126   21  10  04          LXI   H,BDGBF
     0129   09                  DAD   B        ; FORM IDEXED ADR TO TABLE
     012A   77                  MOV   M,A      ; SAVE ID CODE
     012B   21  0A  04          LXI   H,CKSUM
     012E   86                  ADD   M        ; ADD ID TO CHECKSUM
     012F   77                  MOV   M,A
     0130   01  0B  04          LXI   B,BDGIX  ; INCREMENT BADGE TABLE INDEX
     0133   0A                  LDAX  B
     0134   3C                  INR   A
     0135   02                  STAX  B
     0136   FE  11              CPI   17       ; OK IF < 17
     0138   D8                  RC
     0139   21  BB  00          LXI   H,RCVIL  ; ERROR - IDLE RECEIVER
     013C   22  02  04          SHLD  RCV
     013F   C9                  RET
```

Table 5.12. TMS 8080 Design Example Listing (Continued)

```
V3L1 LOC   OB1  OB2  OB3  SOURCE LINES     08:25 AM MON   APR 14, 1975   PAGE   0009
     0140   21   47   01  RCV3E. LXI  H, RCVR4 ; NEXT CHARACTER TO RCVR4
     0143   22   02   04         SHLD RCV
     0146   C9                   RET
                           ;
                           ;      RECEIVE CHECKSUM CHARACTER AND VERIFY
                           ;      IF AGAINST CALCULATED CHECKSUM
                           ;
     0147   21   BB   00  RCVR4. LXI  H, RCVIL ; IDLE RECEIVER
     014A   22   02   04         SHLD RCV
     014D   21   0A   04         LXI  H, CKSUM
     0150   BE                   CMP  M        ; CHECKSUM MATCH
     0151   C0                   RNZ           ; STOP PROCESSING IF ERROR
     0152   21   6A   01         LXI  H, XMTAK ; SET XMITTER TO SEND ACK
     0155   22   04   04         SHLD XMT
     0158   3E   36              MVI  A, 36H   ; UNMASK XMITTER
     015A   32   08   08         STA  IOMSK
     015D   26   00              MVI  H, 0
     015F   6C                   MOV  L, H
     0160   22   08   04         SHLD TMCNT    ; CLEAR TIMER COUNT
     0163   21   DB   00         LXI  H, TMRIL ; IDLE TIMER
     0166   22   00   04         SHLD TMR
     0169   C9                   RET
                           ;
                           ;      XMIT ACK TO CENTRAL CPU TO
                           ;      ACKNOWLEDE ID CODES
                           ;
     016A   3E   06       XMTAK  MVI  A, ACK   ; XMIT ACK
     016C   32   06   08         STA  XMITR
     016F   3E   16              MVI  A, 16H   ; MASK XMIT INTERRUPT
     0171   32   08   08         STA  IOMSK
     0174   21   80   01         LXI  H, READ1 ; SET BADGE INT. TO READ1
     0177   22   0A   04         SHLD INT
     017A   3E   ..              MVI  A, RDY   ; WAIT LITE OFF/READY LITE ON
     017C   32   07   08         STA  OUT
     017F   C9                   RET
```

Table 5.12. TMS 8080 Design Example Listing (Continued)

```
V3L1 LOC   OB1 OB2 OB3 SOURCE LINES    08:25 AM MON  APR 14, 1975   PAGE   0010
     0180                       EJECT
                     ; ********************************************************
                     ;
                     ;            BADGE READ ROUTINE
                     ;
                     ;              DEBOUNCE BADGE INSERTION
                     ;              READ BADGE
                     ;              READ BADGE 100 MSEC LATER / MATCH
                     ;              CHECK IF BADGE ID OC
                     ;
                     ; ********************************************************  ;**
     0180   21  BB  00  READ1: LXI   H, INTIL ; IDLE BADGE INT.
     0183   22  06  04         SHLD  INT
     0186   21  14  00         LXI   H, 20    ; SET TIMER TO 200 MSEC
     0189   CD  90  00         CALL  TMEIT
     018C   21  93  01         LXI   H, READ2 ; TIME OUT TO READ2
     018F   22  00  04         SHLD  TMR
     0192   C9                 RET
                     ;
                     ;       READ BADGE   IGNORE ALL ONES
                     ;
     0193   3A  01  08  READ2: LDA   SCANA    ; READ BADGE NUM A-PART
     0196   32  0C  04         STA   BDGNA
     0199   47                 MOV   B, A
     019A   3A  01  0C         LDA   SCANB    ; READ BADGE NUM B-PART
     019D   32  0D  04         STA   BDGNB
     01A0   FE  FF             CPI   OFFH     ; IGNORE ALL ONES READ
     01A2   C2  AB  01         JNZ   RAD2B
     01A5   78                 MOV   A, B
     01A6   FE  FF             CPI   OFFH
     01A8   CA  B8  01         JZ    RAD2A
     01AB   21  0A  00  RAD2B: LXI   H, 10    ; SET TIMER FOR 100 MSEC
     01AE   CD  90  00         CALL  TMEIT
     01B1   21  BF  01         LXI   H, READ3 ; TIME OUT TO READ3
     01B4   22  00  04         SHLD  TMR
     01B7   C9                 RET
     01B8   21  80  01  RAD2A: LXI   H, READ1 , ARM BADGE INT TO READ1
     01BB   22  06  04         SHLD  INT
     01BE   C9                 RET
                     ;
                     ;       READ BADGE 2ND TIME AND MATCH
                     ;
     01BF   21  0C  04  READ3: LXI   H, BDGNA ; CHECK PART-A
     01C2   3A  01  08         LDA   SCANA
     01C5   BE                 CMP M
     01C6   C2  01  02         JNZ   RAD3M    ; IF NO MATCH - READ ERROR
     01C9   23                 INX   H
     01CA   3A  01  0C         LDA   SCANB    ; CHECK PART-B
     01CD   BE                 CMP   M
     01CE   C2  01  02         JNZ   RAD3M    ; IF NO MATCH - READ ERROR
                     ;
                     ;       CHECK IF MSB 4 BITS IN BADGE BUFFER
                     ;
```

Table 5.12. TMS 8080 Design Example Listing (Continued)

```
V3L1 LOC   OB1  OB2  OB3  SOURCE LINES      08:25 AM MON  APR 14, 1975  PAGE  0011
     01D1   3A   OC   04          LDA   BDGNA    ; ISOLATE BADGE CATAGORY
     01D4   OF                    RRC
     01D5   OF                    RRC
     01D6   OF                    RRC
     01D7   OF                    RRC
     01D8   E6   OF               ANI   OFH
     01DA   21   OB   04          LXI   H, BDGIX
     01DD   4E                    MOV   C, M     ; PICK UP BADGE INDEX
     01DE   06   00               MVI   B, O
     01E0   21   10   04          LXI   H, BDGBF ; INDEX INTO BUFFER
     01E3   09                    DAD   B
     01E4   2B                    DCX   H
                              ;
     01E5   OD           RDCHK:   DCR   C        ; CHECK IF THROUGH LOOKING
     01E6   FA   09   02          JM    RJECT
     01E9   BE                    CMP   M        ; CHECK FOR ID CAT. MATCH
     01EA   CA   F1   01          JZ    OKGO
     01ED   2B                    DCX   H
     01EE   C3   E5   01          JMP   RDCHK
                              ;
                              ;    CATAGORY MATCH
                              ;
     01F1   21   11   02  OKGO:   LXI   H, XMTNO ; XMITER TO SEND BADGE NO.
     01F4   22   04   04          SHLD  XMT
     01F7   AF                    XRA   A        ; CLEAR XMIT POINTER
     01F8   32   OE   04          STA   XMTPT
     01FB   3E   36               MVI   A, 36H   ; UNMASK. XMITTER INTERRUPT
     01FD   32   08   08          STA   IOMSK
     0200   C9                    RET
                              ;
                              ;    READ ERROR
                              ;
     0201   3E   20        RAD3M: MVI   A, REDER ; LITE READ ERROR LITE
     0203   32   07   08          STA   OUT
     0206   C3   4B   02          JMP   ENDIT    ; GO END SEQUENCE
                              ;
                              ;    REJECT
                              ;
     0209   3E   10        RJECT: MVI   A, RJCT  ; LITE REJECT LITE
     020B   32   07   08          STA   OUT
     020E   C3   4B   02          JMP   ENDIT    ; GO END SEQUENCE
```

Table 5.12. TMS 8080 Design Example Listing (Continued)

```
V3L1 LOC   OB1 OB2 OB3 SOURCE LINES    08:25 AM MON  APR 14, 1975  PAGE  0012
     0211                  EJECT
                   ; *************************************************************
                   ;
                   ;        XMIT BADGE # TO CENTRAL CPU THEN
                   ;        OPEAN DOOR
                   ;
                   ; *************************************************************
     0211  21  OE  04  XMTNO: LXI  H, XMTPT ; INCREMENT XMIT POINTER
     0214  7E           MOV  A, M
     0215  3C           INR  A
     0216  77           MOV  M, A
     0217  FE  04       CPI  4        ; 4- SEND CHECKSUM
     0219  CA  38  02    JZ   XTCKM
     021C  FE  03       CPI  3        ; 3- SEND BADGE PART-B
     021E  CA  32  02    JZ   XTBDB
     0221  FE  02       CPI  2        ; 2- SEND BADGE PART-A
     0223  CA  2C  02    JZ   XTBDA
     0226  3E  02       MVI  A, STX   ; SEND STX
     0228  32  06  08  XMTIT: STA  XMITR
     022B  C9           RET
                   ;
     022C  3A  OC  04  XTBDA: LDA  BDGNA
     022F  C3  28  02    JMP  XMTIT
                   ;
     0232  3A  OD  04  XTBDB: LDA  BDGNB
     0235  C3  28  02    JMP  XMTIT
                   ;
     0238  21  OC  04  XTCKM: LXI  H, BDGNA ; ADD UP CHECKSUM
     023B  7E           MOV  A, M
     023C  23           INX  H
     023D  86           ADD  M
     023E  32  06  08    STA  XMITR   ; SEND CHECK SUM
                   ;
                   ;
     0241  3E  09       OPEAN: MVI  A, ENTER+UNLCK  ; OPEAN DOOR - LITE ENTER
     0243  32  07  08    STA  OUT
     0246  3E  16       MVI  A, 16H   ; MASK INTERRUPT
     0248  32  08  08    STA  IOMSK
```

Table 5.12. TMS 8080 Design Example Listing (Continued)

```
V3L1 LOC   OB1 OB2 OB3 SOURCE LINES    08:25 AM MON  APR 14, 1975  PAGE  0013
     024B                   EJECT
                        ; *******************************************************
                        ;
                        ;      END OF BADGE SEQUENCE
                        ;
                        ; *******************************************************
     024B  21  90  01   ENDIT: LXI  H, 400   ; DELAY 4 SEC
     024E  CD  90  00          CALL TMEIT
     0251  21  58  02          LXI  H, END1 ; TIME OUT TO END1
     0254  22  00  04          SHLD TMR
     0257  C9                  RET
                        ;
                        ;      LOOK DOOR  SCAN FOR BADGE REMOVAL
                        ;
     0258  AF           END1:  XRA  A       ; TURN OK OFF - LOCK DOOR SOLENOID
     0259  32  07  08          STA  OUT
                        ;
     025C  3A  01  08   END2:  LDA  SCANA   ; SCAN BADGE
     025F  FE  FF               CPI  OFFH   ; PART-A ALL ONES
     0261  C2  78  02          JNZ  WAITE   ; IF NOT WAIT
     0264  3A  01  0C          LDA  SCANB   ; SCAN PART-B
     0267  FE  FF              CPI  OFFH
     0269  C2  78  02          JNZ  WAITE   ; WAIT IF NOT ALL ONES
                        ;
     026C  3E  02              MVI  A, RDY   ; LITE READY
     026E  32  07  08          STA  OUT
     0271  21  80  01          LXI  H, READ1 ; BADGE INT TO READ1
     0274  22  06  04          SHLD INT
     0277  C9                  RET
                        ;
                        ;
     0278  21  0A  00   WAITE: LXI  H, 10    ; SET TIMER TO 100 MSEC
     027B  CD  90  00          CALL TMEIT
     027E  21  5C  02          LXI  H, END2  , TIME OUT TO END2
     0281  22  00  04          SHLD TMR
     0284  C9                  RET
                        ;
                        ;
                        ; *******************************************************
                        ; *******************************************************
     0285                      END

ASSEMBLY COMPLETE     0000  ERRORS
```

5.3   TMS 9900 PROBLEM

More advanced than any other microprocessor discussed in this book, the TMS 9900 combines minicomputer performance with LSI technology to achieve a step-function in microprocessor computing power. A brief, but sophisticated example of the use of a TMS 9900, illustrates the highest level of design through software of the four examples contained in this book.

5.3.1   Problem Statement

Basically, the example is one of interfacing a terminal to the CPU (TMS 9900) and setting up a particular sequence of character inputs and outputs. Instead of echoing single characters, the task is to have the CPU echo a line of characters. An operator may enter any number of characters up to 72, terminate with a carriage return, and the CPU will send the characters back to the terminal for printout. Before describing the code, it will be instructive to look into the following important foundation topics:

1.   TMS 9900 Characteristics

2.   733 ASR Interface

3.   Assembler for the TMS 9900

5.3.2   Hardware Definition

The TMS 9900 is a 16-bit processor with 69 instructions including byte and bit addressing. The 16-bit word is used to address 32K words or 65K bytes of memory. Processing power comes not only from the 16-bit word length, but also from eight powerful addressing modes and the use of memory as working registers. It is, in fact, this concept called the "Workspace Register" concept that is the most outstanding architectural feature of the TMS 9900. In contrast to the pushdown stack found in many minicomputers and microprocessors, the workspace register file is a contiguous block of 16 words in memory used as working registers. Storage of intermediate results and subroutine return addresses, as well as index register functions, is accomplished in the workspace.

Most important of all is that each small routine, program or subroutine may have its own 16-word workspace. A workspace pointer (a 16-bit register within the arithmetic unit) points to the first word of the appropriate workspace for any given program. This is especially significant in systems where interrupt processing is used, or where multifunction applications require frequent changes of program context. When an interrupt occurs, for example, there is no need to save register contents and a return address is a stack or other block of memory, because they are all in the workspace. The Program Counter, Status Register, and Workspace Pointer (PC, ST, WP) are saved in three words of the workspace, the WP is set to a new value, pointing to the appropriate service routine, and processing resumes around a new set of workspace registers.

The primary impact of the workspace is to give the program designer 16 "working registers" for *every routine and subroutine*; and because the "registers" are actually memory words, there is no need to save and restore register contents when jumping from one routine to another.

Other important features of the TMS 9900 are vectored interrupts (16 levels), an asynchronous I/O bus called TILINE, and a Communications Register Unit (CRU) to accommodate I/O circuit cards for a wide variety of peripherals and general interface requirements.

Instructions for the TMS 9900 may be divided into categories as follows:

	Category	No. Instructions
1.	Data Movement	9
2.	Logical and Arithmetic	32
3.	I/O (a type of data movement)	6
4.	Program Control	18
5.	Special	4
		69

Twenty of these instructions, those used in the example program, are defined (paragraph 5.3.3) to illustrate the instruction versatility and power.

In addition to the TMS 9900, a 733 ASR terminal is required to implement this problem.

5.3.2.1   733 ASR Interface

The interface between the TMS 9900 and the 733 ASR is shown in Figure 5.32. The character output register consists of output lines 0-7. An LDCR instruction is used to transfer a character in memory to the output register.

The character input register consists of input lines 0-7. An STCR instruction is used to transfer a character from the input register to memory. The remaining output lines are individually controlled by SBO and SBZ instructions, and function as command lines. Table 5.13 lists the command lines. The remaining input lines are individually tested by the TB instruction to determine the status of the TTY/EIA module. Table 5.14 lists the TTY/EIA module status lines.

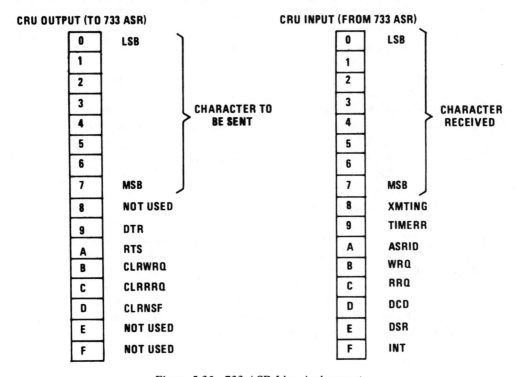

Figure 5.32. 733 ASR Line Assignments

Table 5.13. Command Lines (733 ASR Inputs)

Name	Meaning	Description
DTR	Data terminal ready	Enable 733 ASR operation
RTS	Request to send	Enable 733 ASR to receive characters
CLRWRQ	Clear write request	Clear write request flag
CLRRRQ	Clear read request	Clear read request flag
CLRNSF	Clear new status flag	Clear new status flag interrupt

Table 5.14. TTY/EIA Module Status Lines (733 ASR Outputs)

Name	Meaning	Description
XMTING	Transmit in progress	Module is transmitting to 733 ASR
TIMERR	Timing error	Character received by module before previous character was stored by computer
ASRID	ASR identifier	Logic zero for 733 ASR
WRQ	Write request	Logic one when character has been sent to 733 ASR
RRQ	Read request	Logic one when a character has been received from 733 ASR
DCD	Data carrier detect	Not used for 733 ASR (set to logic one)
DSR	Data set ready	Logic one when DTR has been set and ON LINE/OFF switch on 733 ASR is set to ON LINE position
INT	Interrupt	Logic one when WRQ or RRQ or new status flag is set

The CRU base address used in all I/O operations is determined by the CRU select line wired to the chassis connector for the TTY/EIA module. The standard CRU base address for the 733 ASR is 100_{16}. This value is placed in workspace register 12 prior to any I/O operation with the 733 ASR.

5.3.3 Software Definition

5.3.3.1 Instruction for Example (Order of Appearance)

1. RSET — Reset all I/O devices, and clear the interrupt mask.

2. LWPI — Load workspace pointer immediate. The next word after this instruction contains the address to be set into the WP.

3. LI — Load immediate. The word following this instruction contains the information to be loaded into the specified workspace register.

4. SBO — Set a CRU bit to logical one. Addressing is accomplished by adding a portion of this instruction word to workspace register 12 (WR12).

5. CLR — Clear a memory word. The word is addressed by a workspace register in one of four modes: direct, indirect, indexed, indirect autoincrement.

6. SBZ — Same as SBO, except set bit to zero.

7. TB — Test a bit in the CRU and set EQUAL bit of the status register if it is a one. Addressing is the same as SBO.

8. JNE — Jump if the EQUAL bit of the status register is not set. The 8-bit two's complement value in the instruction word is added to the PC.

9. STCR — Store a specified number of bits in the CRU. Addressing is the same as SBO.

10. MOVB — Move byte from source address to destination address. Two workspace registers are used for addressing.

11. ANDI — Perform logical AND between immediate operand, the word following the instruction, and the specified workspace register. Result in WR.

12. CB — Compare bytes addressed by two WRs. Set appropriate bit in the Status Register (ST).

13. JEQ — Jump if EQUAL bit of ST is set. An 8-bit two's complement number in the operand field is added to the PC.

14. INC — Increment the memory word addressed by the specified WR.

15. CI — Compare the contents of the specified WR with the contents of the word following the instruction, and set appropriate status bits.

16. INCT — Same as INC, except increment by two.

17. LDCR — Load CRU with a specified number of bits from a word specified by a WR. The CRU address is a portion of WR12.

18. DEC — Decrement the memory word addressed by a WR.

19. JGT — Jump if the arithmetic greater than bit of the ST is set. The PC is modified by an 8-bit signed integer in the instruction.

20. JMP — Jump unconditionally. PC is modified by the 8-bit signed integer in the instruction.

Assembler Directives Used

1. EQU — Define a symbol in the label field as the number in the operand field.

2. BSS — Reserve a contiguous block of bytes. A starting address symbol is given in the label field, and the block length is in the operand field.

3. BYTE — Initialize a byte to a given value.

A complete instruction list for the TMS 9900 is contained in Appendix E.

5.3.3.2 Addressing Modes

Further clarification of the instruction set is included with examples of the eight addressing modes.

1. Immediate — Operand is the next word of memory.

    Example: LWPI   WSP
                 LI   1, BUFF

2. Workspace Register — Operand is in a WR.

    Example: MOV 4, 8 — move the word in WR4 to WR8.

3. WR Indirect

    Example: MOV *2, *7 — move the word *addressed by* WR2 to the location *addressed by* WR7.

4. Symbolic Addresses

    Example: MOV @TABLE, @LIST — move the word in symbolic location TABLE (used somewhere as a label) to the symbolic location LIST.

5. Indexed Addressing

    Example: MOV @TABLE (3), @LIST (4)

    Here WR3 and WR4 are index registers used to make the addresses sequentially step through the TABLE and LIST.

6. WR Indirect and Autoincrement

    Example: MOV *2+, *7+

    Here WR2 and WR7 are address pointers (indirect addresses) pointing to locations in two tables. The + symbol means that each register is incremented as a result of the instruction so that it points to the next sequential location in the tables.

7. Displacement Mode

    Example: JMP $−2

    The operand is calculated as a displacement value to be added to (or subtracted from) the PC. This instruction creates a displacement of −2. The displacement value is always a signed integer eight bits long. This gives a range of +128 to −127 as the distance for such a jump.

8. Shift Count Mode (The WRs are addressed with the number of shift positions included.)

    Example: SRL 2, 5

    WR2 will have its contents shifted right by 5 places.

    If WR2 were 8CE3 before, it becomes 0467 afterwards.

        1000 1100 1110 0011 before
        0000 0100 0110 0111 after 5-place shift

5.3.3.3 Assembler Characteristics

An assembler for the TMS 9900 has been written for execution on the TI 990 minicomputer. (The instruction sets for the TI 990 and the TMS 9900 are the same.)

Special remarks, headings, and listing spaces may be obtained by starting a source code card with an asterisk. The assembler simply prints out all characters. The first column of the listing is the card number in the source deck. The second column is the address of the instruction, and the third column is the content of the memory word (or byte) thus addressed. All addresses are relocatable, that is, the first address of this program is 0000, but upon actual loading of the object code into the microprocessor memory, a constant (or offset bias) relocates the instructions.

It is important to note that those instructions which contain an address as a field of the instruction, contain a number which is relocatable as described above. A semicolon (;) follows instruction words which contain relocatable addresses. (Six such cases appear in the listing.)

The next fields of the listing are the source code label, instruction, and operand fields. Note that this assembler will accommodate a label on a separate card from the instruction, and therefore the labels are printed in the listing one line above the related instructions. Instruction mnemonics are as listed in the preceding paragraph (5.3.3.2) and in Appendix E. Operand statements cover a wide range of symbols and expressions. The symbols are as follows:

Symbols	Meaning
,	Term separation
>	The following numbers are in HEX
$	The current value of the location counter
*	Indirect
+	Autoincrement
@	Symbolic memory address

The expressions are best explained as the code is explained in paragraph 5.3.3.4.

Comments for each instruction are listed in the right-hand field of the code lines. Notice that this area is the heart of software documentation, and must be carefully filled in to assist in debugging as well as an overall understanding of the program.

5.3.3.4 Example Program

A terminal connected to the TMS 9900 is used to enter data as a part of some larger application. This example of program development focuses attention on the terminal service routine.

Conceptually, the CPU must go through some kind of initialization, then wait for a character. As each character is received, it is stored in a buffer (up to 72 characters). If the character was a carriage return, terminate the character string with line feed and carriage return, then output the string to the 733 ASR terminal. After this, restart by resetting the buffer address pointer and waiting for a character.

So that the example can stand alone, a direct wait loop is entered when the CPU is waiting for other events, and at the end of the program an instruction loops back to the restart place in the code. If this routine were constructed as a part of a real system, an interrupt technique would probably replace the wait loops, and the final instruction might continue into some other routine before looping back. Otherwise, the example demonstrates a realistic application of the TMS 9900 microprocessor.

5.3.4   Flow Chart

A flow chart is given in Figure 5.33 outlining the details of the program. After initialization, the CPU waits for RRQ to signal a character has been sent from the 733 ASR into the CRU interface card. The character when received must be put into the buffer, then checked to see if it is CR. If not, check to see if 72 characters have been received and if they have not been received, return to A to wait for another character. When a CR is received or 72 characters have been input, add the LF and CR to the buffer and proceed to the output section. Following appropriate protocol, the RRQ and WRQ are reset and RTS (request to send) is set. The CPU sends out one character and waits for a signal from the CRU that transfer is complete.

Notice a software trick is used to compensate for the difference in BAUD rate of the CRU card (1200) and the 733 ASR (300). The same character is repeated three more times. This, in effect, allows time for the 733 ASR to respond properly. After all characters have been sent (four times each), the program counter is returned to A and to the RRQ wait loop.

5.3.5   Problem Coding

Code explanations are as follows — see Table 5.15, pages 0001 through 0004, for the listings.

1. Four EQU statements relate the labels (e.g., DTR) to numerical values (page 0001).

2. The first instruction is at START (PC = 0000). RSET resets the interrupt mask; and LWPI loads the workspace pointer with the address of the first word of the workspace (WSP) identified on page 0003 by the BSS directive reserving 32 bytes of memory. Notice that the LWPI is a two-word instruction, the second of which (006C) is the (relocatable) address of the first byte of the workspace.

3. LI sets the CRU register, WR12, to 100, the address of the card slot in the CRU where the interface card is plugged in. The SBO instructions set the DTR and RTS lines to one (see 733 ASR interface specification).

4. The label BEG corresponds to point D in the flow chart. LI sets WR1 to 008E, the starting address of the character buffer defined on page 0003 by BUFF BSS 80 (reserving 80 bytes of storage). CLR 2 clears WR2, and SBZ WRQ clears the write request.

5. Now look for a character (point A on the flow chart). SBZ RRQ sets the read request to zero. Then TB RRQ and JNE $-2 form the loop "RRQ set?". JNE means jump if not equal to one, and the instruction jumped to is the one, two bytes preceding or the TB instruction.

6. When a character is received, RRQ is 1 and the JNE instruction passes control on to the next instruction: STCR — store the character in the location *indirectly* (*) addressed by WR1. In other words, WR1 holds the address of the place where a character is to be stored.

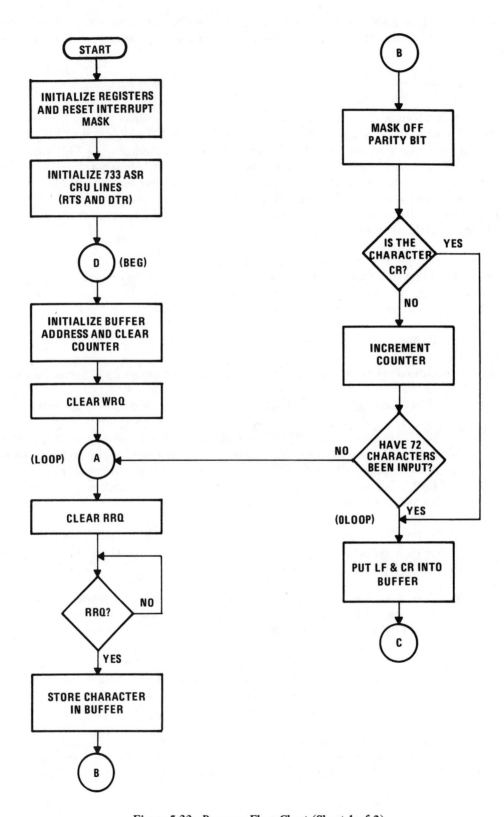

Figure 5.33. Program Flow Chart (Sheet 1 of 2)

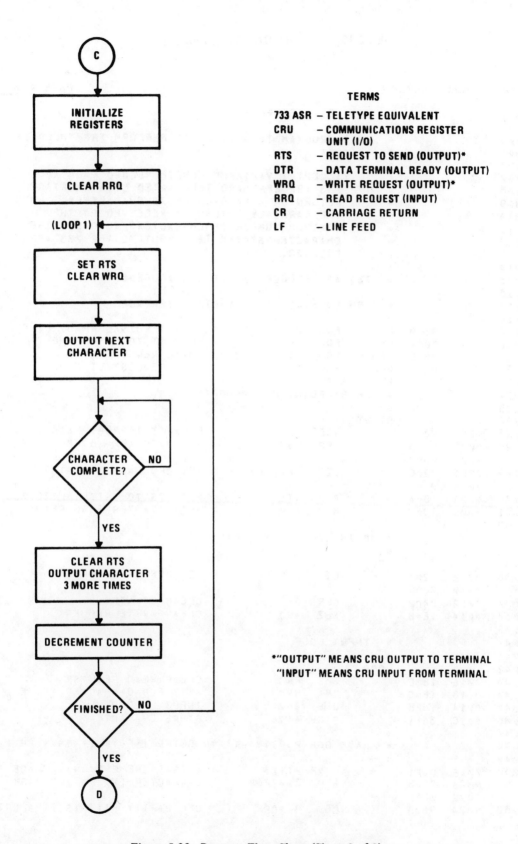

Figure 5.33. Program Flow Chart (Sheet 2 of 2)

Table 5.15. TMS 9900 IDT Sample Program

```
0002                          IDT  'SAMPLE'
0003                    *
0004                    *  THIS PROGRAM IS WRITTEN TO PERFORM THE FOLLOWING
0005                    *    TASK:
0006                    *
0007                    *      ACCEPT A VARIABLE LENGTH RECORD FROM A
0008                    *      733 ASR KEYBOARD TERMINATED BY A CARRIAGE
0009                    *      RETURN OR A MAXIMUM OF 72 CHARACTERS.  WHEN
0010                    *      THE CARRIAGE RETURN IS RECEIVED OR THE
0011                    *      MAXIMUM NUMBER OF CHARACTERS ALLOWED, THE
0012                    *      CHARACTER STRING IS OUTPUT TO THE 733 ASR
0013                    *      PRINTER.
0014                    *
0015                    *  733 ASR PLUGGED IN AT CRU ADDRESS >100
0016                    *
0017                    *  CRU EQUATES FOR TTY-EIA INTERFACE
0018                    *
0019        0009    DTR    EQU  9              DATA TERMINAL READY LINE
0020        000A    RTS    EQU  10             REQUEST TO SEND LINE
0021        000B    WRQ    EQU  11             WRITE REQUEST LINE
0022        000C    RRQ    EQU  12             READ REQUEST LINE
0023                    *
0024                    *  ENTRY POINT FOR PROGRAM
0025                    *
0026                    START
0027  0000  0360              RSET            CLEAR INTERRUPT MASK
0028  0002  02E0              LWPI WSP        SET HARDWARE WORKSPACE REG.
      0004  006C'
0029  0006  020C              LI   12,>100    SET CRU BASE REGISTER
      0008  0100
0030  000A  1D0A              SBO  RTS        SET RTS TO INITIALIZE 733
0031  000C  1D09              SBO  DTR        SET DATA TERMINAL READY
0032                    *
0033                    *  MAIN LOOP OF PROGRAM
0034                    *
0035                    BEG
0036  000E  0201              LI   1,BUFF     SET BUFFER ADDRESS IN R1
      0010  008E'
0037  0012  04C2              CLR  2          CLEAR COUNTER
0038  0014  1E0B              SBZ  WRQ        CLEAR WRITE REQUEST
0039                    *
0040                    *  INPUT LOOP
0041                    *
0042                    LOOP
0043  0016  1E0C              SBZ  RRQ        CLEAR READ REQUEST
0044  0018  1F0C              TB   RRQ        WAIT FOR CHARACTER TO BE
0045  001A  16FE              JNE  $-2        INPUT.  LOOP UNTIL...
0046  001C  3611              STCR *1,8       STORE CHARACTER
0047                    *
0048                    *  MASK OFF PARITY BIT TO DETERMINE IF IT IS A CR
0049                    *
0050  001E  D0F1              MOVB *1+,3       AUTO-INCREMENT WR1. PLACE
0051  0020  0243              ANDI 3,>7F00     CHARACTER IN WR3 AND MASK
      0022  7F00
0052  0024  9803              CB   3,@CR       OFF PARITY BIT. IS IT A CR?
```

Table 5.15. TMS 9900 IDT Sample Program (Continued)

```
      0026  008D'
0053  0028  13A4        JEQ   OLOOP       IF IT IS, GO TO OUTPUT LOOP
0054  002A  05A2        INC   2           NO, INCREMENT COUNTER (WR2)
0055  002C  0282        CI    2,72        HAVE 72 CHARS BEEN INPUT?
      002E  0048
0056  0030  16F2        JNE   LOOP        NO, GO BACK FOR NEXT CHAR.
0057              *
0058              *    INITIALIZE REGISTERS FOR OUTPUT LOOP
0059              *
0060              OLOOP
0061  0032  DC60        MOVB  @LF,*1+     PLACE LINE FEED/CARRIAGE
      0034  008C'
0062  0036  D460        MOVB  @CR,*1      RETURN INTO BUFFER
      0038  008D'
0063  003A  0201        LI    1,BUFF      RESET OUTPUT BUFFER POINTER
      003C  008E'
0064  003E  05C2        INCT  2           INCREMENT COUNT BY TWO TO
0065              *                        INCLUDE CRLF
0066  0040  1E0C        SBZ   RRQ         CLEAR READ REQUEST LINE.
0067              *
0068              *    MAIN OUTPUT LOOP.
0069              *
0070              LOOP1
0071  0042  1D0A        SBO   RTS         SET RTS LINE
0072  0044  1E0B        SBZ   WRQ         CLEAR WRQ LINE
0073  0046  3211        LDCR  *1,8        OUTPUT CHARACTER
0074  0048  1F0B        TB    WRQ         WAIT FOR CHARACTER COMPLETE
0075  004A  16FE        JNE   $-2         LOOP UNTIL CHAR. COMPLETE
0076              *
0077              *    OUTPUT THREE MORE TIMES BECAUSE THE 733 ASR
0078              *      PRINTER PRINTS AT 300 BAUD AND THE CRU CARD IS
0079              *      A 1200 BAUD CARD.
0080              *
0081  004C  1E0A        SBZ   RTS         RESET RTS
0082  004E  1E0B        SBZ   WRQ         CLEAR WRQ
0083  0050  3211        LDCR  *1,8        OUTPUT CHARACTER
0084  0052  1F0B        TB    WRQ         WAIT FOR IT TO COMPLETE
0085  0054  16FE        JNE   $-2         LOOP UNTIL COMPLETE
0086  0056  1E0B        SBZ   WRQ         *
0087  0058  3211        LDCR  *1,8        *
0088  005A  1F0B        TB    WRQ         *
0089  005C  16FE        JNE   $-2         *
0090  005E  1E0B        SBZ   WRQ         *
0091  0060  3231        LDCR  *1+,8       INCREMENT TO NEXT CHARACTER
0092  0062  1F0B        TB    WRQ         *
0093  0064  16FE        JNE   $-2         *
0094              *
0095              *    DECREMENT COUNTER AND CONTINUE OUTPUTTING UNTIL
0096              *      LAST CHARACTER HAS BEEN OUTPUT.
0097              *
0098  0066  0602        DEC   2           DECREMENT COUNTER
0099  0068  15EC        JGT   LOOP1       FINISHED?  NO CONTINUE LOOP
0100  006A  10D1        JMP   BEG         YES, START OVER
0101              *
0102              *    WORKSPACE AND DATA AREA
```

Table 5.15. TMS 9900 IDT Sample Program (Concluded)

```
9900 SAMPLE PROGRAM                                    PAGE 0003

0103                    *
0104  006C       WSP    BSS  32           WORKSPACE
0105  008C   0A  LF     BYTE >0A          LINE FEED IN ASCII
0106  008D   0D  CR     BYTE >0D          CARRIAGE RETURN IN ASCII
0107  008E       BUFF   BSS  80           CHARACTER BUFFER
0108               END  START             TERMINATE ASSEMBLY
0000 ERS
```

```
960 - 980  CONCORDANCE

$                   0045  0075  0085  0089  0093

REG     0035        0100

BUFF    0107        0036  0063

CR      0106        0052  0062

DTR     0019        0031

LF      0105        0061

LOOP    0042        0056

LOOP1   0073        0099

OLOOP   0068        0053

RRQ     0022        0043  0044  0066

RTS     0020        0030  0071  0081

START   0026        0108

WRQ     0021        0038  0072  0074  0082  0084  0086  0088  0090  0092

WSP     0104        0028

THERE ARE    0014  SYMBOLS
```

7. MOVB *1+, 3 means to move the byte addressed by WR1 to WR3, and increment (+) WR1. In order to mask off the parity bit, AND the character with 7F.

    7F00 =   0111 1111 0000 0000

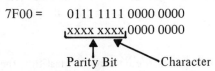

       xxxx xxxx 0000 0000

       Parity Bit   Character

    This is done by ANDI 3, 7F00: AND immediate WR3 with 7F00 (the character is in the most significant byte).

8. Comparing the byte with a CR code is done by CB 3, @CR: Compare byte in WR3 with the symbolic code (@) for CR (found in location 008D as defined on page 0003). Note that the second word of the two-word CB instruction is found on the top of page 0002.

9. Now if the comparison is not equal, JEQ is not taken, INC 2 adds one to WR2, then check to see if 72 characters have been input (CI 2, 72). If not, go back to LOOP.

10. Remember the WR assignments:

    WR1   Pointer to character buffer (BUFF)
    WR2   Character counter
    WR3   Place for checking to see if character is CR

11. There are two ways to get into the output loop (OLOOP). The JEQ OLOOP at the top of page 0002, if the character was CR, and the JNE LOOP, if the number of characters already equals 72 (the jump is not taken and the PC increments to 0032, the first instruction of OLOOP).

12. MOVB @LF, *1+ means move byte identified symbolically (@) by LF, into the byte addressed indirectly (*) by WR1, and increment WR1(+) afterwards. WR1 is the pointer to entries in the buffer. The next MOVB instruction puts CR in the buffers. The LI 1, BUFF returns WR1 content to the starting address of the buffer.

13. INCT 2 adds 2 to the WR2 (byte counter) to take into consideration the LF and CR characters.

14. SBZ RRQ sets RRQ line to zero
    SBO RTS sets RTS to one
    SBZ WRQ sets WRQ to zero
    All the above are part of terminal protocol.

15. LDCR *1, 8 means load the CRU with eight bits, starting with the first bit of the byte addressed (indirectly) by WR1.

16. TB WRQ and JNE $−2 are a wait loop, testing the WRQ line to see if the write operation is complete. When it is one, the JNE no longer jumps back to the TB instruction ($−2), and the program continues.

17. The next 13 instructions repeat the character sent three more times, but with RTS (request to send) set to zero. Thus the 733 ASR is not enabled to receive the characters, and the action is a calculated time delay. In this way a 1200 BAUD interface card is made to serve a 300 BAUD terminal.

18. There is one very important difference in the code for the last time the character is sent. Note the LDCR *1+, 8 instruction. This not only outputs the character addressed by WR1, but the + means to increment WR1. Now WR1 points to the next character to be output.

19. After one character has been sent, DEC 2 decrements WR2 (the byte counter) and the program branches back to LOOP1 to send more characters (via JGT jump if greater than zero).

20. When all characters have been sent, WR2 will have become zero, and JGT LOOP1 no longer directs a jump; the program counter continues on to JMP BEG. This is an unconditional jump back to Ⓓ on the flow chart, the restart point.

21. Page 0003 of the listing gives four directives as described previously and includes an END statement for the assembler.

22. Page 0004 is a cross-reference or concordance of symbols used in the program. Each symbol, $, BEG, BUFF is listed in alphabetical order and the line numbers given to show where each is used. Line numbers are the first column of the listing. These numbers are easier to follow since they are decimal (base 10) numbers, whereas the next column is in hexadecimal (base 16). After going through the TMS 8080 and TMS 9900 problems you can now begin to realize how powerful the TMS 9900 is if you attempt to do the TMS 9900 problem with a TMS 8080.

5.4 SBP0400 PROBLEM

5.4.1 Problem Statement

The scope of this example is simply to highlight the different architecture of the SBP0400, a bit slice processor. One major point made is how the instruction set may be sequenced at the microprogrammed level to provide a tailored solution to a given problem. The scope of this example is *not* intended to demonstrate the cost/performance efficiency of an SBP0400-based system.

5.4.2 Problem Description

An SBP0400-based security access system (Figure 5.34) provides central control governing the locked/unlocked condition of each of 16 remote lock mechanisms. The system functionally consists of: (1) 16 remote lock mechanisms, (2) an Autonomous I/O Controller, (3) a single SBP0400 Processor Element, (4) a fundamental Read-Only-Memory Microsequencer, and (5) a Read-Only-Memory Lookup Table.

Each remote lock mechanism contains: (1) four push buttons, each hardwired to encode one of 16 hexadecimal digits ranging from 0 through F, (2) a single pushbutton which initiates an "access request" condition, (3) a lamp/buzzer which indicates an "access granted" condition, (4) a lamp/buzzer which indicates an "access denied" condition, and (5) sufficient logic to handle serial communication between the lock mechanism and the SBP0400-based central system.

To simplify the detailed description of the SBP0400's function in the system, an autonomous type of I/O controller (Figure 5.35) was chosen to link each lock mechanism to the SBP0400 and associated Microsequencer. Certainly by merely coupling the SBP0400 with an expanded Microsequencer, the SBP0400 could quite comfortably absorb control of the entire I/O function.

The procedure for gaining access through a particular door is initiated by depressing, in sequence, four push buttons on the lock mechanism corresponding to the governing lock combination. Then a fifth push button is depressed initiating an "access request" condition. The SBP0400 is continuously polling the 16 remote lock mechanisms in a sequential manner through the Autonomous I/O Controller. If an "access request" condition is encountered when a particular lock mechanism is polled, the SBP0400 saves the present polling address and, in conjunction with the Microsequencer, proceeds to execute four digit-by-digit comparisons between the four combination digits and the four governing combination digits. If all four comparisons "match", then (1) access is granted through the respective lock mechanism, (2) the associated "access granted" lamp/buzzer is activated,* (3) the "access request" condition is reset, and (4) polling is reinitiated at the next lock mechanism. If *any* of the digit-to-digit comparisons fail: (1) access is denied (the lock remains locked), (2) the associated "access denied" lamp/buzzer is activated,* (3) the "access request" condition is reset, and (4) polling is reinitiated at the next lock mechanism.

5.4.3 Example Problem Flow Chart

Seven unique macroinstructions have been custom developed to provide a tailored solution to this security access problem. The macroinstruction flow is detailed in Figure 5.36. Each macroinstruction consists of from one to 12 machine level microinstructions. A particular

---

*For how long?

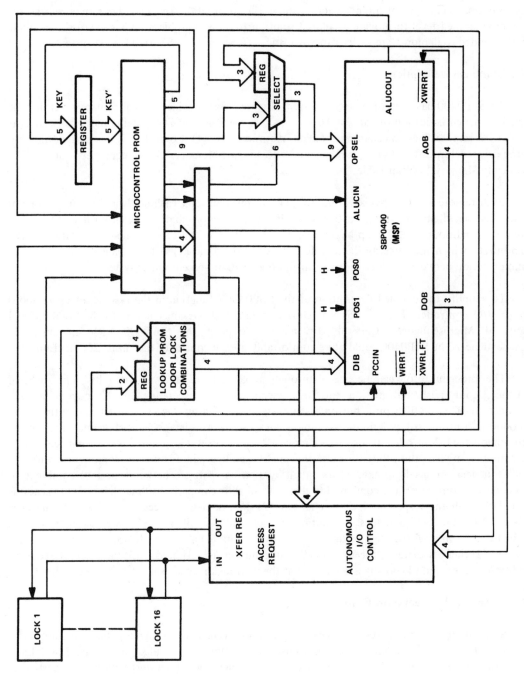

Figure 5.34. SBP0400-Based Security Access System

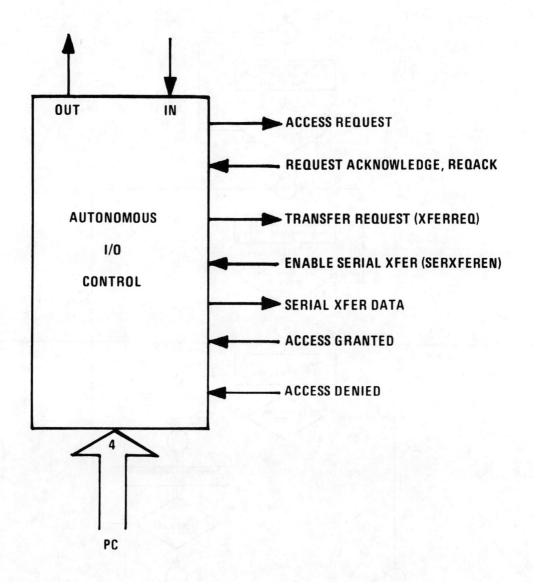

Figure 5.35. I/O Control Block Diagram

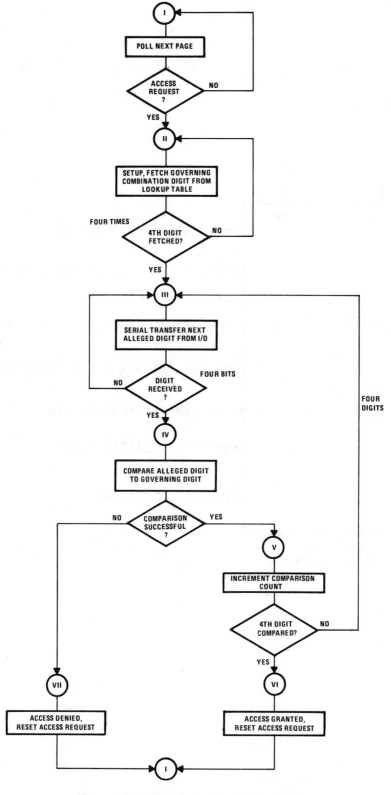

Figure 5.36. Macroinstruction Flow Chart

macroinstruction is executed by sequencing its related microinstruction set. The microinstruction sequence for each macroinstruction is divided into microstates. Each microstate represents the control event in which execution of the related microinstruction is accomplished. The microinstruction flow (sequence) for each macroinstruction is illustrated in Figure 5.37 and detailed below.

5.4.4   Example Problem

As an exercise to enhance understanding of the application of the SBP0400 microprocessor, a subset of the instructions has been isolated. A blank flow chart for the microinstructions is given in Figure 5.38. The steps are numbered as shown in Figure 5.37, the complete microinstruction flow chart.

The steps to be taken are preceded by the setting of 1100 into the XWR. Fill in the blocks to do the following operation (not necessarily in this order):

1.   Load RF4 with 1100

2.   Load RF5 with 0000

3.   Load RFT with 1100

4.   Clear the XWR

5.   Load WR with 1100

Try to fill in the blank flow chart of Figure 5.38 before reading the subsequent sections.

Abbreviations used here are as follows:

RF4 = the fourth register in the SBP0400 register file

XWR = four bit extended working register

WR = four bit working register

Complete description of all elements and signal lines is given in the data in Appendix E for the SBP0400.

Using the block diagram just completed, Figure 5.38, fill in the partial machine code sheet, Figure 5.39, with the operation code words for the SBP0400 to perform the steps. Compare your results with the code in Table 5.16. Note that there can be more than one order for these steps.

5.4.5   Microinstruction Flow Description

5.4.5.1   Macroinstruction I, Microstates 0 through 2

Sixteen lock mechanisms are sequentially polled by the SBP0400's program counter through the Autonomous I/O Controller. When polled, each lock mechanism responds to the Microsequencer, through the Autonomous I/O Controller, with a "service request" status (REQUEST).

MICROSTATES 0 through 2 allow three SBP0400 clock periods for the Autonomous I/O Controller to transmit the polling address and to receive the "service request" status. MICROSTATES 0 and 1 are "do nothing" states included to produce an intentional time delay. In MICROSTATE 2, the "service request" status (REQUEST) of the lock mechanism currently being polled is sensed by the Microsequencer. If service is required (REQUEST = 1), the Microsequencer

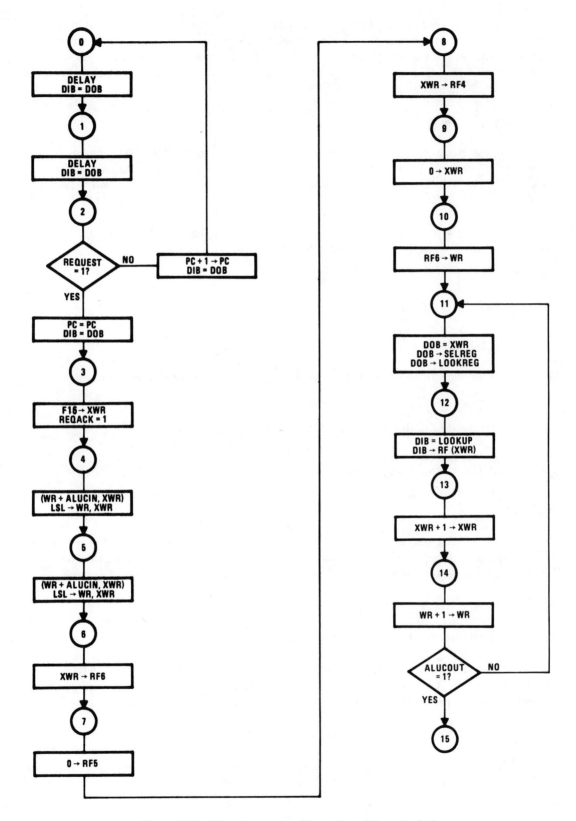

Figure 5.37. Microinstruction Flow Chart (Sheet 1 of 2)

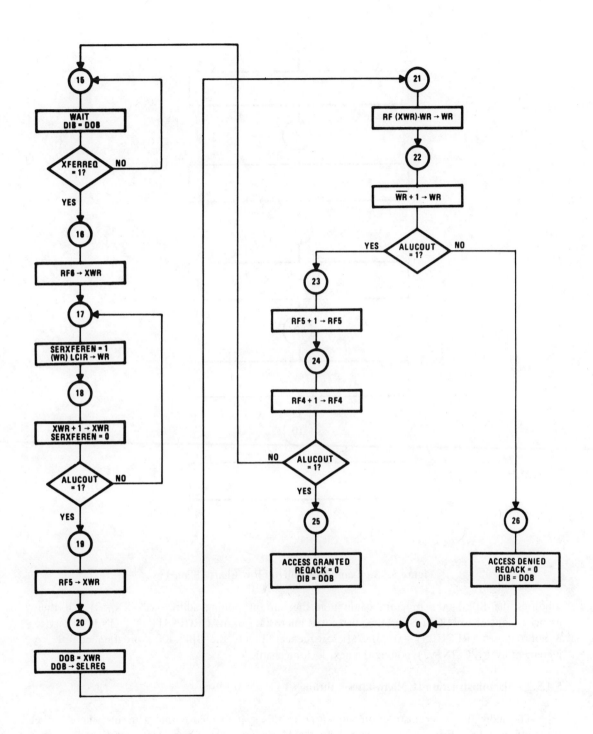

Figure 5.37. Microinstruction Flow Chart (Sheet 2 of 2)

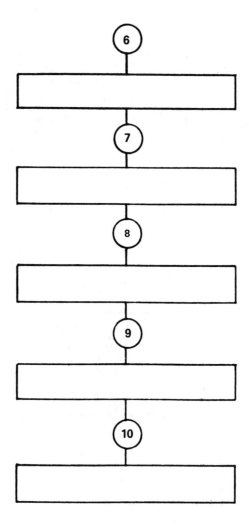

Figure 5.38. Example Problem Flow Chart (Blank)

solidifies the SBP0400's program counter at the current polling address (PCCIN = 0) and then branches control to MICROSTATE 3, the initial microstate of MACROINSTRUCTION II. If service is not required (REQUEST = 0), the Microsequencer directs the SBP0400's program counter to increment by 1 (PCCIN = 1), polling the next lock mechanism.

5.4.5.2 Macroinstruction II, Microstates 3 through 14

The individual microinstruction sequences in this system incorporate a means whereby the completion of four events may be sensed by the Microsequencer. Since incrementation of all the SBP0400's registers may be achieved through the ALU, four "by 1" incrementations of the constant "1100" will force an ALU overflow. This overflow, illustrated below, signifies the completion of four events and, as a result, may be sensed by the Microsequencer.

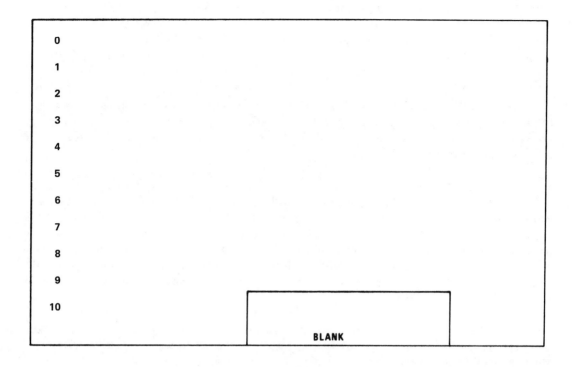

0	
1	
2	
3	
4	
5	
6	
7	
8	
9	
10	BLANK

Figure 5.39. Coding Sheet (Partial)

EVENT 1: 1100 + 1 = 1101 with NO overflow
EVENT 2: 1101 + 1 = 1110 with NO overflow
EVENT 3: 1110 + 1 = 1111 with NO overflow
EVENT 4: 1111 + 1 = 0000 with *OVERFLOW*

The constant "1100" is developed in MICROSTATES 3 through 5. In MICROSTATE 3, all ones (F_{16}) are loaded into the SBP0400's XWR and the Microsequencer acknowledges (REQACK = 1) to the Autonomous I/O Controller the receipt of the "service request" (REQUEST = 1). In MICROSTATE 4, the contents of the XWR in conjunction with the WR are double-precision logical left shifted. Hardwiring the SBP0400's position controls to designate the SBP0400 as occupying a "most significant position" (MSP) and *hardwiring* XWRLFT to XWRRT will result in zeros automatically injected into the LSB of the XWR as the XWR is double-precision logical left shifted. As a result of the shift (in MICROSTATE 4) the XWR = 1110. In MICROSTATE 5, the same shift is repeated resulting in the XWR = 1100, the desired constant.

Note:

Double-precision shifts were utilized in MICROSTATES 4 and 5 because the standard SBP0400 PLA configuration does not provide for standalone shifting of the XWR. Since the contents of the WR are of no consequence at this time, the double-precision logical shift provides a satisfactory means of shifting the XWR.

In a normal double-precision logical left-shift situation, the XWR shift accommodation to the left XWRLFT is usually hardwired, external to the SBP0400, to the WR shift accommodation to the right WRRT. However, in this particular situation, that connection is not made. Rather, XWRLFT is hardwired to XWRRT.

In MICROSTATES 6 through 10, various SBP0400 registers are set up for later use. In MICROSTATE 6, the constant "1100" is nondestructively transferred from the XWR to RF6 (XWR retains 1100 also). In MICROSTATE 7, RF5 is reset to all zeros. In MICROSTATE 8, the constant "1100" is nondestructively transferred from the XWR to RF4. In MICROSTATE 9, the XWR is reset to all zeros. In MICROSTATE 10, the constant "1100" is nondestructively transferred from RF6 to the WR.

In MICROSTATES 11 through 14, four governing combination data words corresponding to the lock mechanism currently being serviced are fetched, in sequence, from the read-only-memory Lookup Table. These data words are stored, in the same sequence, in the SBP0400's register file locations RF0 through RF3.

In MICROSTATE 11, the two LSBs of the XWR are transferred to the two-bit address register of the Lookup Table. The PC, in conjunction with the XWR, consequently provides six bits of address data to the Lookup Table read-only-memory. The four PC bits address a four data word region in the Lookup Table where the governing combination digits of the lock mechanism currently being serviced reside. The two XWR bits address a particular governing combination digit residing in that PC defined region. Also, in MICROSTATE 11, the three LSBs of the XWR are transferred to the Select Register. This transfer allows the XWR to specify a particular register file location for utilization in MICROSTATE 12.

In MICROSTATE 12, one of four governing combination digits is transferred from the Lookup Table ROM to the register file location specified by the XWR via the Select Register. In MICROSTATE 13, the XWR is incremented by one in preparation for fetching the next governing combination digit from the Lookup Table and store that digit in the next succeeding register file location.

In MICROSTATE 14, the number of digits transferred from the Lookup Table to the register file is counted. Initially, the WR = 1100. Each time the microinstruction flow is sequenced through MICROSTATES 11 through 14, the WR is incremented by one. After the fourth governing combination digit has been transferred to the register file, the WR will be incremented by one with the result WR = 0000 with OVERFLOW. The Microsequencer, sensing this overflow, branches control to MICROSTATE 15, the initial microstate of MACROINSTRUCTION III.

5.4.5.3 Macroinstruction III, Microstates 15 through 18

In MICROSTATES 15 through 18, four bits of input data corresponding to one digit of the respective lock mechanism's combination is transferred serially from the Autonomous I/O Controller to the WR.

In MICROSTATE 15, the Microsequencer senses the status of the Autonomous I/O Controller's serial transfer request (SFERREQ). XFERREQ = 1 signifies that the Autonomous I/O Controller has data ready for serial transfer. As a result, the Microsequencer branches to MICROSTATE 16 where the SBP0400 is prepared to receive that data transfer. XFERREQ = 0 signifies that the Autonomous I/O Controller is *not* ready to transfer serial data. Consequently, the Microsequencer holds in MICROSTATE 15 until the Autonomous I/O Controller is ready to transfer data.

In MICROSTATE 16, the constant 1100 is transferred from RF6 to the XWR. This transfer prepares the XWR to track the number of bits serially received by the WR from the Autonomous I/O Controller.

In MICROSTATE 17, the Microsequencer presents a "serial transfer enable" (SERXFEREN = 1) to the Autonomous I/O Controller. SERXFEREN = 1 signifies that the SBP0400 is ready to single-precision, left circulate one bit of serial transfer data into the WR via the WR shift accommodation to the right (WRRT).

Note:

Serial data transfer between the Autonomous I/O Controller and the SBP0400 must be in complement form. This is to compensate for the inversion between the WR and the WR shift accommodation $\overline{WRRT}$.

In MICROSTATE 18, the Microsequencer acknowledges, to the Autonomous I/O Controller, the SBP0400's receipt of one bit. This is characterized by the Microsequencer disabling the "serial transfer enable" (SERXFEREN = 0). Also, in MICROSTATE 18, the XWR is incremented by one. If the fourth of four transfer bits has been received, incrementing the XWR by one will result in XWR = 0000 with OVERFLOW. The Microsequencer, sensing this overflow, branches control to MICROSTATE 19, the initial microstate of MACROINSTRUCTION IV. If less than four transfer bits have been received, the Microsequencer branches control to MICROSTATE 17 where another transfer bit is fetched.

5.4.5.4 Macroinstruction IV, Microstates 19 through 22

The four-bit data word serially transferred from the Autonomous I/O Controller to the WR in MICROSTATES 15 through 18 is one digit of the combination to the lock mechanism currently being serviced. The four governing digits of the respective combination were transferred from the Lookup Table to register file locations RF0 through RF3. These transfers were accomplished in MICROSTATES 3 through 14. The purpose of MICROSTATES 19 through 22 is to compare an alleged combination digit to the appropriate governing digit located in the register file.

In MICROSTATE 19, the contents of RF5 (initially all zeros) is transferred from RF5 to the XWR. This is to prepare the XWR to specify a register file location via the Select Register. In MICROSTATE 20, the contents of the XWR are transferred to the Select Register.

In MICROSTATE 21, an alleged combination digit located in the WR is compared to the respective governing digit located in the register file location specified by the XWR via the Select Register. In MICROSTATE 22, the result of that comparison is tested. If, at this point, the WR contains all zeros, a comparison "match" is indicated; if the WR contains anything other than all zeros, a comparison "mismatch" is indicated. Therefore, performing a "zero check" on the contents of the WR will provide a means by which the comparison result may be sensed by the Microsequencer.

A WR "zero check" is accomplished by complementing the contents of the WR and then incrementing the result by one. If the WR originally contained all zeros, this procedure would force an ALU overflow which may be sensed by the Microsequencer. If an ALU overflow is sensed, the comparison resulted in a "match". Consequently, the Microsequencer will branch control to MICROSTATE 23, the initial microstate of MACROINSTRUCTION V. If an overflow is *not* sensed, the comparison resulted in a "mismatch". Therefore, the Microsequencer will branch control to MICROSTATE 26, the only microinstruction of MACROINSTRUCTION VII.

Note:

"Zero check" illustration

1.   WR = 0: WR = 0101, $\overline{WR}$ = 1010, $\overline{WR}$ + 1 = 1011 with NO overflow

2.   WR = 0: WR = 0000, $\overline{WR}$ = 1111, $\overline{WR}$ + 1 = 0000 with OVERFLOW

5.4.5.5   Macroinstruction V, Microstates 23 and 24

To gain access through a particular lock mechanism, four alleged combination digits must be compared to four corresponding governing digits. The result of each of the four comparisons *must* be a "match". A means of directing which of four governing digits is compared to a particular alleged digit must be provided. Furthermore, a means by which the Microsequencer may sense the completion of four successive "match" comparisons must also be provided.

RF5 is utilized to direct which of four governing digits (register file locations RF0 through RF3) is compared to a particular alleged digit (WR). This is accomplished in MICROSTATES 19 through 21 where: (1) RF5 is transferred to the XWR, (2) the XWR is transferred to the Select Register, and (3) the Select Register specifies a particular register file location for comparison with the WR. Initially, in MICROSTATE 7, RF5 is reset to all zeros. Consequently, the first of the four comparisons utilizes RF0. After each comparison resulting in a "match", the Microsequencer branches control to MICROSTATE 23. In MICROSTATE 23, RF5 is incremented by one. As a result, each succeeding comparison cycle will utilize RF1, . . ., RF3.

RF4 provides the means by which the Microsequencer may sense the completion of four successive "match" comparisons. Initially, in MICROSTATE 8, the constant "1100" is transferred from the XWR to RF4. After each "match", the Microsequencer branches first to MICROSTATE 23, then to MICROSTATE 24. In MICROSTATE 24, RF4 is incremented by one. If an overflow is forced, completion of the fourth comparison is indicated. Consequently, the Microsequencer, sensing this overflow branches control to MICROSTATE 25, the only microinstruction of MACROINSTRUCTION VI. If an overflow is not forced, the Microsequencer branches control back to MICROSTATE 15, the initial microstate of MACROINSTRUCTION III. There, fetching of another alleged combination digit for comparison to the appropriate governing digit is initiated.

5.4.5.6   Macroinstruction VI, Microstate 25

The Microsequencer branches control to MICROSTATE 25 *only* if *all four* alleged-digit to governing-digit comparisons for a particular lock mechanism "match". In MICROSTATE 25, the Microsequencer, via the Autonomous I/O Controller, grants access through the lock mechanism currently being serviced. Also, at this time, the Microsequencer directs the Autonomous I/O Controller to retract the "service request" (REQUEST = 0). The Microsequencer keys this action by deactivating the "service request acknowledge" (REQACK = 0). The Microsequencer then branches control back to MICROSTATE 0 where the next lock mechanism is polled.

5.4.5.7   Macroinstruction VII, Microstate 26

The Microsequencer branches control to MICROSTATE 26 *anytime* an alleged-digit to governing-digit comparison results in a "mismatch". In MICROSTATE 26, the Microsequencer, via the Autonomous I/O Controller, denies access. Also, at this time, the Microsequencer directs the Autonomous I/O Controller to retract the "service request" (REQUEST = 0). The Microsequencer keys this action by deactivating the service request acknowledge (REQACK = 0). The Microsequencer then branches control back to MICROSTATE 0 where the next lock mechanism is polled.

5.4.6 Coding

Table 5.16 is the complete listing of machine code to implement the problem. Note the column labels for guidance on relativity of data for a given circuit mode and the second column to gain information on the microstate relationship of the data to the flow charts.

Table 5.16. Machine Level Code

Macrostate No.	Microstate No.	Request	XFERREQ	ALUCOUT	Present Address Key					REQACK	SERXFEREN	Access Granted	Access Denied	PCCIN	ALUCIN	Select	OP 3	OP 2	OP 1	OP 0	D 1	D 0	S 2	S 1	S 0	Next Address Key					SBP0400 Operation	OP Form OP Type
I	0	X	X	X	L	L	L	L	L	L	L	L	L	L	X	L	H	H	H	H	H	H	L	H	L	L	L	L	L	H	DIB = DOB	III-f.
	1	X	X	X	L	L	L	L	H	L	L	L	L	L	X	L	H	H	H	H	H	H	L	H	L	L	L	L	H	L	DIB = DOB	III-f.
	2	L	X	X	L	L	L	H	L	L	L	L	L	H	X	L	H	H	H	H	H	H	L	H	L	L	L	L	L	L	DIB = DOB	III-f.
	2	H	X	X	L	L	L	H	L	L	L	L	L	L	X	L	H	H	H	H	H	H	L	H	L	L	L	L	H	H	DIB = DOB	III-f.
II	3	X	X	X	L	L	L	H	H	H	L	L	L	L	L	L	L	L	L	L	H	H	H	H	L	L	L	H	L	L	DIB = DOB	III-f.
	4	X	X	X	L	L	H	L	L	H	L	L	L	L	L	L	H	H	H	L	H	H	H	L	H	L	L	H	L	H	(WR + ALUCIN, XWR) LSL → WR, XWR	VI-d.
	5	X	X	X	L	L	H	L	H	H	L	L	L	L	L	L	H	H	H	L	H	H	H	L	H	L	L	H	L	L	(WR + ALUCIN, XWR) LSL → WR, XWR	VI-d.
	6	X	X	X	L	L	H	H	L	H	L	L	L	L	L	L	H	H	H	L	H	L	H	H	L	L	L	H	L	H	XWR → RF6	II-g.
	7	X	X	X	L	L	H	H	H	H	L	L	L	L	H	L	L	L	L	L	L	L	H	L	H	H	L	L	L	L	0 → RF5	I-a.
	8	X	X	X	L	H	L	L	L	H	L	L	L	L	L	L	H	H	H	L	H	L	H	L	L	L	H	L	L	H	XWR → RF4	II-g.
	9	X	X	X	L	H	L	L	H	H	L	L	L	L	H	L	L	L	L	L	H	H	H	H	L	L	H	L	H	L	0 → XWR	I-g.
	10	X	X	X	L	H	L	H	L	H	L	L	L	L	L	L	H	H	H	L	H	H	L	H	L	L	H	L	L	H	RF6 → WR	I-b.
	11	X	X	X	L	H	L	H	H	H	L	L	L	L	L	L	H	H	H	L	H	H	L	H	L	L	H	L	L	L	DOB = XWR	II-l.
	12	X	X	X	L	H	H	L	L	H	L	L	L	L	X	H	H	H	H	H	H	L	X	W	R	L	H	H	L	L	DIB → RF (XWR)	III-a.
	13	X	X	X	L	H	H	L	H	H	L	L	L	L	H	L	L	H	L	L	H	H	H	W	H	L	H	H	H	L	XWR + 1 → XWR	I-g.
	14	X	X	L	L	H	H	H	L	L	L	L	L	L	L	L	L	H	L	L	L	H	X	X	X	L	H	L	H	H	WR + 1 → WR	I-b.
	14	X	X	H	L	H	H	H	L	L	L	L	L	L	L	L	L	H	L	L	L	H	X	X	X	L	H	H	H	H	WR + 1 → WR	I-b.
III	15	X	L	X	L	H	H	H	H	H	L	L	L	L	X	L	H	H	H	H	H	H	L	H	L	L	H	H	H	H	DIB = DOB	III-f.
	15	X	H	X	L	H	H	H	H	H	L	L	L	L	X	L	H	H	H	H	H	H	L	H	L	L	L	L	L	L	DIB = DOB	III-f.
	16	X	X	X	H	L	L	L	L	H	L	L	L	L	X	L	H	H	H	H	H	H	L	H	L	L	L	L	L	L	RF6 → XWR	III-c.
	17	X	X	X	H	L	L	L	H	H	H	L	L	L	H	L	H	H	H	L	H	H	H	L	H	L	L	L	L	L	(WR) LCIR → WR	V-d.
	18	X	X	L	H	L	L	H	L	L	L	L	L	L	H	L	L	H	L	L	H	H	H	H	L	H	L	L	L	L	XWR + 1 → XWR	I-g.
	18	X	X	H	H	L	L	H	L	L	L	L	L	L	H	L	L	H	L	L	H	H	H	H	L	H	L	L	H	H	XWR + 1 → XWR	I-g.
IV	19	X	X	X	H	L	L	H	H	H	L	L	L	L	X	L	L	L	L	H	H	L	H	L	H	H	L	H	L	L	RF5 → XWR	III-c.
	20	X	X	X	H	L	H	L	L	L	L	L	L	L	L	L	L	L	L	L	H	H	H	H	H	H	L	H	L	H	DOB = XWR	I-h.
	21	X	X	X	H	L	H	L	H	L	L	L	L	H	H	L	L	L	L	H	X	W	R	H	L	H	L	H	L	L	RF (XWR) − WR → WR	I-b.
	22	X	X	L	H	L	H	H	L	L	L	L	L	L	H	L	L	H	L	H	L	X	X	X	H	H	L	L	L	L	$\overline{WR}$ + 1 → XWR	I-b.
	22	X	X	H	H	L	H	H	L	L	L	L	L	L	H	L	L	H	L	H	L	X	X	X	H	L	H	H	H	H	$\overline{WR}$ + 1 → WR	I-b.
V	23	X	X	X	H	L	H	H	H	H	L	L	L	L	L	H	L	L	H	H	L	L	L	H	L	H	H	H	L	L	L	RF5 + 1 → RF5	I-a.
	24	X	X	L	H	H	L	L	L	L	L	L	L	L	H	L	L	H	H	L	L	L	H	L	L	H	L	H	L	L	RF4 + 1 → RF4	I-a.
	24	X	X	H	H	H	L	L	L	L	L	L	L	L	H	L	L	H	H	L	L	L	H	L	L	H	H	L	L	H	RF4 + 1 → RF4	I-a.
VI	25	X	X	X	H	H	L	L	H	L	L	L	H	L	X	L	H	H	H	H	H	H	L	H	L	L	L	L	L	L	DIB = DOB	III-f.
VII	26	X	X	X	H	H	L	H	L	L	L	L	H	L	X	L	H	H	H	H	H	H	L	H	L	L	L	L	L	L	DIB = DOB	III-f.

5.5 SUMMARY

In working through the four examples of simple software programs for typical microprocessors, you should now have a feel for the problems involved. How much time does it take? How much do I have to allocate in resources? What are typical milestones by which to monitor progress? What approach is best for my problem? etc., ...

This is, of course, a limited view of one who has observed and not participated in the work. However, it should be sufficient to enable you to begin work with microprocessors with direction and purpose.

APPENDIX A

NUMBER SYSTEMS AND BINARY ARITHMETIC

NUMBER SYSTEMS

In order to understand the elements of computer arithmetic, it is first necessary to develop the concept of number systems. Since it is relatively easy to design electromechanical and electronic circuits which exhibit the characteristic of two stable states, a binary system, or a number system with base two, has universally been adopted as the number system for computers.

In order to more easily understand this concept, a review of the base-ten system may be illuminating. The two fundamental concepts of the base-ten number system are that ten different symbols are used, and there is positional significance when writing a string of these symbols. When the number of objects to be counted is less than ten, only one digit is required. When that number exceeds ten, two or more digits are used in conjunction. This may be contrasted with the Roman numeral system which contains the specific symbols I, V, X, L, C, and M, but yet does not possess positional significance, and therefore requires no 0. Positional significance in the base-ten system may be illustrated as shown in Table A-1 in which each position dictates multiplication by a power of ten. Obviously, numbers may be as large as desired by simply increasing the number of positions. No additional characters other than 0 through 9 are required. In the Roman numeral system, new symbols are added for additional integer possibility.

Table A-1. Positional Significance of the Base Ten Number System

Position	4	3	2	1
Name	Thousands	Hundreds	Tens	Units
Significance	10^3	10^2	10^1	10^0
Examples:	$1 \times 10^3 + 2 \times 10^2 + 3 \times 10^1 + 4 \times 10^0 = 1234$			
	$2 \times 10^3 + 0 \times 10^2 + 4 \times 10^1 + 8 \times 10^0 = 2048$			

In the binary system there are only two symbols, but counting is carried out in the same manner as in the decimal or base-ten system. The fundamental difference is that more positions are required to accomplish given results. An example of this is shown in Table A-2. Note that in the base-ten system the first digit counted through each of the symbols before a second position was required. The same is true in base two and this point was reached after only two symbols. Thus, by the time the count of eight (decimal) is reached, four binary positions are required. Positional significance in the base-two system is shown in Table A-3. Note that the significance of each position is that the base of the number system is raised to the power corresponding to its position.

It should be obvious from this that given enough positions, the binary system is capable of representing numerical quantities as large as desired. But what about negative numbers? The technique for handling signed numbers is to assign a sign-bit and typically let it have a value of 1 for negative numbers. It is also typical to find the sign-bit in the most significant bit position. There are

Table A-2. Counting in Bases Ten and Two

Base 10	Base 2
0	0
1	1
2	10
3	11
4	100
5	101
6	110
7	111
8	1000
9	1001
10	1010
11	1011
12	1100
13	1101
14	1110
15	1111
16	1 0000
17	1 0001

Table A-3. Positional Significance in the Base Two Number System

Position	7	6	5	4	3	2	1
Significance	2^6	2^5	2^4	2^3	2^2	2^1	2^0

Examples:

$$1 \times 2^6 + 0 \times 2^5 + 1 \times 2^4 + 1 \times 2^3 + 1 \times 2^2 + 0 \times 2^1 + 1 \times 2^0 = 1011101$$

$$1 \times 2^6 + 1 \times 2^5 + 0 \times 2^4 + 0 \times 2^3 + 1 \times 2^2 + 1 \times 2^1 + 0 \times 2^0 = 1100110$$

two systems that commonly have been used to represent a full range of binary numbers, and they are called the one's complement and the two's complement systems. In the one's complement system, a negative number is developed by changing each of the ones to zeros and the zeros to ones for a given quantity. This is known as complementing a number, and it is shown in Table A-4. Notice, however, that the complement of zero is all ones. This means there would necessarily be two representations for zero. While some machines have been built using one's complement arithmetic, two's complement arithmetic is more commonly used. In two's complement notation, a negative number is achieved by complementing a positive number and then adding one. This eliminates the confusion of two representations of zero as well as facilitating the counting aspect, that is, a counter would not have to be incremented twice while passing through zero.

Table A-5 illustrates that with four binary bits, it is possible to represent a total of 16 different combinations and these may be labeled from −8 through +7. Notice again that all of the negative numbers have a one for the most significant bit. Thus, for negative number representation in binary arithmetic, the most significant bit is typically a one and is in effect, the sign-bit. Table A-5 also illustrates that if 16 binary bits are used, integers from −32,768 to +32,767 may be represented.

Table A-4. Negative Number Representation

Base 10	Signed Binary	1's Complement	2's Complement
4	0100	0100	0100
3	0011	0011	0011
2	0010	0010	0010
1	0001	0001	0001
0	0000	(0000)	0000
		(1111)	
−1	1001	1110	1111
−2	1010	1101	1110
−3	1011	1100	1101
−4	1100	1011	1100
−5	1101	1010	1011

Table A-5. Binary Number Ranges

4 Bit Range		16 Bit Range				
Base 10	Base 2	Base 2				Base 10
7	0111	0111	1111	1111	1111	32,767
6	0110	0111	1111	1111	1110	32,766
5	0101	.	.	.	.	.
4	0100	.	.	.	.	.
3	0011	0000	0000	0000	0111	7
2	0010	.	.	.	.	.
1	0001	0000	0000	0000	0001	1
0	0000	0000	0000	0000	0000	0
−1	1111	1111	1111	1111	1111	−1
−2	1110	1111	1111	1111	1110	−2
−3	1101	.	.	.	.	.
−4	1100	.	.	.	.	.
−5	1011	1111	1111	1111	1000	−8
−6	1010	.	.	.	.	.
−7	1001	.	.	.	.	.
−8	1000	1000	0000	0000	0000	−32,768

When the required range of numbers exceeds the limit of the computer word, a double-length word is often used, provided the arithmetic unit is designed to handle this double-length word. Table A-6 shows the integer range for various word lengths. The most common method for handling very large numbers is the double-word technique. The double-word data format for handling such numbers requires special instruction in the instruction set and double-word facility within the ALU (Arithmetic and Logic Unit). This technique is called *double precision* arithmetic.

Table A-6. Integer Range for Word Length

Word Length (bits)	No. of Values	Positive Integer Range	Positive and Negative Integer Range
8	256	0 to 255	− 128 to 127
9	512	0 to 511	− 256 to 255
10	1 024	0 to 1 023	− 512 to 511
11	2 048	0 to 2 047	− 1 024 to 1 023
12	4 096	0 to 4 095	− 2 048 to 2 047
13	8 192	0 to 8 191	− 4 096 to 4 095
14	16 384	0 to 16 383	− 8 192 to 8 191
15	32 768	0 to 32 767	− 16 384 to 16 383
16	65 536	0 to 65 535	− 32 768 to 32 767
24	16 777 216	0 to 16 777 215	− 8 388 604 to 8 388 607
32	4 294 967 396	0 to 4 294 967 395	− 2147 483 648 to 2147 483 647

Another technique for expanding the range of numbers beyond that achieved with double precision (see Table A-6 for examples) is the *floating point* arithmetic concept. Two words are usually combined to include a binary fraction or *mantissa* and an *exponent*. The exponent is usually applied to the base ten and specifies a number by which the mantissa is to be multiplied. Only six binary bits are required to give this multiplier the range of 10^{-32} to 10^{32}.

In addition to the positive/negative integer range one's complement, and two's complement numbering, it is common to find three coding schemes in digital systems. The three most common coding methods and their relationship to each other are shown in Table A-7.

In base eight, there are only eight unique symbols, 0 through 7. In base 16, there are 16 unique symbols, 0 through 9 and A through F. Base eight is convenient because each digit represents three binary bits and requires no new symbols. In base 16, each digit represents four binary bits. Octal and hexadecimal representations are used for converting three or four binary bits into a single character for simplification and ease of written information. It is easier to write 3D, for example, than 00101101. Octal and hexadecimal numbers can be easily determined from binary numbers by inspection after a little practice.

In Table A-8, two binary numbers are translated to their corresponding octal and hexadecimal representations. Notice in the first case, groups of four bits are used and in the second case, groups of three bits are used. While it is generally easier to learn base eight or octal notation because there are no new symbols involved, the hexadecimal system is superior because one character represents four binary bits, and a substantial amount of computer arithmetic and digital communication is based on eight-bit bytes. Two hex characters can represent a byte while three characters are needed in octal notation.

Table A-7. Number Coding Schemes

Decimal	Binary	Octal	Hexadecimal	Binary Coded Decimal
0	00000	00	0 0	0000 0000
1	00001	01	0 1	0000 0001
2	00010	02	0 2	0000 0010
3	00011	03	0 3	0000 0011
4	00100	04	0 4	0000 0100
5	00101	05	0 5	0000 0101
6	00110	06	0 6	0000 0110
7	00111	07	0 7	0000 0111
8	01000	10	0 8	0000 1000
9	01001	11	0 9	0000 1001
10	01010	12	0 A	0001 0000
11	01011	13	0 B	0001 0001
12	01100	14	0 C	0001 0010
13	01101	15	0 D	0001 0011
14	01110	16	0 E	0001 0100
15	01111	17	0 F	0001 0101
16	10000	20	1 0	0001 0110

Table A-8. Binary/Hexadecimal/Octal Conversion

Binary/Hexadecimal

Binary	0000	0010	1010	0011
Hex	0	2	A	3
Binary	0001	0100	1100	1110
Hex	1	4	C	E

Binary/Octal

Binary	0	000	001	010	100	011
Octal	0	0	1	2	4	3
Binary	0	001	010	011	001	110
Octal	0	1	2	3	1	6

Another numbering system translation frequently required is between base ten and base two; the bridge between these two number systems is the use of the BCD (binary coded decimal) system. BCD numbers are binary numbers that are easily translated by inspection into decimal numbers. The primary disadvantage is the inefficiency of hardware utilization and the extra logic required to perform counting and arithmetic operations. This is because there are 16 possible states for four binary bits, but only ten are used for BCD codes.

Table A-9 shows three common BCD codes. While this system is, in some ways, inconvenient from the standpoint of binary arithmetic, it has certain advantages in man-machine interfaces where decimal numbers are used both for input and readout. In order to overcome these disadvantages, many computers and microprocessors include special instructions for performing BCD arithmetic. This means that in such systems it is not necessary to translate between BCD and binary before performing arithmetic operations, and, therefore, a substantial amount of computing time is saved. One of the most common applications of BCD arithmetic is in modern electronic calculators.

Table A-9. Binary/BCD/Excess 3 Conversion

Decimal	BCD Code 8, 4, 2, 1	BCD "Excess 3" Code	Excess 3 Gray
0	0000	0011	0010
1	0001	0100	0110
2	0010	0101	0111
3	0011	0110	0101
4	0100	0111	0100
5	0101	1000	1100
6	0110	1001	1101
7	0111	1010	1111
8	1000	1011	1110
9	1001	1100	1010
Illegal	1010	1101	1011
Codes	1011	1110	1001
	1100	1111	1000
	1101	0000	0000
	1110	0001	0001
	1111	0010	0011

When it is necessary to make straight conversion between binary and decimal systems, two methods are generally used. The first is to simply add the powers of two represented by the ones in the binary number to achieve the corresponding decimal number. Table A-10 shows this conversion for several binary numbers. A faster method, shown in Table A-11, is accomplished by developing a string of decimal numbers for each position in the binary number to be converted. The first number is always one, the second and subsequent numbers are achieved by doubling and adding one as shown in the examples. The new number is always double the previous number and one is added if there is a one in that position in the binary word. As shown in the examples, the last decimal number in the string is the decimal equivalent of the binary number. The formulas at the bottom of Table A-11 give the mathematical basis for those algorithm. X_i represents the decimal number for position i of the binary number, and A_i is the binary bit at the same position.

Conversion of decimal numbers to binary is shown in Table A-12. The approach is to subtract powers of two starting with the largest number possible. To convert 163, the process starts by subtracting 128 (the largest possible power of two that can be subtracted). The result is 35, and the largest power of two that can now be subtracted is 32. The next two steps show subtracting 2 and 1 which are the powers of two: 2^1 and 2^0. The binary number is now constructed by writing 1's in the position corresponding to the powers of two subtracted, and filling in zeros elsewhere. Decimal 163 becomes 10100011 in binary.

Table A-10. Binary-to-Decimal Conversion

Position Significance		2^6	2^5	2^4	2^3	2^2	2^1	2^0		
Decimal Equivalent		64	32	16	8	4	2	1		
Examples:	1)	1	0	0	1	1	0	0	=	64 + 8 + 4 = 76
	2)	0	1	0	1	1	0	1	=	32 + 8 + 4 + 1 = 45
	3)	1	1	1	1	1	1	1	=	64 + 32 + 16 + 8 + 4 + 2 + 1 = 127
	4)	1	0	0	0	0	1	0	=	64 + 2 = 66

Table A-11. Binary-to-Decimal Conversion — Faster Method

Binary No. (a)	1)	1	0	0	1	1	0	0	=	76
Doubling		—	2	4	8	18	38	76		
Adding (x)		1	2	4	9	19	38	76		
	2)	0	1	0	1	1	0	1	=	45
			1	2	5	11	22	45		
	3)	1	1	1	1	1	1	1	=	127
		1	3	7	15	31	63	127		
	4)	1	0	0	0	0	1	0	=	66
		1	2	4	8	16	33	66		

$$X_0 = A_0$$
$$X_1 = 2X_0 + A_1$$
$$X_2 = 2X_1 + A_2$$
$$X_3 = 2X_2 + A_3$$
$$X_i = 2X_{i-1} + A_i$$

Table A-12. Decimal-to-Binary Conversion

Position Significance		2^7	2^6	2^5	2^4	2^3	2^2	2^1	2^0
Decimal Equivalent		128	64	32	16	8	4	2	1
Example:	163 =	1	0	1	0	0	0	1	1

$$-128 \quad 2^7$$
$$35$$
$$- 32 \quad 2^5$$
$$3$$
$$- 2 \quad 2^1$$
$$1$$
$$- 1 \quad 2^0$$
$$0$$

Table A-12. Decimal-to-Binary Conversion (Concluded)

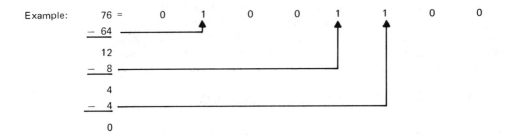

BINARY ARITHMETIC

The basic arithmetic functions in a binary system are performed in a manner similar to a decimal system.

Table A-13 gives an example and the basic rules for binary addition. Since there are only two symbols, 0 and 1, the basic rules are very simple. Decimal, hexadecimal, and octal notations have been included to further demonstrate the process of addition. Carries are noted with a in this example. Binary addition and subtraction of larger numbers are more easily written in hexadecimal notation.

Table A-13. Binary Addition

Decimal	Binary	Hexadecimal	Binary	Octal
	a a a		a a a	
52	0011 0100	34	00 110 100	064
54	0011 0110	36	00 110 110	066
106	0110 1010	6A	01 101 010	152
	0 + 0 = 0			
	0 + 1 = 1			
	1 + 1 = 10			
	Basic Rules			

a — Carries are generated at these positions

Table A-14 gives two examples of binary addition in hexadecimal: one with carries, and one without carries.

Table A-14. Hexadecimal Addition

```
  8   B   A   7   9   6
  7   3   3   5   2   4     (No Carries)
 ───────────────────────
  F   E   D   C   B   A


      a   a   a   a   a        (Carries)
  6   7   8   9   A   B
  A   B   C   D   E   F
 ───────────────────────
1 1   3   5   7   9   A
```

A-8

In most computer arithmetic units, subtraction is accomplished via complementing and adding. Table A-15 shows a purely arithmetic representation. Table A-16 shows the two's complement method for subtraction. In the example, the negative binary number is converted to its two's complement and then added to the other binary number. The carry, if any, from the most significant bit is ignored. This is a significant benefit for two's complement arithmetic since in one's complement arithmetic this carry cannot be ignored and circuitry must be included to accomplish what is known as an end around carry.

Table A-15. Binary Subtraction

Decimal	Binary	Hexadecimal	Binary	Octal
	aa a			
106	0110 1010	6A	001 101 010	152
− 52	− 0011 0100	−34	− 000 110 100	− 64
54	0011 0110	36	000 110 110	66

$$0 - 0 = 0$$
$$1 - 0 = 1$$
$$1 - 1 = 0$$
$$10 - 1 = 1$$

Basic Rules

a — Borrows are generated at these positions

Table A-16. Two's Complement Binary Subtraction

Decimal	Binary	2's Complement Binary	
106	0110 1010	0110 1010)	Add
− 52	− 0011 0100	1100 1100)	
54	0011 0110	1 0011 0110	

↑
Ignore

Complementing the Subtrahend

	0011 0110	Subtrahend
	1100 1011	Complement (1's complement)
	1100 1100	Complement + 1 (2's complement)

52	0011 0100	0011 0100
−106	− 0110 1010	1001 0110
− 54	1100 1010	1100 1010

One's complement = 0011 0101
Two's complement = 0011 0110 = 54

Binary multiplication uses very simple, basic rules. They are:

0 x 0 = 0

0 x 1 = 0

1 x 0 = 0

1 x 1 = 1

In multiplying binary numbers, the process can be seen as a series of shifts and adds. Table A-17 shows an example. If the least significant bit of the multiplier is a one, *add* the multiplicand into the accumulator. Each bit of the multiplier is likewise tested and the multiplicand is added at each step where the bit is a one. Also, for each position, the multiplicand is shifted left before adding.

One important fact in the concept of binary multiplication is that the product may require twice as many bit positions as the multiplier and multiplicand. In the example, two four bit numbers were multiplied producing an eight bit product.

Table A-17. Binary Multiplication

Binary		Decimal
1100	Multiplican	12
X 1011	Multiplier	X 11
1100	Add	12
1100	Shift and Add	12
100100	Partial Product	132
1100	Shift, Shift, Add	
10000100	Product	

Binary division is in general the same as decimal division insofar as the arithmetic sequence is concerned. An example is shown in Table A-18. The divisor is subtracted from the dividend starting with the highest order position. The divisor is then shifted right and a test is made to see if the divisor is less than the remainder. If so, subtraction is performed; if not, another shift is required. The quotient is developed by writing 1's for each position at which subtraction takes place, and zeros elsewhere (for steps involving shift only).

Table A-18. Binary Division

Binary		Decimal
101		5
101 ⟌ 11010		5 ⟌ 26
101	Subtract	25
110		1
101	Shift, Shift, Subtract	
1	Remainder	

APPENDIX B

BOOLEAN ALGEBRA

Most designers of digital systems are initimately familiar with the concepts of Boolean algebra. A summary of these concepts as they apply to digital computing is useful here. The basic AND, OR, NAND, and NOR gates are shown in Table B-1 along with their corresponding truth tables. The truth tables give the binary state of the output for all states of the inputs. While the logic diagram approach has classically been used to describe the Boolean algebra concepts, computer system designers approach Boolean algebra from a different aspect. First, consider the purely algebraic notation.

Table B-2 gives the symbols or Boolean algebra notation. The + sign is used for OR, overscore signals a complement function, and two letters adjacent to one another signal the AND function. Parentheses indicate standard algebraic groupings, and the $\oplus$ symbol indicates the **exclusive** OR function. The fundamental rules given in an equation form in Table B-2 describe the combinatorial algebra in its purest form.

Truth tables are given for equations 5 and 6 since they are not as easily recognized as the others. Notice that in all of these equations the variables A, B, and C are two valued functions, that is, they may be either 1 or 0. Equations 7 through 10 are especially significant because they are used quite often in digital computer logic steps.

Table B-3 shows what takes place when logic functions are implemented by computer. An AND instruction will do bit-by-bit Boolean algebraic ANDing and this must not be confused with binary addition in which the numeric values are added and carries generated. While four-bit binary words used are for the examples in Table B-3, it is clear that binary words of any length could be used. The importance of logical operations on binary words is that this technique provides a very powerful method for testing conditions prior to branching in programs. That is, in addition to sequential steps, programs require the ability to establish the status of a word or a particular bit before branching into a new string of instructions.

It is a well known theorem in combinatorial logic that all functions can be implemented with NAND gates or with NOR gates. In other words, given the AND function with the inversion capability, all logic functions can be implemented. Applying this to a stored program digital computer, all computer logic functions can be implemented given the AND function and the complement function.

Table B-4 describes the OR function implemented using only the AND and complement capabilities. From equation 11 of Table B-2, the OR function may be rewritten as shown in Table B-4 equation 2. Two 4-bit binary words are used for the example. Note that in complementing each of the words, ones replace zeros and zeros replace ones. Step 2 is simply an AND function on the two words resulting from step 1, and step 3 is simply complementing the result of step 2.

Table B-1. Basic AND, OR, NAND, and NOR Gates

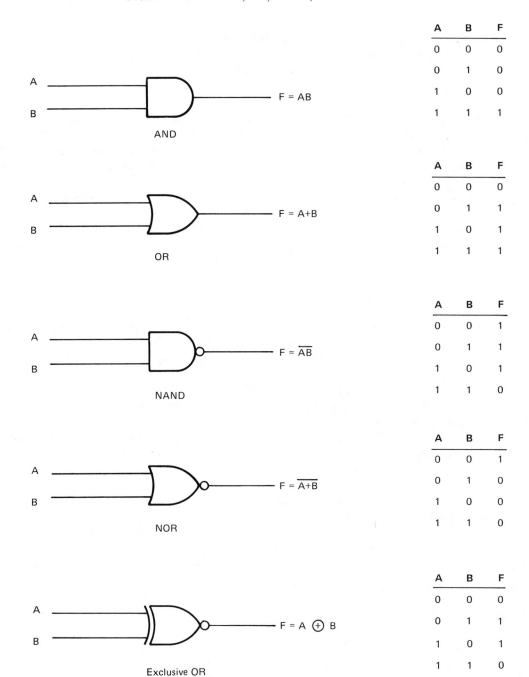

A	B	F
0	0	0
0	1	0
1	0	0
1	1	1

A ——
B ——
$F = AB$
AND

A	B	F
0	0	0
0	1	1
1	0	1
1	1	1

A ——
B ——
$F = A+B$
OR

A	B	F
0	0	1
0	1	1
1	0	1
1	1	0

A ——
B ——
$F = \overline{AB}$
NAND

A	B	F
0	0	1
0	1	0
1	0	0
1	1	0

A ——
B ——
$F = \overline{A+B}$
NOR

A	B	F
0	0	0
0	1	1
1	0	1
1	1	0

A ——
B ——
$F = A \oplus B$
Exclusive OR

Table B-2. Symbols for Boolean Algebra Notation

$+, ^-, ( ), \oplus$

$+$ OR

$^-$ Complement (inverse)

$( )$ Algebraic group

$\oplus$ Exclusive OR (XOR)

Fundamental Rules

1.	A + B	= B + A	A OR B
2.	AB	= BA	A AND B
3.	(A + B) + C	= A + (B + C)	
4.	A (BC)	= (AB) C	
5.	A (B+C)	= AB + AC	
5a.	A (A+B)	= AA + AB = A + AB = A	

A	B	C	A (B+C)	AB	AC
0	0	0	0	0	0
0	0	1	0	0	0
0	1	0	0	0	0
0	1	1	0	0	0
1	0	0	0	0	0
1	0	1	1	0	1
1	1	0	1	1	0
1	1	1	1	1	1

6.   A + B (A + C)   =   A + BC

A	B	C	A + B (A + C)	BC
0	0	0	0	0
0	0	1	0	0
0	1	0	0	0
0	1	1	1	1
1	0	0	1	0
1	0	1	1	0
1	1	0	1	0
1	1	1	1	1

7.	$A\overline{A}$	= 0	
7a.	$A + \overline{A}$	= 1	
8.	A+0	= A	
8a.	A + 1	= 1	
9.	(A) (1)	= A	
9a.	(A) (0)	= 0	
10.	A+A	= A	
10a.	AA	= A	
11.	$\overline{(A+B)}$	= $\overline{A}\ \overline{B}$	DeMorgan's Theorem
11a.	$\overline{A}\ \overline{B}$	= $\overline{A+B}$	
11b.	(A+B) (C+D)	= $\overline{\overline{AB} + \overline{CD}}$	

Table B-2. Symbols for Boolean Algebra Notation (Continued)

12. $A \oplus B$ $= \overline{AB}\ (A + B)$ Exclusive OR

A	B	$A \oplus B$	AB	A + B
0	0	0	1	0
0	1	1	1	1
1	0	1	1	1
1	1	0	0	1

Table B-3. Boolean Algebra Performed on Binary Words

A	A_1	A_2	A_3	A_4
B	B_1	B_2	B_3	B_4
A + B	$A_1 + B_1$	$A_2 + B_2$	$A_3 + B_3$	$A_4 + B_4$
AB	$A_1 B_1$	$A_2 B_2$	$A_3 B_3$	$A_4 B_4$
$A \oplus B$	$A_1 \oplus B_1$	$A_2 \oplus B_2$	$A_3 \oplus B_3$	$A_4 \oplus B_4$

Examples:

$$A = 0\ 1\ 0\ 1$$
$$B = \underline{0\ 0\ 1\ 1}$$
$$A + B = 0\ 1\ 1\ 1$$
$$AB = 0\ 0\ 0\ 1$$
$$A \oplus B = 0\ 1\ 1\ 0$$

Using the result of this example, develop the exclusive OR function. Example 2 shows that by ANDing and complementing, the first step can be developed: "not A and B," then using the OR function, develop "A or B". By ANDing these two, the exclusive OR function can be achieved. These examples demonstrate the use of Boolean algebra in four-bit binary words and show how Boolean algebra is used in digital computers.

Table B-5 shows three common uses for logic instructions. The first is to generate a word to be used as a mask. Suppose you wish to observe the contents of a word "A", but are only interested in the lower order four bits. A word "B" is set up with ones in the lower order four bits and zeros elsewhere. The AND function between A and B yields all zeros except for those locations where B contained ones. This step usually precedes a test-for-0 instruction. That is, an instruction that would direct the computer to execute a branch whenever a content of a word is 0. In this case, had the lower order four bits been all zeros, then the mask would have generated a word of zeros which then would be the condition tested for in the branch on zero instructions.

Table B-4. OR Functions

OR	Function	F	$=$	$A + B$		(1)
		F	$=$	$\overline{\overline{A}\,\overline{B}}$	(See EQ 11)	(2)
XOR	Function	F	$=$	$\overline{AB}\,(A + B)$	(See EQ 12)	(3)
		F	$=$	$\overline{AB}\,(\overline{\overline{A}\,\overline{B}})$		(4)

Examples:

1. **OR Function**

	A	0 0 1 1
	B	0 1 0 1

Step 1.   Complement

	$\overline{A}$	1 1 0 0
	$\overline{B}$	1 0 1 0

Step 2.   AND

	$\overline{A}\,\overline{B}$	1 0 0 0

Step 3.   Complement

	$\overline{\overline{A}\,\overline{B}}$	0 1 1 1	$= A + B$

2. **XOR Function**

	A	0 0 1 1	
	B	0 1 0 1	
AND	AB	0 0 0 1	
COMPL.	$\overline{AB}$	1 1 1 0	
OR	A+B	0 1 1 1	From previous examples
AND	$\overline{AB}$ (A+B)	0 1 1 0	$= A + B$

Table B-5. Use of Mask, Exclusive OR, and Complement Instructions

	A	1 1 0 1	1 0 1 0
	B (mask)	0 0 0 0	1 1 1 1

Examples:

1.	AB	0 0 0 0	1 0 1 0
2.	A $\oplus$ A	0 0 0 0	0 0 0 0
3.	$\overline{A}$	0 0 1 0	1 1 0 1
4.	A + B	1 1 0 1	1 1 1 1

The second example in Table B-5 demonstrates the effect of an exclusive OR function on two identical words. The result is obviously 0. The third example in Table B-5 demonstrates the use of the complement function.

In general, discussions of Boolean algebra in combinatorial logic include sequential logic such as shift registers and counters. However, in digital computer applications, sequential logic takes on a new dimension. In effect one must consider the content of a given word in memory and the way it changes in time in a different manner from simply applying clock pulses to a counter or shift register. Any word in memory can be used as a counter simply by bringing it into the accumulator of the arithmetic unit adding one and storing it again. In order to utilize an incrementing word in a control system environment for example, this word must be sent out to the output circuits using an output instruction. The frequency at which this takes place is a function of the computer instruction cycles, that is, the frequency with which this particular word is incremented. Only the basics of Boolean algebra and simple links to digital processing functions have been shown in this appendix. For a more comprehensive treatment, refer to Franz E. Hohn, *Applied Boolean Algebra* (Macmillan, 1966).

APPENDIX C

TABLES AND DATA

HEXADECIMAL ARITHMETIC

ADDITION TABLE

0	1	2	3	4	5	6	7	8	9	A	B	C	D	E	F
1	02	03	04	05	06	07	08	09	0A	0B	0C	0D	0E	0F	10
2	03	04	05	06	07	08	09	0A	0B	0C	0D	0E	0F	10	11
3	04	05	06	07	08	09	0A	0B	0C	0D	0E	0F	10	11	12
4	05	06	07	08	09	0A	0B	0C	0D	0E	0F	10	11	12	13
5	06	07	08	09	0A	0B	0C	0D	0E	0F	10	11	12	13	14
6	07	08	09	0A	0B	0C	0D	0E	0F	10	11	12	13	14	15
7	08	09	0A	0B	0C	0D	0E	0F	10	11	12	13	14	15	16
8	09	0A	0B	0C	0D	0E	0F	10	11	12	13	14	15	16	17
9	0A	0B	0C	0D	0E	0F	10	11	12	13	14	15	16	17	18
A	0B	0C	0D	0E	0F	10	11	12	13	14	15	16	17	18	19
B	0C	0D	0E	0F	10	11	12	13	14	15	16	17	18	19	1A
C	0D	0E	0F	10	11	12	13	14	15	16	17	18	19	1A	1B
D	0E	0F	10	11	12	13	14	15	16	17	18	19	1A	1B	1C
E	0F	10	11	12	13	14	15	16	17	18	19	1A	1B	1C	1D
F	10	11	12	13	14	15	16	17	18	19	1A	1B	1C	1D	1E

MULTIPLICATION TABLE

1	2	3	4	5	6	7	8	9	A	B	C	D	E	F
2	04	06	08	0A	0C	0E	10	12	14	16	18	1A	1C	1E
3	06	09	0C	0F	12	15	18	1B	1E	21	24	27	2A	2D
4	08	0C	10	14	18	1C	20	24	28	2C	30	34	38	3C
5	0A	0F	14	19	1E	23	28	2D	32	37	3C	41	46	4B
6	0C	12	18	1E	24	2A	30	36	3C	42	48	4E	54	5A
7	0E	15	1C	23	2A	31	38	3F	46	4D	54	5B	62	69
8	10	18	20	28	30	38	40	48	50	58	60	68	70	78
9	12	1B	24	2D	36	3F	48	51	5A	63	6C	75	7E	87
A	14	1E	28	32	3C	46	50	5A	64	6E	78	82	8C	96
B	16	21	2C	37	42	4D	58	63	6E	79	84	8F	9A	A5
C	18	24	30	3C	48	54	60	6C	78	84	90	9C	A8	B4
D	1A	27	34	41	4E	5B	68	75	82	8F	9C	A9	B6	C3
E	1C	2A	38	46	54	62	70	7E	8C	9A	A8	B6	C4	D2
F	1E	2D	3C	4B	5A	69	78	87	96	A5	B4	C3	D2	E1

TABLE OF POWERS OF SIXTEEN$_{10}$

16^n	n	16^{-n}
1	0	$0.10000\ 00000\ 00000\ 00000 \times 10$
16	1	$0.62500\ 00000\ 00000\ 00000 \times 10^{-1}$
256	2	$0.39062\ 50000\ 00000\ 00000 \times 10^{-2}$
4 096	3	$0.24414\ 06250\ 00000\ 00000 \times 10^{-3}$
65 536	4	$0.15258\ 78906\ 25000\ 00000 \times 10^{-4}$
1 048 576	5	$0.95367\ 43164\ 06250\ 00000 \times 10^{-6}$
16 777 216	6	$0.59604\ 64477\ 53906\ 25000 \times 10^{-7}$
268 435 456	7	$0.37252\ 90298\ 46191\ 40625 \times 10^{-8}$
4 294 967 296	8	$0.23283\ 06436\ 53869\ 62891 \times 10^{-9}$
68 719 476 736	9	$0.14551\ 91522\ 83668\ 51807 \times 10^{-10}$
1 099 511 627 776	10	$0.90949\ 47017\ 72928\ 23792 \times 10^{-12}$
17 592 186 044 416	11	$0.56843\ 41886\ 08080\ 14870 \times 10^{-13}$
281 474 976 510 656	12	$0.35527\ 13678\ 80050\ 09294 \times 10^{-14}$
4 503 599 627 370 496	13	$0.22204\ 46049\ 25031\ 30808 \times 10^{-15}$
72 057 594 037 927 936	14	$0.13877\ 78780\ 78144\ 56755 \times 10^{-16}$
1 152 921 504 606 846 976	15	$0.86736\ 17379\ 88403\ 54721 \times 10^{-18}$

TABLE OF POWERS OF TEN$_{16}$

10^n	n	10^{-n}
1	0	$1.0000\ 0000\ 0000\ 0000$
A	1	$0.1999\ 9999\ 9999\ 999A$
64	2	$0.28F5\ C28F\ 5C28\ F5C3 \times 16^{-1}$
3E8	3	$0.4189\ 374B\ C6A7\ EF9E \times 16^{-2}$
2710	4	$0.68DB\ 8BAC\ 710C\ B296 \times 16^{-3}$
1 86A0	5	$0.A7C5\ AC47\ 1B47\ 8423 \times 16^{-4}$
F 4240	6	$0.10C6\ F7A0\ B5ED\ 8D37 \times 16^{-4}$
98 9680	7	$0.1AD7\ F29A\ BCAF\ 4858 \times 16^{-5}$
5F5 E100	8	$0.2AF3\ 1DC4\ 6118\ 73BF \times 16^{-6}$
3B9A CA00	9	$0.44B8\ 2FA0\ 9B5A\ 52CC \times 16^{-7}$
2 540B E400	10	$0.6DF3\ 7F67\ 5EF6\ EADF \times 16^{-8}$
17 4876 E800	11	$0.AFEB\ FF0B\ CB24\ AAFF \times 16^{-9}$
E8 D4A5 1000	12	$0.1197\ 9981\ 2DEA\ 1119 \times 16^{-9}$
918 4E72 A000	13	$0.1C25\ C268\ 4976\ 81C2 \times 16^{-10}$
5AF3 107A 4000	14	$0.2D09\ 370D\ 4257\ 3604 \times 16^{-11}$
3 8D7E A4C6 8000	15	$0.480E\ BE7B\ 9D58\ 566D \times 16^{-12}$
23 86F2 6FC1 0000	16	$0.734A\ CA5F\ 6226\ F0AE \times 16^{-13}$
163 4578 5D8A 0000	17	$0.B877\ AA32\ 36A4\ B449 \times 16^{-14}$
DE0 B6B3 A764 0000	18	$0.1272\ 5DD1\ D243\ ABA1 \times 16^{-14}$
8AC7 2304 89E8 0000	19	$0.1D83\ C94F\ B6D2\ AC35 \times 16^{-15}$

TABLE OF POWERS OF TWO

2^n	n	2^{-n}

2^n			n	2^{-n}							
		1	0	1.0							
		2	1	0.5							
		4	2	0.25							
		8	3	0.125							
		16	4	0.062	5						
		32	5	0.031	25						
		64	6	0.015	625						
		128	7	0.007	812	5					
		256	8	0.003	906	25					
		512	9	0.001	953	125					
	1	024	10	0.000	976	562	5				
	2	048	11	0.000	488	281	25				
	4	096	12	0.000	244	140	625				
	8	192	13	0.000	122	070	312	5			
	16	384	14	0.000	061	035	156	25			
	32	768	15	0.000	030	517	578	125			
	65	536	16	0.000	015	258	789	062	5		
	131	072	17	0.000	007	629	394	531	25		
	262	144	18	0.000	003	814	697	265	625		
	524	288	19	0.000	001	907	348	632	812	5	
1	048	576	20	0.000	000	953	674	316	406	25	
2	097	152	21	0.000	000	476	837	158	203	125	
4	194	304	22	0.000	000	238	418	579	101	562	5
8	388	608	23	0.000	000	119	209	289	550	781	25
16	777	216	24	0.000	000	059	604	644	775	390	625
33	554	432	25	0.000	000	029	802	322	387	695	312 5
67	108	864	26	0.000	000	014	901	161	193	847	656 25
134	217	728	27	0.000	000	007	450	580	596	923	828 125
268	435	456	28	0.000	000	003	725	290	298	461	914 062 5
536	870	912	29	0.000	000	001	862	645	149	230	957 031 25
1 073	741	824	30	0.000	000	000	931	322	574	615	478 515 625
2 147	483	648	31	0.000	000	000	465	661	287	307	739 257 812 5

HEXADECIMAL—DECIMAL INTEGER
CONVERSION TABLE

The table appearing on the following pages provides a means for direct conversion of decimal integers in the range of 0 to 4095 and for hexadecimal integers in the range of 0 to FFF.

To convert numbers above those ranges, add table values to the figures below:

Hexadecimal	Decimal	Hexadecimal	Decimal
01 000	4 096	20 000	131 072
02 000	8 192	30 000	196 608
03 000	12 288	40 000	262 144
04 000	16 384	50 000	327 680
05 000	20 480	60 000	393 216
06 000	24 576	70 000	458 752
07 000	28 672	80 000	524 288
08 000	32 768	90 000	589 824
09 000	36 864	A0 000	655 360
0A 000	40 960	B0 000	720 896
0B 000	45 056	C0 000	786 432
0C 000	49 152	D0 000	851 968
0D 000	53 248	E0 000	917 504
0E 000	57 344	F0 000	983 040
0F 000	61 440	100 000	1 048 576
10 000	65 536	200 000	2 097 152
11 000	69 632	300 000	3 145 728
12 000	73 728	400 000	4 194 304
13 000	77 824	500 000	5 242 880
14 000	81 920	600 000	6 291 456
15 000	86 016	700 000	7 340 032
16 000	90 112	800 000	8 388 608
17 000	94 208	900 000	9 437 184
18 000	98 304	A00 000	10 485 760
19 000	102 400	B00 000	11 534 336
1A 000	106 496	C00 000	12 582 912
1B 000	110 592	D00 000	13 631 488
1C 000	114 688	E00 000	14 680 064
1D 000	118 784	F00 000	15 728 640
1E 000	122 880	1 000 000	16 777 216
1F 000	126 976	2 000 000	33 554 432

	0	1	2	3	4	5	6	7	8	9	A	B	C	D	E	F
000	0000	0001	0002	0003	0004	0005	0006	0007	0008	0009	0010	0011	0012	0013	0014	0015
010	0016	0017	0018	0019	0020	0021	0022	0023	0024	0025	0026	0027	0028	0029	0030	0031
020	0032	0033	0034	0035	0036	0037	0038	0039	0040	0041	0042	0043	0044	0045	0046	0047
030	0048	0049	0050	0051	0052	0053	0054	0055	0056	0057	0058	0059	0060	0061	0062	0063
040	0064	0065	0066	0067	0068	0069	0070	0071	0072	0073	0074	0075	0076	0077	0078	0079
050	0080	0081	0082	0083	0084	0085	0086	0087	0088	0089	0090	0091	0092	0093	0094	0095
060	0096	0097	0098	0099	0100	0101	0102	0103	0104	0105	0106	0107	0108	0109	0110	0111
070	0112	0113	0114	0115	0116	0117	0118	0119	0120	0121	0122	0123	0124	0125	0126	0127
080	0128	0129	0130	0131	0132	0133	0134	0135	0136	0137	0138	0139	0140	0141	0142	0143
090	0144	0145	0146	0147	0148	0149	0150	0151	0152	0153	0154	0155	0156	0157	0158	0159
0A0	0160	0161	0162	0163	0164	0165	0166	0167	0168	0169	0170	0171	0172	0173	0174	0175
0B0	0176	0177	0178	0179	0180	0181	0182	0183	0184	0185	0186	0187	0188	0189	0190	0191
0C0	0192	0193	0194	0195	0196	0197	0198	0199	0200	0201	0202	0203	0204	0205	0206	0207
0D0	0208	0209	0210	0211	0212	0213	0214	0215	0216	0217	0218	0219	0220	0221	0222	0223
0E0	0224	0225	0226	0227	0228	0229	0230	0231	0232	0233	0234	0235	0236	0237	0238	0239
0F0	0240	0241	0242	0243	0244	0245	0246	0247	0248	0249	0250	0251	0252	0253	0254	0255
100	0256	0257	0258	0259	0260	0261	0262	0263	0264	0265	0266	0267	0268	0269	0270	0271
110	0272	0273	0274	0275	0276	0277	0278	0279	0280	0281	0282	0283	0284	0285	0286	0287
120	0288	0289	0290	0291	0292	0293	0294	0295	0296	0297	0298	0299	0300	0301	0302	0303
130	0304	0305	0306	0307	0308	0309	0310	0311	0312	0313	0314	0315	0316	0317	0318	0319
140	0320	0321	0322	0323	0324	0325	0326	0327	0328	0329	0330	0331	0332	0333	0334	0335
150	0336	0337	0338	0339	0340	0341	0342	0343	0344	0345	0346	0347	0348	0349	0350	0351
160	0352	0353	0354	0355	0356	0357	0358	0359	0360	0361	0362	0363	0364	0365	0366	0367
170	0368	0369	0370	0371	0372	0373	0374	0375	0376	0377	0378	0379	0380	0381	0382	0383
180	0384	0385	0386	0387	0388	0389	0390	0391	0392	0393	0394	0395	0396	0397	0398	0399
190	0400	0401	0402	0403	0404	0405	0406	0407	0408	0409	0410	0411	0412	0413	0414	0415
1A0	0416	0417	0418	0419	0420	0421	0422	0423	0424	0425	0426	0427	0428	0429	0430	0431
1B0	0432	0433	0434	0435	0436	0437	0438	0439	0440	0441	0442	0443	0444	0445	0446	0447
1C0	0448	0449	0450	0451	0452	0453	0454	0455	0456	0457	0458	0459	0460	0461	0462	0463
1D0	0464	0465	0466	0467	0468	0469	0470	0471	0472	0473	0474	0475	0476	0477	0478	0479
1E0	0480	0481	0482	0483	0484	0485	0486	0487	0488	0489	0490	0491	0492	0493	0494	0495
1F0	0496	0497	0498	0499	0500	0501	0502	0503	0504	0505	0506	0507	0508	0509	0510	0511
200	0512	0513	0514	0515	0516	0517	0518	0519	0529	0521	0522	0523	0524	0525	0526	0527
210	0528	0529	0530	0531	0532	0533	0534	0535	0536	0537	0538	0539	0540	0541	0542	0543
220	0544	0545	0546	0547	0548	0549	0550	0551	0552	0553	0554	0555	0556	0557	0558	0559
230	0560	0561	0562	0563	0564	0565	0566	0567	0568	0569	0570	0571	0572	0573	0574	0575
240	0576	0577	0578	0579	0580	0581	0582	0583	0584	0585	0586	0587	0588	0589	0590	0591
250	0592	0593	0594	0595	0596	0597	0598	0599	0600	0601	0602	0603	0604	0605	0606	0607
260	0608	0609	0610	0611	0612	0613	0614	0615	0616	0617	0618	0619	0620	0621	0622	0623
270	0624	0625	0626	0627	0628	0629	0630	0631	0632	0633	0634	0635	0636	0637	0638	0639
280	0640	0641	0642	0643	0644	0645	0646	0647	0648	0649	0650	0651	0652	0653	0654	0655
290	0656	0657	0658	0659	0660	0661	0662	0663	0664	0665	0666	0667	0668	0669	0670	0671
2A0	0672	0673	0674	0675	0676	0677	0678	0679	0680	0681	0682	0683	0684	0685	0686	0687
2B0	0688	0689	0690	0691	0692	0693	0694	0695	0696	0697	0698	0699	0700	0701	0702	0703
2C0	0704	0705	0706	0707	0708	0709	0710	0711	0712	0713	0714	0715	0716	0717	0718	0719
2D0	0720	0721	0722	0723	0724	0725	0726	0727	0728	0729	0730	0731	0732	0733	0734	0735
2E0	0736	0737	0738	0739	0740	0741	0742	0743	0744	0745	0746	0747	0748	0749	0750	0751
2F0	0752	0753	0754	0755	0756	0757	0758	0759	0760	0761	0762	0763	0764	0765	0766	0767

	0	1	2	3	4	5	6	7	8	9	A	B	C	D	E	F
300	0768	0769	0770	0771	0772	0773	0774	0775	0776	0777	0778	0779	0780	0781	0782	0783
310	0784	0785	0786	0787	0788	0789	0790	0791	0792	0793	0794	0795	0796	0797	0798	0799
320	0800	0801	0802	0803	0804	0805	0806	0807	0808	0809	0810	0811	0812	0813	0814	0815
330	0816	0817	0818	0819	0820	0821	0822	0823	0824	0825	0826	0827	0828	0829	0830	0831
340	0832	0833	0834	0835	0836	0837	0838	0839	0840	0841	0842	0843	0844	0845	0846	0847
350	0848	0849	0850	0851	0852	0853	0854	0855	0856	0857	0858	0859	0860	0861	0862	0863
360	0864	0865	0866	0867	0868	0869	0870	0871	0872	0873	0874	0875	0876	0877	0878	0879
370	0880	0881	0882	0883	0884	0885	0886	0887	0888	0889	0890	0891	0892	0893	0894	0895
380	0896	0897	0898	0899	0900	0901	0902	0903	0904	0905	0906	0907	0908	0909	0910	0911
390	0912	0913	0914	0915	0916	0917	0918	0919	0920	0921	0922	0923	0924	0925	0926	0927
3A0	0928	0929	0930	0931	0932	0933	0934	0935	0936	0937	0938	0939	0940	0941	0942	0943
3B0	0944	0945	0946	0947	0948	0949	0950	0951	0952	0953	0954	0955	0956	0957	0958	0959
3C0	0960	0961	0962	0963	0964	0965	0966	0967	0968	0969	0970	0971	0972	0973	0974	0975
3D0	0976	0977	0978	0979	0980	0981	0982	0983	0984	0985	0986	0987	0988	0989	0990	0991
3E0	0992	0993	0994	0995	0996	0997	0998	0999	1000	1001	1002	1003	1004	1005	1006	1007
3F0	1008	1009	1010	1011	1012	1013	1014	1015	1016	1017	1018	1019	1020	1021	1022	1023
400	1024	1025	0126	0127	1028	1029	1030	1031	1032	1033	1034	1035	1036	1037	1038	1039
410	1040	1041	1042	1043	1044	1045	1046	1047	1048	1049	1050	1051	1052	1053	1054	1055
420	1056	1057	1058	1059	1060	1061	1062	1063	1064	1065	1066	1067	1068	1069	1070	1071
430	1072	1073	1074	1075	1076	1077	1078	1079	1080	1081	1082	1083	1084	1085	1086	1087
440	1088	1089	1090	1091	1092	1093	1094	1095	1096	1097	1098	1099	1100	1101	1102	1103
450	1104	1105	1106	1107	1108	1109	1110	1111	1112	1113	1114	1115	1116	1117	1118	1119
460	1120	1121	1122	1123	1124	1125	1126	1127	1128	1129	1130	1131	1132	1133	1134	1135
470	1136	1137	1138	1139	1140	1141	1142	1143	1144	1145	1146	1147	1148	1149	1150	1151
480	1152	1153	1154	1155	1156	1157	1158	1159	1160	1161	1162	1163	1164	1165	1166	1167
490	1168	1169	1170	1171	1172	1173	1174	1175	1176	1177	1178	1179	1180	1181	1182	1183
4A0	1184	1185	1186	1187	1188	1189	1190	1191	1192	1193	1194	1195	1196	1197	1198	1199
4B0	1200	1201	1202	1203	1204	1205	1206	1207	1208	1209	1210	1211	1212	1213	1214	1215
4C0	1216	1217	1218	1219	1220	1221	1222	1223	1224	1225	1226	1227	1228	1229	1230	1231
4D0	1232	1233	1234	1235	1236	1237	1238	1239	1240	1241	1242	1243	1244	1245	1246	1247
4E0	1248	1249	1250	1251	1252	1253	1254	1255	1256	1257	1258	1259	1260	1261	1262	1263
4F0	1264	1265	1266	1267	1268	1269	1270	1271	1272	1273	1274	1275	1276	1277	1278	1279
500	1280	1281	1282	1283	1284	1285	1286	1287	1288	1289	1290	1291	1291	1293	1294	1295
510	1296	1297	1298	1299	1399	1301	1302	1303	1304	1305	1306	1307	1308	1309	1310	1311
520	1312	1313	1314	1315	1316	1317	1318	1319	1329	1321	1322	1323	1324	1325	1326	1327
530	1328	1329	1330	1331	1332	1333	1334	1335	1336	1337	1338	1339	1340	1341	1342	1343
540	1344	1345	1346	1347	1348	1349	1350	1351	1352	1353	1354	1355	1356	1367	1358	1359
550	1360	1361	1362	1363	1364	1365	1366	1367	1368	1369	1370	1371	1372	1373	1374	1375
560	1376	1377	1378	1379	1380	1381	1382	1383	1384	1385	1386	1387	1388	1389	1390	1391
570	1392	1393	1394	1395	1396	1397	1398	1399	1400	1401	1402	1403	1404	1405	1406	1407
580	1408	1409	1410	1411	1412	1413	1414	1415	1416	1417	1418	1419	1429	1421	1422	1423
590	1324	1425	1426	1427	1428	1429	1430	1431	1432	1433	1434	1435	1436	1437	1438	1439
5A0	1440	1441	1442	1443	1444	1445	1446	1447	1448	1449	1450	1451	1452	1453	1454	1455
3B0	1456	1457	1458	1459	1460	1461	1462	1463	1464	1465	1466	1467	1468	1469	1470	1471
5C0	1472	1473	1474	1475	1476	1477	1478	1479	1480	1481	1482	1483	1484	1485	1486	1487
5D0	1488	1489	1490	1491	1492	1493	1494	1495	1496	1497	1498	1499	1500	1501	1502	1503
5E0	1504	1505	1506	1507	1508	1509	1510	1511	1512	1513	1514	1515	1516	1517	1518	1519
5F0	1520	1521	1522	1523	1524	1515	1526	1527	1528	1529	1530	1531	1532	1533	1534	1535

	0	1	2	3	4	5	6	7	8	9	A	B	C	D	E	F
600	1536	1537	1538	1539	1540	1541	1542	1543	1544	1545	1546	1547	1548	1549	1550	1551
610	1552	1553	1554	1555	1556	1557	1558	1559	1560	1561	1562	1563	1564	1565	1566	1567
620	1568	1569	1570	1571	1572	1573	1574	1575	1576	1577	1578	1579	1580	1581	1582	1583
630	1584	1585	1586	1587	1588	1589	1590	1591	1592	1592	1594	1595	1596	1597	1598	1599
640	1600	1601	1602	1603	1604	1605	1606	1607	1608	1609	1610	1611	1612	1613	1614	1615
650	1616	1617	1618	1619	1620	1621	1622	1623	1624	1625	1626	1627	1628	1629	1630	1631
660	1632	1633	1634	1635	1636	1637	1638	1639	1640	1641	1642	1643	1644	1645	1646	1647
670	1648	1649	1650	1651	1652	1653	1654	1655	1656	1657	1658	1659	1660	1661	1662	1663
680	1664	1665	1666	1667	1668	1669	1670	1671	1672	1673	1674	1675	1676	1677	1678	1679
690	1680	1681	1682	1683	1684	1685	1686	1687	1688	1689	1690	1691	1692	1693	1694	1695
6A0	1696	1697	1698	1699	1700	1701	1702	1703	1704	1705	1706	1707	1708	1709	1710	1711
6B0	1712	1713	1714	1715	1716	1717	1718	1719	1720	1721	1722	17231	1724	1725	1726	1727
6C0	1728	1729	1730	1731	1732	1733	1734	1735	1736	1737	1738	1739	1740	1741	1742	1743
6D0	1744	1745	1746	1747	1748	1749	1750	1751	1752	1753	1754	1755	1756	1757	1758	1759
6E0	1760	1761	1762	1763	1764	1765	1766	1767	1768	1769	1770	1771	1772	1773	1774	1775
6F0	1776	1777	1778	1779	1780	1781	1782	1783	1784	1785	1786	1787	1788	1789	1790	1791
700	1792	1793	1794	1795	1796	1797	1798	1799	1800	1801	8102	1803	1804	1805	1806	1807
710	1808	1809	1810	1811	1812	1813	1814	1815	1816	1817	1818	1819	1820	1821	1822	1823
720	1824	1825	1826	1827	1818	1829	1830	1831	1832	1833	1834	1835	1836	1837	1838	1839
730	1840	1841	1842	1843	1844	1845	1846	1847	1848	1849	1850	1851	1852	1853	1854	1855
740	1856	1857	1858	1859	1860	1861	1862	1863	1864	1865	1866	1867	1868	1869	1870	1871
750	1872	1873	1874	1875	1876	1877	1878	1879	1880	1881	1882	1883	1884	1885	1886	1887
760	1888	1889	1890	1891	1892	1893	1894	1895	1896	1897	1898	1899	1900	1909	1902	1903
770	1904	1905	1906	1907	1908	1909	1910	1911	1912	1913	1914	1915	1916	1917	1918	1919
780	1920	1921	1922	1923	1924	1925	1926	1927	1928	1929	1930	1931	1932	1933	1934	1935
790	1936	1937	1938	1939	1940	1941	1942	1943	1944	1945	1946	1947	1948	1949	1950	1951
7A0	1952	1953	1954	1955	1956	1957	1958	1959	1960	1961	1962	1963	1964	1965	1966	1967
7B0	1968	1969	1970	1971	1972	1973	1974	1975	1976	1977	1978	1979	1980	1981	1982	1983
7C0	1984	1985	1986	1987	1988	1989	1990	1991	1992	1993	1994	1995	1996	1997	1998	1999
7D0	2000	2001	2002	2003	2004	2005	2006	2007	2008	2009	2010	2011	2012	2013	2014	2015
7E0	2016	2017	2018	2019	2020	2021	2022	2023	2024	2025	2026	2027	2028	2029	2030	2031
7F0	2032	2033	2034	2035	2036	2037	2038	2039	2040	2041	2042	2043	2044	2045	2046	2047
800	2048	2049	2050	2051	2052	2053	2054	2055	2056	2057	2058	2059	2060	2061	2062	2063
810	2064	2065	2066	2067	2068	2069	2070	2071	2072	2073	2074	2075	2076	2077	2078	2079
820	2080	2081	2082	2083	2084	2085	2086	2087	2088	2089	2090	2091	2092	2093	2094	2095
830	2096	2097	2098	2099	2100	2101	2102	2103	2104	2105	2106	2107	2108	2109	2110	2111
840	2112	2113	2114	2115	2116	2117	2118	2119	2120	2121	2122	2123	2124	2125	2126	2127
850	2128	2129	2130	2131	2132	2133	2134	2135	2136	2137	2138	2139	2140	2141	2142	2143
860	2144	2145	2146	2147	2148	2149	2150	2151	2152	2153	2154	2155	2156	2157	2158	2159
870	2160	2161	2162	2163	2164	2165	2166	2167	2168	2169	2170	2171	2172	2173	2174	2175
880	2176	2177	2178	2179	2180	2181	2182	2183	2184	2185	2186	2187	2188	2189	2190	2191
890	2192	2193	2194	2195	2196	2197	2198	2199	2200	2201	2202	2203	2204	2205	2206	2207
8A0	2208	2209	2210	2211	2212	2213	2214	2215	2216	2217	2218	2219	2220	2221	2222	2223
8B0	2224	2225	2226	2227	2228	2229	2230	2231	2232	2233	2234	2235	2236	2237	2238	2239
8C0	2240	2241	2242	2243	2244	2245	2246	2247	2248	2249	2250	2251	2252	2253	2254	2255
8D0	2256	2257	2258	2259	2260	2261	2262	2263	2264	2265	2266	2267	2268	2269	2270	2271
8E0	2272	2273	2274	2275	2276	2277	2278	2279	2280	2281	2282	2283	2284	2285	2286	2287
8F0	2288	2289	2290	2291	2292	2293	2294	2295	2296	2297	2298	2299	2300	2301	2302	2303

	0	1	2	3	4	5	6	7	8	9	A	B	C	D	E	F
900	2304	2305	2306	2307	2308	2309	2310	2311	2312	2313	2314	2315	2316	2317	2318	2319
910	2320	2321	2322	2323	2324	2325	2326	2327	2328	2329	2330	2331	2332	2333	2334	2335
920	2336	2337	2338	2339	2340	2341	2342	2343	2344	2345	2346	2347	2348	2349	2350	2351
930	2352	2353	2354	2355	2356	2357	2358	2359	2360	2361	2362	2363	2364	2365	2366	2367
940	2368	2369	2370	2371	2372	2373	2374	2375	2376	2377	2378	2379	2380	2381	2382	2383
950	2384	2385	2386	2387	2388	2389	2390	2391	2392	2393	2394	2395	3496	2397	2398	2399
960	2400	2401	2402	2403	2404	2405	2406	2407	2408	2409	2410	2411	2412	2413	2414	2415
970	2416	2417	2418	2419	2420	2421	2422	2423	2424	2425	2426	2427	2428	2429	2430	2431
980	2432	2433	2434	24351	2436	2437	2438	2439	2440	2441	2442	2443	2444	2445	2446	2447
990	2448	2449	2450	2451	2452	2453	2454	2455	2456	2457	2458	2459	2460	2461	2462	2463
9A0	2464	2465	2466	2467	2468	2469	2479	2471	2472	2473	2474	2475	2476	2477	2478	2479
9B0	2480	2481	2482	2483	2484	2485	2486	2487	2488	2489	2490	2491	2492	2493	2494	2495
9C0	2496	2497	2498	2499	2500	2501	2502	2503	2504	2505	2506	2507	2508	2509	2510	2511
9D0	2512	2513	2514	2515	2516	2517	2518	2519	2520	2521	2522	2523	2524	2525	2526	2527
9E0	2528	2529	2530	2531	2532	2533	2534	2535	2536	2537	2538	2539	2540	2541	2542	2543
9F0	2544	2545	2546	2547	2548	2549	2550	2551	2552	2553	2554	2555	2556	2557	2558	2559
A00	2560	2561	2562	2563	2564	2565	2566	2567	2568	2569	2570	2571	2572	2573	2574	2575
A10	2576	2577	2578	2579	2580	2581	2582	2583	2584	2585	2586	2587	2588	2589	2590	2591
A20	2592	2593	2594	2595	2596	2597	2598	2599	2600	2601	2602	2603	2604	2605	2606	2607
A30	2608	2609	2610	2611	2612	2613	2614	2615	2626	2617	2618	2619	2620	2621	2622	2623
A40	2624	2625	2626	2627	2628	2629	2630	2631	2632	2633	2634	2635	2636	2637	2638	2639
A50	2640	2641	2642	2643	2644	2645	2646	2647	2648	2649	2650	2651	2652	2653	2654	2655
A60	2656	2657	2658	2659	2660	2661	2662	2663	2664	2665	2666	2667	2668	2669	2670	2671
A70	2672	2673	2674	2675	2676	2677	2678	2679	2680	2681	2682	2683	2684	2685	2686	2687
A80	2688	2689	2690	2691	2692	2693	2694	2695	2696	2697	2698	2699	2700	2701	2702	2703
A90	2704	2705	2706	2707	2708	2709	2710	2711	2712	2713	2714	2715	2716	2717	2718	2719
AA0	2720	2721	2722	2723	2724	2725	2726	2727	2728	2729	2730	2731	2732	2733	2734	2735
Ab0	2736	2737	2738	2739	2740	2741	2742	2743	2744	2745	2746	2747	2748	2749	2750	2751
AC0	2752	2753	2754	2755	2756	2757	2758	2759	2760	2761	2762	2763	2764	2765	2766	2767
AD0	2768	2769	2770	2771	2772	2773	2774	2775	2776	2777	2778	2779	2780	2781	2782	2783
AE0	2784	2785	2786	2787	2788	2789	2790	2791	2792	2793	2794	2795	2796	2797	2798	2799
AF0	2800	2801	2802	2803	2804	2805	2806	2807	2808	2809	2810	2811	2812	2813	2814	2815
B00	2816	2817	2818	2819	2820	2821	2822	2823	2824	2825	2826	2827	2828	2829	2830	2831
B10	2832	2833	2834	2835	2836	2837	2838	2839	2840	2841	2842	2843	2844	2845	2846	2847
B20	2848	2849	2850	2851	2852	2853	2854	2855	2856	2857	2858	2859	2860	2861	2862	2863
B30	2864	2865	2866	2867	2868	2869	2870	2871	2872	2873	2874	2875	2876	2877	2878	2879
B40	2880	2881	2882	2883	2884	2885	2886	2887	2888	2889	2890	2891	2892	2893	2894	2895
B50	2896	2897	2898	2899	2900	2901	2902	2903	2904	2905	2906	2907	2908	2909	2910	2911
B60	2912	2913	2914	2915	2916	2917	2918	2919	2920	2921	2922	2923	2924	2925	2926	2927
B70	2928	2929	2930	2931	2932	2933	2934	2935	2936	2937	2938	2939	2940	2941	2942	2943
B80	2944	2945	2946	2947	2948	2949	2950	2951	2952	2953	2954	2955	2956	2957	2958	2959
B90	2960	2961	2962	2963	2964	2965	2966	2967	2968	2969	2970	2971	2972	2973	2974	2975
BA0	2976	2977	2978	2979	2980	2981	2982	2983	2984	2985	2986	2987	2988	2989	2990	2991
BB0	2992	2993	2994	2995	2996	2997	2998	2999	3000	3001	3002	3003	3004	3005	3006	3007
BC0	3008	3009	3010	3011	3012	3013	3014	3015	3016	3017	3018	3019	3020	3021	3022	3023
BD0	3024	3025	3026	3027	3028	3029	3030	3031	3032	3033	3034	3035	3036	3037	3038	3039
BE0	3040	3041	3042	3043	3044	3045	3046	3047	3048	3049	3050	3051	3052	3053	3054	3055
BF0	3056	3057	3058	3059	3060	3061	3062	3063	3064	3065	3066	3067	3068	3069	3070	3071

	0	1	2	3	4	5	6	7	8	9	A	B	C	D	E	F
C00	3072	3073	3074	3075	3076	3077	3078	3079	3080	3081	3082	3083	3084	3085	3086	3087
C10	3088	3089	3090	3091	3092	3093	3094	3095	3096	3097	3098	3099	3100	3101	3102	3103
C20	3104	3105	3106	3107	3108	3109	3110	3111	3112	3113	3114	3115	3116	3117	3118	3119
C30	3120	3121	3122	3123	3124	3125	3126	3127	3128	3129	3130	3131	3132	3133	3134	3135
C40	3136	3137	3138	3139	3140	3141	3142	3143	3144	3145	3146	3147	3148	3149	3150	3151
C50	3152	3153	3154	3155	3156	3157	3158	3159	3160	3161	3162	3163	3164	3165	3166	3167
C60	3168	3169	3170	3171	3172	3173	3174	3175	3176	3177	3178	3179	3180	3181	3182	3183
C70	3184	3185	3186	3187	3188	3189	3190	3191	3192	3193	3194	3195	3196	3197	3198	3199
C80	3200	3201	3202	3203	3204	3205	3206	3207	3208	3209	3210	3211	3212	3213	3214	3215
C90	3216	3217	3218	3219	3220	3221	3222	3223	3224	3225	3226	3227	3228	3229	3230	3231
CA0	3232	3233	3234	3235	3236	3237	3238	3239	3240	3241	3242	3243	3244	3245	3246	3247
CB0	3248	3249	3250	3251	3252	3253	3254	3255	3256	3257	3258	3259	3260	3261	3262	3263
CC0	3264	3265	3266	3267	3268	3269	3270	3271	3272	3273	3274	3275	3276	3277	3278	3279
CD0	3280	3281	3282	3283	3284	3285	3286	3287	3288	3289	3290	3291	3292	3293	3294	3295
CE0	3296	3297	3298	3299	3300	3301	3302	3303	3304	3305	3306	3307	3308	3309	3310	3311
CF0	3312	3313	3314	3315	3316	3317	3318	3319	3320	3321	3322	3323	3324	3325	3326	3327
D00	3328	3329	3330	3331	3332	3333	3334	3335	3336	3337	3338	3339	3340	3341	3342	3343
D10	3344	3345	3346	3347	3348	3349	3350	3351	3352	3353	3354	3355	3356	3357	3358	3359
D20	3360	3361	3362	3363	3364	3365	3366	3367	3368	3369	3370	3371	3372	3373	3374	3375
D30	3376	3377	3378	3379	3380	3381	3382	3383	3384	3385	3386	3387	3388	3389	3390	3391
D40	3392	3393	3394	3395	3396	3397	3398	3399	3400	3401	3402	3403	3404	3405	3406	3407
D50	3408	3409	3410	3411	3412	3413	3414	3415	3416	3417	3418	3419	3420	3421	3422	3423
D60	3424	3425	3426	3427	3428	3429	3430	3431	3432	3433	3434	3435	3436	3437	3438	3439
D70	3440	3441	3442	3443	3444	3445	3446	3447	3448	3449	3450	3451	3452	3453	3454	3455
D80	3456	3457	3458	3459	3460	3461	3462	3463	3464	3465	3466	3467	3468	3469	3470	3471
D90	3472	3473	3474	3475	3476	3477	3478	3479	3480	3481	3482	3483	3484	3485	3486	3487
DA0	3488	3489	3490	3491	3492	3493	3494	3495	3496	3497	3498	3499	3500	3501	3502	3503
DB0	3504	3505	3506	3507	3508	3509	3510	3511	3512	3513	3514	3515	3516	3517	3518	3519
DC0	3520	3521	3522	3523	3524	3525	3526	3527	3528	3529	3530	3531	3532	3533	3534	3535
DD0	3536	3537	3538	3539	3540	3541	3542	3543	3544	3545	3546	3547	3548	3549	3550	3551
DE0	3552	3553	3554	3555	3556	3557	3558	3559	3560	3561	3562	3563	3564	3565	3566	3567
DF0	3568	3569	3570	3571	3572	3573	3574	3575	3576	3577	3578	3579	3580	3581	3582	3583
E00	3584	3585	3586	3587	3588	3589	3590	3591	3592	3593	3594	3595	3596	3597	3598	3599
E10	3600	3601	3602	3603	3604	3605	3606	3607	3608	3609	3610	3611	3612	3613	3614	3615
E20	3616	3617	3618	3619	3620	3621	3622	3623	3624	3625	3626	3627	3628	3629	3630	3631
E30	3632	3633	3634	3635	3636	3637	3638	3639	3640	3641	3642	3643	3644	3645	3646	3647
E40	3648	3649	3650	3651	3652	3653	3654	3655	3656	3657	3658	3659	3660	3661	3662	3663
E50	3664	3665	3666	3667	3668	3669	3670	3671	3672	3673	3674	3675	3676	3677	3678	3679
E60	3680	3681	3682	3683	3684	3685	3686	3687	3688	3689	3690	3691	3692	3693	3694	3695
E70	3696	3697	3698	3699	3700	3701	3702	3703	3704	3705	3706	3707	3708	3709	3710	3711
E80	3712	3713	3714	3715	3716	3717	3718	3719	3720	3721	3722	3723	3724	3725	3726	3727
E90	3728	3729	3730	3731	3732	3733	3734	3735	3736	3737	3738	3739	3740	3741	3742	3743
EA0	3744	3745	3746	3747	3748	3749	3750	3751	3752	3753	3754	3755	3756	3757	3758	3759
EB0	3760	3761	3762	3763	3764	3765	3766	3767	3768	3769	3770	3771	3772	3773	3774	3775

	0	1	2	3	4	5	6	7	8	9	A	B	C	D	E	F
EC0	3776	3777	3778	3779	3780	3781	3782	3783	3784	3785	3786	3787	3788	3789	3790	3791
ED0	3792	3793	3794	3795	3796	3797	3798	3799	3800	3801	3802	3803	3804	3805	3806	3807
EE0	3808	3809	3810	3811	3812	3813	3814	3815	3816	3817	3818	3819	3820	3821	3822	3823
EF0	3824	3825	3826	3827	3828	3829	3830	3831	3832	3833	3834	3835	3836	3837	3838	3839
F00	3840	3841	3842	3843	3844	3845	3846	3847	3848	3849	3850	3851	3852	3853	3854	3855
F10	3856	3857	3858	3859	3860	3861	3862	3863	3864	3865	3866	3867	3868	3869	3870	3871
F20	3872	3873	3874	3875	3876	3877	3878	3879	3880	3881	3882	3883	3884	3885	3886	3887
F30	3888	3889	3890	3891	3892	3893	3894	3895	3896	3897	3898	3899	3900	3901	3902	3903
F40	3904	3905	3906	3907	3908	3909	3910	3911	3912	3913	3914	3915	3916	3917	3918	3919
F50	3920	3921	3922	3923	3924	3925	3926	3927	3928	3929	3930	3931	3932	3933	3934	3935
F60	3936	3937	3938	3939	3940	3941	3942	3943	3944	3945	3946	3947	3948	3949	3950	3951
F70	3952	3953	3954	3955	3956	3957	3958	3959	3960	3961	3962	3963	3964	3965	3966	3967
F80	3968	3969	3970	3971	3972	3973	3974	3975	3976	3977	3978	3979	3980	3981	3982	3983
F90	3984	3985	3986	3987	3988	3989	3990	3991	3992	3993	3994	3995	3996	3997	3998	3999
FA0	4000	4001	4002	4003	4004	4005	4006	4007	4008	4009	4010	4011	4012	4013	4014	4015
FB0	4016	4017	4018	4019	4020	4021	4022	4023	4024	4025	4026	4027	4028	4029	4030	4031
FC0	4032	4033	4034	4035	4036	4037	4038	4039	4040	4041	4042	4043	4044	4045	4046	4047
FD0	4048	4049	4050	4051	4052	4053	4054	4055	4056	4057	4058	4059	4060	4061	4062	4063
FE0	4064	4065	4066	4067	4068	4069	4070	4071	4072	4073	4074	4075	4076	4077	4078	4079
FF0	4080	4081	4082	4083	4084	4085	4086	4087	4088	4089	4090	4091	4092	4093	4094	4095

HEXADECIMAL–DECIMAL FRACTION CONVERSION TABLE

Hexadecimal	Decimal	Hexadecimal	Decimal	Hexadecimal	Decimal	Hexadecimal	Decimal
.00 00 00 00	.00000 00000	.40 00 00 00	.25000 00000	.80 00 00 00	.50000 00000	.C0 00 00 00	.75000 00000
.01 00 00 00	.00390 62500	.41 00 00 00	.25390 62500	.81 00 00 00	.50390 62500	.C1 00 00 00	.75390 62500
.02 00 00 00	.00781 25000	.42 00 00 00	.25781 25000	.82 00 00 00	.50781 25000	.C2 00 00 00	.75781 25000
.03 00 00 00	.01171 87500	.43 00 00 00	.26171 87500	.83 00 00 00	.51171 87500	.C3 00 00 00	.76171 87500
.04 00 00 00	.01562 50000	.44 00 00 00	.26562 50000	.84 00 00 00	.51562 50000	.C4 00 00 00	.76562 50000
.05 00 00 00	.01953 12500	.45 00 00 00	.26953 12500	.85 00 00 00	.51953 12500	.C5 00 00 00	.76953 12500
.06 00 00 00	.02343 75000	.46 00 00 00	.27343 75000	.86 00 00 00	.52343 75000	.C6 00 00 00	.77343 75000
.07 00 00 00	.02734 37500	.47 00 00 00	.27734 37500	.87 00 00 00	.52734 37500	.C7 00 00 00	.77734 37500
.08 00 00 00	.03125 00000	.48 00 00 00	.28125 00000	.88 00 00 00	.53125 00000	.C8 00 00 00	.78125 00000
.09 00 00 00	.03515 62500	.49 00 00 00	.28515 62500	.89 00 00 00	.53515 62500	.C9 00 00 00	.78515 62500
.0A 00 00 00	.03906 25000	.4A 00 00 00	.28906 25000	.8A 00 00 00	.53906 25000	.CA 00 00 00	.78906 25000
.0B 00 00 00	.04296 87500	.4B 00 00 00	.29296 87500	.8B 00 00 00	.54296 87500	.CB 00 00 00	.79296 87500
.0C 00 00 00	.04687 50000	.4C 00 00 00	.29687 50000	.8C 00 00 00	.54687 50000	.CC 00 00 00	.79687 50000
.0D 00 00 00	.05078 12500	.4D 00 00 00	.30078 12500	.8D 00 00 00	.55078 12500	.CD 00 00 00	.80078 12500
.0E 00 00 00	.05468 75000	.4E 00 00 00	.30468 75000	.8E 00 00 00	.55468 75000	.CE 00 00 00	.80468 75000
.0F 00 00 00	.05859 37500	.4F 00 00 00	.30859 37500	.8F 00 00 00	.55859 37500	.CF 00 00 00	.80859 37500
.10 00 00 00	.06250 00000	.50 00 00 00	.31250 00000	.90 00 00 00	.56250 00000	.D0 00 00 00	.81250 00000
.11 00 00 00	.06640 62500	.51 00 00 00	.31640 62500	.91 00 00 00	.56640 62500	.D1 00 00 00	.81640 62500
.12 00 00 00	.07031 25000	.52 00 00 00	.32031 25000	.92 00 00 00	.57031 25000	.D2 00 00 00	.82031 25000
.13 00 00 00	.07421 87500	.53 00 00 00	.32421 87500	.93 00 00 00	.57421 87500	.D3 00 00 00	.82421 87500
.14 00 00 00	.07812 50000	.54 00 00 00	.32812 50000	.94 00 00 00	.57812 50000	.D4 00 00 00	.82812 50000
.15 00 00 00	.08203 12500	.55 00 00 00	.33203 12500	.95 00 00 00	.58203 12500	.D5 00 00 00	.83203 12500
.16 00 00 00	.08593 75000	.56 00 00 00	.33593 75000	.96 00 00 00	.58593 75000	.D6 00 00 00	.83593 75000
.17 00 00 00	.08984 37500	.57 00 00 00	.33984 37500	.97 00 00 00	.58984 37500	.D7 00 00 00	.83984 37500
.18 00 00 00	.09375 00000	.58 00 00 00	.34375 00000	.98 00 00 00	.59375 00000	.D8 00 00 00	.84375 00000
.19 00 00 00	.09765 62500	.59 00 00 00	.34765 62500	.99 00 00 00	.59765 62500	.D9 00 00 00	.84765 62500
.1A 00 00 00	.10156 25000	.5A 00 00 00	.35156 25000	.9A 00 00 00	.60156 25000	.DA 00 00 00	.85156 25000
.1B 00 00 00	.10546 87500	.5B 00 00 00	.35546 87500	.9B 00 00 00	.60546 87500	.DB 00 00 00	.85546 87500
.1C 00 00 00	.10937 50000	.5C 00 00 00	.35937 50000	.9C 00 00 00	.60937 50000	.DC 00 00 00	.85937 50000
.1D 00 00 00	.11328 12500	.5D 00 00 00	.36328 12500	.9D 00 00 00	.61328 12500	.DD 00 00 00	.86328 12500
.1E 00 00 00	.11718 75000	.5E 00 00 00	.36718 75000	.9E 00 00 00	.61718 75000	.DE 00 00 00	.86718 75000
.1F 00 00 00	.12109 37500	.5F 00 00 00	.37109 37500	.9F 00 00 00	.62109 37500	.DF 00 00 00	.87109 37500
.20 00 00 00	.12500 00000	.60 00 00 00	.37500 00000	.A0 00 00 00	.62500 00000	.E0 00 00 00	.87500 00000
.21 00 00 00	.12890 62500	.61 00 00 00	.37890 62500	.A1 00 00 00	.62890 62500	.E1 00 00 00	.87890 62500
.22 00 00 00	.13281 25000	.62 00 00 00	.38281 25000	.A2 00 00 00	.63281 25000	.E2 00 00 00	.88281 25000
.23 00 00 00	.13671 87500	.63 00 00 00	.38671 87500	.A3 00 00 00	.63671 87500	.E3 00 00 00	.88671 87500
.24 00 00 00	.14062 50000	.64 00 00 00	.39062 50000	.A4 00 00 00	.64062 50000	.E4 00 00 00	.89062 50000
.25 00 00 00	.14453 12500	.65 00 00 00	.39453 12500	.A5 00 00 00	.64453 12500	.E5 00 00 00	.89453 12500
.26 00 00 00	.14843 75000	.66 00 00 00	.39843 75000	.A6 00 00 00	.64843 75000	.E6 00 00 00	.89843 75000
.27 00 00 00	.15234 37500	.67 00 00 00	.40234 37500	.A7 00 00 00	.65234 37500	.E7 00 00 00	.90234 37500
.28 00 00 00	.15625 00000	.68 00 00 00	.40625 00000	.A8 00 00 00	.65625 00000	.E8 00 00 00	.90625 00000
.29 00 00 00	.16015 62500	.69 00 00 00	.41015 62500	.A9 00 00 00	.66015 62500	.E9 00 00 00	.91015 62500
.2A 00 00 00	.16406 25000	.6A 00 00 00	.41406 25000	.AA 00 00 00	.66406 25000	.EA 00 00 00	.91406 25000
.2B 00 00 00	.16796 87500	.6B 00 00 00	.41796 87500	.AB 00 00 00	.66796 87500	.EB 00 00 00	.91796 87500
.2C 00 00 00	.17187 50000	.6C 00 00 00	.42187 50000	.AC 00 00 00	.67187 50000	.EC 00 00 00	.92187 50000
.2D 00 00 00	.17578 12500	.6D 00 00 00	.42578 12500	.AD 00 00 00	.67578 12500	.ED 00 00 00	.92578 12500
.2E 00 00 00	.17968 75000	.6E 00 00 00	.42968 75000	.AE 00 00 00	.67968 75000	.EE 00 00 00	.92968 75000
.2F 00 00 00	.18359 37500	.6F 00 00 00	.43359 37500	.AF 00 00 00	.68359 37500	.EF 00 00 00	.93359 37500
.30 00 00 00	.18750 00000	.70 00 00 00	.43750 00000	.B0 00 00 00	.68750 00000	.F0 00 00 00	.93750 00000
.31 00 00 00	.19140 62500	.71 00 00 00	.44140 62500	.B1 00 00 00	.69140 62500	.F1 00 00 00	.94140 62500
.32 00 00 00	.19531 25000	.72 00 00 00	.44531 25000	.B2 00 00 00	.69531 25000	.F2 00 00 00	.94531 25000
.33 00 00 00	.19921 87500	.73 00 00 00	.44921 87500	.B3 00 00 00	.69921 87500	.F3 00 00 00	.94921 87500
.34 00 00 00	.20312 50000	.74 00 00 00	.45312 50000	.B4 00 00 00	.70312 50000	.F4 00 00 00	.95312 50000
.35 00 00 00	.20703 12500	.75 00 00 00	.45703 12500	.B5 00 00 00	.70703 12500	.F5 00 00 00	.95703 12500
.36 00 00 00	.21093 75000	.76 00 00 00	.46093 75000	.B6 00 00 00	.71093 75000	.F6 00 00 00	.96093 75000
.37 00 00 00	.21484 37500	.77 00 00 00	.46484 37500	.B7 00 00 00	.71484 37500	.F7 00 00 00	.96484 37500
.38 00 00 00	.21875 00000	.78 00 00 00	.46875 00000	.B8 00 00 00	.71875 00000	.F8 00 00 00	.96875 00000
.39 00 00 00	.22265 62500	.79 00 00 00	.47265 62500	.B9 00 00 00	.72265 62500	.F9 00 00 00	.97265 62500
.3A 00 00 00	.22656 25000	.7A 00 00 00	.47656 25000	.BA 00 00 00	.72656 25000	.FA 00 00 00	.97656 25000
.3B 00 00 00	.23046 87500	.7B 00 00 00	.48046 87500	.BB 00 00 00	.73046 87500	.FB 00 00 00	.98046 87500
.3C 00 00 00	.23437 50000	.7C 00 00 00	.48437 50000	.BC 00 00 00	.73437 50000	.FC 00 00 00	.98437 50000
.3D 00 00 00	.23828 12500	.7D 00 00 00	.48828 12500	.BD 00 00 00	.73828 12500	.FD 00 00 00	.98828 12500
.3E 00 00 00	.24218 75000	.7E 00 00 00	.49218 75000	.BE 00 00 00	.74218 75000	.FE 00 00 00	.99218 75000
.3F 00 00 00	.24609 37500	.7F 00 00 00	.49609 37500	.BF 00 00 00	.74609 37500	.FF 00 00 00	.99609 37500

HEXADECIMAL–DECIMAL FRACTION CONVERSION TABLE (cont.)

Hexadecimal	Decimal	Hexadecimal	Decimal	Hexadecimal	Decimal	Hexadecimal	Decimal
.00 00 00 00	.00000 00000	.00 40 00 00	.00097 65625	.00 80 00 00	.00195 31250	.00 C0 00 00	.00292 96875
.00 01 00 00	.00001 52587	.00 41 00 00	.00099 18212	.00 81 00 00	.00196 83837	.00 C1 00 00	.00294 49462
.00 02 00 00	.00003 05175	.00 42 00 00	.00100 70800	.00 82 00 00	.00198 36425	.00 C2 00 00	.00296 02050
.00 03 00 00	.00004 57763	.00 43 00 00	.00102 23388	.00 83 00 00	.00199 89013	.00 C3 00 00	.00297 54638
.00 04 00 00	.00006 10351	.00 44 00 00	.00103 75976	.00 84 00 00	.00201 41601	.00 C4 00 00	.00299 07226
.00 05 00 00	.00007 62939	.00 45 00 00	.00105 28564	.00 85 00 00	.00202 94189	.00 C5 00 00	.00300 59814
.00 06 00 00	.00009 15527	.00 46 00 00	.00106 81152	.00 86 00 00	.00204 46777	.00 C6 00 00	.00302 12402
.00 07 00 00	.00010 68115	.00 47 00 00	.00108 33740	.00 87 00 00	.00205 99365	.00 C7 00 00	.00303 64990
.00 08 00 00	.00012 20703	.00 48 00 00	.00109 86328	.00 88 00 00	.00207 51953	.00 C8 00 00	.00305 17578
.00 09 00 00	.00013 73291	.00 49 00 00	.00111 38916	.00 89 00 00	.00209 04541	.00 C9 00 00	.00306 70166
.00 0A 00 00	.00015 25878	.00 4A 00 00	.00112 91503	.00 8A 00 00	.00210 57128	.00 CA 00 00	.00308 22753
.00 0B 00 00	.00016 78466	.00 4B 00 00	.00114 44091	.00 8B 00 00	.00212 09716	.00 CB 00 00	.00309 75341
.00 0C 00 00	.00018 31054	.00 4C 00 00	.00115 96679	.00 8C 00 00	.00213 62304	.00 CC 00 00	.00311 27929
.00 0D 00 00	.00019 83642	.00 4D 00 00	.00117 49267	.00 8D 00 00	.00215 14892	.00 CD 00 00	.00312 80517
.00 0E 00 00	.00021 36230	.00 4E 00 00	.00119 01855	.00 8E 00 00	.00216 67480	.00 CE 00 00	.00314 33105
.00 0F 00 00	.00022 88818	.00 4F 00 00	.00120 54443	.00 8F 00 00	.00218 20068	.00 CF 00 00	.00315 85693
.00 10 00 00	.00024 41406	.00 50 00 00	.00122 07031	.00 90 00 00	.00219 72656	.00 D0 00 00	.00317 38281
.00 11 00 00	.00025 93994	.00 51 00 00	.00123 59619	.00 91 00 00	.00221 25244	.00 D1 00 00	.00318 90869
.00 12 00 00	.00027 46582	.00 52 00 00	.00125 12207	.00 92 00 00	.00222 77832	.00 D2 00 00	.00320 43457
.00 13 00 00	.00028 99169	.00 53 00 00	.00126 64794	.00 93 00 00	.00224 30419	.00 D3 00 00	.00321 96044
.00 14 00 00	.00030 51757	.00 54 00 00	.00128 17382	.00 94 00 00	.00225 83007	.00 D4 00 00	.00323 48632
.00 15 00 00	.00032 04345	.00 55 00 00	.00129 69970	.00 95 00 00	.00227 35595	.00 D5 00 00	.00325 01220
.00 16 00 00	.00033 56933	.00 56 00 00	.00131 22558	.00 96 00 00	.00228 88183	.00 D6 00 00	.00326 53808
.00 17 00 00	.00035 09521	.00 57 00 00	.00132 75146	.00 97 00 00	.00230 40771	.00 D7 00 00	.00328 06396
.00 18 00 00	.00036 62109	.00 58 00 00	.00134 27734	.00 98 00 00	.00231 93359	.00 D8 00 00	.00329 58984
.00 19 00 00	.00038 14697	.00 59 00 00	.00135 80322	.00 99 00 00	.00233 45947	.00 D9 00 00	.00331 11572
.00 1A 00 00	.00039 67285	.00 5A 00 00	.00137 32910	.00 9A 00 00	.00234 98535	.00 DA 00 00	.00332 64160
.00 1B 00 00	.00041 19873	.00 5B 00 00	.00138 85498	.00 9B 00 00	.00236 51123	.00 DB 00 00	.00334 16748
.00 1C 00 00	.00042 72460	.00 5C 00 00	.00140 38085	.00 9C 00 00	.00238 03710	.00 DC 00 00	.00335 69335
.00 1D 00 00	.00044 25048	.00 5D 00 00	.00141 90673	.00 9D 00 00	.00239 56298	.00 DD 00 00	.00337 21923
.00 1E 00 00	.00045 77636	.00 5E 00 00	.00143 43261	.00 9E 00 00	.00241 08886	.00 DE 00 00	.00338 74511
.00 1F 00 00	.00047 30224	.00 5F 00 00	.00144 95849	.00 9F 00 00	.00242 61474	.00 DF 00 00	.00340 27099
.00 20 00 00	.00048 82812	.00 60 00 00	.00146 48437	.00 A0 00 00	.00244 14062	.00 E0 00 00	.00341 79687
.00 21 00 00	.00050 35400	.00 61 00 00	.00148 01025	.00 A1 00 00	.00245 66650	.00 E1 00 00	.00343 32275
.00 22 00 00	.00051 87988	.00 62 00 00	.00149 53613	.00 A2 00 00	.00247 19238	.00 E2 00 00	.00344 84863
.00 23 00 00	.00053 40576	.00 63 00 00	.00151 06201	.00 A3 00 00	.00248 71826	.00 E3 00 00	.00346 37451
.00 24 00 00	.00054 93164	.00 64 00 00	.00152 58789	.00 A4 00 00	.00250 24414	.00 E4 00 00	.00347 90039
.00 25 00 00	.00056 45751	.00 65 00 00	.00154 11376	.00 A5 00 00	.00251 77001	.00 E5 00 00	.00349 42626
.00 26 00 00	.00057 98339	.00 66 00 00	.00155 63964	.00 A6 00 00	.00253 29589	.00 E6 00 00	.00350 95214
.00 27 00 00	.00059 50927	.00 67 00 00	.00157 16552	.00 A7 00 00	.00254 82177	.00 E7 00 00	.00352 47802
.00 28 00 00	.00061 03515	.00 68 00 00	.00158 69140	.00 A8 00 00	.00256 34765	.00 E8 00 00	.00354 00390
.00 29 00 00	.00062 56103	.00 69 00 00	.00160 21728	.00 A9 00 00	.00257 87353	.00 E9 00 00	.00355 52978
.00 2A 00 00	.00064 08691	.00 6A 00 00	.00161 74316	.00 AA 00 00	.00259 39941	.00 EA 00 00	.00357 05566
.00 2B 00 00	.00065 61279	.00 6B 00 00	.00163 26904	.00 AB 00 00	.00260 92529	.00 EB 00 00	.00358 58154
.00 2C 00 00	.00067 13867	.00 6C 00 00	.00164 79492	.00 AC 00 00	.00262 45117	.00 EC 00 00	.00360 10742
.00 2D 00 00	.00068 66455	.00 6D 00 00	.00166 32080	.00 AD 00 00	.00263 97705	.00 ED 00 00	.00361 63330
.00 2E 00 00	.00070 19042	.00 6E 00 00	.00167 84667	.00 AE 00 00	.00265 50292	.00 EE 00 00	.00363 15917
.00 2F 00 00	.00071 71630	.00 6F 00 00	.00169 37255	.00 AF 00 00	.00267 02880	.00 EF 00 00	.00364 68505
.00 30 00 00	.00073 24218	.00 70 00 00	.00170 89843	.00 B0 00 00	.00268 55468	.00 F0 00 00	.00366 21093
.00 31 00 00	.00074 76806	.00 71 00 00	.00172 42421	.00 B1 00 00	.00270 08056	.00 F1 00 00	.00367 73681
.00 32 00 00	.00076 29394	.00 72 00 00	.00173 95019	.00 B2 00 00	.00271 60644	.00 F2 00 00	.00369 26269
.00 33 00 00	.00077 81982	.00 73 00 00	.00175 47607	.00 B3 00 00	.00273 13232	.00 F3 00 00	.00370 78857
.00 34 00 00	.00079 34570	.00 74 00 00	.00177 00195	.00 B4 00 00	.00274 65820	.00 F4 00 00	.00372 31445
.00 35 00 00	.00080 87158	.00 75 00 00	.00178 52783	.00 B5 00 00	.00276 18408	.00 F5 00 00	.00373 84033
.00 36 00 00	.00082 39746	.00 76 00 00	.00180 05371	.00 B6 00 00	.00277 70996	.00 F6 00 00	.00375 36621
.00 37 00 00	.00083 92333	.00 77 00 00	.00181 57958	.00 B7 00 00	.00279 23583	.00 F7 00 00	.00376 89208
.00 38 00 00	.00085 44921	.00 78 00 00	.00183 10546	.00 B8 00 00	.00280 76171	.00 F8 00 00	.00378 41796
.00 39 00 00	.00086 97509	.00 79 00 00	.00184 63134	.00 B9 00 00	.00282 28759	.00 F9 00 00	.00379 94384
.00 3A 00 00	.00088 50097	.00 7A 00 00	.00186 15722	.00 BA 00 00	.00283 81347	.00 FA 00 00	.00381 46972
.00 3B 00 00	.00090 02685	.00 7B 00 00	.00187 68310	.00 BB 00 00	.00285 33935	.00 FB 00 00	.00382 99560
.00 3C 00 00	.00091 55273	.00 7C 00 00	.00189 20898	.00 BC 00 00	.00286 86523	.00 FC 00 00	.00384 52148
.00 3D 00 00	.00093 07861	.00 7D 00 00	.00190 73486	.00 BD 00 00	.00288 39111	.00 FD 00 00	.00386 04736
.00 3E 00 00	.00094 60449	.00 7E 00 00	.00192 26074	.00 BE 00 00	.00289 91699	.00 FE 00 00	.00387 57324
.00 3F 00 00	.00096 13037	.00 7F 00 00	.00193 78662	.00 BF 00 00	.00291 44287	.00 FF 00 00	.00389 09912

Hexadecimal	Decimal	Hexadecimal	Decimal	Hexadecimal	Decimal	Hexadecimal	Decimal
.00 00 00 00	.00000 00000	.00 00 40 00	.00000 38146	.00 00 80 00	.00000 76293	.00 00 C0 00	.00001 14440
.00 00 01 00	.00000 00596	.00 00 41 00	.00000 38743	.00 00 81 00	.00000 76889	.00 00 C1 00	.00001 15036
.00 00 02 00	.00000 01192	.00 00 42 00	.00000 39339	.00 00 82 00	.00000 77486	.00 00 C2 00	.00001 15633
.00 00 03 00	.00000 01788	.00 00 43 00	.00000 39935	.00 00 83 00	.00000 78082	.00 00 C3 00	.00001 16229
.00 00 04 00	.00000 02384	.00 00 44 00	.00000 40531	.00 00 84 00	.00000 78678	.00 00 C4 00	.00001 16825
.00 00 05 00	.00000 02980	.00 00 45 00	.00000 41127	.00 00 85 00	.00000 79274	.00 00 C5 00	.00001 17421
.00 00 06 00	.00000 03576	.00 00 46 00	.00000 41723	.00 00 86 00	.00000 79870	.00 00 C6 00	.00001 18017
.00 00 07 00	.00000 04172	.00 00 47 00	.00000 42319	.00 00 87 00	.00000 80466	.00 00 C7 00	.00001 18613
.00 00 08 00	.00000 04768	.00 00 48 00	.00000 42915	.00 00 88 00	.00000 81062	.00 00 C8 00	.00001 19209
.00 00 09 00	.00000 05364	.00 00 49 00	.00000 43511	.00 00 89 00	.00000 81658	.00 00 C9 00	.00001 19805
.00 00 0A 00	.00000 05960	.00 00 4A 00	.00000 44107	.00 00 8A 00	.00000 82254	.00 00 CA 00	.00001 20401
.00 00 0B 00	.00000 06556	.00 00 4B 00	.00000 44703	.00 00 8B 00	.00000 82850	.00 00 CB 00	.00001 20997
.00 00 0C 00	.00000 07152	.00 00 4C 00	.00000 45299	.00 00 8C 00	.00000 83446	.00 00 CC 00	.00001 21593
.00 00 0D 00	.00000 07748	.00 00 4D 00	.00000 45895	.00 00 8D 00	.00000 84042	.00 00 CD 00	.00001 22189
.00 00 0E 00	.00000 08344	.00 00 4E 00	.00000 46491	.00 00 8E 00	.00000 84638	.00 00 CE 00	.00001 22785
.00 00 0F 00	.00000 08940	.00 00 4F 00	.00000 47087	.00 00 8F 00	.00000 85234	.00 0C CF 00	.00001 23381
.00 00 10 00	.00000 09536	.00 00 50 00	.00000 47683	.00 00 90 00	.00000 85830	.00 00 D0 00	.00001 23977
.00 00 11 00	.00000 10132	.00 00 51 00	.00000 48279	.00 00 91 00	.00000 86426	.00 00 D1 00	.00001 24573
.00 00 12 00	.00000 10728	.00 00 52 00	.00000 48875	.00 00 92 00	.00000 87022	.00 00 D2 00	.00001 25169
.00 00 13 00	.00000 11324	.00 00 53 00	.00000 49471	.00 00 93 00	.00000 87618	.00 00 D3 00	.00001 25765
.00 00 14 00	.00000 11920	.00 00 54 00	.00000 50067	.00 00 94 00	.00000 88214	.00 00 D4 00	.00001 26361
.00 00 15 00	.00000 12516	.00 00 55 00	.00000 50663	.00 00 95 00	.00000 88810	.00 00 D5 00	.00001 26957
.00 00 16 00	.00000 13113	.00 00 56 00	.00000 51259	.00 00 96 00	.00000 89406	.00 00 D6 00	.00001 27553
.00 00 17 00	.00000 13709	.00 00 57 00	.00000 51856	.00 00 97 00	.00000 90003	.00 00 D7 00	.00001 28149
.00 00 18 00	.00000 14305	.00 00 58 00	.00000 52452	.00 00 98 00	.00000 90599	.00 00 D8 00	.00001 28746
.00 00 19 00	.00000 14901	.00 00 59 00	.00000 53048	.00 00 99 00	.00000 91195	.00 00 D9 00	.00001 29342
.00 00 1A 00	.00000 15497	.00 00 5A 00	.00000 53644	.00 00 9A 00	.00000 91791	.00 00 DA 00	.00001 29938
.00 00 1B 00	.00000 16093	.00 00 5B 00	.00000 54240	.00 00 9B 00	.00000 92387	.00 00 DB 00	.00001 30534
.00 00 1C 00	.00000 16689	.00 00 5C 00	.00000 54836	.00 00 9C 00	.00000 92983	.00 00 DC 00	.00001 31130
.00 00 1D 00	.00000 17285	.00 00 5D 00	.00000 55432	.00 00 9D 00	.00000 93579	.00 00 DD 00	.00001 31726
.00 00 1E 00	.00000 17881	.00 00 5E 00	.00000 56028	.00 00 9E 00	.00000 94175	.00 00 DE 00	.00001 32322
.00 00 1F 00	.00000 18477	.00 00 5F 00	.00000 56624	.00 00 9F 00	.00000 94771	.00 00 DF 00	.00001 32918
.00 00 20 00	.00000 19073	.00 00 60 00	.00000 57220	.00 00 A0 00	.00000 95367	.00 00 E0 00	.00001 33514
.00 00 21 00	.00000 19669	.00 00 61 00	.00000 57816	.00 00 A1 00	.00000 95963	.00 00 E1 00	.00001 34110
.00 00 22 00	.00000 20265	.00 00 62 00	.00000 58412	.00 00 A2 00	.00000 96559	.00 00 E2 00	.00001 34706
.00 00 23 00	.00000 20861	.00 00 63 00	.00000 59008	.00 00 A3 00	.00000 97155	.00 00 E3 00	.00001 35302
.00 00 24 00	.00000 21457	.00 00 64 00	.00000 59604	.00 00 A4 00	.00000 97751	.00 00 E4 00	.00001 35898
.00 00 25 00	.00000 22053	.00 00 65 00	.00000 60200	.00 00 A5 00	.00000 98347	.00 00 E5 00	.00001 36494
.00 00 26 00	.00000 22649	.00 00 66 00	.00000 60796	.00 00 A6 00	.00000 98943	.00 00 E6 00	.00001 37090
.00 00 27 00	.00000 23245	.00 00 67 00	.00000 61392	.00 00 A7 00	.00000 99539	.00 00 E7 00	.00001 37686
.00 00 28 00	.00000 23841	.00 00 68 00	.00000 61988	.00 00 A8 00	.00001 00135	.00 00 E8 00	.00001 38282
.00 00 29 00	.00000 24437	.00 00 69 00	.00000 62584	.00 00 A9 00	.00001 00731	.00 00 E9 00	.00001 38878
.00 00 2A 00	.00000 25033	.00 00 6A 00	.00000 63180	.00 00 AA 00	.00001 01327	.00 00 EA 00	.00001 39474
.00 00 2B 00	.00000 25629	.00 00 6B 00	.00000 63776	.00 00 AB 00	.00001 01923	.00 00 EB 00	.00001 40070
.00 00 2C 00	.00000 26226	.00 00 6C 00	.00000 64373	.00 00 AC 00	.00001 02519	.00 00 EC 00	.00001 40666
.00 00 2D 00	.00000 26822	.00 00 6D 00	.00000 64969	.00 00 AD 00	.00001 03116	.00 00 ED 00	.00001 41263
.00 00 2E 00	.00000 27418	.00 00 6E 00	.00000 65565	.00 00 AE 00	.00001 03712	.00 00 EE 00	.00001 41859
.00 00 2F 00	.00000 28014	.00 00 6F 00	.00000 61661	.00 00 AF 00	.00001 04308	.00 00 EF 00	.00001 42455
.00 00 30 00	.00000 28610	.00 00 70 00	.00000 66757	.00 00 B0 00	.00001 04904	.00 00 F0 00	.00001 43051
.00 00 31 00	.00000 29206	.00 00 71 00	.00000 67353	.00 00 B1 00	.00001 05500	.00 00 F1 00	.00001 43647
.00 00 32 00	.00000 29802	.00 00 72 00	.00000 67949	.00 00 B2 00	.00001 06096	.00 00 F2 00	.00001 44243
.00 00 33 00	.00000 30398	.00 00 73 00	.00000 68545	.00 00 B3 00	.00001 06692	.00 00 F3 00	.00001 44839
.00 00 34 00	.00000 30994	.00 00 74 00	.00000 69141	.00 00 B4 00	.00001 07228	.00 00 F4 00	.00001 45435
.00 00 35 00	.00000 31590	.00 00 75 00	.00000 69737	.00 00 B5 00	.00001 07884	.00 00 F5 00	.00001 46031
.00 00 36 00	.00000 32186	.00 00 76 00	.00000 70333	.00 00 B6 00	.00001 08480	.00 00 F6 00	.00001 46627
.00 00 37 00	.00000 32782	.00 00 77 00	.00000 70929	.00 00 B7 00	.00001 09076	.00 00 F7 00	.00001 47223
.00 00 38 00	.00000 33378	.00 00 78 00	.00000 71525	.00 00 B8 00	.00001 09672	.00 00 F8 00	.00001 47819
.00 00 39 00	.00000 33974	.00 00 79 00	.00000 75121	.00 00 B9 00	.00001 10268	.00 00 F9 00	.00001 48415
.00 00 3A 00	.00000 34570	.00 00 7A 00	.00000 72717	.00 00 BA 00	.00001 10864	.00 00 FA 00	.00001 49011
.00 00 3B 00	.00000 35166	.00 00 7B 00	.00000 73313	.00 00 BB 00	.00001 11460	.00 00 FB 00	.00001 49607
.00 00 3C 00	.00000 35762	.00 00 7C 00	.00000 73909	.00 00 BC 00	.00001 12056	.00 00 FC 00	.00001 50203
.00 00 3D 00	.00000 36358	.00 00 7D 00	.00000 74505	.00 00 BD 00	.00001 12652	.00 00 ED 00	.00001 50799
.00 00 3E 00	.00000 36954	.00 00 7E 00	.00000 75101	.00 00 BE 00	.00001 13248	.00 00 FE 00	.00001 51395
.00 00 3F 00	.00000 37550	.00 00 7F 00	.00000 75697	.00 00 BF 00	.00001 13844	.00 00 FF 00	.00001 51991

HEXADECIMAL–DECIMAL FRACTION CONVERSION TABLE

Hexadecimal	Decimal	Hexadecimal	Decimal	Hexadecimal	Decimal	Hexadecimal	Decimal
.00 00 00 00	.00000 00000	.00 00 00 40	.00000 00149	.00 00 00 80	.00000 00298	.00 00 00 C0	.00000 00447
.00 00 00 01	.00000 00002	.00 00 00 41	.00000 00151	.00 00 00 81	.00000 00300	.00 00 00 C1	.00000 00449
.00 00 00 02	.00000 00004	.00 00 00 42	.00000 00153	.00 00 00 82	.00000 00302	.00 00 00 C2	.00000 00451
.00 00 00 03	.00000 00006	.00 00 00 43	.00000 00155	.00 00 00 83	.00000 00305	.00 00 00 C3	.00000 00454
.00 00 00 04	.00000 00009	.00 00 00 44	.00000 00158	.00 00 00 84	.00000 00307	.00 00 00 C4	.00000 00456
.00 00 00 05	.00000 00011	.00 00 00 45	.00000 00160	.00 00 00 85	.00000 00309	.00 00 00 C5	.00000 00458
.00 00 00 06	.00000 00013	.00 00 00 46	.00000 00162	.00 00 00 86	.00000 00311	.00 00 00 C6	.00000 00461
.00 00 00 07	.00000 00016	.00 00 00 47	.00000 00165	.00 00 00 87	.00000 00314	.00 00 00 C7	.00000 00463
.00 00 00 08	.00000 00018	.00 00 00 48	.00000 00167	.00 00 00 88	.00000 00316	.00 00 00 C8	.00000 00465
.00 00 00 09	.00000 00020	.00 00 00 49	.00000 00169	.00 00 00 89	.00000 00318	.00 00 00 C9	.00000 00467
.00 00 00 0A	.00000 00023	.00 00 00 4A	.00000 00172	.00 00 00 8A	.00000 00321	.00 00 00 CA	.00000 00470
.00 00 00 0B	.00000 00025	.00 00 00 4B	.00000 00174	.00 00 00 8B	.00000 00323	.00 00 00 CB	.00000 00472
.00 00 00 0C	.00000 00027	.00 00 00 4C	.00000 00176	.00 00 00 8C	.00000 00325	.00 00 00 CC	.00000 00474
.00 00 00 0D	.00000 00030	.00 00 00 4D	.00000 00179	.00 00 00 8D	.00000 00328	.00 00 00 CD	.00000 00477
.00 00 00 0E	.00000 00032	.00 00 00 4E	.00000 00181	.00 00 00 8E	.00000 00330	.00 00 00 CE	.00000 00479
.00 00 00 0F	.00000 00034	.00 00 00 4F	.00000 00183	.00 00 00 8F	.00000 00332	.00 00 00 CF	.00000 00481
.00 00 00 10	.00000 00037	.00 00 00 50	.00000 00186	.00 00 00 90	.00000 00335	.00 00 00 D0	.00000 00484
.00 00 00 11	.00000 00039	.00 00 00 51	.00000 00188	.00 00 00 91	.00000 00337	.00 00 00 D1	.00000 00486
.00 00 00 12	.00000 00041	.00 00 00 52	.00000 00190	.00 00 00 92	.00000 00339	.00 00 00 D2	.00000 00488
.00 00 00 13	.00000 00044	.00 00 00 53	.00000 00193	.00 00 00 93	.00000 00342	.00 00 00 D3	.00000 00491
.00 00 00 14	.00000 00046	.00 00 00 54	.00000 00195	.00 00 00 94	.00000 00344	.00 00 00 D4	.00000 00493
.00 00 00 15	.00000 00048	.00 00 00 55	.00000 00197	.00 00 00 95	.00000 00346	.00 00 00 D5	.00000 00495
.00 00 00 16	.00000 00051	.00 00 00 56	.00000 00200	.00 00 00 96	.00000 00349	.00 00 00 D6	.00000 00498
.00 00 00 17	.00000 00053	.00 00 00 57	.00000 00202	.00 00 00 97	.00000 00351	.00 00 00 D7	.00000 00500
.00 00 00 18	.00000 00055	.00 00 00 58	.00000 00204	.00 00 00 98	.00000 00353	.00 00 00 D8	.00000 00502
.00 00 00 19	.00000 00058	.00 00 00 59	.00000 00207	.00 00 00 99	.00000 00356	.00 00 00 D9	.00000 00505
.00 00 00 1A	.00000 00060	.00 00 00 5A	.00000 00209	.00 00 00 9A	.00000 00358	.00 00 00 DA	.00000 00507
.00 00 00 1B	.00000 00062	.00 00 00 5B	.00000 00211	.00 00 00 9B	.00000 00360	.00 00 00 DB	.00000 00509
.00 00 00 1C	.00000 00065	.00 00 00 5C	.00000 00214	.00 00 00 9C	.00000 00363	.00 00 00 DC	.00000 00512
.00 00 00 1D	.00000 00067	.00 00 00 5D	.00000 00216	.00 00 00 9D	.00000 00365	.00 00 00 DD	.00000 00514
.00 00 00 1E	.00000 00069	.00 00 00 5E	.00000 00218	.00 00 00 9E	.00000 00367	.00 00 00 DE	.00000 00516
.00 00 00 1F	.00000 00072	.00 00 00 5F	.00000 00221	.00 00 00 9F	.00000 00370	.00 00 00 DF	.00000 00519
.00 00 00 20	.00000 00074	.00 00 00 60	.00000 00223	.00 00 00 A0	.00000 00372	.00 00 00 E0	.00000 00521
.00 00 00 21	.00000 00076	.00 00 00 61	.00000 00225	.00 00 00 A1	.00000 00374	.00 00 00 E1	.00000 00523
.00 00 00 22	.00000 00079	.00 00 00 62	.00000 00228	.00 00 00 A2	.00000 00377	.00 00 00 E2	.00000 00526
.00 00 00 23	.00000 00081	.00 00 00 63	.00000 00230	.00 00 00 A3	.00000 00379	.00 00 00 E3	.00000 00528
.00 00 00 24	.00000 00083	.00 00 00 64	.00000 00232	.00 00 00 A4	.00000 00381	.00 00 00 E4	.00000 00530
.00 00 00 25	.00000 00086	.00 00 00 65	.00000 00235	.00 00 00 A5	.00000 00384	.00 00 00 E5	.00000 00533
.00 00 00 26	.00000 00088	.00 00 00 66	.00000 00237	.00 00 00 A6	.00000 00386	.00 00 00 E6	.00000 00535
.00 00 00 27	.00000 00090	.00 00 00 67	.00000 00239	.00 00 00 A7	.00000 00388	.00 00 00 E7	.00000 00537
.00 00 00 28	.00000 00093	.00 00 00 68	.00000 00242	.00 00 00 A8	.00000 00391	.00 00 00 E8	.00000 00540
.00 00 00 29	.00000 00095	.00 00 00 69	.00000 00244	.00 00 00 A9	.00000 00393	.00 00 00 E9	.00000 00542
.00 00 00 2A	.00000 00097	.00 00 00 6A	.00000 00246	.00 00 00 AA	.00000 00395	.00 00 00 EA	.00000 00544
.00 00 00 2B	.00000 00100	.00 00 00 6B	.00000 00249	.00 00 00 AB	.00000 00398	.00 00 00 EB	.00000 00547
.00 00 00 2C	.00000 00102	.00 00 00 6C	.00000 00251	.00 00 00 AC	.00000 00400	.00 00 00 EC	.00000 00549
.00 00 00 2D	.00000 00104	.00 00 00 6D	.00000 00253	.00 00 00 AD	.00000 00402	.00 00 00 ED	.00000 00551
.00 00 00 2E	.00000 00107	.00 00 00 6E	.00000 00256	.00 00 00 AE	.00000 00405	.00 00 00 EE	.00000 00554
.00 00 00 2F	.00000 00109	.00 00 00 6F	.00000 00258	.00 00 00 AF	.00000 00407	.00 00 00 EF	.00000 00556
.00 00 00 30	.00000 00111	.00 00 00 70	.00000 00260	.00 00 00 B0	.00000 00409	.00 00 00 F0	.00000 00558
.00 00 00 31	.00000 00114	.00 00 00 71	.00000 00263	.00 00 00 B1	.00000 00412	.00 00 00 F1	.00000 00561
.00 00 00 32	.00000 00116	.00 00 00 72	.00000 00265	.00 00 00 B2	.00000 00414	.00 00 00 F2	.00000 00563
.00 00 00 33	.00000 00118	.00 00 00 73	.00000 00267	.00 00 00 B3	.00000 00416	.00 00 00 F3	.00000 00565
.00 00 00 34	.00000 00121	.00 00 00 74	.00000 00270	.00 00 00 B4	.00000 00419	.00 00 00 F4	.00000 00568
.00 00 00 35	.00000 00123	.00 00 00 75	.00000 00272	.00 00 00 B5	.00000 00421	.00 00 00 F5	.00000 00570
.00 00 00 36	.00000 00125	.00 00 00 76	.00000 00274	.00 00 00 B6	.00000 00423	.00 00 00 F6	.00000 00572
.00 00 00 37	.00000 00128	.00 00 00 77	.00000 00277	.00 00 00 B7	.00000 00426	.00 00 00 F7	.00000 00575
.00 00 00 38	.00000 00130	.00 00 00 78	.00000 00279	.00 00 00 B8	.00000 00428	.00 00 00 F8	.00000 00577
.00 00 00 39	.00000 00132	.00 00 00 79	.00000 00281	.00 00 00 B9	.00000 00430	.00 00 00 F9	.00000 00579
.00 00 00 3A	.00000 00135	.00 00 00 7A	.00000 00284	.00 00 00 BA	.00000 00433	.00 00 00 FA	.00000 00582
.00 00 00 3B	.00000 00137	.00 00 00 7B	.00000 00286	.00 00 00 BB	.00000 00435	.00 00 00 FB	.00000 00584
.00 00 00 3C	.00000 00139	.00 00 00 7C	.00000 00288	.00 00 00 BC	.00000 00437	.00 00 00 FC	.00000 00586
.00 00 00 3D	.00000 00142	.00 00 00 7D	.00000 00291	.00 00 00 BD	.00000 00440	.00 00 00 FD	.00000 00589
.00 00 00 3E	.00000 00144	.00 00 00 7E	.00000 00293	.00 00 00 BE	.00000 00442	.00 00 00 FE	.00000 00591
.00 00 00 3F	.00000 00146	.00 00 00 7F	.00000 00295	.00 00 00 BF	.00000 00444	.00 00 00 FF	.00000 00593

COMMON MATHEMATICAL CONSTANTS

Constant	Decimal Value			Hexadecimal Value	
π	3.14159	26535	89793	3.243F	6A89
π^{-1}	0.31830	98861	83790	0.517C	C1B7
$\sqrt{\pi}$	1.77245	38509	05516	1.C5BF	891C
$\ln\pi$	1.14472	98858	49400	1.250D	048F
e	2.71828	18284	59045	2.B7E1	5163
e^{-1}	0.36787	94411	71442	0.5E2D	58D9
$\sqrt{e}$	1.64872	12707	00128	1.A612	98E2
$\log_{10}e$	0.43429	44819	03252	0.6F2D	EC55
$\log_2 e$	1.44269	50408	88963	1.7154	7653
γ	0.57721	56649	01533	0.93C4	67E4
$\ln\gamma$	−0.54953	93129	81645	−0.8CAE	9BC1
$\sqrt{2}$	1.41421	35623	73095	1.6A09	E668
$\ln 2$	0.69314	71805	59945	0.B172	17F8
$\log_{10}2$	0.30102	99956	63981	0.4D10	4D42
$\sqrt{10}$	3.16227	76601	68379	3.298B	075C
$\ln 10$	2.30258	40929	94046	2.4D76	3777

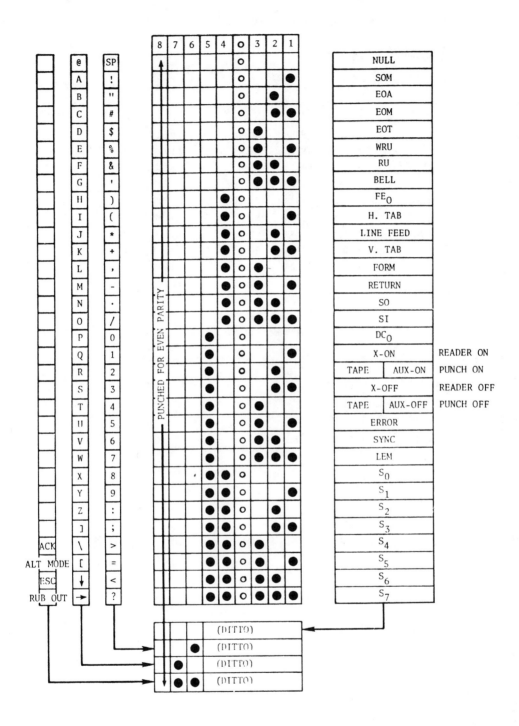

CHARACTER ARRANGEMENT (ASCII) FOR PAPER TAPE

APPENDIX D

FLOW CHART SYMBOLS

The following symbol definitions are those followed in the sample programs of this book. They represent a subset typical of most flow chart effort. For a more complete treatment of the subject, refer to IBM standard flow chart template X20-8020-1 U/M 010 available from most college bookstores or office supply houses.

Symbol	Label	Function
▭	Process	Used to describe a process such as: "calculate the $\sqrt{A}$" or "clear buffer and initialize address register."
▱	Input/Output	Used for input/output operations such as: Output next character (frequently a programmer will just use the process symbol for this type of function).
⏢	Manual Operation	Used for such operations as: "load data tape A" or "remove card deck C and transport to reader 2."
◇	Decision	Used to denote branch or jump conditions typically stated as a question. If the answer to the question is yes, then one path is pursued, if no, then another path is taken.
⬭	Interrupt	Used to signify abrupt changes in the program such as END or START.
◯	Connector	Used with a number or letter to connect various noncontiguous parts of a flow chart together.

APPENDIX E

This appendix consists of excerpted material from various Texas Instruments publications and a reference sheet which are applicable to the Microprocessor Sample Programs.

TMS 1000 Microcomputer
TMS 8080 Microprocessor
TMS 5501 Multifunction Input/Output Controller
TMS 9900 Microprocessor
SBP 0400 Microprogrammer Instruction Manual
Memory Devices Reference Sheet

TMS 1000 Data

TABLE OF CONTENTS

1. INTRODUCING A ONE-CHIP MICROCOMPUTER
   1.1 Description E-5
   1.2 Applications E-6
   1.3 Design Support E-8

2. TMS1000-SERIES OPERATION
   2.1 ROM Operation E-9
   2.2 RAM Operation E-9
   2.3 Arithmetic Logic Unit Operation E-9
   2.4 Input E-10
   2.5 Output E-10
   2.6 The Instruction Programmable Logic Array E-11
   2.7 Timing Relationships E-11
   2.8 Software Summary E-11
   2.9 Sample Program E-13
   2.10 Power-On E-14

LIST OF ILLUSTRATIONS

Figure 1 . . . TMS1000-Series Logic Blocks E-5
Figure 2 . . . Block Diagram of Typical Application — Terminal Controller E-7
Figure 3 . . . TMS1000-Series Algorithm Development E-8
Figure 4 . . . ALU and Associated Data Paths E-9
Figure 5 . . . Machine Instruction Flowchart — BCD-Addition Subroutine E-15

TMS 1000 NC, TMS 1200 NC MICROCOMPUTERS

1. INTRODUCING A ONE-CHIP MICROCOMPUTER

1.1 DESCRIPTION

The TMS1000 series is a family of P-channel MOS four-bit microcomputers with a ROM, a RAM, and an arithmetic logic unit on a single semiconductor chip. The TMS1000 family is unique in the field of microprocessors because this device is a single-chip binary computer. A customer's specification determines the software that is reproduced during wafer processing by a single-level mask technique that defines a fixed ROM pattern. This versatile one-chip computer is very cost effective and capable of performing a myriad of complex functions.

Key features of the TMS1000 series are:

- 8192-bit Read-Only Memory (ROM) on chip
- 256-bit Random-Access Memory (RAM) on chip
- Arithmetic Logic Unit (ALU) and 2 four-bit working registers on chip
- Conditional branching and subroutines
- Four-bit parallel data input
- 11 latched control/data-strobe outputs in a 28-pin package
- 13 latched control/data-strobe outputs in a 40-pin package
- 8 parallel data outputs and output programmable logic array (PLA)
- Programmable instruction decoder
- On-chip oscillator, or external synchronization if desired
- Single-power-supply operation (15 V)

TMS1000 SERIES	
DEVICE	PACKAGE
TMS1000NC	28-Pin DIP
TMS1200NC	40-Pin DIP

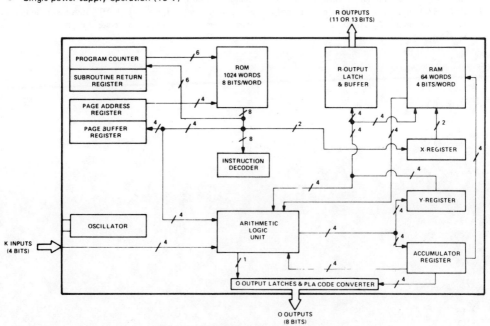

FIGURE 1—TMS1000-SERIES LOGIC BLOCKS

The microcomputer's ROM program controls data input, storage, processing, and output. Data processing takes place in the arithmetic logic unit. K input data goes into the ALU, as shown in Figure 1, and is stored in the four-bit accumulator. The accumulator output accesses the output latches, the RAM storage cells, and the adder input. Data storage in the 256-bit RAM is organized into 64 words, four bits per word. The four-bit words are conveniently grouped into four 16-word files addressed by a two-bit register. A four-bit register addresses one of the 16 words in a file by ROM control.

The O outputs and the R outputs are the output channels. The eight parallel O outputs are decoded from five data latches. The O outputs serve many applications because the decoder is a programmable logic array (PLA) that is modified by changing the gate-level mask tooling. Each of the thirteen R outputs of the TMS1200NC and the eleven R outputs on the TMS1000NC has an individual storage element that can be set or reset by program control. The R outputs send status or enable signals to external devices. The R outputs strobe the O outputs to displays, to other TMS1000 series chips, or to TTL and other interface circuits. The same R outputs multiplex data into the K inputs whenever necessary.

There are 43 basic instructions that handle I/O, constant data from the ROM, bit control, internal data transfer, arithmetic processing, branching, looping, and subroutines. The eight-bit instruction word performs 256 unique operations for maximum efficiency. Section 2.7 defines the standard instruction set, which is optimized for most programs. Microprogramming for special applications is possible, and the operations of the instruction set can be modified by the same mask-tooling step that programs the ROM and the O output PLA.

1.2 APPLICATIONS

One major advantage of the TMS1000 series is flexibility. The TMS1000 series is effective in applications such as printer controllers, data terminals, remote sensing systems, cash registers, appliance controls, and automotive applications. A data terminal is a useful example. In Figure 2, a sample interconnect diagram shows how the R outputs control a universal asynchronous receiver/transmitter (UART), display scan, and keyboard scan. The ROM controls data output to the appropriate display digit or to the transmitter section of the UART. A routine in the ROM program controls selection of incoming data through the K-input ports. Two dedicated R outputs (load and ready reset) control the UART's transmit and receive modes. The remaining R outputs both scan the display and select inputs. The SN74157 TTL devices multiplex eight bits of the incoming data word, four bits of UART status and the four key input lines. Through the TMS1000 series' versatility, a wide range of systems realize reduced costs, fewer parts, and high reliability.

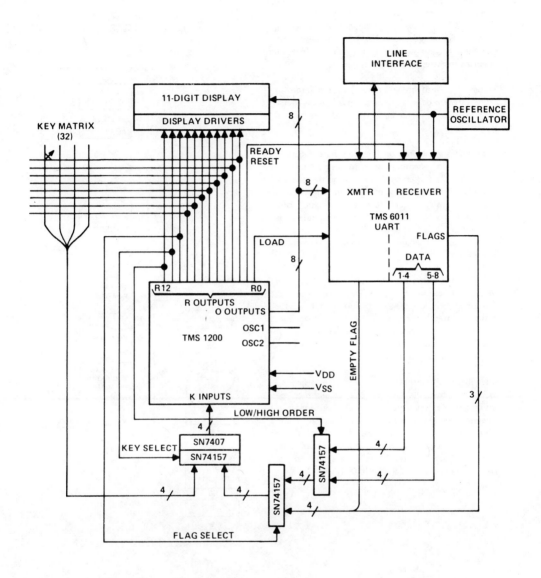

NOTE: Discrete components for level shifting and other functions are not shown

FIGURE 2—BLOCK DIAGRAM OF TYPICAL APPLICATION—TERMINAL CONTROLLER

1.3 DESIGN SUPPORT

Through a staff of experienced application programmers, Texas Instruments will, upon request,
assist customers in evaluating applications, in training
designers to program the TMS1000 series and in
simulating programs. TI will also contract to write
programs to customer's specifications.

TI has developed an assembler and simulator for
aiding software designs. These programs are available
on nationwide time-sharing systems and at TI computer facilities.

A TMS1000 series program (see flowchart, Figure 3)
is written in assembly language using standard
mnemonics. The assembler converts the source code
(assembly language program) into machine code,
which is transferred to a software simulation program. Also the assembler produces a machine code
object deck. The object deck is used to produce a
tape for hardware simulation or a tape for generating
prototype tooling.

The TMS1000 series programs are checked by software and hardware simulation. The software simulation offers the advantages of printed outputs for
instruction traces or periodic outputs. The hardware
simulation offers the designer the advantages of
real-time simulation and testing asynchronous inputs.
A software user's guide is available.

After the algorithms have been checked and approved
by the customer, the final object code and machine
option statements are supplied to TI. A gate mask is
generated and slices produced. After assembly and
testing, the prototypes are shipped to the customer
for approval. Upon receiving final approval, the part
is released for volume production at the required rate
as one unique version of the TMS1000 family.

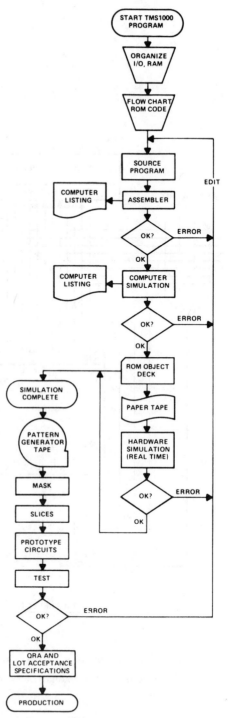

FIGURE 3—TMS1000-SERIES ALGORITHM DEVELOPMENT

2. TMS1000-SERIES OPERATION

2.1 ROM OPERATION

The sequence of the 1024 eight-bit ROM instructions determines the device operation. There are 16 pages of instructions with 64 instructions on each page. After power-up the program execution starts at a fixed instruction address. Then a shift-register program counter sequentially addresses each ROM instruction on a page. A conditional branch or call subroutine instruction may alter the six-bit program-counter address to transfer software control. One level of subroutine return address is stored in the subroutine return register. The page address register (four bits) holds the current address for one of the 16 ROM pages. To change pages, a constant from the ROM loads into the page buffer register (four bits), and upon a successful branch or call, the page buffer loads into the page address register. The page buffer register also holds the return page address in the call subroutine mode.

2.2 RAM OPERATION

There are 256 addressable bits of RAM storage available. The RAM is comprised of four files, each file containing 16 four-bit words. The RAM is addressed by the Y register and the X register. The Y register selects one of the 16 words in a file and is completely controllable by the arithmetic unit. The TMS1000 series has instructions that: Compare Y to a constant, set Y to a constant, increment or decrement Y, and/or perform data transfer to or from Y. Two bits in the X register select one of the four 16-word files. The X register is set to a constant or is complemented. A four-bit data word goes to the RAM location addressed by X and Y from the accumulator or from the constants in the ROM. The RAM output words go to the arithmetic unit and can be operated on and loaded into Y or the accumulator in one instruction interval. Any selected bit in the RAM can be set, reset, or tested.

2.3 ARITHMETIC LOGIC UNIT OPERATION

Arithmetic and logic operations are performed by the four-bit adder and associated logic. The arithmetic unit performs logical comparison, arithmetic comparison, add, and subtract functions. The arithmetic unit and interconnects are shown in Figure 4. The operations are performed on two sets of inputs, P and N. The two four-bit parallel inputs may be added together or logically compared. The accumulator has an inverted output to the N selector for subtraction by two's complement arithmetic. The other N inputs are from the true output of the accumulator, the RAM, constants, and the K inputs. The P inputs come from the Y register, the RAM, the constants, and the K inputs.

Addition and subtraction results are stored in either the Y register or the accumulator. An arithmetic function may cause a carry output to the status logic. Logical comparison may generate an output to status. If the comparison functions are used, only the status bit affects the program control, and neither the Y register's nor the accumulator register's contents are affected. If the status feedback is a logic one, which is the normal state, then the conditional branch or call is executed. If an instruction calls for a carry output to status and the carry does not occur, then status will go to a zero state for one instruction cycle. Likewise, if an instruction calls for the logical-comparison function and the bits compared are all equal, then status will go to a zero state for one instruction cycle. If status is a logic zero, then branches and calls are not performed.

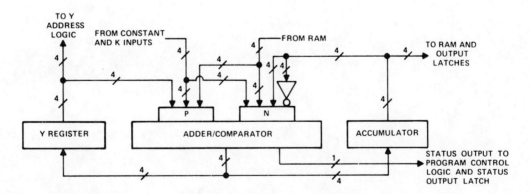

FIGURE 4—ALU AND ASSOCIATED DATA PATHS

2.4 INPUT

There are four data inputs to the TMS1000-series circuit, K1, K2, K4, and K8. Each time an input word is requested, the data path from the K inputs is enabled to the adder. The inputs are either tested for a high level ($\approx V_{SS}$), or the input data are stored in the accumulator for further use. The R outputs usually multiplex inputs such as keys and other data. Other input interfaces are possible. An external device that sends data out to the K-input bus at a fixed rate may be used with the TMS1000 series when an initiating "handshake" signal is given from an R output. Data from the K inputs is stored periodically in synchronization with the predetermined data rate of the external device. Thus, multiple four-bit words can be requested and stored with only one R output supplying the control signal.

2.5 OUTPUT

There are two output channels with multiple purposes, the R outputs and the O outputs. Thirteen latches store the R output data. The eight parallel O outputs come from a five-bit-to-eight-bit code converter, which is the O-output PLA.

The R outputs are individually addressed by the Y register. Each addressed bit can be set or reset. The R outputs are normally used to multiplex inputs and strobe O output data to displays, external memories, and other devices. Also, one R output can strobe other R outputs that represent variable data, because every R output may be set or reset individually. For example, the Y register addresses each latch in turn, the variable data R outputs are set or reset, and finally, the data strobe R latch is set.

The eight O outputs usually send out display or binary data that are encoded from the O output latches. The O latches contain five bits. Four bits load from the accumulator in parallel. The fifth bit comes from the status latch, which is selectively loaded from the adder output (see Figure 4). The load output command sends the status latch and accumulator information into the five output latches. The five bits are available in true or complementary form to 20 programmable-input NAND gates in the O output PLA. Each NAND gate can simultaneously select any combination of O0 thru O7 as an output. The user defines this PLA's decoding to suit an optimum output configuration. As an illustration, the O output PLA can encode any 16 characters of eight-segment display information and additionally can transfer out a four-bit word of binary data.

2.6 THE INSTRUCTION PROGRAMMABLE LOGIC ARRAY

The programmable instruction decode is defined by the instruction PLA. Thirty programmable-input NAND gates decode the eight bits of instruction word. Each NAND gate output selects a combination of 16 microinstructions. The 16 microinstructions control the arithmetic unit, status logic, status latch, and write inputs to the RAM.

As an example, the "add eight to the accumulator, results to accumulator" instruction can be modified to perform a "add eight to the Y register, results to Y" instruction. Modifications that take away an instruction that is not used very often are desirable if the modified instructions save ROM words by increasing the efficiency of the instruction repertoire. A programmer's reference manual is available to explain PLA programming and the TMS1000-series operation in detail.

2.7 TIMING RELATIONSHIPS

Six oscillator pulses constitute one instruction cycle. All instructions are executed in one instruction cycle. The actual machine cycle period is determined by either a fixed external resistor and capacitor connected to the OSC1 and OSC2 pins (refer to Section 3.5), or an external clock input frequency.

2.8 SOFTWARE SUMMARY

The following table defines the TMS1000 series' standard instruction set with a description, mnemonic, and status effect. The mnemonics were defined for easy reference to the functional description. Eighteen mnemonics use an identifier to indicate the condition that satisfies the status requirement for a successful branch or call if the instruction is followed immediately by a branch or call command. "C" means that if the instruction generates a carry (status = one), then a following branch or call is executed. If a branch instruction does not follow or if there is no carry (status = zero), then the program counter proceeds to the next address without changing the normal counting sequence. "N" means that if no borrow (equal to a carry in two's complement aritmetic) is generated, an ensuing branch or call is taken. "Z" indicates that if the two's complement of zero in the accumulator (instruction CPAIZ) is attempted with a branch or call following, then the branch or call is taken. "1", "LE", "NE", and "NEZ" are used to indicate conditions for branch and call for seven test instructions. The test instructions do not modify data at all; tests are used solely in conjunction with subsequent branches or calls.

If an instruction that does not affect status is placed between an instruction that does affect status and a branch or call instruction, then the branch or call is always performed. This is true because status always returns to its normal state (status = one) after one instruction cycle, and branches and calls are taken if status equals one.

TMS1000-SERIES STANDARD INSTRUCTION SET

FUNCTION	MNEMONIC	STATUS EFFECTS C	STATUS EFFECTS N	DESCRIPTION
Register to Register	TAY			Transfer accumulator to Y register.
	TYA			Transfer Y register to accumulator.
	CLA			Clear accumulator.
Transfer Register to Memory	TAM			Transfer accumulator to memory.
	TAMIY			Transfer accumulator to memory and increment Y register.
	TAMZA			Transfer accumulator to memory and zero accumulator.
Memory to Register	TMY			Transfer memory to Y register.
	TMA			Transfer memory to accumulator.
	XMA			Exchange memory and accumulator.
Arithmetic	AMAAC	Y		Add memory to accumulator, results to accumulator. If carry, one to status.
	SAMAN	Y		Subtract accumulator from memory, results to accumulator. If no borrow, one to status.
	IMAC	Y		Increment memory and load into accumulator. If carry, one to status.
	DMAN	Y		Decrement memory and load into accumulator. If no borrow, one to status.
	IA			Increment accumulator, no status effect.
	IYC	Y		Increment Y register. If carry, one to status.
	DAN	Y		Decrement accumulator. If no borrow, one to status.
	DYN	Y		Decrement Y register. If no borrow, one to status.
	A8AAC	Y		Add 8 to accumulator, results to accumulator. If carry, one to status.
	A10AAC	Y		Add 10 to accumulator, results to accumulator. If carry, one to status.
	A6AAC	Y		Add 6 to accumulator, results to accumulator. If carry, one to status.
	CPAIZ	Y		Complement accumulator and increment. If then zero, one to status.
Arithmetic Compare	ALEM	Y		If accumulator less than or equal to memory, one to status.
	ALEC	Y		If accumulator less than or equal to a constant, one to status
Logical Compare	MNEZ		Y	If memory not equal to zero, one to status.
	YNEA		Y	If Y register not equal to accumulator, one to status.
	YNEC		Y	If Y register not equal to a constant, one to status
Bits in Memory	SBIT			Set memory bit.
	RBIT			Reset memory bit.
	TBIT1		Y	Test memory bit. If equal to one, one to status.
Constants	TCY			Transfer constant to Y register.
	TCMIY			Transfer constant to memory and increment Y.
Input	KNEZ		Y	If K inputs not equal to zero, one to status.
	TKA			Transfer K inputs to accumulator.
Output	SETR			Set R output addressed by Y.
	RSTR			Reset R output addressed by Y.
	TDO			Transfer data from accumulator and status latch to O outputs.
	CLO			Clear O-output register.
RAM 'X' Addressing	LDX			Load 'X' with a constant.
	COMX			Complement 'X'.
ROM Addressing	BR			Branch on status = one.
	CALL			Call subroutine on status = one.
	RETN			Return from subroutine.
	LDP			Load page buffer with constant.

NOTES: C Y (Yes) means that if there is a carry out of the MSB, status output goes to the one state. If no carry is generated, status output goes to the zero state.

N Y (Yes) means that if the bits compared are not equal, status output goes to the one state. If the bits are equal, status output goes to the zero state.

A zero in status remains through the next instruction cycle only. If the next instruction is a branch or call and status is a zero, then the branch or call is not executed.

2.9 SAMPLE PROGRAM

The following example shows register addition of up to fifteen BCD digits. The add subroutine (flow charted in Figure 5) can use the entire RAM, which is divided into two pairs of registers. The definition of registers, for the purpose of illustration, is expanded to include the concept of a variable-length word that is a subset of a 16-digit file. Addition proceeds from the least-significant digit (LSD) to the most-significant digit (MSD), and carry ripples through the accumulator. The decrement-Y instruction is used to index the numbers in a register. The initial Y value sets the address for the LSD's of two numbers to be added. Thus, if Y equals eight at the start, the LSD is defined to be stored in M(X,8), [M(X, Y) ≡ contents of RAM word location X equals 0, 1, 2, or 3, and Y equals 0 to 15]. If Y is eight initially, M(X,7) is the next-most-significant digit.

RAM DATA MAP BEFORE EXECUTING SAMPLE ROUTINE

FILE ADDRESS	REGISTER	0	1	2	3	4	5	6	7	8	9	10	11	12	13	14	15
		OV	MSD							LSD							
X = 00	D	0	9	8	7	6	5	4	3	2	(hatched)	(hatched)	(hatched)	(hatched)	(hatched)	(hatched)	(hatched)
		OV	MSD														LSD
X = 01	E	0	1	2	3	4	5	6	7	8	9	0	1	2	3	4	5
		OV	MSD														LSD
X = 10	F	0	5	4	3	2	1	0	9	8	7	6	5	4	3	2	1
		OV	MSD							LSD							
X = 11	G	0	8	7	6	5	4	3	2	1	(hatched)	(hatched)	(hatched)	(hatched)	(hatched)	(hatched)	(hatched)

In the preceeding RAM register assignment map, registers D and G are nine digits long, and registers E and F are 16 digits long. The sample routine calls the D plus G → D subroutine and the E plus F → E subroutine. After executing the two subroutines, the RAM contents are the following:

RAM DATA MAP AFTER EXECUTING SAMPLE ROUTINE

FILE ADDRESS	REGISTER	0	1	2	3	4	5	6	7	8	9	10	11	12	13	14	15
		OV	MSD							LSD							
X = 00	D	1	8	6	4	1	9	7	5	3	(hatched)	(hatched)	(hatched)	(hatched)	(hatched)	(hatched)	(hatched)
		OV	MSD														LSD
X = 01	E	0	6	6	6	6	6	7	7	7	6	6	6	6	6	6	6
		OV	MSD														LSD
X = 10	F	0	5	4	3	2	1	0	9	8	7	6	5	4	3	2	1
		OV	MSD							LSD							
X = 11	G	0	8	7	6	5	4	3	2	1	(hatched)	(hatched)	(hatched)	(hatched)	(hatched)	(hatched)	(hatched)

NOTE: Cross-hatched areas indicate locations in the RAM that are unaffected by executing the example routine.

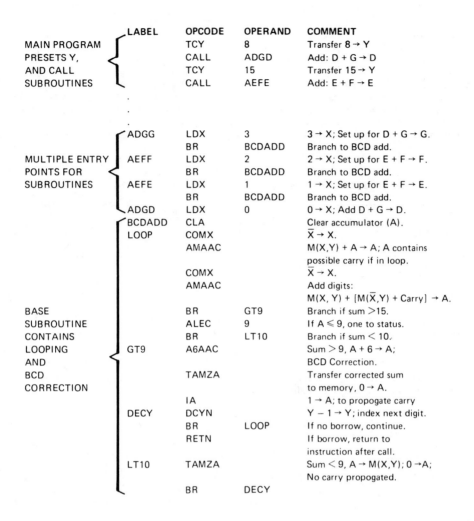

	LABEL	OPCODE	OPERAND	COMMENT
MAIN PROGRAM PRESETS Y, AND CALL SUBROUTINES		TCY	8	Transfer 8 → Y
		CALL	ADGD	Add: D + G → D
		TCY	15	Transfer 15 → Y
		CALL	AEFE	Add: E + F → E
	.			
	.			
	.			
MULTIPLE ENTRY POINTS FOR SUBROUTINES	ADGG	LDX	3	3 → X; Set up for D + G → G.
		BR	BCDADD	Branch to BCD add.
	AEFF	LDX	2	2 → X; Set up for E + F → F.
		BR	BCDADD	Branch to BCD add.
	AEFE	LDX	1	1 → X; Set up for E + F → E.
		BR	BCDADD	Branch to BCD add.
	ADGD	LDX	0	0 → X; Add D + G → D.
BASE SUBROUTINE CONTAINS LOOPING AND BCD CORRECTION	BCDADD	CLA		Clear accumulator (A).
	LOOP	COMX		$\bar{X}$ → X.
		AMAAC		M(X,Y) + A → A; A contains possible carry if in loop.
		COMX		$\bar{X}$ → X.
		AMAAC		Add digits: M(X, Y) + [M($\bar{X}$,Y) + Carry] → A.
		BR	GT9	Branch if sum >15.
		ALEC	9	If A ≤ 9, one to status.
		BR	LT10	Branch if sum < 10.
	GT9	A6AAC		Sum > 9, A + 6 → A; BCD Correction.
		TAMZA		Transfer corrected sum to memory, 0 → A.
		IA		1 → A; to propogate carry
	DECY	DCYN		Y − 1 → Y; index next digit.
		BR	LOOP	If no borrow, continue.
		RETN		If borrow, return to instruction after call.
	LT10	TAMZA		Sum < 9, A → M(X,Y); 0 →A; No carry propogated.
		BR	DECY	

Note that there are four entry points to the base subroutine (ADGG, ADGD, AEFF, AEFE). The main program can call two of the other possible subroutines that store the addition results differently. These subroutines have applications in floating-point arithmetic, multiplication, division, and subtraction routines.

2.10 POWER-ON

The TMS1000 series has a built-in power-on latch, which resets the program counter upon the proper application of power. After power-up the chip resets and begins execution at a fixed ROM address. The system reset depends on the ROM program after the starting address. For power supplies with slow rise times or noisy conditions, an external network connected to the test pin may be necessary.

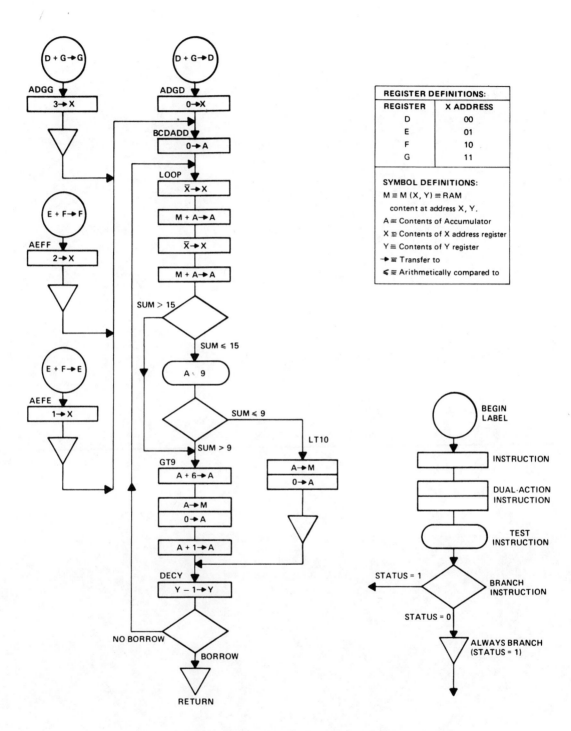

FIGURE 5—MACHINE INSTRUCTION FLOWCHART—BCD-ADDITION SUBROUTINE

TMS 8080 Data

TABLE OF CONTENTS

1. **ARCHITECTURE**
   - 1.1 Introduction E-18
   - 1.2 The Stack E-18
   - 1.3 Registers E-18
   - 1.4 The Arithmetic Unit E-19
   - 1.5 Status and Control E-19
   - 1.6 I/O Operations E-19
   - 1.7 Instruction Timing E-19

2. **TMS 8080 INSTRUCTION SET**
   - 2.1 Instruction Formats E-22
   - 2.2 Instruction Set Description E-23
     - 2.2.1 Instruction Symbols E-23
     - 2.2.2 Accumulator Group Instructions E-24
     - 2.2.3 Input/Output Instructions E-25
     - 2.2.4 Machine Instructions E-25
     - 2.2.5 Program Counter and Stack Control Instructions E-26
     - 2.2.6 Register Group Instructions E-27
   - 2.3 Instruction Set Opcodes Alphabetically Listed E-28

LIST OF ILLUSTRATIONS

Figure 1   TMS 8080 Functional Block Diagram E-18
Figure 2   Voltage Waveforms E-33

TMS 8080 MICROPROCESSOR

1. ARCHITECTURE

1.1 INTRODUCTION

The TMS 8080 is an 8-bit parallel central processing unit (CPU) fabricated on a single chip using a high-speed N-channel silicon-gate process. (See Figure 1). A complete microcomputer system with a 2-μs instruction cycle can be formed by interfacing this circuit with any appropriate memory. Separate 8-bit data and 16-bit address buses simplify the interface and allow direct addressing of 65,536 bytes of memory. Up to 256 input and 256 output ports are also provided with direct addressing. Control signals are brought directly out of the processor and all signals, excluding clocks, are TTL compatible.

1.2 THE STACK

The TMS 8080 incorporates a stack architecture in which a portion of external memory is used as a pushdown stack for storing data from working registers and internal machine status. A 16-bit stack pointer (SP) is provided to facilitate stack location in the memory and to allow almost unlimited interrupt handling capability. The CALL and RST (restart) instructions use the SP to store the program counter (PC) into the stack. The RET (return) instruction uses the SP to acquire the previous PC value. Additional instructions allow data from registers and flags to be saved in the stack.

1.3 REGISTERS

The TMS 8080 has three categories of registers: general registers, program control registers, and internal registers. The general registers and program control registers are listed in Table 1. The internal registers are not accessible by the programmer. They include the instruction register, which holds the present instruction, and several temporary storage registers to hold internal data or latch input and output addresses and data.

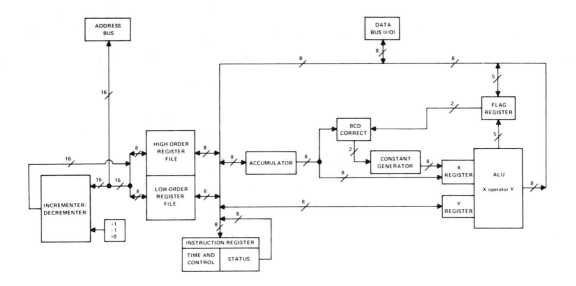

FIGURE 1—TMS 8080 FUNCTIONAL BLOCK DIAGRAM

1.4 THE ARITHMETIC UNIT

Arithmetic operations are performed in an 8-bit parallel arithmetic unit that has both binary and decimal capabilities. Four testable internal flag bits are provided to facilitate program control, and a fifth flag is used for decimal corrections. Table 2 defines these flags and their operation. Decimal corrections are performed with the DAA instruction. The DAA corrects the result of binary arithmetic operation on BCD data as shown in Table 3.

1.5 STATUS AND CONTROL

Two types of status are provided by the TMS8080. Certain status is indicated by dedicated control lines. Additional status is transmitted on the data bus during the beginning of each instruction cycle (machine cycle). Table 4 indicates the pin functions of the TMS8080. Table 5 defines the status information that is presented during the beginning of each machine cycle (SYNC time) on the data bus.

1.6 I/O OPERATIONS

Input/output operations (I/O) are performed using the IN and OUT instructions. The second byte of these instructions indicates the device address (256 device addresses). When an IN instruction is executed, the input device address appears in duplicate on A7 through A0 and A15 through A8, along with $\overline{WO}$ and INP status on the data bus. The addressed input device then puts its input data on the data bus for entry into the accumulator. When an OUT instruction is executed, the same operation occurs except that the data bus has OUT status and then has output data.

Direct memory access channels (DMA) can be OR-tied directly with the data and address buses through the use of the HOLD and HLDA (hold acknowledge) controls. When a HOLD request is accepted by the CPU, HLDA goes high, the address and data lines are forced to a high-impedance or "floating" condition, and the CPU stops until the HOLD request is removed.

Interfacing with different speed memories is easily accomplished by use of the WAIT and READY pins. During each machine cycle, the CPU polls the READY input and enters a wait condition until the READY line becomes true. When the WAIT output pin is high, it indicates that the CPU has entered the wait state.

Designing interrupt driven systems is simplified through the use of vectored interrupts. At the end of each instruction, the CPU polls the INT input to determine if an interrupt request is being made. This action does not occur if the CPU is in the HOLD state or if interrupts are disabled. The INTE output indicates if the interrupt logic is enabled (INTE is high). When a request is honored, the INTA status bit becomes high, and an RST instruction may be inserted to force the CPU to jump to one of eight possible locations. Enabling or disabling interrupts is controlled by special instructions (EI or DI). The interrupt input is automatically disabled when an interrupt request is accepted or when a RESET signal is received.

1.7 INSTRUCTION TIMING

The execution time of the instructions varies depending on the operation required and the number of memory references needed. A machine cycle is defined to be a memory referencing operation and is either 3, 4, or 5 state times long. A state time (designated S) is a full cycle of clocks $\phi 1$ and $\phi 2$. (NOTE: The exception to this rule is the DAD instruction, which consists of 1 memory reference in 10 state times). The first machine cycle (designated M1) is either 4 or 5 state times long and is the "instruction fetch" cycle with the program counter appearing on the address bus. The CPU then continues with as many M cycles as necessary to complete the execution of the instruction (up to a maximum of 5). Thus the instruction execution time varies from 4 state times (several including ADDr) to 18 (XTHL). The WAIT or HOLD conditions may affect the execution time since they can be used to control the machine (for example to "single step") and the HALT instruction forces the CPU to stop until an interrupt is received. As the instruction execution is completed (or in the HALT state) the INT pin is polled for an interrupt. In the event of an interrupt, the PC will not be incremented during the next M1 and an RST instruction can be inserted.

TABLE 1
TMS 8080 REGISTERS

NAME	DESIGNATOR	LENGTH	PURPOSE
Accumulator	A	8	Used for arithmetic, logical, and I/O operations
B Register	B	8	General or most significant 8 bits of double register BC
C Register	C	8	General or least significant 8 bits of double register BC
D Register	D	8	General or most significant 8 bits of double register DE
E Register	E	8	General or least significant 8 bits of double register DE
H Register	H	8	General or most significant 8 bits of double register HL
L Register	L	8	General or least significant 8 bits of double register HL
Program Counter	PC	16	Contains address of next byte to be fetched
Stack Pointer	SP	16	Contains address of the last byte of data saved in the memory stack
Flag Register	F	5	Five flags (C, Z, S, P, C1)

NOTE: Registers B and C may be used together as a single 16-bit register, likewise, D and E, and H and L.

TABLE 2
FLAG DESCRIPTIONS

SYMBOL	TESTABLE	DESCRIPTION
C	YES	C is the carry/borrow out of the MSB (most significant bit) of the ALU (Arithmetic Logic Unit). A TRUE condition (C = 1) indicates overflow for addition or underflow for subtraction.
Z	YES	A TRUE condition (Z = 1) indicates that the output of the ALU is equal to zero.
S	YES	A TRUE condition (S = 1) indicates that the MSB of the ALU output is equal to a one (1).
P	YES	A TRUE condition (P = 1) indicates that the output of the ALU has even parity (the number of bits equal to one is even).
C1	NO	C1 is the carry out of the fourth bit of the ALU (TRUE condition). C1 is used only for BCD correction with the DAA instruction.

TABLE 3
FUNCTION OF THE DAA INSTRUCTION

Assume the accumulator (A) contains two BCD digits, X and Y

	7	4	3	0
ACC		X		Y

ACCUMULATOR BEFORE DAA				ACCUMULATOR AFTER DAA			
C	$A_7 \ldots A_4$	C1	$A_3 \ldots A_0$	C	$A_7 \ldots A_4$	C1	$A_3 \ldots A_0$
0	$X < 10$	0	$Y < 10$	0	X	0	Y
0	$X < 10$	1	$Y < 10$	0	X	0	$Y + 6$
0	$X < 9$	0	$Y \geqslant 10$	0	$X + 1$	1	$Y + 6$
1	$X < 10$	0	$Y < 10$	1	$X + 6$	0	Y
1	$X < 10$	1	$Y < 10$	1	$X + 6$	0	$Y + 6$
1	$X < 10$	0	$Y \geqslant 10$	1	$X + 7$	1	$Y + 6$
0	$X \geqslant 10$	0	$Y < 10$	1	$X + 6$	0	Y
0	$X \geqslant 10$	1	$Y < 10$	1	$X + 6$	0	$Y + 6$
0	$X \geqslant 9$	0	$Y \geqslant 10$	1	$X + 7$	1	$Y + 6$

NOTE: The corrections shown in Table 3 are sufficient for addition. For subtraction, the programmer must account for the borrow condition that can occur and give erroneous results. The most straight forward method is to set $A = 99_{16}$ and carry = 1. Then add the minuend to A after subtracting the subtrahend from A.

TABLE 4
TMS 8080 PIN DEFINITIONS

SIGNATURE	PIN	I/O	DESCRIPTION
A15 (MSB)	36	OUT	A15 through A0 comprise the address bus. True memory or I/O device addresses appear on
A14	39	OUT	this 3-state bus during the first state time of each instruction cycle.
A13	38	OUT	
A12	37	OUT	
A11	40	OUT	
A10	1	OUT	
A9	35	OUT	
A8	34	OUT	
A7	33	OUT	
A6	32	OUT	
A5	31	OUT	
A4	30	OUT	
A3	29	OUT	
A2	27	OUT	
A1	26	OUT	
A0 (LSB)	25	OUT	
D7 (MSB)	6	IN/OUT	D7 through D0 comprise the bidirectional 3-state data bus. Memory, status, or I/O data is
D6	5	IN/OUT	transferred on this bus.
D5	4	IN/OUT	
D4	3	IN/OUT	
D3	7	IN/OUT	
D2	8	IN/OUT	
D1	9	IN/OUT	
D0 (LSB)	10	IN/OUT	
V_{SS}	2		Ground reference
V_{BB}	11		Supply voltage (−5 V nominal)
V_{CC}	20		Supply voltage (5 V nominal)
V_{DD}	28		Supply voltage (12 V nominal)
ϕ1	22	IN	Phase 1 clock.
ϕ2	15	IN	Phase 2 clock. See page 19 for ϕ1 and ϕ2 timing.
RESET	12	IN	Reset. When active (high) for a minimum of 3 clock cycles, the RESET input causes the TMS 8080 to be reset. PC is cleared, interrupts are disabled, and after RESET, instruction execution starts at memory location 0. To prevent a lockup condition, a HALT instruction must not be used in location 0.
HOLD	13	IN	Hold signal. When active (high) HOLD causes the TMS 8080 to enter a hold state and float (put the 3-state address and data bus in a high-impedance state). The chip acknowledges entering the hold state with the HLDA signal and will not accept interrupts until it leaves the hold state.
INT	14	IN	Interrupt request. When active (high) INT indicates to the TMS 8080 that an interrupt is being requested. The TMS 8080 polls INT during a HALT or at the end of an instruction. The request will be accepted except when INTE is low or the CPU is in the HOLD condition.
INTE	16	OUT	Interrupts enabled. INTE indicates that an interrupt will be accepted by the TMS 8080 unless it is in the hold state. INTE is set to a high logic level by the EI (Enable Interrupt) instruction and reset to a low logic level by the DI (Disable Interrupt) instruction. INTE is also reset when an interrupt is accepted and by a high on RESET.
DBIN	17	OUT	Data bus in. DBIN indicates whether the data bus is in an input or an output mode. (high = input, low = output).

TABLE 4 (CONTINUED)

SIGNATURE	PIN	I/O	DESCRIPTION
$\overline{\text{WR}}$	18	OUT	Write. When active (low) $\overline{\text{WR}}$ indicates a write operation on the data bus to memory or to an I/O port.
SYNC	19	OUT	Synchronizing control line. When active (high) SYNC indicates the beginning of each machine cycle of the TMS 8080. Status information is also present on the data bus during SYNC for external latches.
HLDA	21	OUT	Hold acknowledge. When active (high) HLDA indicates that the TMS 8080 is in a hold state.
READY	23	IN	Ready control line. An active (high) level indicates to the TMS 8080 that an external device has completed the transfer of data to or from the data bus. READY is used in conjunction with WAIT for different memory speeds.
WAIT	24	OUT	Wait status. When active (high) WAIT indicates that the TMS 8080 has entered a wait state pending a READY signal from memory.

TABLE 5

TMS 8080 STATUS

SIGNATURE	DATA BUS BIT	DESCRIPTION
INTA	D0	Interrupt acknowledge.
$\overline{\text{WO}}$	D1	Indicates that current machine cycle will be a read (input) (high = read) or a write (output) (low = write) operation.
STACK	D2	Indicates that address is stack address from the SP.
HLTA	D3	HALT instruction acknowledge.
OUT	D4	Indicates that the address bus has an output device address and the data bus has output data.
M1	D5	Indicates instruction acquisition for first byte.
INP	D6	Indicates address bus has address of input device.
MEMR	D7	Indicates that data bus will be used for memory read data.

2. TMS 8080 INSTRUCTION SET

2.1 INSTRUCTION FORMATS

TMS 8080 instructions are either one, two, or three bytes long and are stored as binary integers in successive memory locations in the format shown below.

One-Byte Instructions

| D7 D6 D5 D4 D3 D2 D1 D0 | OP CODE

Two-Byte Instructions

| D7 D6 D5 D4 D3 D2 D1 D0 | OP CODE

| D7 D8 D5 D4 D3 D2 D1 D0 | OPERAND

Three-Byte Instructions

| D7 D6 D5 D4 D3 D2 D1 D0 | OP CODE

| D7 D6 D5 D4 D3 D2 D1 D0 | LOW ADDRESS OR OPERAND 1

| D7 D6 D5 D4 D3 D2 D1 D0 | HIGH ADDRESS OR OPERAND 2

2.2 INSTRUCTION SET DESCRIPTION

Operations resulting from the execution of TMS 8080 instructions are described in this section. The flags that are affected by each instruction are given after the description.

2.2.1 INSTRUCTION SYMBOLS

SYMBOL	DESCRIPTION	
$<b_2>$	Second byte of instruction	
$<b_3>$	Third byte of instruction	

r_a	Register #	Register Name
	000	B
	001	C
	010	D
	011	E
	100	H
	101	L
	111	A

r_b	Register #	Register Name
	00	BC
	01	DE
	10	HL
	11	SP

r_c	Register #	Register Name
	0	BC
	1	DE

r_d	Register #	Register Name
	00	BC
	01	DE
	10	HL

Symbol	Description	
r_{dL}	Least significant 8 bits of r_d	
r_{dH}	Most significant 8 bits of r_d	
f	Flags	True condition
	Zero (Z)	Result is zero
	Carry (C)	Carry/borrow out of MSB is one
	Parity (P)	Parity of result is even
	Sign (S)	MSB of result is one
	Carry 1(C1)	Carry out of fourth bit is one
M	Memory address defined by registers H and L	
( )	Contents of specified address or register	
[ ]	Contents at address contained in specified register	
←	Is transferred to	
↔	Exchange	
Am	Bit m of A register (accumulator)	
‖	Flags affected	
b_2	Single byte immediate operand	
b_3b_2	Double byte immediate operand	
$(nnn)_8$	(nnn) is an octal (base 8) number	

2.2.2 ACCUMULATOR GROUP INSTRUCTIONS

MNEMONIC	OPERANDS	BYTES	M CYCLES/ STATES	DESCRIPTION
ACI	b_2	2	2/7	$(A) \leftarrow (A) + <b_2>+(carry)$, add the second byte of the instruction and the contents of the carry flag to register A and place in A. $\{C,Z,S,P,C1\}$
ADC	M	1	2/7	$(A) \leftarrow (A) + (M) + (carry)$. $\{C,Z,S,P,C1\}$
ADC	r_a	1	1/4	$(A) \leftarrow (A) + (r_a) + (carry)$. $\{C,Z,S,P,C1\}$
ADD	M	1	2/7	$(A) \leftarrow (A) + (M)$, add the contents of M to register A and place in A. $\{C,Z,S,P,C1\}$
ADD	r_a	1	1/4	$(A) \leftarrow (A) + (r_a)$. $\{C,Z,S,P,C1\}$
ADI	b_2	2	2/7	$(A) \leftarrow (A) + <b_2>$. $\{C,Z,S,P,C1\}$
ANA	M	1	2/7	$(A) \leftarrow (A)$ AND (M), take the logical AND of M and register A and place in A. The carry flag will be reset low. $\{C,Z,S,P,C1\}$
ANA	r_a	1	1/4	$(A) \leftarrow (A)$ AND (r_a). $\{C,Z,S,P,C1\}$
ANI	b_2	2	2/7	$(A) \leftarrow (A)$ AND $<b_2>$. $\{C,Z,S,P,C1\}$
CMA		1	1/4	$(A) \leftarrow (\overline{A})$, complement A.
CMC		1	1/4	$(carry) \leftarrow (\overline{carry})$, complement the carry flag. $\{C\}$
CMP	M	1	2/7	$(A) - (M)$, compare the contents of M to register A and set the flags accordingly. $\{C,Z,S,P,C1\}$ $(A) = (M)$ $Z = 1$ $(A) \neq (M)$ $Z = 0$ $(A) < (M)$ $C = 1$ $(A) > (M)$ $C = 0$
CMP	r_a	1	1/4	$(A) - (r_a)$. $\{C,Z,S,P,C1\}$
CPI	b_2	2	2/7	$(A)-<b_2>$. $\{C,Z,S,P,C1\}$
DAA		1	1/4	$(A)\leftarrow$ BCD correction of (A). The 8 bit A contents is corrected to form two 4 bit BCD digits after a binary arithmetic operation. A fifth flag C1 indicates the overflow from A_3. The carry flag C indicates the overflow from A_7 (See Table 3). $\{C,Z,S,P,C1\}$
DAD	r_b	1	1/10	$(HL) \leftarrow (HL) + (r_b)$, add the contents of double register r_b to double register HL and place in HL. $\{C\}$
LDA	b_3b_2	3	4/13	$(A)\leftarrow[<b_3> <b_2>]$
LDAX	r_c	1	2/7	$(A)\leftarrow[(r_c)]$
ORA	M	1	2/7	$(A) \leftarrow (A)$ OR (M), take the logical OR of the contents of M and register A and place in A. The carry flag will be reset. $\{C,Z,S,P,C1\}$
ORA	r_a	1	1/4	$(A) \leftarrow (A)$ OR (r_a). $\{C,Z,S,P,C1\}$
ORI	b_2	2	2/7	$(A) \leftarrow (A)$ OR $<b_2>$. $\{C,Z,S,P,C1\}$
RAL		1	1/4	$A_{m+1}\leftarrow A_m$, $A_0\leftarrow(carry)$, $(carry)\leftarrow(A_7)$. Shift the contents of register A to the left one bit through the carry flag. $\{C\}$
RAR		1	1/4	$A_m\leftarrow A_m+1$, $A_7\leftarrow(carry)$, $(carry)\leftarrow A_0$. $\{C\}$
RLC		1	1/4	$A_{m+1}\leftarrow A_m$, $A_0\leftarrow A_7$ $(carry)\leftarrow(A_7)$. Shift the contents of register A to the left one bit. Shift A_7 into A and into the carry flag. $\{C\}$
RRC		1	1/4	$A_m\leftarrow A_{m+1}$, $A_7\leftarrow A_0$, $(carry)\leftarrow(A_0)$. $\{C\}$

MNEMONIC	OPERANDS	BYTES	M CYCLES/ STATES	DESCRIPTION
SBB	M	1	2/7	$(A) \leftarrow (A) - (M) - (carry)$, subtract the contents of M and the contents of the carry flag from register A and place in A. Two's complement subtraction is used and a true borrow causes the carry flag to be set (underflow condition). $\{C,Z,S,P,C1\}$
SBB	r_a	1	1/4	$(A) \leftarrow (A) - (r_a) - (carry)$. $\{C,Z,S,P,C1\}$
SBI	b_2	2	2/7	$(A) \leftarrow (A) - <b_2> - (carry)$. $\{C,Z,S,P,C1\}$
STA	$b_3 b_2$	3	4/13	$[<b_3> <b_2>] \leftarrow (A)$, store contents of A in memory address given in bytes 2 and 3.
STAX	r_c	1	2/7	$[(r_c)] \leftarrow (A)$, store contents of A in memory address given in BC or DE.
STC		1	1/4	$(carry) \leftarrow 1$, set carry flag to a 1 (true condition).
SUB	M	1	2/7	$(A) \leftarrow (A) - (M)$, subtract the contents of M from register A and place in A. Two's complement subtraction is used and a true borrow causes the carry flag to be set (underflow condition). $\{C,Z,S,P,C1\}$
SUB	r_a	1	1/4	$(A) \leftarrow (A) - (r_a)$. $\{C,Z,S,P,C1\}$
SUI	b_2	2	2/7	$(A) \leftarrow (A) - <b_2>$. $\{C,Z,S,P,C1\}$
XRA	M	1	2/7	$(A) \leftarrow (A)$ XOR (M), take the exclusive OR of the contents of M and register A and place in A. The carry flag will be reset. $\{C,Z,S,P,C1\}$
XRA	r_a	1	1/4	$(A) \leftarrow (A)$ XOR (r_a). $\{C,Z,S,P,C1\}$
XRI	b_2	2	2/7	$(A) \leftarrow (A)$ XOR $<b_2>$. $\{C,Z,S,P,C1\}$

2.2.3 INPUT/OUTPUT INSTRUCTIONS

MNEMONIC	OPERANDS	BYTES	M CYCLES/ STATES	DESCRIPTION
IN	b_2	2	3/10	$(A) \leftarrow$ (input data from data bus), byte 2 is sent on bits A7-A0 and A15-A8 as the input device address. INP status is given on the data bus.
OUT	b_2	2	3/10	(Output data) $\leftarrow (A)$, byte 2 is sent on bits A7-A0 and A15-A8 as the output device address. OUT status is given on the data bus.

2.2.4 MACHINE INSTRUCTIONS

MNEMONIC	OPERANDS	BYTES	M CYCLES/ STATES	DESCRIPTION
HLT		1	2/7	Halt, all machine operations stop. All registers are maintained. Only an interrupt can return the TMS 8080 to the run mode. Note that a HLT should not be placed in location zero, otherwise after the reset pin is active, the TMS 8080 will enter a nonrecoverable state (until power is removed), i.e., in halt with interrupts disabled. This condition also occurs if a HLT is executed while interrupts are disabled. HLTA status is given on the data bus.
NOP		1	1/4	$(PC) \leftarrow (PC) + 1$, no operation.

2.2.5 PROGRAM COUNTER AND STACK CONTROL INSTRUCTIONS

MNEMONIC	OPERANDS	BYTES	M CYCLES/ STATES	DESCRIPTION
CALL	b3b2	3	5/17	[(SP)−1] [(SP)−2]←(PC), (SP)←(SP)−2, (PC)←<b3> <b2>, transfer PC to the stack address given by SP, decrement SP twice, and jump unconditionally to address given in bytes 2 and 3.
Conditional call instructions for true flags:				
(f)			5/17 (Pass)	If (f) = 1, [(SP)−1] [(SP)−2]←(PC), (SP)←(SP)−2, (PS)←<b3> <b2>, otherwise (PC)←(PC)+3. If the flag specified, f, is 1, then execute a call. Otherwise, execute the next instruction.
CC (carry)	b3b2	3	3/11 (Fail)	
CPE (parity)	b3b2	3		
CM (sign)	b3b2	3		
CZ (zero)	b3b2	3		
Conditional call instructions for false flags:				
(f)			5/17 (Pass)	If (f) = 0, [(SP)−1] [(SP)−2]←(PC), (SP)←(SP)−2, (PC)←<b3> <b2>, otherwise (PC)←(PC)+3.
CNC (carry)	b3b2	3	3/11 (Fail)	
CPO (parity)	b3b2	3		
CP (sign)	b3b2	3		
CNZ (zero)	b3b2	3		
DI		1	1/4	Disable interrupts. INTE is driven false to indicate that no interrupts will be accepted.
EI		1	1/4	Enable interrupts. INTE is driven true to indicate that an interrupt will be accepted. Execution of this instruction is delayed to allow the next instruction to be executed before the INT input is polled.
JMP	b3b2	3	3/10	(PC)←<b3> <b2>, jump unconditionally to address given in bytes 2 and 3.
Conditional jump instructions for true flags:				
(f)			3/10	If (f) = 1, (PC)←<b3><b2>, otherwise (PC)←(PC)+3. If the flag specified, f, is 1, execute a JMP. Otherwise, execute the next instruction.
JC (carry)	b3b2	3		
JPE (parity)	b3b2	3		
JM (sign)	b3b2	3		
JZ (zero)	b3b2	3		
Conditional jump instructions for false flags:				
(f)			3/10	If (f) = 0, (PC)←<b3> <b2>, othewise (PC)←(PC)+3.
JNC (carry)	b3b2	3		
JPO (parity)	b3b2	3		
JM (sign)	b3b2	3		
JNZ (zero)	b3b2	3		
PCHL		1	1/5	(PC)←(HL)
POP	PSW	1	3/10	(F)←[(SP)], (A)←[(SP)+1], (SP)←(SP)+2, restore the last stack values addressed by SP into A and F. Increment SP twice.
POP	rd	1	3/10	(rdL)←[(SP)], (rdH)←[(SP)+1], (SP)←(SP)+2.
PUSH	PSW	1	3/11	[(SP)−1]←(A), [(SP)−2]←(F), (SP)←(SP)−2, save the contents of A and F into the stack addressed by SP. Decrement SP twice.
PUSH	rd	1	3/11	[(SP)−1]←(rdL), [(SP)−2]←(rdH), (SP)←(SP)−2.
RET		1	3/10	(PC)←[(SP)] [(SP)+1], (SP)←(SP)+2, return to program at memory address given by last values in the stack. The SP is incremented by two.

MNEMONIC	OPERANDS	BYTES	M CYCLES/ STATES	DESCRIPTION
Conditional return instructions for true flags:				
(f)			3/11 (Pass)	If (f) = 1, (PC)←[(SP)] [(SP+1], (SP)←(SP)+2. If the flag specified, f, is 1, execute a RET. Otherwise, execute the next instruction.
RC (carry)	C	1	1/5 (Fail)	
RPE (parity)	P	1		
RM (sign)	S	1		
RZ (zero)	Z	1		
Conditional return instructions for false flags:				
(f)			3/11 (Pass)	If (f) = 0, (PC)←[(SP)] [(SP)+1] , (SP)←(SP)+2.
RNC (carry)	C	1	1/5 (Fail)	
RPO (parity)	P	1		
RP (sign)	S	1		
RNZ (zero)	Z	1		
RST		1	3/11	[(SP)−1] [(SP)−2] ←(PC) (SP)←(SP)−2, (PC)←0000R0$_8$ where R is a 3 bit field in RST (RST=3R7$_8$). Transfer PC to the stack address given by SP, decrement SP twice, and jump to the address specified by R.
SPHL		1	1/5	(SP)←(HL).

2.2.6 REGISTER GROUP INSTRUCTIONS

MNEMONIC	OPERANDS	BYTES	M CYCLES/ STATES	DESCRIPTION
DCR	M	1	3/10	(M)←(M)−1, decrement the contents of memory location specified by H and L. {Z,S,P,C1}
DCR	r_a	1	1/5	(r_a)←(r_a)−1, decrement the contents of register r_a. {Z,S,P,C1}
DCX	r_b	1	1/5	(r_b)←(r_b)−1, decrement double registers BC, DE, HL, or SP.
INR	M	1	3/10	(M)←(M)+1, increment the contents of memory location specified by H and L. {Z,S,P,C1}
INR	r_a	1	1/5	(r_a)←(r_a)+1, increment the contents of register r_a. {Z,S,P,C1}
INX	r_b	1	1/5	(r_b)←(r_b)+1, increment double registers BC, DE, HL, or SP.
LHLD	b_3b_2	3	5/16	(L)←[<b_3> <b_2>] ; (H)← [<b_3> <b_2>+1], load registers H and L with contents of the two memory locations specified by bytes 3 and 2.
LXI	$r_b b_3 b_2$	3	3/10	(r_{bH})←<b_3>; (r_{bL})←<b_2>, load double registers BC, DE, HL, or SP immediate with bytes 3, 2, respectively.
MVI	M,b_2	2	3/10	(M)←<b_2>, store immediate byte 2 in the address specified by HL
MVI	$r_a b_2$	2	2/7	(r_a)←<b_2>, load register r_a immediate with byte 2 of the instruction.
MOV	Mr_a	1	2/7	(M)←(r_a), store register r_a in the memory location addressed by H and L.
MOV	r_aM	1	2/7	(r_a)←(M), load register r_a with contents of memory addressed by HL.
MOV	$r_{a1} r_{a2}$	1	1/5	(r_{a1})←(r_{a2}), load register r_{a1} with contents of r_{a2}, r_{a2} contents remain unchanged.
SHLD	b_3b_2	3	5/16	[<b_3> <b_2>] ←(L); [<b_3> <b_2>+1)] ←(H), store the contents of H and L into two successive memory locations specified by bytes 3 and 2.
XCHG		1	1/4	(H)↔(D); (L)↔(E), exchange double registers HL and DE
XTHL		1	5/18	(L)↔[(SP)] , (H)↔[(SP)+1] , (SP)=(SP), exchange the top of the stack with register HL.

2.3 INSTRUCTION SET OPCODES ALPHABETICALLY LISTED

MNEMONIC	BYTES	DESCRIPTION	REGISTER AFFECTED	POSITIVE-LOGIC HEX OPCODE D7–D4	D3–D0	CLOCK CYCLES*
ACI	2	Add immediate to A with carry[†]		C	E	7
ADC M	1	Add memory to A with carry[†]		8	E	7
ADC r	1	Add register to A with carry[†]	B	8	8	4
			C	8	9	
			D	8	A	
			E	8	B	
			H	8	C	
			L	8	D	
			A	8	F	
ADD M	1	Add memory to A[†]		8	6	7
ADD r	1	Add register to A[†]	B	8	0	4
			C	8	1	
			D	8	2	
			E	8	3	
			H	8	4	
			L	8	5	
			A	8	7	
ADI	2	Add immediate to A[†]		C	6	7
ANA M	1	AND memory with A[†]		A	6	7
ANAr	1	AND register with A[†]	B	A	0	4
			C	A	1	
			D	A	2	
			E	A	3	
			H	A	4	
			L	A	5	
			A	A	7	
ANI	2	AND immediate with A[†]		E	6	7
CALL	3	Call unconditional		C	D	17
CC	3	Call on carry		D	C	11/17
CM	3	Call on minus		F	C	11/17
CMA	1	Complement A		2	F	4
CMC	1	Complement carry[‡]		3	F	4
CMP M	1	Compare memory with A[†]		B	E	7
CMP r	1	Compare register with A				
			B	B	8	4
			C	B	9	
			D	B	A	
			E	B	B	
			H	B	C	
			L	B	D	
			A	B	F	
CNC	3	Call on no carry		D	4	11/17
CNZ	3	Call on no zero		C	4	11/17
CP	3	Call on positive		F	4	11/17
CPE	3	Call on parity even		E	C	11/17
CPI	2	Compare immediate with A[†]		F	E	7
CPO	3	Call on parity odd		E	4	11/17
CZ	3	Call on zero		C	C	11/17
DAA	1	Decimal adjust A[†]		2	7	4

*Two possible cycle times (11/17) indicate instruction cycles dependent on condition flags.
[†]All flags (C, Z, S, P, C1) affected.
[‡]Only carry flag affected.

MNEMONIC	BYTES	DESCRIPTION	REGISTER AFFECTED	POSITIVE-LOGIC HEX OPCODE D7–D4	D3–D0	CLOCK CYCLES
DAD B	1	Add B&C to H&L ‡		0	9	10
DAD C	1	Add D&E to H&L ‡		1	9	10
DAD H	1	Add H&L to H&L ‡		2	9	10
DAD SP	1	Add stack pointer to H&L ‡		3	9	10
DCR M	1	Decrement Memory §		3	5	10
DCR r	1	Decrement Register §	B	0	5	5
			C	0	D	
			D	1	5	
			E	1	D	
			H	2	5	
			L	2	D	
			A	3	D	
DCX B	1	Decrement B&C		0	B	5
DCX D	1	Decrement D&E		1	B	5
DCX H	1	Decrement H&L		2	B	5
DCX SP	1	Decrement stack pointer		3	B	5
DI	1	Disable interrupts		F	3	4
EI	1	Enable interrupts		F	B	4
HLT	1	Halt		7	6	7
IN	2	Input		D	B	10
INR M	1	Increment memory §		3	4	10
INR r	1	Increment register §	B	0	4	5
			C	0	C	
			D	1	4	
			E	1	C	
			H	2	4	
			L	2	C	
			A	3	C	
INX B	1	Increment B&C register		0	3	5
INX D	1	Increment D&E register		1	3	5
INX H	1	Increment H&L register		2	3	5
INX SP	1	Increment stack pointer		3	3	5
JC	3	Jump on carry		D	A	10
JM	3	Jump on minus		F	A	10
JMP	3	Jump unconditional		C	3	10
JNC	3	Jump on no carry		D	2	10
JNZ	3	Jump on no zero		C	2	10
JP	3	Jump on positive		F	2	10
JPE	3	Jump on parity even		E	A	10
JPO	3	Jump on parity odd		E	2	10
JZ	3	Jump on zero		C	A	10
LDA	1	Load A direct		3	A	13
LDAX B	1	Load A indirect		0	A	7
LDAX D	1	Load A indirect		1	A	7
LHLD	3	Load H&L direct		2	A	16
LXI B	3	Load immediate register pair B&C		0	1	10
LXI D	3	Load immediate register pair D&E		1	1	10
LXI H	3	Load immediate register		2	1	10
LXI SP	3	Load immediate stack pointer		3	1	10

‡ Only carry flag affected.
§ All flags except carry affected.

MNEMONIC	BYTES	DESCRIPTION	REGISTER AFFECTED	POSITIVE-LOGIC HEX OPCODE D7–D4	POSITIVE-LOGIC HEX OPCODE D3–D0	CLOCK CYCLES
MOV M,r	1	Move register to memory	B	7	0	7
			C	7	1	
			D	7	2	
			E	7	3	
			H	7	4	
			L	7	5	
			A	7	7	
MOV r,M	1	Move memory to register	B	4	6	7
			C	4	E	
			D	5	6	
			E	5	E	
			H	6	6	
			L	6	E	
			A	7	E	
MOV r_1, r_2	1	Move register to register	B,B	4	0	5
			B,C	4	1	
			B,D	4	2	
			B,E	4	3	
			B,H	4	4	
			B,L	4	5	
			B,A	4	7	
			C,B	4	8	
			C,C	4	9	
			C,D	4	A	
			C,E	4	B	
			C,H	4	C	
			C,L	4	D	
			C,A	4	F	
			D,B	5	0	
			D,C	5	1	
			D,D	5	2	
			D,E	5	3	
			D,H	5	4	
			H,L	5	5	
			D,A	5	7	
			E,B	5	8	
			E,C	5	9	
			E,D	5	A	
			E,E	5	B	
			E,H	5	C	
			E,L	5	D	
			E,A	5	F	
			H,B	6	0	
			H,C	6	1	
			H,D	6	2	
			H,E	6	3	
			H,H	6	4	
			H,L	6	5	
			H,A	6	7	
			L,B	6	8	

MNEMONIC	BYTES	DESCRIPTION	REGISTER AFFECTED	POSITIVE-LOGIC HEX OPCODE D7–D4	POSITIVE-LOGIC HEX OPCODE D3–D0	CLOCK CYCLES*
MOV r_1, r_2	1	Move register to register (continued)	L,C	6	9	
			L,D	6	A	
			L,E	6	B	
			L,H	6	C	
			L,L	6	D	
			L,A	6	F	
			A,B	7	8	
			A,C	7	9	
			A,D	7	A	
			A,E	7	B	
			A,H	7	C	
			A,L	7	D	
			A,A	7	F	
MVI M	2	Move immediate memory		3	6	10
MVI r	2	Move immediate register	B	0	6	7
			C	0	E	
			D	1	6	
			E	1	E	
			H	2	6	
			L	2	E	
			A	3	E	
NOP	1	No operation	4	0	0	4
ORA M	1	OR memory with A[†]		B	6	7
ORA r	1	OR register with A[†]	B	B	0	4
			C	B	1	
			D	B	2	
			E	B	3	
			H	B	4	
			L	B	5	
			A	B	7	
ORI	2	OR immediate with A[†]	F	6		7
OUT	2	Output	D	3		10
PCHL	1	H&L to program counter	E	9		5
POP B	1	Pop register pair B&C off stack	C	1		10
POP D	1	Pop register pair D&E off stack	D	1		10
POP H	1	Pop register pair H&L off stack	E	1		10
POP PSW	1	Pop A and flags off stack[†]	F	1		10
PUSH B	1	Push register pair B&C	C	5		11
PUSH D	1	Push register pair D&C	D	5		11
PUSH H	2	Push register pair H&L on stack	E	5		11
PUSH PSW	1	Push A and Flags on stack	F	5		11
RAL	1	Rotate A left through carry [‡]	1	7		4
RAR	1	Rotate A right through carry[‡]	1	F		4
RC	1	Return on carry	D	8		5/11
RET	1	Return	C	9		10
RLC	1	Rotate A left[‡]	0	7		4
RM	1	Return on minus	F	8		5/11
RNC	1	Return on no carry	D	0		5/11
RNZ	1	Return on no zero	C	0		5/11
RP	1	Return on positive	F	0		5/11

* Two possible cycles times (11/17) indicate instruction cycles dependent on condition flags.
[†] All flags (C, Z, S, P, C1) affected.
[‡] Only carry flag affected.

MNEMONIC	BYTES	DESCRIPTION	REGISTER AFFECTED	POSITIVE-LOGIC HEX OPCODE D7–D4	D3–D0	CLOCK CYCLES*
RPE	1	Return on parity even		E	8	5/11
RPO	1	Return on parity odd		E	0	5/11
RRC	1	Rotate A right‡		0	F	4
RST	1	Restart				11
			PC←0000_{16}	C	7	
			PC←0008_{16}	C	F	
			PC←0010_{16}	D	7	
			PC←0018_{16}	D	F	
			PC←0020_{16}	E	7	
			PC←0028_{16}	E	F	
			PC←0030_{16}	F	7	
			PC←0038_{16}	F	F	
RZ	1	Return on Zero		C	8	5/11
SBB M	1	Subtract memory from A with borrow[†]		9	E	7
SBB r	1	Subtract register from A with borrow[†]	B	9	8	4
			C	9	9	
			D	9	A	
			E	9	B	
			H	9	C	
			L	9	D	
			A	9	F	
SBI	2	Subtract immediate from A with borrow[†]		D	E	7
SHLD	3	Store H&L direct		2	2	16
SPHL	1	H&L to stack pointer		F	9	5
STA	3	Store A direct		3	2	13
STAX B	1	Store A indirect		0	2	7
STAX D	1	Store A indirect		1	2	7
STC	1	Set carry‡		3	7	4
SUB M	1	Subtract memory from A[†]		9	6	7
SUB r	1	Subtract register from A[†]	B	9	0	4
			C	9	1	
			D	9	2	
			E	9	3	
			H	9	4	
			L	9	5	
			A	9	7	
SUI	2	Subtract immediate from A[†]		D	6	7
XCHG	1	Exchange D&E, H&L registers		E	B	4
XRA M	1	Exclusive OR memory with A[†]		A	E	7
XRA r	1	Exclusive OR register with A[†]	B	A	8	4
			C	A	9	
			D	A	A	
			E	A	B	
			H	A	C	
			L	A	D	
			A	A	F	
XRI	2	Exclusive OR immediate with A[†]		E	E	7
XTHL	1	Exchange top of stack H&L		E	3	18

* Two possible cycles times (11/17) indicate instruction cycles dependent on condition flags.

[†] All flags (C, Z, S, P, C1) affected.

‡ Only carry flag affected.

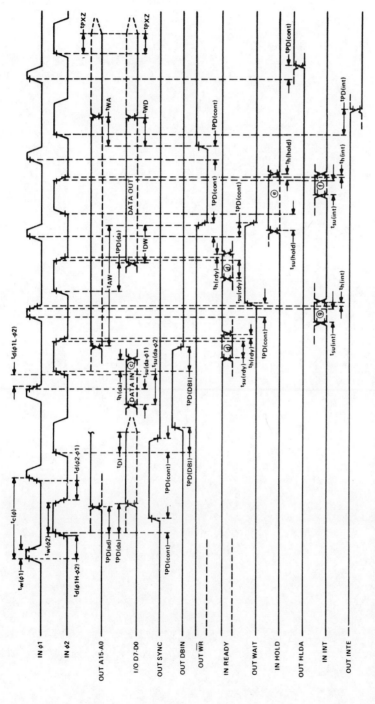

NOTES: a. This timing diagram shows timing relationships only, it does not represent any specific machine cycle.

b. Time measurements are made at the following reference voltages: Clock, $V_{ref(H)}$ = 9.5 V, $V_{ref(L)}$ = 1 V. Other inputs, $V_{ref(H)}$ = 2 V, $V_{ref(L)}$ = 0.8 V.

c. Data in must be stable for this period when DBIN is high during S3. Requirements for both $t_{su(da-\phi1)}$ and $t_{su(da-\phi2)}$ must be satisfied.

d. The ready signal must be stable for this period during S2 or SW. This requires external synchronization.

e. The hold signal must be stable for this period during S2 or SW when entering the hold mode and during S3, S4, S5 and SWH when in the hold mode. This requires external synchronization.

f. The interrupt signal must be stable during this period on the last clock cycle of any instruction to be recognized on the following instruction. External synchronization is not required.

g. During halt mode only, timing is with respect to the clock 1 falling edge.

FIGURE 2 – VOLTAGE WAVEFORMS (SEE NOTES A AND B)

E-33

TMS 5501 Data

TABLE OF CONTENTS

1. **INTRODUCTION**

    1.1 Description E-36
    1.2 Summary of Operation E-37
    1.3 Applications E-38

2. **OPERATIONAL AND FUNCTIONAL DESCRIPTION**

    2.1 Interface Signals E-40
    2.2 TMS 5501 Commands E-42
        2.2.1   Read Receiver Buffer E-43
        2.2.2   Read External Input Lines E-43
        2.2.3   Read Interrupt Address E-43
        2.2.4   Read TMS 5501 Status E-43
        2.2.5   Issue Discrete Commands E-44
        2.2.6   Load Rate Register E-45
        2.2.7   Load Transmitter Buffer E-46
        2.2.8   Load Output Port E-46
        2.2.9   Load Mask Register E-46
        2.2.10 Load Timer n E-46

LIST OF ILLUSTRATIONS

Figure 1   TMS 5501 Block Diagram E-36
Figure 2   Access Control System Block Diagram E-39
Figure 3   Data Bus Assignments for TMS 5501 Status E-43
Figure 4   Discrete Command Format E-44
Figure 5   Data Bus Assignments for Rate Commands E-45
Figure 6   Read Cycle Timing E-46
Figure 7   Write Cycle Timing E-47
Figure 8   Sensor/Interrupt Timing E-47

TMS 5501 MULTIFUNCTION INPUT/OUTPUT CONTROLLER

1. INTRODUCTION

1.1 DESCRIPTION

The TMS 5501 is a multifunction input/output circuit for use with TI's TMS 8080 CPU. It is fabricated with the same N-channel silicon-gate process as the TMS 8080 and has compatible timing, signal levels, and power supply requirements. The TMS 5501 provides a TMS 8080 microprocessor system with an asynchronous communications interface, data I/O buffers, interrupt control logic, and interval timers.

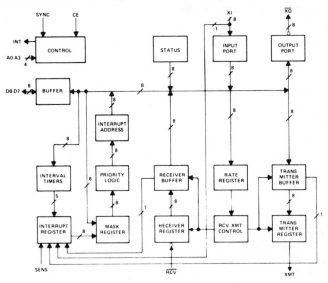

FIGURE 1—TMS 5501 BLOCK DIAGRAM

The I/O section of the TMS 5501 contains an eight-bit parallel input port and a separate eight-bit parallel output port with storage register. Five programmable interval timers provide time intervals from 64 μs to 16.32 ms.

The interrupt system allows the processor to effectively communicate with the interval timers, external signals, and the communications interface by providing TMS 8080-compatible interrupt logic with masking capability.

Data transfers between the TMS 5501 and the CPU are carried by the data bus and controlled by the interrupt, chip enable, sync, and address lines. The TMS 8080 uses four of its memory-address lines to select one of 14 commands to which the TMS 5501 will respond. These commands allow the CPU to:

     ···· read the receiver buffer
     ···· read the input port
     ···· read the interrupt address
     ···· read TMS 5501 status
     ···· issue discrete commands
     ···· load baud rate register
     ···· load the transmitter buffer
     ···· load the output port
     ···· load the mask register
     ···· load an interval timer

The commands are generated by executing memory referencing instructions such as MOV (register to memory) with the memory address being the TMS 5501 command. This provides a high degree of flexibility for I/O operations by letting the systems programmer use a variety of instructions.

1.2 SUMMARY OF OPERATION

Addressing the TMS 5501

A convenient method for addressing the TMS 5501 is to tie the chip enable input to the highest order address line of the CPU's 16-bit address bus and the four TMS 5501 address inputs to the four lowest order bits of the bus. This, of course, limits the system to 32,768 words of memory but in many applications the full 65,536 word memory addressing capability of the TMS 8080 is not required.

Communications Functions

The communications section of the TMS 5501 is an asynchronous transmitter and receiver for serial communications and provides the following functions:

Programmable baud rate — A CPU command selects a baud rate of 110, 150, 300, 1200, 2400, 4800, or 9600 baud.

Incoming character detection — The receiver detects the start and stop bits of an incoming character and places the character in the receive buffer.

Character transmission — The transmitter generates start and stop bits for a character received from the CPU and shifts it out.

Status and command signals — Via the data bus, the TMS 5501 signals the status of: framing error and overrun error flags; data in the receiver and transmitter buffers; start and data bit detectors; and end-of-transmission (break) signals from external equipment. It also issues break signals to external equipment.

Data Interface

The TMS 5501 moves data between the CPU and external devices through its internal data bus, input port, and output port. When data is present on the bus that is to be sent to an external device, a Load Output Port (LOP) command from the CPU puts the data on the $\overline{XO}$ pins of the TMS 5501 by latching it in the output port. The data remains in the port until another LOP command is received. When the CPU requires data that is present on the External Input (XI) lines, it issues a command that gates the data onto the internal data bus of the TMS 5501 and consequently onto the CPU's data bus at the correct time during the CPU cycles.

Interval Timers

To start a countdown by any of the five interval timers, the program selects the particular timer by an address to the TMS 5501 and loads the required interval into the timer via the data bus. Loading the timer activates it and it counts down in increments of 64 microseconds. The 8-bit counters provide intervals that vary in duration from 64 to 16,320 microseconds. Much longer intervals can be generated by cascading the timers through software. When a timer reaches zero, it generates an interrupt that typically will be used to point to a subroutine that performs a servicing function such as polling a peripheral or scanning a keyboard. Loading an interval value of zero causes an immediate interrupt. A new value loaded while the interval timer is counting overrides the previous value and the interval timer starts counting down the new interval. When an interval timer reaches zero it remains inactive until a new interval is loaded.

Servicing Interrupts

The TMS 5501 provides a TMS 8080 system with several interrupt control functions by receiving external interrupt signals, generating interrupt signals, masking out undersired interrupts, establishing the priority of interrupts, and generating RST instructions for the TMS 8080. An external interrupt is received on pin 22, SENS. An additional external interrupt can be received on pin 32, XI 7, if selected by a discrete command from the TMS 8080 (See Figure 4). The TMS 5501 generates an interrupt when any of the five interval timers count to zero. Interrupts are also generated when the receiver buffer is loaded and when the transmitter buffer is empty.

When an interrupt signal is received by the interrupt register from a particular source, a corresponding bit is set and gated to the mask register. A pattern will have previously been set in the mask register by a load-mask-register command from the TMS 8080. This pattern determines which interrupts will pass through to the priority logic. The priority logic allows an interrupt to generate an RST instruction to the TMS 8080 only if there is no higher priority interrupt that has not been accepted by the TMS 8080. The TMS 5501 prioritizes interrupts in the order shown below:

> 1st — Interval Timer #1
> 2nd — Interval Timer #2
> 3rd — External Sensor
> 4th — Interval Timer #3
> 5th — Receiver Buffer Loaded
> 6th — Transmitter Buffer Emptied
> 7th — Interval Timer #4
> 8th — Interval Timer #5 or an External Input (XI 7)

The highest priority interrupt passes through to the interrupt address logic, which generates the RST instruction to be read by the TMS 8080. See Table 3 for relationship of interrupt sources to RST instructions and Figures 6 and 8 for timing relationships.

The TMS 5501 provides two methods of servicing interrupts; an interrupt-driven system or a polled-interrupt system. In an interrupt-driven system, the INT signal of the TMS 5501 is tied to the INT input of the TMS 8080. The sequence of events will be: (1) The TMS 5501 receives (or generates) an interrupt signal and readies the appropriate RST instruction. (2) The TMS 5501 INT output, tied to the TMS 8080 INT input, goes high signaling the TMS 8080 that an interrupt has occured. (3) If the TMS 8080 is enabled to accept interrupts, it sets the INTA (interrupt acknowledge) status bit high at SYNC time of the next machine cycle. (4) If the TMS 5501 has previously received an interrupt-acknowledge-enable command from the CPU (see Bit 3, Paragraph 2.2.5), the RST instruction is transferred to the data bus.

In a polled-interrupt system, INT is not used and the sequence of events will be: (1) The TMS 5501 receives (or generates) an interrupt and readies the RST instruction. (2) The TMS 5501 interrupt-pending status bit (see Bit 5, Paragraph 2.2.4) is set high (the interrupt-pending status bit and the INT output go high simultaneously). (3) At the prescribed time, the TMS 8080 polls the TMS 5501 to see if an interrupt has occurred by issuing a read-TMS 5501-status command and reading the interrupt-pending bit. (4) If the bit is high, the TMS 8080 will then issue a read-interrupt-address command, which causes the TMS 5501 to transfer the RST instruction to the data bus as data for the instruction being executed by the TMS 8080.

1.3 APPLICATIONS

Communications Terminals

The functions of the TMS 5501 make it particularly useful in TMS 8080-based communications terminals and generally applicable in systems requiring periodic or random servicing of interrupts, generation of control signals to external devices, buffering of data, and transmission and reception of asynchronous serial data. As an example, a system configuration such as shown in Figure 2 can function as the controller for a terminal that governs employee entrance into a plant or security areas within a plant. Each terminal is identified by a central computer through ID switches. The central system supplies each terminal's RAM with up to 16 employee access categories applicable to that terminal. These categories are compared with an employee's badge character when he inserts his badge into the badge sensor. If a

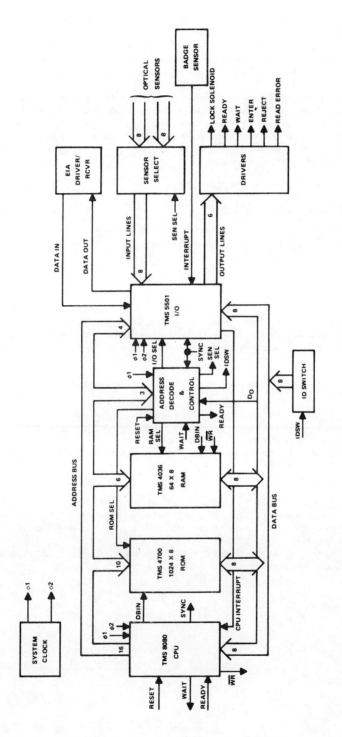

FIGURE 2—ACCESS CONTROL SYSTEM BLOCK DIAGRAM

match is not found, a reject light will be activated. If a match is found, the terminal will transmit the employee's badge number and access category to the central system, and a door unlock solenoid will be activated for 4 seconds. The central computer then may take the transmitted information and record it along with time and date of access.

The TMS 4700 is a 1024 x 8 ROM that contains the system program, and the TMS 4036 is a 64 x 8 RAM that serves as the stack for the TMS 8080 and storage for the access category information. TTL circuits control chip-enable information carried by the address bus. Signals from the CPU gate the address bits from the ROM, the RAM, or the TMS 5501 onto the data bus at the correct time in the CPU cycle. The clock generator consists of four TTL circuits along with a crystal, needed to maintain accurate serial data assembly and disassembly with the central computer.

The TMS 5501 handles the asynchronous serial communication between the TMS 8080 and the central system and gates data from the badge reader onto the data bus. It also gates control and status data from the TMS 8080 to the door lock and badge reader and controls the time that the door lock remains open. The TMS 5501 signals the TMS 8080 when the badge reader or the communication lines need service. The functions that the TMS 5501 is to perform are selected by an address from the TMS 8080 with the highest order address line tied to the TMS 5501 chip enable input and the four lowest order lines tied to the address inputs.

2. OPERATIONAL AND FUNCTIONAL DESCRIPTION

This detailed description of the TMS 5501 consists of:

INTERFACE SIGNALS — a definition of each of the circuit's external connections

COMMANDS — the address required to select each of the TMS 5501 commands and a description of the response to the command.

2.1 INTERFACE SIGNALS

The TMS 5501 communicates with the TMS 8080 via four address lines: a chip enable line, an eight-bit bidirectional data bus, an interrupt line, and a sync line. It communicates with system components other than the CPU via eight external inputs, eight external outputs, a serial receiver input, a serial transmitter output, and an external sensor input. Table 1 defines the TMS 5501 pin assignments and describes the function of each pin.

TABLE 1
TMS 5501 PIN ASSIGNMENTS AND FUNCTIONS

SIGNATURE	PIN	DESCRIPTION
		INPUTS
CE	18	Chip enable—When CE is low, the TMS 5501 address decoding is inhibited, which prevents execution of any of the TMS 5501 commands.
A3	17	Address bus—A3 through A0 are the lines that are addressed by the TMS 8080 to select a particular
A2	16	TMS 5501 function.
A1	15	
A0	14	
SYNC	19	Synchronizing signal—The SYNC signal is issued by the TMS 8080 and indicates the beginning of a machine cycle and availability of machine status. When the SYNC signal is active (high), the TMS 5501 will monitor the data bus bits DO (interrupt acknowledge) and D1 ($\overline{WO}$, data output function).
$\overline{RCV}$	5	Receiver serial data input line—$\overline{RCV}$ must be held in the inactive (high) state when not receiving data. A transition from high to low will activate the receive circuitry.

TABLE 1 (continued)
TMS 5501 PIN ASSIGNMENTS AND FUNCTIONS

SIGNATURE	PIN	DESCRIPTION

INPUTS

SIGNATURE	PIN	DESCRIPTION
XI 0	39	External inputs—These eight external inputs are gated to the data bus when the read-external-inputs function is addressed. External input n is gated to data bus bit n without conversion.
XI 1	38	
XI 2	37	
XI 3	36	
XI 4	35	
XI 5	34	
XI 6	33	
XI 7	32	
SENS	22	External interrupt sensing — A transition from low to high at SENS sets a bit in the interrupt register, which, if enabled, generates an interrupt to the TMS 8080.

OUTPUTS

SIGNATURE	PIN	DESCRIPTION
$\overline{XO}$ 0	24	External outputs—These eight external outputs are driven by the complement of the output register; i.e., if output register bit n is loaded with a high (low) from data bus bit n by a load-output register command, the external output n will be a low (high). The external outputs change only when a load-output-register function is addressed.
$\overline{XO}$ 1	25	
$\overline{XO}$ 2	26	
$\overline{XO}$ 3	27	
$\overline{XO}$ 4	28	
$\overline{XO}$ 5	29	
$\overline{XO}$ 6	30	
$\overline{XO}$ 7	31	
XMT	40	Transmitter serial data output line—This line remains high when the TMS 5501 is not transmitting.

DATA BUS INPUT/OUTPUT

SIGNATURE	PIN	DESCRIPTION
D0	13	Data bus — Data transfers between the TMS 5501 and the TMS 8080 are made via the 8-bit bidirectional data bus. D0 is the LSB. D7 is the MSB.
D1	12	
D2	11	
D3	10	
D4	9	
D5	8	
D6	7	
D7	6	
INT	23	Interrupt—When active (high), the INT output indicates that at least one of the interrupt conditions has occurred and that its corresponding mask-register bit is set.

POWER AND CLOCKS

SIGNATURE	PIN	DESCRIPTION
V_{SS}	4	Ground reference
V_{BB}	1	Supply voltage (−5 V nominal)
V_{CC}	2	Supply voltage (5 V nominal)
V_{DD}	3	Supply voltage (12 V nominal)
$\phi 1$	20	Phase 1 clock
$\phi 2$	21	Phase 2 clock

2.2 TMS 5501 COMMANDS

The TMS 5501 operates as memory device for the TMS 8080. Functions are initiated via the TMS 8080 address bus and the TMS 5501 address inputs. Address decoding to determine the command function being issued is defined in Table 2.

TABLE 2
COMMAND ADDRESS DECODING
When Chip Enable Is High

A3	A2	A1	A0	COMMAND	FUNCTION	PARAGRAPH
L	L	L	L	Read receiver buffer	$RBn \rightarrow Dn$	2.2.1
L	L	L	H	Read external inputs	$XIn \rightarrow Dn$	2.2.2
L	L	H	L	Read interrupt address	$RST \rightarrow Dn$	2.2.3
L	L	H	H	Read TMS 5501 status	$(Status) \rightarrow Dn$	2.2.4
L	H	L	L	Issue discrete commands	See Figure 4	2.2.5
L	H	L	H	Load rate register	See Figure 4	2.2.6
L	H	H	L	Load transmitter buffer	$Dn \rightarrow TBn$	2.2.7
L	H	H	H	Load output port	$Dn \rightarrow \overline{XO}n$	2.2.8
H	L	L	L	Load mask register	$Dn \rightarrow MRn$	2.2.9
H	L	L	H	Load interval timer 1	$Dn \rightarrow Timer\ 1$	2.2.10
H	L	H	L	Load interval timer 2	$Dn \rightarrow Timer\ 2$	2.2.10
H	L	H	H	Load interval timer 3	$Dn \rightarrow Timer\ 3$	2.2.10
H	H	L	L	Load interval timer 4	$Dn \rightarrow Timer\ 4$	2.2.10
H	H	L	H	Load interval timer 5	$Dn \rightarrow Timer\ 5$	2.2.10
H	H	H	L	No function		
H	H	H	H	No function		

$RBn \equiv$ Receiver buffer bit n
$Dn \equiv$ Data bus I/O terminal n
$XIn \equiv$ External input terminal n
$RST \equiv 11\ (IA_2)\ (IA_1)\ (IA_0)\ 1\ 1\ 1$ (see Table 3)
$TBn \equiv$ Transmit buffer bit n
$\overline{XO}n \equiv$ Output register bit n
$MRn \equiv$ Mask register bit n

TABLE 3
RST INSTRUCTIONS

DATA BUS BIT								INTERRUPT CAUSED BY
0	1	2	3	4	5	6	7	
H	H	H	L	L	L	H	H	Interval Timer 1
H	H	H	H	L	L	H	H	Interval Timer 2
H	H	H	L	H	L	H	H	External Sensor
H	H	H	H	H	L	H	H	Interval Timer 3
H	H	H	L	L	H	H	H	Receiver Buffer
H	H	H	H	L	H	H	H	Transmitter Buffer
H	H	H	L	H	H	H	H	Interval Timer 4
H	H	H	H	H	H	H	H	Interval Timer 5 or X17

The following paragraphs define the functions of the TMS 5501 commands.

2.2.1 Read receiver buffer

Addressing the read-receiver-buffer function causes the receiver buffer contents to be transferred to the TMS 8080 and clears the receiver-buffer-loaded flag.

2.2.2 Read external input lines

Addressing the read-external-inputs function transfers the states of the eight external input lines to the TMS 8080.

2.2.3 Read interrupt address

Addressing the read interrupt address function transfers the current highest priority interrupt address onto the data bus as read data. After the read operation is completed, the corresponding bit in the interrupt register is reset.

If the read-interrupt-address function is addressed when there is no interrupt pending, a false interrupt address will be read. TMS 5501 status function should be addressed in order to determine whether or not an interrupt condition is pending.

2.2.4 Read TMS 5501 status

Addressing the read-TMS 5501-status function gates the various status conditions of the TMS 5501 onto the data bus. The status conditions, available as indicated in Figure 3, are described in the following paragraphs.

BIT:	7	6	5	4	3	2	1	0
	START BIT DETECT	FULL BIT DETECT	INTRPT PENDING	XMIT BUFFER EMPTY	RCV BUFFER LOADED	SERIAL RCVD	OVERRUN ERROR	FRAME ERROR

FIGURE 3—DATA BUS ASSIGNMENTS FOR TMS 5501 STATUS

Bit 0, framing error

A high in bit 0 indicates that a framing error was detected on the last character received (either one or both stop bits were in error). The framing error flag is updated at the end of each character. Bit 0 of the TMS 5501 status will remain high until the next valid character is received.

Bit 1, overrun error

A high in bit 1 indicates that a new character was loaded into the receiver buffer before a previous character was read out. The overrun error flag is cleared each time the read-I/O-status function is addressed or a reset command is issued.

Bit 2, serial received data

Bit 2 monitors the receiver serial data input line. This line is provided as a status input for use in detecting a break and for test purposes. Bit 2 is normally high when no data is being received.

Bit 3, receiver buffer loaded

A high in bit 3 indiciates that the receiver buffer is loaded with a new character. The receiver-buffer-loaded flag remains high until the read-receiver-buffer function is addressed (at which time the flag is cleared). The reset function also clears this flag.

Bit 4, transmitter buffer empty

A high in bit 4 indicates that the transmitter buffer register is empty and ready to accept a character. Note, however, that the serial transmitter register may be in the process of shifting out a character. The reset function sets the transmitter-buffer-empty flag high.

Bit 5, interrupt pending

A high in bit 5 indicates that one or more of the interrupt conditions has occured and the corresponding interrupt is enabled. This bit is the status of the interrupt signal INT.

Bit 6, full bit detected

A high in bit 6 indicates that the first data bit of a receive-data character has been detected. This bit remains high until the entire character has been received or until a reset is issued and is provided for test purposes.

Bit 7, start bit detected

A high in bit 7 indicates that the start bit of an incoming data character has been detected. This bit remains high until the entire character has been received or until a reset is issued and is provided for test purposes.

2.2.5 Issue discrete commands

Addressing the discrete command function causes the TMS 5501 to interpret the data bus information according to the following descriptions. See Figure 4 for the discrete command format. Bits 1 through 5 are latched until a different discrete command is received.

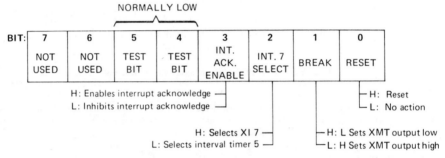

FIGURE 4–DISCRETE COMMAND FORMAT

Bit 0, reset

A high in bit 0 will cause the following:

1) The receiver buffer and register are cleared to the search mode including the receiver-buffer-loaded flag, the start-bit-detected flag, the full-bit-detected flag, and the overrun-error flag. The receiver buffer is not cleared and will contain the last character received.

2) The transmitter data output is set high (marking). The transmitter-buffer-empty flag is set high indicating that the transmitter buffer is ready to accept a character from the TMS 8080.

3) The interrupt register is cleared except for the bit corresponding to the transmitter buffer interrupt, which is set high.

4) The interval timers are inhibited.

A low in bit 0 causes no action. The reset function has no affect on the output port, the external inputs, interrupt acknowledge enable, the mask register, the rate register, the transmitter register, or the transmitter buffer.

Bit 1, break

A low in bit 1 causes the transmitter data output to be reset low (spacing).

If bit 0 and bit 1 are both high, the reset function will override.

Bit 2, interrupt 7 select

Interrupt 7 may be generated either by a low to high transition of external input 7 or by interval timer 5.

A high in bit 2 selects the interrupt 7 source to be the transition of external input 7. A low in bit 2 selects the interrupt 7 source to be interval timer 5.

Bit 3, interrupt acknowledge enable

The TMS 5501 decodes data bus (CPU status) bit 0 at SYNC of each machine cycle to determine if an interrupt acknowledge is being issued.

A high in bit 3 enables the TMS 5501 to accept the interrupt acknowledge decode. A low in bit 3 causes the TMS 5501 to ignore the interrupt acknowledge decode.

Bit 4 and bit 5 are used only during testing of the TMS 5501. For correct system operation both bits must be kept low.

Bit 6 and bit 7 are not used and can assume any value.

2.2.6 Load rate register

Addressing the load-rate-register function causes the TMS 5501 to load the rate register from the data bus and interpret the data bits (See Figure 5) as follows.

BIT:	7	6	5	4	3	2	1	0
	STOP	9600	4800	2400	1200	300	150	110
	BIT(s)	baud	baud	baud	baud	baud	baud	baud

—H: One stop bit
—L: Two stop bits

FIGURE 5—DATA BUS ASSIGNMENTS FOR RATE COMMANDS

Bits 0 through 6, rate select

The rate select bits (bits 0 through 6) are mutually exclusive, i.e., only one bit may be high. A high in bits 0 through 6 will select the baud rate for both the transmitter and receiver circuitry as defined below and in Figure 5:

Bit 0   110 baud
Bit 1   150 baud
Bit 2   300 baud
Bit 3   1200 baud
Bit 4   2400 baud
Bit 5   4800 baud
Bit 6   9600 baud

If more than one bit is high, the highest rate indicated will result. If bits 0 through 6 are all low, both the receiver and the transmitter circuitry will be inhibited.

Bit 7, stop bits

Bit 7 determines whether one or two stop bits are to be used by both the transmitter and receiver circuitry. A high in bit 7 selects one stop bit. A low in bit 7 selects two stop bits.

2.2.7 Load transmitter buffer

Addressing the load-transmitter-buffer function transfers the state of the data bus into the transmitter buffer.

2.2.8 Load output port

Addressing the load-output-port function transfers the state of the data bus into the output port. The data is latched and remains on $\overline{XO}\,0$ through $\overline{XO}\,7$ as the complement of the data bus until new data is loaded.

2.2.9 Load mask register

Addressing the load-mask-register function loads the contents of the data bus into the mask register. A high in data bus bit n enables interrupt n. A low inhibits the corresponding interrupt.

2.2.10 Load timer n

Addressing the load-timer-n function loads the contents of the data bus into the appropriate interval timer. Time intervals of from 64 μs (data bus = LLLLLLLH) to 16,320 μs (data bus HHHHHHHH) are counted in 64-μs, steps. When the count of interval timer n reaches 0, the bit in the interrupt register that corresponds to timer n is set and an interrupt is generated. Loading all lows causes an interrupt immediately.

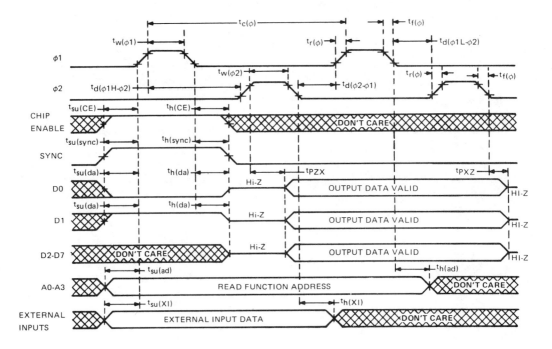

NOTE: For ϕ1 or ϕ2 inputs, high and low timing points are 90% and 10% of $V_{IH(\phi)}$. All other timing points are the 50% level.

FIGURE 6—READ CYCLE TIMING

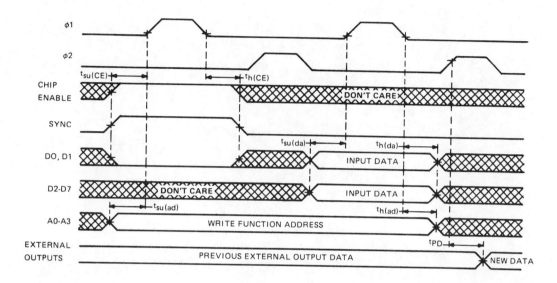

NOTE: For φ1 and φ2 inputs, high and low timing points are 90% and 10% of $V_{IH(\phi)}$. All other timing points are the 50% level.

FIGURE 7—WRITE CYCLE TIMING

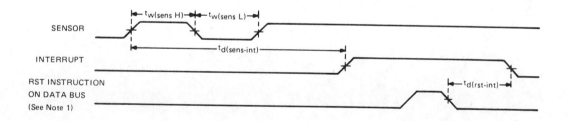

NOTES: 1. The RST instruction occurs during the output data valid time of the read cycle.
2. All timing points are 50% of V_{IH}.

FIGURE 8—SENSOR/INTERRUPT TIMING

TMS 9900 Data
TABLE OF CONTENTS

1. **INTRODUCTION**
   1.1 Description E-51
   1.2 Key Features E-51

2. **ARCHITECTURE**
   2.1 Registers and Memory E-51
   2.2 Interrupts E-54
   2.3 Input/Output E-55
   2.4 Single-Bit CRU Operations E-56
   2.5 Multiple-Bit CRU Operations E-56
   2.6 External Instructions E-58
   2.7 Load Function E-59
   2.8 TMS 9900 Pin Description E-61
   2.9 Timing E-63
       2.9.1 Memory E-63
       2.9.2 Hold E-63
       2.9.3 CRU E-66

3. **TMS 9900 INSTRUCTION SET**
   3.1 Definition E-66
   3.2 Addressing Modes E-66
       3.2.1 Workspace Register Addressing R E-66
       3.2.2 Workspace Register Indirect Addressing *R E-66
       3.2.3 Workspace Register Indirect Auto Increment Addressing *R+ E-66
       3.2.4 Symbolic (Direct) Addressing @Label E-68
       3.2.5 Indexed Addressing @Table (R) E-68
       3.2.6 Immediate Addressing E-68
       3.2.7 Program Counter Relative Addressing E-68
       3.2.8 CRU Relative Addressing E-68
   3.3 Terms and Definitions E-69
   3.4 Status Register E-69
   3.5 Instructions E-70
       3.5.1 Dual Operand Instructions with Multiple Addressing Modes for Source and Destination Operand. E-70
       3.5.2 Dual Operand Instructions with Multiple Addressing Modes for the Source Operand
             and Workspace Register Addressing for the Destination E-71
       3.5.3 Extended Operation (XOP) Instruction E-72
       3.5.4 Single Operand Instructions E-72
       3.5.5 CRU Multiple-Bit Instructions E-73
       3.5.6 CRU Single-Bit Instructions E-73
       3.5.7 Jump Instructions E-73
       3.5.8 Shift Instructions E-74
       3.5.9 Immediate Register Instructions E-74
       3.5.10 Internal Register Load Immediate Instructions E-75
       3.5.11 Internal Register Store Instructions E-75
       3.5.12 Return Workspace Pointer (RTWP) Instruction E-75
       3.5.13 External Instructions E-75
   3.6 TMS 9900 Instruction Execution Times E-76

LIST OF ILLUSTRATIONS

Figure 1   Architecture E-52

Figure 2   Memory Map E-53

Figure 3   TMS 9900 Interrupt Interface E-56

Figure 4   TMS 9900 Single-Bit CRU Address Development E-57

Figure 5   TMS 9900 LDCR/STCR Data Transfers E-57

Figure 6   TMS 9900 16-Bit Input/Output Interface E-58

Figure 7   External Instruction Decode Logic E-59

Figure 8   TMS 9900 CPU Flow Chart E-60

Figure 9   TMS 9900 Memory Bus Timing E-64

Figure 10   TMS 9900 Hold Timing E-65

Figure 11   TMS 9900 CRU Interface Timing E-67

Figure 12   Clock Timing E-77

Figure 13   Signal Timing E-78

LIST OF TABLES

Table 1 Interrupt Level Data E-55

Table 2 TMS 9900 Pin Assignments and Functions E-61

Table 3 Instruction Execution Times E-76

1. INTRODUCTION

1.1 DESCRIPTION

The TMS 9900 microprocessor is a single-chip 16-bit central processing unit (CPU) produced using N-channel silicon-gate MOS technology (see Figure 1). The instruction set of the TMS 9900 includes the capabilities offered by full minicomputers. The unique memory-to-memory architecture features multiple register files, resident in memory, which allow faster response to interrupts and increased programming flexibility. The separate bus structure simplifies the system design effort. Texas Instruments provides a compatible set of MOS and TTL memory and logic function circuits to be used with a TMS 9900 system. The system is fully supported by software and a complete prototyping system.

1.2 KEY FEATURES

- 16-Bit Instruction Word
- Full Minicomputer Instruction Set Capability Including Multiply and Divide
- Up to 65,536 Bytes of Memory
- 3-MHz Speed
- Advanced Memory-to-Memory Architecture
- Separate Memory, I/O, and Interrupt-Bus Structures
- 16 General Registers
- 16 Prioritized Interrupts
- Programmed and DMA I/O Capability
- N-Channel Silicon-Gate Technology

2. ARCHITECTURE

The memory word of the TMS 9900 is 16 bits long. Each word is also defined as 2 bytes of 8 bits. The instruction set of the TMS 9900 allows both word and byte operands. Thus, all memory locations are on even address boundaries and byte instructions can address either the even or odd byte. The memory space is 65,536 bytes or 32,768 words. The word and byte formats are shown below.

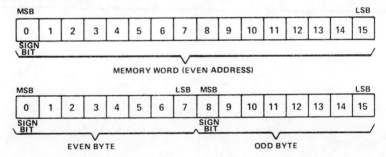

2.1 REGISTERS AND MEMORY

The TMS 9900 employs an advanced memory-to-memory architecture. Blocks of memory designated as workspace replace internal-hardware registers with program-data registers. The TMS 9900 memory map is shown in Figure 2. The first 32 words are used for interrupt trap vectors. The next contiguous block of 32 memory words is used by the extended operation (XOP) instruction for trap vectors. The last two memory words, $FFFC_{16}$ and $FFFE_{16}$, are used for the trap vector of the LOAD signal. The remaining memory is then available for programs, data, and workspace registers. If desired, any of the special areas may also be used as general memory.

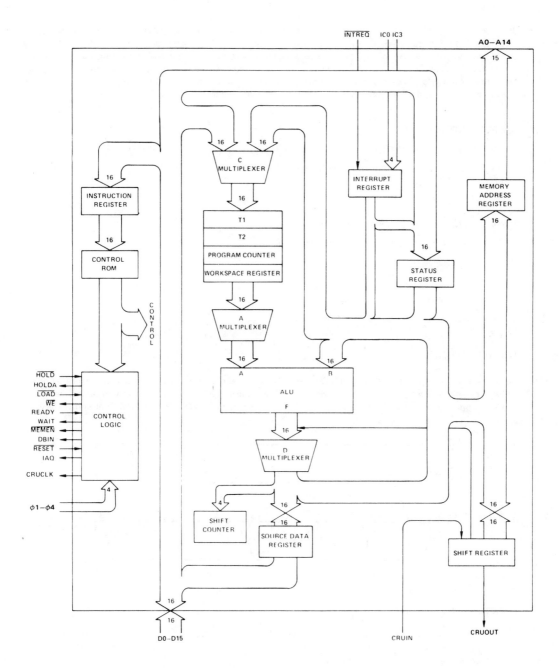

FIGURE 1 — ARCHITECTURE

E-52

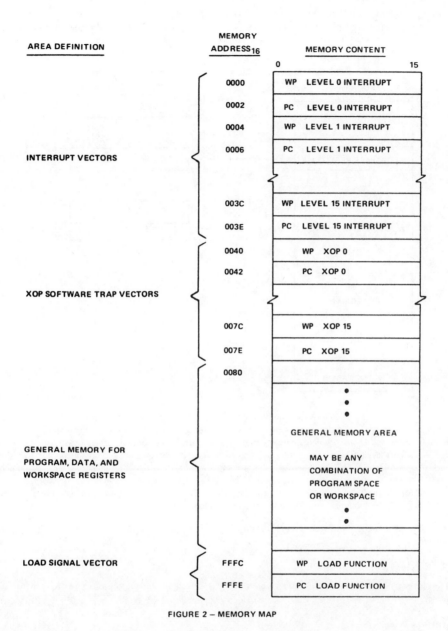

FIGURE 2 – MEMORY MAP

Three internal registers are accessible to the user. The program counter (PC) contains the address of the instruction following the current instruction being executed. This address is referenced by the processor to fetch the next instruction from memory and is then automatically incremented. The status register (ST) contains the present state of the processor and will be further defined in Section 3.4. The workspace pointer (WP) contains the address of the first word in the currently active set of workspace registers.

A workspace-register file occupies 16 contiguous memory words in the general memory area (see Figure 2). Each workspace register may hold data or addresses and function as operand registers, accumulators, address registers, or index registers. During instruction execution, the processor addresses any register in the workspace by adding the register number to the contents of the workspace pointer and initiating a memory request for the word. The relationship between the workspace pointer and its corresponding workspace is shown below.

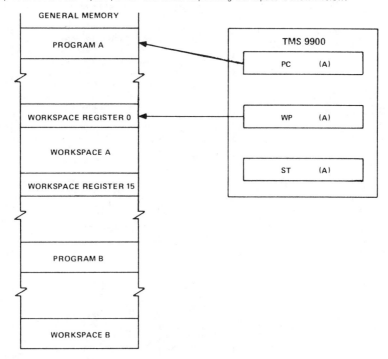

The workspace concept is particularly valuable during operations that require a context switch, which is a change from one program environment to another (as in the case of an interrupt) or to a subroutine. Such an operation, using a conventional multi-register arrangement, requires that at least part of the contents of the register file be stored and reloaded. A memory cycle is required to store or fetch each word. By exchanging the program counter, status register, and workspace pointer, the TMS 9900 accomplishes a complete context switch with only three store cycles and three fetch cycles. After the switch the workspace pointer contains the starting address of a new 16-word workspace in memory for use in the new routine. A corresponding time saving occurs when the original context is restored. Instructions in the TMS 9900 that result in a context switch include:

1. Branch and Load Workspace Pointer (BLWP)

2. Return from Subroutine (RTWP)

3. Extended Operation (XOP).

Device interrupts, $\overline{\text{RESET}}$, and $\overline{\text{LOAD}}$ also cause a context switch by forcing the processor to trap to a service subroutine.

2.2   INTERRUPTS

The TMS 9900 employs 16 interrupt levels with the highest priority level 0 and lowest level 15. Level 0 is reserved for the $\overline{\text{RESET}}$ function and all other levels may be used for external devices. The external levels may also be shared by several device interrupts, depending upon system requirements.

The TMS 9900 continuously compares the interrupt code (IC0 through IC3) with the interrupt mask contained in status-register bits 12 through 15. When the level of the pending interrupt is less than or equal to the enabling mask level (higher or equal priority interrupt), the processor recognizes the interrupt and initiates a context switch following completion of the currently executing instruction. The processor fetches the new context WP and PC from the interrupt vector locations. Then, the previous context WP, PC, and ST are stored in workspace registers 13, 14, and 15, respectively, of the new workspace. The TMS 9900 then forces the interrupt mask to a value that is one less than the level of the interrupt being serviced, except for level-zero interrupt, which loads zero into the mask. This allows only interrupts of higher priority to interrupt a service routine. The processor also inhibits interrupts until the first instruction of the service routine has been executed to preserve program linkage should a higher priority interrupt occur. All interrupt requests should remain active until recognized by the processor in the device-service routine. The individual service routines must reset the interrupt requests before the routine is complete.

If a higher priority interrupt occurs, a second context switch occurs to service the higher priority interrupt. When that routine is complete, a return instruction (RTWP) restores the first service routine parameters to the processor to complete processing of the lower-priority interrupt. All interrupt subroutines should terminate with the return instruction to restore original program parameters. The interrupt-vector locations, device assignment, enabling-mask value, and the interrupt code are shown in Table 1.

TABLE 1
INTERRUPT LEVEL DATA

Interrupt Level	Vector Location (Memory Address In Hex)	Device Assignment	Interrupt Mask Values To Enable Respective Interrupts (ST12 thru ST15)	Interrupt Codes IC0 thru IC3
(Highest priority) 0	00	Reset	0 through F*	0000
1	04	External device	1 through F	0001
2	08		2 through F	0010
3	0C		3 through F	0011
4	10		4 through F	0100
5	14		5 through F	0101
6	18		6 through F	0110
7	1C		7 through F	0111
8	20		8 through F	1000
9	24		9 through F	1001
10	28		A through F	1010
11	2C		B through F	1011
12	30		C through F	1100
13	34		D through F	1101
14	38		E and F	1110
(Lowest priority) 15	3C	External device	F only	1111

*Level 0 can not be disabled.

The TMS 9900 interrupt interface utilizes standard TTL components as shown in Figure 3. Note that for eight or less external interrupts a single SN74148 is required and for one external interrupt INTREQ is used as the interrupt signal with a hard-wired code IC0 through IC3.

2.3 INPUT/OUTPUT

The TMS 9900 utilizes a versatile direct command-driven I/O interface designated as the communications-register unit (CRU). The CRU provides up to 4096 directly addressable input bits and 4096 directly addressable output bits. Both input and output bits can be addressed individually or in fields of from 1 to 16 bits. The TMS 9900 employs three dedicated I/O pins (CRUIN, CRUOUT, and CRUCLK) and 12 bits (A3 through A14) of the address bus to interface with the CRU system. The processor instructions that drive the CRU interface can set, reset, or test any bit in the CRU array or move between memory and CRU data fields.

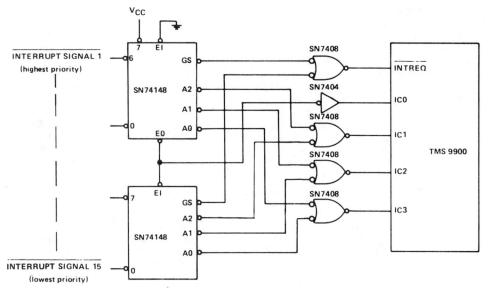

FIGURE 3 — TMS 9900 INTERRUPT INTERFACE

2.4 SINGLE-BIT CRU OPERATIONS

The TMS 9900 performs three single-bit CRU functions: test bit (TB), set bit to one (SBO), and set bit to zero (SBZ). To identify the bit to be operated upon, the TMS 9900 develops a CRU-bit address and places it on the address bus, A3 to A14.

For the two output operations (SBO and SBZ), the processor also generates a CRUCLK pulse, indicating an output operation to the CRU device, and places bit 7 of the instruction word on the CRUOUT line to accomplish the specified operation (bit 7 is a one for SBO and a zero for SBZ). A test-bit instruction transfers the addressed CRU bit from the CRUIN input line to bit 2 of the status register (EQUAL).

The TMS 9900 develops a CRU-bit address for the single-bit operations from the CRU-base address contained in workspace register 12 and the signed displacement count contained in bits 8 through 15 of the instruction. The displacement allows two's complement addressing from base minus 128 bits through base plus 127 bits. The base address from W12 is added to the signed displacement specified in the instruction and the result is loaded onto the address bus. Figure 4 illustrates the development of a single-bit CRU address.

2.5 MULTIPLE-BIT CRU OPERATIONS

The TMS 9900 performs two multiple-bit CRU operations: store communications register (STCR) and load communications register (LDCR). Both operations perform a data transfer from the CRU-to-memory or from memory-to-CRU as illustrated in Figure 5. Although the figure illustrates a full 16-bit transfer operation, any number of bits from 1 through 16 may be involved. The LDCR instruction fetches a word from memory and right-shifts it to serially transfer it to CRU output bits. If the LDCR involves eight or fewer bits, those bits come from the right-justified field within the addressed byte of the memory word. If the LDCR involves nine or more bits, those bits come from the right-justified field within the whole memory word. When transferred to the CRU interface, each successive bit receives an address that is sequentially greater than the address for the previous bit. This addressing mechanism results in an order reversal of the bits; that is, bit 15 of the memory word (or bit 7) becomes the lowest addressed bit in the CRU and bit 0 becomes the highest addressed bit in the CRU field.

An STCR instruction transfers data from the CRU to memory. If the operation involves a byte or less transfer, the transferred data will be stored right-justified in the memory byte with leading bits set to zero. If the operation involves from nine to 16 bits, the transferred data is stored right-justified in the memory word with leading bits set to zero.

E-56

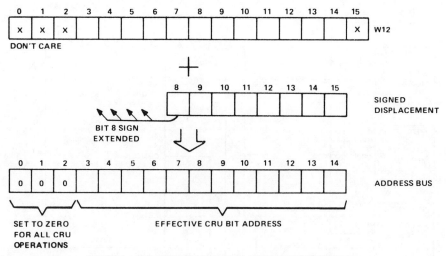

FIGURE 4 – TMS 9900 SINGLE-BIT CRU ADDRESS DEVELOPMENT

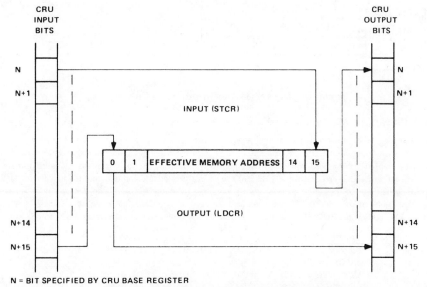

N = BIT SPECIFIED BY CRU BASE REGISTER

FIGURE 5 – TMS 9900 LDCR/STCR DATA TRANSFERS

When the input from the CRU device is complete, the first bit from the CRU is the least-significant-bit position in the memory word or byte.

Figure 6 illustrates how to implement a 16-bit input and a 16-bit output register in the CRU interface. CRU address are decoded as needed to implement up to 256 such 16-bit interface registers. In system application, however, only the exact number of interface bits needed to interface specific peripheral devices are implemented. It is not necessary have a 16-bit interface register to interface an 8-bit device.

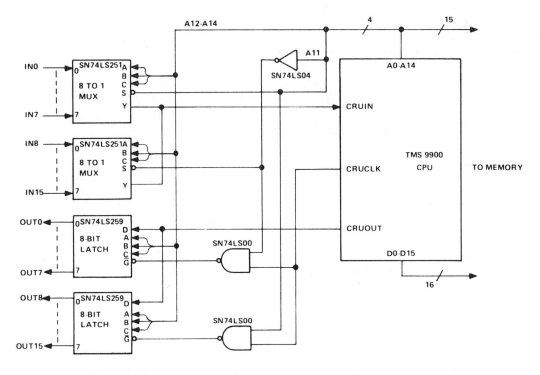

FIGURE 6 — TMS 9900 16-BIT INPUT/OUTPUT INTERFACE

2.6 EXTERNAL INSTRUCTIONS

The TMS 9900 has five external instructions that allow user-defined external functions to be initiated under program control. These instructions are CKON, CKOF, RSET, IDLE, and LREX. These mnemonics, except for IDLE, relate to functions implemented in the 990 minicomputer and do not restrict use of the instructions to initiate various user-defined functions. IDLE also causes the TMS 9900 to enter the idle state and remain until an interrupt, $\overline{\text{RESET}}$, or $\overline{\text{LOAD}}$ occurs. When any of these five instructions are executed by the TMS 9900, a unique 3-bit code appears on the most-significant 3 bits of the address bus (A0 through A2) along with a CRUCLK pulse. When the TMS 9900 is in an idle state, the 3-bit code and CRUCLK pulses occur repeatedly until the idle state is terminated. The codes are:

EXTERNAL INSTRUCTION	A0	A1	A2
LREX	H	H	H
CKOF	H	H	L
CKON	H	L	H
RSET	L	H	H
IDLE	L	H	L

Figure 7 illustrates typical external decode logic to implement these instructions. Note that a signal is generated to inhibit CRU decodes during external instructions.

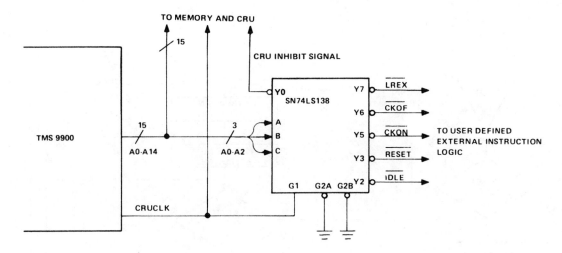

FIGURE 7 — EXTERNAL INSTRUCTION DECODE LOGIC

2.7 LOAD FUNCTION

The $\overline{\text{LOAD}}$ signal allows cold-start ROM loaders and front panels to be implemented for the TMS 9900. When active, $\overline{\text{LOAD}}$ causes the TMS 9900 to initiate an interrupt sequence immediately following the instruction being executed. Memory location FFFC is used to obtain the vector (WP and PC). The old PC, WP and ST are loaded into the new workspace and the interrupt mask is set to 0000. Then, program execution resumes using the new PC and WP.

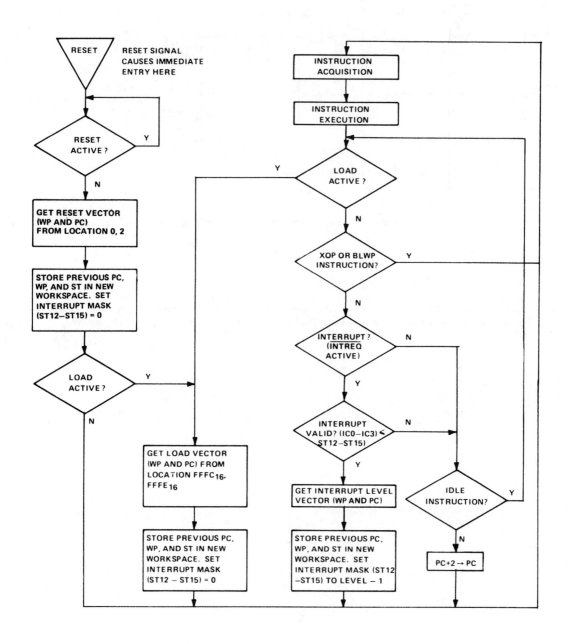

FIGURE 8 – TMS 9900 CPU FLOW CHART

2.8 TMS 9900 PIN DESCRIPTION

Table 2 defines the TMS 9900 pin assignments and describes the function of each pin.

TABLE 2
TMS 9900 PIN ASSIGNMENTS AND FUNCTIONS

SIGNATURE	PIN	I/O	DESCRIPTION
			ADDRESS BUS
A0 (MSB)	24	OUT	A0 through A14 comprise the address bus.
A1	23	OUT	This 3-state bus provides the memory-
A2	22	OUT	address vector to the external-memory
A3	21	OUT	system when MEMEN is active and I/O-bit
A4	20	OUT	addresses and external-instruction addresses
A5	19	OUT	to the I/O system when MEMEN is inactive.
A6	18	OUT	The address bus assumes the high-impedance
A7	17	OUT	state when HOLDA is active.
A8	16	OUT	
A9	15	OUT	
A10	14	OUT	
A11	13	OUT	
A12	12	OUT	
A13	11	OUT	
A14 (LSB)	10	OUT	
			DATA BUS
D0 (MSB)	41	I/O	D0 through D15 comprise the bidirectional
D1	42	I/O	3-state data bus. This bus transfers memory
D2	43	I/O	data to (when writing) and from (when
D3	44	I/O	reading) the external-memory system when
D4	45	I/O	MEMEN is active. The data bus assumes the
D5	46	I/O	high-impedance state when HOLDA is
D6	47	I/O	active.
D7	48	I/O	
D8	49	I/O	
D9	50	I/O	
D10	51	I/O	
D11	52	I/O	
D12	53	I/O	
D13	54	I/O	
D14	55	I/O	
D15 (LSB)	56	I/O	
			POWER SUPPLIES
V_{BB}	1		Supply voltage (−5 V NOM)
V_{CC}	2		Supply voltage (5 V NOM)
V_{DD}	27		Supply voltage (12 V NOM)
V_{SS}	26		Ground reference
			CLOCKS
$\phi 1$	8	IN	Phase-1 clock
$\phi 2$	9	IN	Phase-2 clock
$\phi 3$	28	IN	Phase-3 clock
$\phi 4$	25	IN	Phase-4 clock

TMS 9900 PIN ASSIGNMENTS

V_{BB}	1		64	HOLD
V_{CC}	2		63	MEMEN
WAIT	3		62	READY
LOAD	4		61	WE
HOLDA	5		60	CRUCLK
RESET	6		59	NC
IAQ	7		58	NC
$\phi 1$	8		57	NC
$\phi 2$	9		56	D15
A14	10		55	D14
A13	11		54	D13
A12	12		53	D12
A11	13		52	D11
A10	14		51	D10
A9	15		50	D9
A8	16		49	D8
A7	17		48	D7
A6	18		47	D6
A5	19		46	D5
A4	20		45	D4
A3	21		44	D3
A2	22		43	D2
A1	23		42	D1
A0	24		41	D0
$\phi 4$	25		40	NC
V_{SS}	26		39	NC
V_{DD}	27		38	NC
$\phi 3$	28		37	NC
DBIN	29		36	IC0
CRUOUT	30		35	IC1
CRUIN	31		34	IC2
INTREQ	32		33	IC3

NC — No connection

TABLE 2 (CONTINUED)

SIGNATURE	PIN	I/O	DESCRIPTION
			BUS CONTROL
DBIN	29	OUT	Data bus in. When active (high), DBIN indicates that the TMS 9900 has disabled its output buffers to allow the memory to place memory-read data on the data bus during MEMEN. DBIN remains low in all other cases except when HOLDA is active.
MEMEN	63	OUT	Memory enable. When active (low), MEMEN indicates that the address bus contains a memory address.
WE	61	OUT	Write enable. When active (low), WE indicates that memory-write data is available from the TMS 9900 to be written into memory.
CRUCLK	60	OUT	CRU clock. When active (high), CRUCLK indicates that external interface logic should sample the output data on CRUOUT or should decode external instructions on A0 through A2.
CRUIN	31	IN	CRU data in. CRUIN, normally driven by 3-state or open-collector devices, receives input data from external interface logic. When the processor executes a STCR or TB instruction, it samples CRUIN for the level of the CRU input bit specified by the address bus (A3 through A14).
CRUOUT	30	OUT	CRU data out. Serial I/O data appears on the CRUOUT line when an LDCR, SBZ, or SBO instruction is executed. The data on CRUOUT should be sampled by external I/O interface logic when CRUCLK goes active (high).
			INTERRUPT CONTROL
INTREQ	32	IN	Interrupt request. When active (low), INTREQ indicates that an external interrupt is requested. If INTREQ is active, the processor loads the data on the interrupt-code-input lines IC0 through IC3 into the internal interrupt-code-storage register. The code is compared to the interrupt mask bits of the status register. If equal or higher priority than the enabled interrupt level (interrupt code equal or less than status register bits 12 through 15) the TMS 9900 interrupt sequence is initiated. If the comparison fails, the processor ignores the request. INTREQ should remain active and the processor will continue to sample IC0 through IC3 until the program enables a sufficiently low priority to accept the request interrupt.
IC0 (MSB) IC1 IC2 IC3 (LSB)	36 35 34 33	IN IN IN IN	Interrupt codes. IC0 is the MSB of the interrupt code, which is sampled when INTREQ is active. When IC0 through IC3 are LLLH, the highest external-priority interrupt is being requested and when HHHH, the lowest-priority interrupt is being requested.
			MEMORY CONTROL
HOLD	64	IN	Hold. When active (low), HOLD indicates to the processor that an external controller (e.g., DMA device) desires to utilize the address and data buses to transfer data to or from memory. The TMS 9900 enters the hold state following a hold signal when it has completed its present memory cycle.* The processor then places the address and data buses in the high-impedance state (along with WE, MEMEN, and DBIN) and responds with a hold-acknowledge signal (HOLDA). When HOLD is removed, the processor returns to normal operation.
HOLDA	5	OUT	Hold acknowledge. When active (high), HOLDA indicates that the processor is in the hold state and the address and data buses and memory control outputs (WE, MEMEN, and DBIN) are in the high-impedance state.
READY	62	IN	Ready. When active (high), READY indicates that memory will be ready to read or write during the next clock cycle. When not-ready is indicated during a memory operation, the TMS 9900 enters a wait state and suspends internal operation until the memory systems indicate ready.
WAIT	3	OUT	Wait. When active (high), WAIT indicates that the TMS 9900 has entered a wait state because of a not-ready condition from memory.

*If the cycle following the present memory cycle is also a memory cycle, it, too, is completed before the TMS9900 enters the hold state. The maximum number of consecutive memory cycles is two.

TABLE 2 (CONCLUDED)

SIGNATURE	PIN	I/O	DESCRIPTION
			TIMING AND CONTROL
IAQ	7	OUT	Instruction acquisition. IAQ is active (high) during any memory cycle when the TMS 9900 is acquiring an instruction. IAQ can be used to detect illegal op codes.
$\overline{\text{LOAD}}$	4	IN	Load. When active (low), $\overline{\text{LOAD}}$ causes the TMS 9900 to execute a nonmaskable interrupt with memory address FFFC$_{16}$ containing the trap vector (WP and PC). The load sequence begins after the instruction being executed is completed. $\overline{\text{LOAD}}$ will also terminate an idle state. If $\overline{\text{LOAD}}$ is active during the time $\overline{\text{RESET}}$ is released, then the $\overline{\text{LOAD}}$ trap will occur after the $\overline{\text{RESET}}$ function is completed. $\overline{\text{LOAD}}$ should remain active for one instruction period. IAQ can be used to determine instruction boundaries. This signal can be used to implement cold-start ROM loaders. Additionally, front-panel routines can be implemented using CRU bits as front-panel-interface signals and software-control routines to control the panel operations.
$\overline{\text{RESET}}$	6	IN	Reset. When active (low), $\overline{\text{RESET}}$ causes the processor to be reset and inhibits $\overline{\text{WE}}$ and CRUCLK. When $\overline{\text{RESET}}$ is released, the TMS 9900 then initiates a level-zero interrupt sequence that acquires WP and PC from locations 0000 and 0002, sets all status register bits to zero, and starts execution. $\overline{\text{RESET}}$ will also terminate an idle state. $\overline{\text{RESET}}$ must be held active for a minimum of three clock cycles.

2.9 TIMING

2.9.1 MEMORY

A basic memory read and write cycle is shown in Figure 9. The read cycle is shown with no wait states and the write cycle is shown with one wait state.

$\overline{\text{MEMEN}}$ goes active (low) during each memory cycle. At the same time that $\overline{\text{MEMEN}}$ is active, the memory address appears on the address bus bits A0 through A14. If the cycle is a memory-read cycle, DBIN will go active (high) at the same time $\overline{\text{MEMEN}}$ and A0 through A14 become valid. The memory-write signal $\overline{\text{WE}}$ will remain inactive (high) during a read cycle. If the read cycle is also an instruction acquisition cycle, IAQ will go active (high) during the cycle.

The READY signal, which allows extended memory cycles, is shown high during $\phi1$ of the second clock cycle of the read operation. This indicates to the TMS 9900 that memory-read data will be valid during $\phi1$ of the next clock cycle. If READY is low during $\phi1$, then the TMS 9900 enters a wait state suspending internal operation until a READY is sensed during a subsequent $\phi1$. The memory read data is then sampled by the TMS 9900 during the next $\phi1$, which completes the memory-read cycle.

At the end of the read cycle, $\overline{\text{MEMEN}}$ and DBIN go inactive (high and low, respectively). The address bus may also change at this time, however, the data bus remains in the input mode for one clock cycle after the read cycle.

A write cycle is similar to the read cycle with the exception that $\overline{\text{WE}}$ goes active (low) as shown and valid write data appears on the data bus at the same time the address appears. The write cycle is shown as an example of a one-wait-state memory cycle. READY is low during $\phi1$ resulting in the WAIT signal shown.

2.9.2 HOLD

Other interfaces may utilize the TMS 9900 memory bus by using the hold operation (illustrated in Figure 10) of the TMS 9900. When $\overline{\text{HOLD}}$ is active (low), the TMS 9900 enters the hold state at the next available non-memory cycle. Considering that there can be a maximum of two consecutive memory cycles, the maximum delay between $\overline{\text{HOLD}}$ going active to HOLDA going active (high) could be $t_{c(\phi)}$ (for setup) + (4+W) $t_{c(\phi)}$ + $t_{c(\phi)}$ (delay for HOLDA), where W is the number of wait states per memory cycle and $t_{c(\phi)}$ is the clock cycle time. When the TMS 9900 has entered the hold state, HOLDA goes active (high) and A0 through A15, D0 through D15 DBIN, $\overline{\text{MEMEN}}$, and $\overline{\text{WE}}$ go into a high-impedance state to allow other devices to use the memory buses. When $\overline{\text{HOLD}}$ goes inactive (high), the TMS 9900 resumes processing as shown. If hold occurs during a CRU operation, the TMS 9900 uses an extra clock cycle (after the removal of the $\overline{\text{HOLD}}$ signal) to reassert the CRU address providing the normal setup times for the CRU bit transfer that was interrupted.

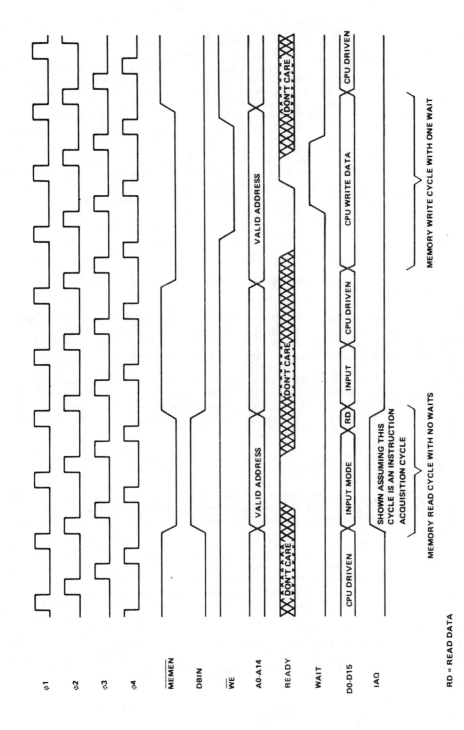

$\phi 1$

$\phi 2$

$\phi 3$

$\phi 4$

$\overline{\text{MEMEN}}$

DBIN

$\overline{\text{WE}}$

A0-A14

READY

WAIT

D0-D15

IAQ

RD = READ DATA

FIGURE 9 – TMS 9900 MEMORY BUS TIMING

E-64

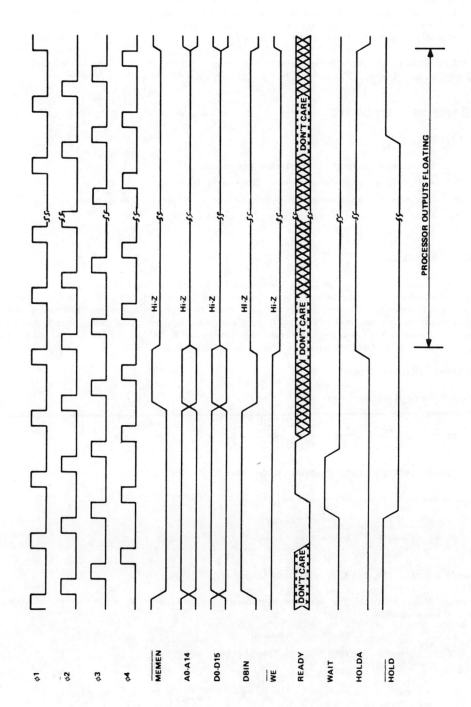

FIGURE 10 – TMS 9900 HOLD TIMING

φ1
φ2
φ3
φ4

MEMEN
A0-A14
D0-D15
DBIN
WE
READY
WAIT
HOLDA
HOLD

Hi-Z
Hi-Z
Hi-Z
Hi-Z
Hi-Z

DON'T CARE
DON'T CARE
DON'T CARE

PROCESSOR OUTPUTS FLOATING

E-65

2.9.3 CRU

CRU interface timing is shown in Figure 11. The timing for transferring two bits out and one bit in is shown. These transfers would occur during the execution of a CRU instruction. The other cycles of the instruction execution are not illustrated. To output a CRU bit, the CRU-bit address is placed on the address bus A0 through A14 and the actual bit data on CRUOUT. During the second clock cycle a CRU pulse is supplied by CRUCLK. This process is repeated until the number of bits specified by the instruction are completed.

The CRU input operation is similar in that the bit address appears on A0 through A14. During the subsequent cycle the TMS 9900 accepts the bit input data as shown. No CRUCLK pulses occur during a CRU input operation.

3. TMS 9900 INSTRUCTION SET

3.1 DEFINITION

Each TMS 9900 instruction performs one of the following operations:

- Arithmetic, logical, comparison, or manipulation operations on data
- Loading or storage of internal registers (program counter, workspace pointer, or status)
- Data transfer between memory and external devices via the CRU
- Control functions.

3.2 ADDRESSING MODES

TMS 9900 instructions contain a variety of available modes for addressing random-memory data (e.g., program parameters and flags), or formatted memory data (character strings, data lists, etc.). The following figures graphically describe the derivation of the effective address for each addressing mode. The applicability of addressing modes to particular instructions is described in Section 3.5 along with the description of the operations performed by the instruction. The symbols following the names of the addressing modes [R, *R, *R+, @ LABEL, or @ TABLE (R)] are the general forms used by TMS 9900 assemblers to select the addressing mode for register R.

3.2.1 WORKSPACE REGISTER ADDRESSING   R

Workspace Register R contains the operand.

3.2.2 WORKSPACE REGISTER INDIRECT ADDRESSING   *R

Workspace Register R contains the address of the operand.

3.2.3 WORKSPACE REGISTER INDIRECT AUTO INCREMENT ADDRESSING   *R+

Workspace Register R contains the address of the operand. After acquiring the operand, the contents of workspace register R are incremented.

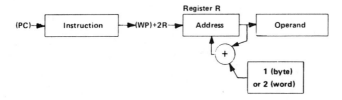

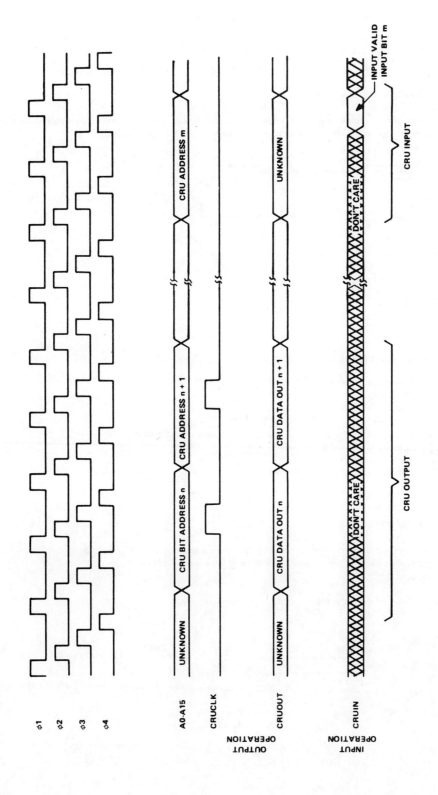

FIGURE 11 — TMS 9900 CRU INTERFACE TIMING

3.2.4 SYMBOLIC (DIRECT) ADDRESSING   @ LABEL

The word following the instruction contains the address of the operand.

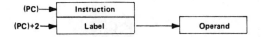

3.2.5 INDEXED ADDRESSING   @ TABLE (R)

The word following the instruction contains the base address. Workspace register R contains the index value.   The sum of the base address and the index value results in the effective address of the operand.

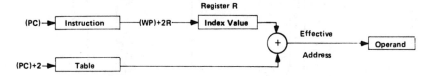

3.2.6 IMMEDIATE ADDRESSING

The word following the instruction contains the operand.

3.2.7 PROGRAM COUNTER RELATIVE ADDRESSING

The 8-bit signed displacement in the right byte (bits 8 through 15) of the instruction is multiplied by 2 and added to the updated contents of the program counter. The result is placed in the PC.

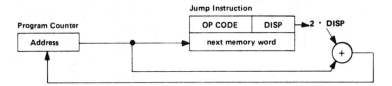

3.2.8 CRU RELATIVE ADDRESSING

The 8-bit signed displacement in the right byte of the instruction is added to the CRU base address (bits 3 through 14 of the workspace register 12). The result is the CRU address of the selected CRU bit.

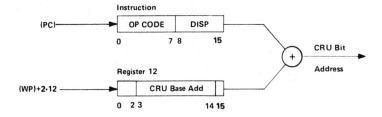

3.3 TERMS AND DEFINITIONS

The following terms are used in describing the instructions of the TMS 9900:

TERM	DEFINITION
B	Byte indicator (1=byte, 0 = word)
C	Bit count
D	Destination address register
DA	Destination address
IOP	Immediate operand
LSB(n)	Least significant (right most) bit of (n)
MSB(n)	Most significant (left most) bit of (n)
N	Don't care
PC	Program counter
Result	Result of operation performed by instruction
S	Source address register
SA	Source address
ST	Status register
STn	Bit n of status register
T_D	Destination address modifier
T_S	Source address modifier
W	Workspace register
WRn	Workspace register n
(n)	Contents of n
a $\rightarrow$ b	a is transferred to b
|n|	Absolute value of n
+	Arithmetic addition
−	Arithmetic subtraction
AND	Logical AND
OR	Logical OR
$\oplus$	Logical exclusive OR
$\overline{n}$	Logical complement of n

3.4 STATUS REGISTER

The status register contains the interrupt mask level and information pertaining to the instruction operation.

0	1	2	3	4	5	6	7	8	9	10	11	12	13	14	15
ST0	ST1	ST2	ST3	ST4	ST5	ST6		not used (=0)				ST12	ST13	ST14	ST15
L>	A>	=	C	O	P	X							Interrupt Mask		

BIT	NAME	INSTRUCTION	CONDITION TO SET BIT TO 1
ST0	LOGICAL GREATER THAN	C,CB	If MSB(SA) = 1 and MSB(DA) = 0, or if MSB(SA) = MSB(DA) and MSB of (DA) − (SA) = 1
		CI	If MSB(W) = 1 and MSB of IOP = 0, or if MSB(W) = MSB of IOP and MSB of IOP − (W) = 1
		ABS	If (SA) ≠ 0
		All Others	If result ≠ 0
ST1	ARITHMETIC GREATER THAN	C,CB	If MSB(SA) = 0 and MSB(DA) = 1, or if MSB(SA) = MSB(DA) and MSB(DA) − (SA) = 1
		CI	If MSB(W) = 0 and MSB of IOP = 1, or if MSB(W) = MSB of IOP and MSB of IOP − (W) = 1
		ABS	If MSB(SA) = 0 and (SA) ≠ 0
		All Others	If MSB of result = 0 and result ≠ 0

— Continued

BIT	NAME	INSTRUCTION	CONDITION TO SET BIT TO 1
ST2	EQUAL	C, CB	If (SA) = (DA)
		C1	If (W) = IOP
		COC	If (SA) and $(\overline{DA})$ = 0
		CZC	If (SA) and (DA) = 0
		TB	If CRUIN = 1
		ABS	If (SA) = 0
		All others	If result = 0
ST3	CARRY	A, AB, ABS, AI, DEC, DECT, INC, INCT, NEG, S, SB	If CARRY OUT = 1
		SLA, SRA, SRC, SRL	If last bit shifted out = 1
ST4	OVERFLOW	A, AB	If MSB(SA) = MSB(DA) and MSB of result $\neq$ MSB(DA)
		AI	If MSB(W) = MSB of IOP and MSB of result $\neq$ MSB(W)
		S, SB	If MSB(SA) $\neq$ MSB(DA) and MSB of result $\neq$ MSB(DA)
		DEC, DECT	If MSB(SA) = 1 and MSB of result = 0
		INC, INCT	If MSB(SA) = 0 and MSB of result = 1
		SLA	If MSB changes during shift
		DIV	If MSB(SA) = 0 and MSB(DA) = 1, or if MSB(SA) = MSB(DA) and MSB of (DA) − (SA) = 0
		ABS, NEG	If (SA) = 8000_{16}
ST5	PARITY	CB, MOVB	If (SA) has odd number of 1's
		LDCR, STCR	If $1 \leqslant C \leqslant 8$ and (SA) has odd number of 1's
		AB, SB, SOCB, SZCB	If result has odd number of 1's
ST6	XOP	XOP	If XOP instruction is executed
ST12–ST15	INTERRUPT MASK	LIMI	If corresponding bit of IOP is 1
		RTWP	If corresponding bit of WR15 is 1

3.5 INSTRUCTIONS

3.5.1 Dual Operand Instructions with Multiple Addressing Modes for Source and Destination Operand

0	1	2	3	4	5	6	7	8	9	10	11	12	13	14	15

General format:

OP CODE	B	T_D	D	T_S	S

If B = 1 the operands are bytes and the operand addresses are byte addresses. If B = 0 the operands are words and the operand addresses are word addresses.

The addressing mode for each operand is determined by the T field of that operand.

T_S OR T_D	S OR D	ADDRESSING MODE	NOTES
00	0, 1, . . . 15	Workspace register	1
01	0, 1, . . . 15	Workspace register indirect	
10	0	Symbolic	4
10	1, 2, . . . 15	Indexed	2,4
11	0, 1, . . . 15	Workspace register indirect auto-increment	3

NOTES: 1. When a workspace register is the operand of a byte instruction (bit 3 = 1), the left byte (bits 0 through 7) is the operand and the right byte (bits 8 through 15) is unchanged.

2. Workspace register 0 may not be used for indexing.

3. The workspace register is incremented by 1 for byte instructions (bit 3 = 1) and is incremented by 2 for word instructions (bit 3 = 0).

4. When T_S = T_D = 10, two words are required in addition to the instruction word. The first word is the source operand base address and the second word is the destination operand base address.

MNEMONIC	OP CODE			B 3	MEANING	RESULT COMPARED TO 0	STATUS BITS AFFECTED	DESCRIPTION
	0	1	2					
A	1	0	1	0	Add	Yes	0-4	(SA)+(DA) → (DA)
AB	1	0	1	1	Add bytes	Yes	0-5	(SA)+(DA) → (DA)
C	1	0	0	0	Compare	No	0-2	Compare (SA) to (DA) and set appropriate status bits
CB	1	0	0	1	Compare bytes	No	0-2,5	Compare (SA) to (DA) and set appropriate status bits
S	0	1	1	0	Subtract	Yes	0-4	(DA) − (SA) → (DA)
SB	0	1	1	1	Subtract bytes	Yes	0-5	(DA) − (SA) → (DA)
SOC	1	1	1	0	Set ones corresponding	Yes	0-2	(DA) OR (SA) → (DA)
SOCB	1	1	1	1	Set ones corresponding bytes	Yes	0-2,5	(DA) OR (SA) → (DA)
SZC	0	1	0	0	Set zeroes corresponding	Yes	0-2	(DA) AND ($\overline{SA}$) → (DA)
SZCB	0	1	0	1	Set zeroes corresponding bytes	Yes	0-2,5	(DA) AND ($\overline{SA}$) → (DA)
MOV	1	1	0	0	Move	Yes	0-2	(SA) → (DA)
MOVB	1	1	0	1	Move bytes	Yes	0-2,5	(SA) → (DA)

3.5.2 Dual Operand Instructions with Multiple Addressing Modes for the Source Operand and Workspace Register Addressing for the Destination

General format:

0 1 2 3 4 5	6 7 8 9	10 11	12 13 14 15
OP CODE	D	T_S	S

The addressing mode for the source operand is determined by the T_S field.

T_S	S	ADDRESSING MODE	NOTES
00	0, 1, . . . 15	Workspace register	
01	0, 1, . . . 15	Workspace register indirect	
10	0	Symbolic	
10	1, 2, . . . 15	Indexed	1
11	0, 1, . . . 15	Workspace register indirect auto increment	2

NOTES: 1. Workspace register 0 may not be used for indexing.
2. The workspace register is incremented by 2.

MNEMONIC	OP CODE 0 1 2 3 4 5	MEANING	RESULT COMPARED TO 0	STATUS BITS AFFECTED	DESCRIPTION
COC	0 0 1 0 0 0	Compare ones corresponding	No	2	Test (D) to determine if 1's are in each bit position where 1's are in (SA). If so, set ST2.
CZC	0 0 1 0 0 1	Compare zeros corresponding	No	2	Test (D) to determine if 0's are in each bit position where 1's are in (SA). If so, set ST2.
XOR	0 0 1 0 1 0	Exclusive OR	Yes	0-2	(D) $\oplus$ (SA) → (D)
MPY	0 0 1 1 1 0	Multiply	No		Multiply unsigned (D) by unsigned (SA) and place unsigned 32-bit product in D (most significant) and D+1 (least significant). If WR15 is D, the next word in memory after WR15 will be used for the least significant half of the product.
DIV	0 0 1 1 1 1	Divide	No	4	If unsigned (SA) is less than or equal to unsigned (D), perform no operation and set ST4. Otherwise, divide unsigned (D) and (D+1) by unsigned (SA). Quotient → (D), remainder → (D+1). If D = 15, the next word in memory after WR 15 will be used for the remainder.

3.5.3 Extended Operation (XOP) Instruction

	0	1	2	3	4	5	6	7	8	9	10	11	12	13	14	15
General format:	0	0	1	0	1	1		D			T_S			S		

The T_S and S fields provide multiple mode addressing capability for the source operand. When the XOP is executed, ST6 is set and the following transfers occur:

$(40_{16} + 4D) \rightarrow (WP)$
$(42_{16} + 4D) \rightarrow (PC)$
$SA \rightarrow (new\ WR11)$
$(old\ WP) \rightarrow (new\ WR13)$
$(old\ PC) \rightarrow (new\ WR14)$
$(old\ ST) \rightarrow (new\ WR15)$

The TMS 9900 does not test interrupt requests ($\overline{INTREQ}$) upon completion of the XOP instruction.

3.5.4 Single Operand Instructions

	0	1	2	3	4	5	6	7	8	9	10	11	12	13	14	15
General format:					OP CODE						T_S			S		

The T_S and S fields provide multiple mode addressing capability for the source operand.

MNEMONIC	OP CODE 0 1 2 3 4 5 6 7 8 9	MEANING	RESULT COMPARED TO 0	STATUS BITS AFFECTED	DESCRIPTION
B	0 0 0 0 0 1 0 0 0 1	Branch	No	—	$SA \rightarrow (PC)$
BL	0 0 0 0 0 1 1 0 1 0	Branch and link	No	—	$(PC) \rightarrow (WR11)$; $SA \rightarrow (PC)$
BLWP	0 0 0 0 0 1 0 0 0 0	Branch and load workspace pointer	No	—	$(SA) \rightarrow (WP)$;$(SA+1) \rightarrow (PC)$; (old WP) $\rightarrow$ (new WR13); (old PC) $\rightarrow$ (new WR14); (old ST) $\rightarrow$ (new WR15); the interrupt input ($\overline{INTREQ}$) is not tested upon completion of the BLWP instruction.
CLR	0 0 0 0 0 1 0 0 1 1	Clear operand	No	—	$0 \rightarrow (SA)$
SETO	0 0 0 0 0 1 1 1 0 0	Set to ones	No	—	$FFFF_{16} \rightarrow (SA)$
INV	0 0 0 0 0 1 0 1 0 1	Invert	Yes	0-2	$\overline{(SA)} \rightarrow (SA)$
NEG	0 0 0 0 0 1 0 1 0 0	Negate	Yes	0-4	$-(SA) \rightarrow (SA)$
ABS	0 0 0 0 0 1 1 1 0 1	Absolute value*	No	0-4	$|(SA)| \rightarrow (SA)$
SWPB	0 0 0 0 0 1 1 0 1 1	Swap bytes	No	—	(SA), bits 0 thru 7 $\rightarrow$ (SA), bits 8 thru 15; (SA), bits 8 thru 15 $\rightarrow$ (SA), bits 0 thru 7.
INC	0 0 0 0 0 1 0 1 1 0	Increment	Yes	0-4	$(SA) + 1 \rightarrow (SA)$
INCT	0 0 0 0 0 1 0 1 1 1	Increment by two	Yes	0-4	$(SA) + 2 \rightarrow (SA)$
DEC	0 0 0 0 0 1 1 0 0 0	Decrement	Yes	0-4	$(SA) - 1 \rightarrow (SA)$
DECT	0 0 0 0 0 1 1 0 0 1	Decrement by two	Yes	0-4	$(SA) - 2 \rightarrow (SA)$
X†	0 0 0 0 0 1 0 0 1 0	Execute	No	—	Execute the instruction at SA.

*Operand is compared to zero for status bit.

†If additional memory words for the execute instruction are required to define the operands of the instruction located at SA, these words will be accessed from PC and the PC will be updated accordingly. The instruction acquisition signal (IAQ) will not be true when the TMS 9900 accesses the instruction at SA. Status bits are affected in the normal manner for the instruction executed.

3.5.5 CRU Multiple-Bit Instructions

0	1	2	3	4	5	6	7	8	9	10	11	12	13	14	15

General format:

OP CODE	C	T$_S$	S

The C field specifies the number of bits to be transferred. If C = 0, 16 bits will be transferred. The CRU base register (WR12, bits 3 through 14) defines the starting CRU bit address. The bits are transferred serially and the CRU address is incremented with each bit transfer, although the contents of WR12 is not affected. T$_S$ and S provide multiple mode addressing capability for the source operand. If 8 or fewer bits are transferred (C = 1 through 8), the source address is a byte address. If 9 or more bits are transferred (C = 0, 9 through 15), the source address is a word address. If the source is addressed in the workspace register indirect auto increment mode, the workspace register is incremented by 1 if C = 1 through 8, and is incremented by 2 otherwise.

MNEMONIC	OP CODE 0 1 2 3 4 5	MEANING	RESULT COMPARED TO 0	STATUS BITS AFFECTED	DESCRIPTION
LDCR	0 0 1 1 0 0	Load communcation register	Yes	0-2,5[†]	Beginning with LSB of (SA), transfer the specified number of bits from (SA) to the CRU.
STCR	0 0 1 1 0 1	Store communcation register	Yes	0-2,5[†]	Beginning with LSB of (SA), transfer the specified number of bits from the CRU to (SA). Load unfilled bit positions with 0.

[†]ST5 is affected only if $1 \leqslant C \leqslant 8$.

3.5.6 CRU Single-Bit Instructions

0	1	2	3	4	5	6	7	8	9	10	11	12	13	14	15

General format:

OP CODE	SIGNED DISPLACEMENT

CRU relative addressing is used to address the selected CRU bit.

MNEMONIC	OP CODE 0 1 2 3 4 5 6 7	MEANING	STATUS BITS AFFECTED	DESCRIPTION
SBO	0 0 0 1 1 1 0 1	Set bit to one	–	Set the selected CRU output bit to 1.
SBZ	0 0 0 1 1 1 1 0	Set bit to zero	–	Set the selected CRU output bit to 0.
TB	0 0 0 1 1 1 1 1	Test bit	2	If the selected CRU input bit = 1, set ST2.

3.5.7 Jump Instructions

0	1	2	3	4	5	6	7	8	9	10	11	12	13	14	15

General format:

OP CODE	DISPLACEMENT

Jump instructions cause the PC to be loaded with the value selected by PC relative addressing if the bits of ST are at specified values. Otherwise, no operation occurs and the next instruction is executed since PC points to the next instruction. The displacement field is a word count to be added to PC. Thus, the jump instruction has a range of −128 to 127 words from memory-word address following the jump instruction. No ST bits are affected by jump instruction.

MNEMONIC	OP CODE 0 1 2 3 4 5 6 7	MEANING	ST CONDITION TO LOAD PC
JEQ	0 0 0 1 0 0 1 1	Jump equal	ST2 = 1
JGT	0 0 0 1 0 1 0 1	Jump greater than	ST1 = 1
JH	0 0 0 1 1 0 1 1	Jump high	ST0 = 1 and ST2 = 0
JHE	0 0 0 1 0 1 0 0	Jump high or equal	ST0 = 1 or ST2 = 1
JL	0 0 0 1 1 0 1 0	Jump low	ST0 = 0 and ST2 = 0
JLE	0 0 0 1 0 0 1 0	Jump low or equal	ST0 = 0 or ST2 = 1
JLT	0 0 0 1 0 0 0 1	Jump less than	ST1 = 0 and ST2 = 0
JMP	0 0 0 1 0 0 0 0	Jump unconditional	unconditional
JNC	0 0 0 1 0 1 1 1	Jump no carry	ST3 = 0
JNE	0 0 0 1 0 1 1 0	Jump not equal	ST2 = 0
JNO	0 0 0 1 1 0 0 1	Jump no overflow	ST4 = 0
JOC	0 0 0 1 1 0 0 0	Jump on carry	ST3 = 1
JOP	0 0 0 1 1 1 0 0	Jump odd parity	ST5 = 1

3.5.8 Shift Instructions

General format:

0	1	2	3	4	5	6	7	8	9	10	11	12	13	14	15
			OP CODE						C				W		

If C = 0, bits 12 through 15 of WR0 contain the shift count. If C = 0 and bits 12 through 15 of WR0 = 0, the shift count is 16.

MNEMONIC	OP CODE 0 1 2 3 4 5 6 7	MEANING	RESULT COMPARED TO 0	STATUS BITS AFFECTED	DESCRIPTION
SLA	0 0 0 0 1 0 1 0	Shift left arithmetic	Yes	0-4	Shift (W) left. Fill vacated bit positions with 0.
SRA	0 0 0 0 1 0 0 0	Shift right arithmetic	Yes	0-3	Shift (W) right. Fill vacated bit positions with original MSB of (W).
SRC	0 0 0 0 1 0 1 1	Shift right circular	Yes	0-3	Shift (W) right. Shift previous LSB into MSB.
SRL	0 0 0 0 1 0 0 1	Shift right logical	Yes	0-3	Shift (W) right. Fill vacated bit positions with 0's.

3.5.9 Immediate Register Instructions

General format:

0	1	2	3	4	5	6	7	8	9	10	11	12	13	14	15
				OP CODE							N		W		
				IOP											

MNEMONIC	OP CODE 0 1 2 3 4 5 6 7 8 9 10	MEANING	RESULT COMPARED TO 0	STATUS BITS AFFECTED	DESCRIPTION
AI	0 0 0 0 0 0 1 0 0 0 1	Add immediate	Yes	0-4	(W) + IOP → (W)
ANDI	0 0 0 0 0 0 1 0 0 1 0	AND immediate	Yes	0-2	(W) AND IOP → (W)
CI	0 0 0 0 0 0 1 0 1 0 0	Compare immediate	Yes	0-2	Compare (W) to IOP and set appropriate status bits
LI	0 0 0 0 0 0 1 0 0 0 0	Load immediate	Yes	0-2	IOP → (W)
ORI	0 0 0 0 0 0 1 0 0 1 1	OR immediate	Yes	0-2	(W) OR IOP → (W)

3.5.10 Internal Register Load Immediate Instructions

General format:

0	1	2	3	4	5	6	7	8	9	10	11	12	13	14	15
OP CODE											N				
IOP															

MNEMONIC	OP CODE											MEANING	DESCRIPTION
	0	1	2	3	4	5	6	7	8	9	10		
LWPI	0	0	0	0	0	0	1	0	1	1	1	Load workspace pointer immediate	IOP → (WP), no ST bits affected
LIMI	0	0	0	0	0	0	1	1	0	0	0	Load interrupt mask	IOP, bits 12 thru 15 → ST12 thru ST15

3.5.11 Internal Register Store Instructions

General format:

0	1	2	3	4	5	6	7	8	9	10	11	12	13	14	15
OP CODE											N		W		

No ST bits are affected.

MNEMONIC	OP CODE											MEANING	DESCRIPTION
	0	1	2	3	4	5	6	7	8	9	10		
STST	0	0	0	0	0	0	1	0	1	1	0	Store status register	(ST) → (W)
STWP	0	0	0	0	0	0	1	0	1	0	1	Store workspace pointer	(WP) → (W)

3.5.12 Return Workspace Pointer (RTWP) Instruction

General format:

0	1	2	3	4	5	6	7	8	9	10	11	12	13	14	15
0	0	0	0	0	0	1	1	1	0	0	N				

The RTWP instruction causes the following transfers to occur:

(WR15) → (ST)
(WR14) → (PC)
(WR13) → (WP)

3.5.13 External Instructions

General format:

0	1	2	3	4	5	6	7	8	9	10	11	12	13	14	15
OP CODE											N				

External instructions cause the three most-significant address lines (A0 through A2) to be set to the below-described levels and the CRUCLK line to be pulsed, allowing external control functions to be initiated.

MNEMONIC	OP CODE											MEANING	STATUS BITS AFFECTED	DESCRIPTION	ADDRESS BUS		
	0	1	2	3	4	5	6	7	8	9	10				A0	A1	A2
IDLE	0	0	0	0	0	0	1	1	0	1	0	Idle	—	Suspend TMS 9900 instruction execution until an interrupt, LOAD, or RESET occurs	L	H	L
RSET	0	0	0	0	0	0	1	1	0	1	1	Reset	12–15	0 → ST12 thru ST15	L	H	H
CKOF	0	0	0	0	0	0	1	1	1	1	0	User defined		— — —	H	H	L
CKON	0	0	0	0	0	0	1	1	1	0	1	User defined		— — —	H	L	H
LREX	0	0	0	0	0	0	1	1	1	1	1	User defined		— — —	H	H	H

3.6 TMS 9900 INSTRUCTION EXECUTION TIMES

Instruction execution times for the TMS 9900 are a function of:

1) Clock cycle time, $t_{c(\phi)}$

2) Addressing mode used where operands have multiple addressing mode capability

3) Number of wait states required per memory access.

Table 3 lists the number of clock cycles and memory accesses required to execute each TMS 9900 instruction. For instructions with multiple addressing modes for either or both operands, the table lists the number of clock cycles and memory accesses with all operands addressed in the workspace-register mode. To determine the additional number of clock cycles and memory accesses required for modified addressing, add the appropriate values from the referenced tables. The total instruction-execution time for an instruction is:

$$T = t_{c(\phi)} \quad (C + W \cdot M)$$

where:

T = total instruction execution time;

$t_{c(\phi)}$ = clock cycle time;

C = number of clock cycles for instruction execution plus address modification;

W = number of required wait states per memory access for instruction execution plus address modification;

M = number of memory accesses.

TABLE 3
INSTRUCTION EXECUTION TIMES

INSTRUCTION	CLOCK CYCLES C	MEMORY ACCESS M	ADDRESS MODIFICATION[†] SOURCE	DEST	INSTRUCTION	CLOCK CYCLES C	MEMORY ACCESS M	ADDRESS MODIFICATION[†] SOURCE	DEST
A	14	4	A	A	LWPI	10	2	–	–
AB	14	4	B	B	MOV	14	4	A	A
ABS (MSB = 0)	12	2	A	–	MOVB	14	4	B	B
(MSB = 1)	14	3	A	–	MPY	52	5	A	–
AI	14	4	–	–	NEG	12	3	A	–
ANDI	14	4	–	–	ORI	14	4	–	–
B	8	2	A	–	RSET	12	1	–	–
BL	12	3	A	–	RTWP	14	4	–	–
BLWP	26	6	A	–	S	14	4	A	A
C	14	3	A	A	SB	14	4	B	B
CB	14	3	B	B	SBO	12	2	–	–
CI	14	3	–	–	SBZ	12	2	–	–
CKOF	12	1	–	–	SETO	10	3	A	–
CKON	12	1	–	–	Shift (C≠0)	12+2C	3	–	–
CLR	10	3	A	–	(C=0, Bits 12–15				
COC	14	3	A	–	of WRO=0)	52	4	–	–
CZC	14	3	A	–	(C=0, Bits 12–15				
DEC	10	3	A	–	of WRP=N≠0)	20+2N	4	–	–
DECT	10	3	A	–	SOC	14	4	A	A
DIV (ST4 is set)	16	3	A	–	SOCB	14	4	B	B
DIV (ST4 is reset)*	92-124	6	A	–	STCR (C=0)	60	4	A	–
IDLE	12	1	–	–	(1⩽C⩽7)	42	4	B	–
INC	10	3	A	–	(C=8)	44	4	B	–
INCT	10	3	A	–	(9⩽C⩽15)	58	4	A	–
INV	10	3	A	–	STST	8	2	–	–
Jump (PC is					STWP	8	2	–	–
changed)	10	1	–	–	SWPB	10	3	A	–
(PC is not					SZC	14	4	A	A
changed)	8	1	–	–	SZCB	14	4	B	B
LDCR (C = 0)	52	3	A	–	TB	12	2	–	–
(1⩽C⩽8)	20+2C	3	B	–	X **	8	2	A	–
(9⩽C⩽15)	20+2C	3	A	–	XOP	44	8	A	–
LI	12	3	–	–	XOR	14	4	A	–
LIMI	16	3	–	–					
LREX	12	1	–	–					
RESET function	28	6	–	–	Undefined op codes				
LOAD function	24	6	–	–	0000-01FF,0320-	6	1	–	–
Interrupt context					033F,0C00-0FFF,				
switch	24	6	–	–	0780-07FF				

*Execution time is dependent upon the partial quotient after each clock cycle during execution.

**Execution time is added to the execution time of the instruction located at the source address.

[†]The letters A and B refer to the respective tables that follow.

ADDRESS MODIFICATION – TABLE A

ADDRESSING MODE	CLOCK CYCLES C	MEMORY ACCESSES M
WR (T_S or T_D = 00)	0	0
WR indirect (T_S or T_D = 01)	4	1
WR indirect auto-increment (T_S or T_D = 11)	8	2
Symbolic (T_S or T_D = 10, S or D = 0)	8	1
Indexed (T_S or T_D = 10, S or D ≠ 0)	8	2

ADDRESS MODIFICATION – TABLE B

ADDRESSING MODE	CLOCK CYCLES C	MEMORY ACCESSES M
WR (T_S or T_D = 00)	0	0
WR indirect (T_S or T_D = 01)	4	1
WR indirect auto-increment (T_S or T_D = 11)	6	2
Symbolic (T_S or T_D = 10, S or D = 0)	8	1
Indexed (T_S or T_D = 10, S or D ≠ 0)	8	2

As an example, the instruction MOVB is used in a system with $t_{c(\phi)}$ = 0.333 μs and no wait states are required to access memory. Both operands are addressed in the workspace register mode:

$$T = t_{c(\phi)} (C + W \cdot M) = 0.333 (14 + 0 \cdot 4) \ \mu s = 4.662 \ \mu s.$$

If two wait states per memory access were required, the execution time is:

$$T = 0.333 (14 + 2 \cdot 4) \ \mu s = 7.326 \ \mu s.$$

If the source operand was addressed in the symbolic mode and two wait states were required:

$$T = t_{c(\phi)} (C + W \cdot M)$$
$$C = 14 + 8 = 22$$
$$M = 4 + 1 = 5$$
$$T = 0.333 (22 + 2 \cdot 5) \ \mu s = 10.656 \ \mu s.$$

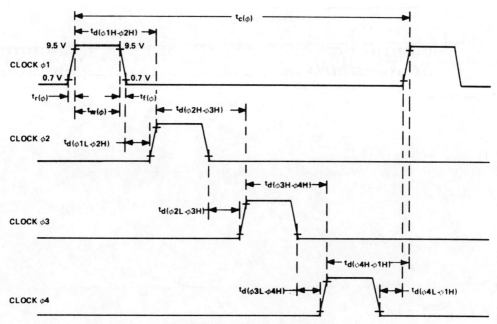

NOTE: All timing and voltage levels shown on ϕ1 applies to ϕ2, ϕ3, and ϕ4 in the same manner.

FIGURE 12 – CLOCK TIMING

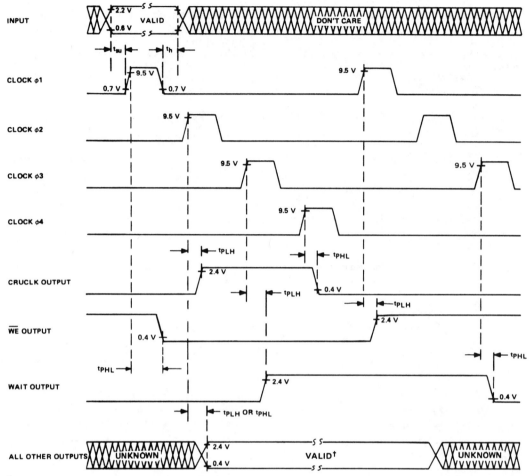

† The number of cycles over which input/output data must/will remain valid can be determined from Section 3.9. Note that in all cases data should not change during φ1.

FIGURE 13—SIGNAL TIMING

SBP 0400 Data

TABLE OF CONTENTS

1. **ARCHITECTURE** **E-82**
   - a. Programmable Logic Array E-83
   - b. Operation Register E-83
   - c. Arithmetic Logic Unit E-83
   - d. Relative Position Control E-87
   - e. Register Files E-88
   - f. Program Counter Register E-90
   - g. Address-Out Multiplexer E-92
   - h. A Bus E-92
   - i. B Bus E-95
   - j. Working Register E-95
   - k. Extended Working Register E-95
   - l. Data-Out Multiplexer E-98
   - m. Data-Out I Multiplexer E-99
   - n. Data-Out J Multiplexer E-101
   - o. Extended Working Register Multiplexer E-101
   - p. Extended Working Register K Multiplexer E-102
   - q. Extended Working Register L Multiplexer E-102
   - r. Working Register Multiplexer E-102

2. **DATA HANDLING** **E-103**
   - a. WR Single-Precision Shifts/Circulates E-103
   - b. WR, XWR Double-Precision Shifts/Circulates . . . E-106
   - c. Single-Signed Double-Precision RSA E-111
   - d. Double-Signed Double-Precision RSA E-111
   - e. Single-Signed Double-Precision LSA E-114
   - f. Double-Signed Double-Precision LSA E-114
   - g. Compound-Function WR, XWR Double-Precision Shifts/Circulates E-114

3. **INSTRUCTIONS** **E-117**
   - a. Operation Forms E-117
   - b. Operation Field E-118
   - c. Single-Length Addition — Form II ALU Operations E-120
   - d. Transfer — Form III Operations E-120
   - e. Add Subtract with Double-Precision Shift/Circulate — Form IV ALU Operations E-120
   - f. Shifts/Circulates with Active Carry — Form V and VI ALU Operations E-120
   - g. D-Field E-121
   - h. S-Field E-121
   - i. Operation Form I E-122

TABLE OF CONTENTS (Continued)

3.   j.   Operation Form II E-122

k.   Operation Form III E-122

l.   Operation Form IV E-123

m.   Operation Form V E-124

n.   Operation Form VI E-124

LIST OF ILLUSTRATIONS

Figure 3.4   SBP 0400 Functional Block Diagram E-84

Figure 3.5   Programmable Logic Array (PLA) E-85

Figure 3.6   Arithmetic Logic Unit (ALU) E-86

Figure 3.7   Single-Level Look-Ahead E-88

Figure 3.8   Typical Register File Store Sequence E-91

Figure 3.9   16-Bit Program Counter E-93

Figure 3.10   12-Bit Program Counter E-94

Figure 3.11   Right-Shift Logical — Single-Precision (RSL — SP) E-105

Figure 3.12   Left-Shift Logical — Single-Precision (LSL — SP) E-105

Figure 3.13   Right-Shift Arithmetic — Single-Precision (RSA — SP) E-107

Figure 3.14   Left-Shift Arithmetic — Single-Precision (LSA — SP) E-107

Figure 3.15   Right-Circulate — Single-Precision (RCIR — SP) E-108

Figure 3.16   Left-Circulate — Single-Precision (LCIR — SP) E-108

Figure 3.17   Right-Shift Logical — Double-Precision (RSL — DP) E-110

Figure 3.18   Left-Shift Logical — Double-Precision (LSL — DP) E-110

Figure 3.19   Right-Shift Arithmetic — Single-Sign/Double-Precision

                 (RSA — SS/DP) E-112

Figure 3.20   Right-Shift Arithmetic — Double-Sign/Double-Precision

                 (RSA — DS/DP) E-112

Figure 3.21   Left-Shift Arithmetic — Single-Sign/Double-Precision

                 (LSA — SS/DP) E-113

Figure 3.22   Left-Shift Arithmetic — Double-Sign/Double-Precision

                 (LSA — DS/DP) E-113

Figure 3.23   Right-Circulate — Double-Precision (RCIR — DP) E-115

Figure 3.24   Left-Circulate — Double-Precision (LCIR — DP) E-115

Figure 3.25   Nine-Bit Microinstruction (Operation-Select Word) E-117

LIST OF TABLES

Table 3.2   ALU Function-Select Table E-87
Table 3.3   Position Control Functions E-89
Table 3.4   RF Source Operands E-89
Table 3.5   RF Destination Operands E-90
Table 3.6   Program Counter Incrementation E-92
Table 3.7   Working Register Source Operands E-96
Table 3.8   Working Register Destination Operands E-97
Table 3.9   Extended Working Register Source Operands E-98
Table 3.10   Working Register Destination Operands E-99
Table 3.11   DO MUX Transfers E-100
Table 3.12   DO IMUX Transfers to $\overline{\text{WRLFT}}$ E-100
Table 3.13   DO JMUX Transfers to $\overline{\text{WRRT}}$ E-101
Table 3.14   XWR MUX Transfers E-102
Table 3.15   XWR KMUX Transfers to $\overline{\text{XWRLFT}}$ E-103
Table 3.16   XWR LMUX Transfers to $\overline{\text{XWRRT}}$ E-103
Table 3.17   WR Single-Precision Shifts/Circulates E-104
Table 3.18   WR, XWR Double-Precision Shifts/Circulates E-109
Table 3.19   Compound-Function WR, XWR Double-Precision
              Shifts/Circulates E-116
Table 3.20   ALU Function-Select Table E-118
Table 3.21   D-Field Register-File Select E-121
Table 3.22   Register-File Selection Table E-121
Table 3.23   Operation Form I E-122
Table 3.24   Operation Form II E-123
Table 3.25   Operation Form III E-123
Table 3.26   Operation Form IV E-124
Table 3.27   Operation Form V E-124
Table 3.28   Operation Form VI E-125
Table 3.29   Data-In Bus Source Operands E-126
Table 3.30   Extended Working Register Source Operands E-127
Table 3.31   Register File Source Operands E-127
Table 3.32   Working Register Source Operands E-128

The SBP 0400 is a 4-bit expandable parallel binary processor element monolithically integrating 1660 functional gates within a 40-pin package. This controller/processor building block combines Integrated Injection Logic (I^2L) with a microprogrammable bit-slice architecture to offer a high degree of usability and flexibility. In the following three subsections, the architecture, data handling, and instructions (operation-select word) are discussed.

1. Architecture

Primary among the SBP 0400 architectural features are:

- Microprogrammable, bit-slice design expandable in 4-bit multiples
- Parallel access to all control, data, and address functions
- 16-operation arithmetic logic unit (ALU) with symmetrical subtraction and full carry look-ahead capability
- 8-word general register file including independent program counter with incrementer
- Two 4-bit working registers for both single- and double-length operations
- Dual scaled shifters with on-chip handling of end conditions
- Versatile factory programmable logic array (PLA) generates on-chip control transformation

The functional power of the SBP 0400 is characterized in its ability to perform, within a single clock cycle, any one of its repertoire of 512 standard operations. Included in the repertoire are:

- Operand modifications or combination via eight arithmetic or eight Boolean functions on the ALU
- Single- or double-precision logical shifts or circulates
- Single- or double-precision arithmetic shifts of single- or double-signed binary words
- Single clock ALU/shift combinations to simplify implementation of iterative multiple and nonrestore divide algorithms
- Special select operations and transfers

Additional SBP 0400 features are:

- Internal operation register and independent program counter access control provide instruction look-ahead capability (pipelining)

- Relative position control defines bit-slice rank in N-bit applications

- Serial and parallel access to or from working registers

- Word or byte incrementation of program counter

- ALU bypass for direct register-file access

A listing of the input/output function of each pin of the 40-pin SBP 0400 is included as Appendix A.

Figure 3.4 shows a complete functional block diagram of the SBP 0400; however, a better understanding of the architecture can be obtained by looking at each major function separately.

a. PROGRAMMABLE LOGIC ARRAY (PLA)

The programmable logic array, or PLA (Figure 3.5), is a factory-programmable block of combinational logic forming the operation transformation control center. The PLA decodes the 9-bit microinstruction (operation-select word) input lines to generate a 20-bit present microinstruction which is stored in the operation register (OR). The stored instruction conditions the appropriate functional-blocks, bus-enable, and/or bus-selects for execution of the decoded instruction.

The standard factory PLA program provides the SBP 0400 with a flexible, universal set of microinstructions.

b. OPERATION REGISTER (OR)

The 20-bit operation register (OR) is D-type edge-triggered flip-flops which, on each positive transition of the clock, latches the present PLA output. The OR, as loaded, continuously enables the various functional blocks for execution of the present microinstruction, while the PLA can be decoding/translating the next instruction.

c. ARITHMETIC LOGIC UNIT (ALU)

The 4-bit, parallel, binary arithmetic logic unit (ALU) provides the arithmetic/Boolean operand combination/modification mechanism (Figure 3.6). The ALU performs, as directed by the OR, one of eight arithmetic operations or one of eight Boolean operations on either or both of two operands as detailed in Table 3.2. The two operands are bused, one each, to the input ports of the ALU via the A and B bus. The A input port of the ALU has access to the register file bus and data-in bus through the A multiplexer. The B input port of the ALU has access to the data-in bus, working register and extended working register buses through the B multiplexer.

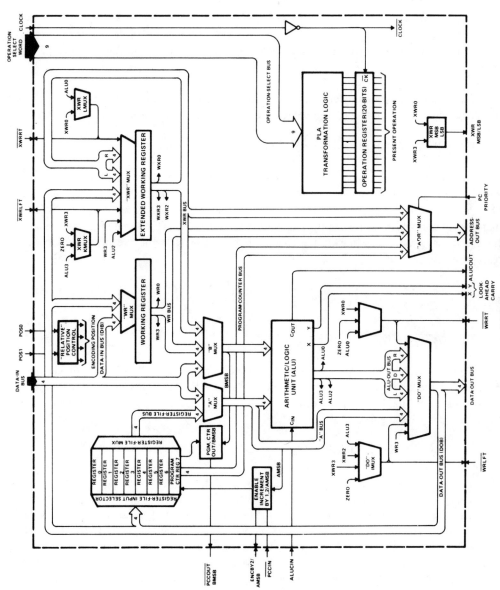

Figure 3.4. SBP 0400 Functional Block Diagram

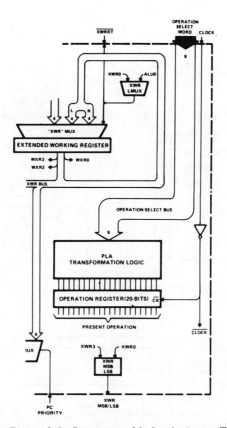

Figure 3.5. Programmable Logic Array (PLA)

In general, both the ALU mode and function is specified via the 4-bit OP-Field (OP3-OP0) of the 9-bit microinstruction. This field is presented to the PLA via the input lines. The PLA translates OP3-OP0 into a 4-bit micro-operation field which ultimately selects the ALU function via the OR. The OP3-bit functions similarly to an ALU mode control in that 1) a low-logic level places the ALU in an arithmetic mode, and 2) a high-logic level places the ALU in a logic mode. OP2-OP0 select a particular function within the specified ALU mode. A complete discussion of operation codes is presented later in the manual.

Functionally similar to the popular TTL ALUs, such as the SN54S/75S181 and SN54S/74S281, the SBP 0400 arithmetic functions include symmetrical forms of subtract operands by which either A minus B or B minus A can be employed to simplify the microprogram. (See Table 3.2)

Other arithmetic-type functions include simple A plus B, A plus B plus carry-in, preset all high, clear all low, and direct symmetrical generation of complements (1's or 2's) for either A or B.

Logic functions performed on two source operands include AND, OR, exclusive-OR or NOR, and four symmetrical mixed combinatorial functions of A and B data. The full capabilities of the processor are shown in Table 3.2.

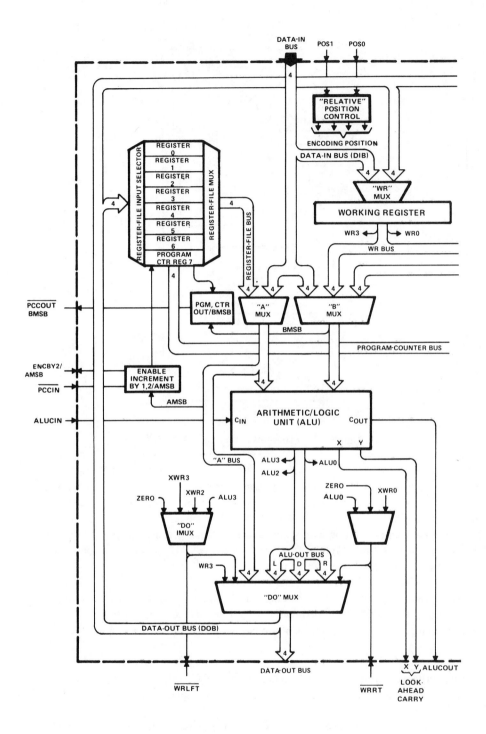

Figure 3.6. Arithmetic Logic Unit (ALU)

Table 3.2. ALU Function-Select Table

ALU OP-Field				Active High Data	
OP3	OP2	OP1	OP0	ALUCIN = H (With Carry)	ALUCIN = L (No Carry)
Arithmetic					
L	L	L	L	Fn = L	Fn = H
L	L	L	H	Fn = B minus A	Fn = B minus A minus 1
L	L	H	L	Fn = A minus B	Fn = A minus B minus 1
L	L	H	H	Fn = A plus B plus 1	Fn = A plus B
L	H	L	L	Fn = B plus 1	Fn = B
L	H	L	H	Fn = $\overline{B}$ plus 1	Fn = $\overline{B}$
L	H	H	L	Fn = A plus 1	Fn = A
L	H	H	H	Fn = $\overline{A}$ plus 1	Fn = $\overline{A}$
Logic					
H	L	L	L	Fn = AnBn	
H	L	L	H	Fn = An $\oplus$ Bn	
H	L	H	L	Fn = $\overline{An \oplus Bn}$	
H	L	H	H	Fn = $\overline{A}$nBn	
H	H	L	L	Fn = An$\overline{B}$n	
H	H	L	H	Fn = An + $\overline{B}$n	
H	H	H	L	Fn = $\overline{A}$n + Bn	
H	H	H	H	Fn = An + Bn	

ALU Carry and Look-Ahead Generator Functions

The SBP 0400 has accommodations for ALU ripple carry-in (ALUCIN) and ALU ripple carry-out (ALUCOUT). In order to facilitate look-ahead carry generation across expanded word sizes, each SBP 0400 has output accommodations for both ALU carry-generate data Y and ALU carry-propagate data X.

d.   RELATIVE POSITION CONTROL (POS1, POS0)

The 2-bit relative position control, as a function of the SBP 0400's individual rank in an expanded word length system (Figure 3.7), indicates the manner in which data shifts are accomplished throughout the interconnected SBP 0400s, and a particular assignment for each of

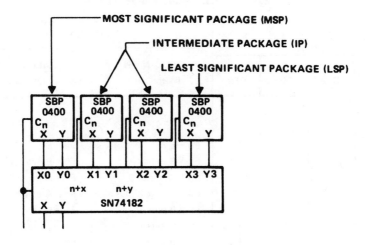

Figure 3.7. Single-Level Look-Ahead

the 0400's individual multipurpose input/output (I/O) accommodations. The input switches POS1 and POS0 encode the position information and dictate the multipurpose input/output accommodation assignments shown in Table 3.3.

The relative position function also provides specific control over incrementation of the program counter, data routing through the three DO multiplexers and the three XWR multiplexers (including the XWR MSB/LSB output), the AMSB output, and the BMSB output. Details of the position control for these functions are included with their individual descriptions on the following pages.

e.   REGISTER FILES (RF0-RF7)

The register file is an 8-word by 4-bit set of D-type edge-triggered registers. Any one of the eight registers may be selected as an operand source and/or destination. Register selection is accomplished via the 3-bit, S-Field (S2-S0) of the microinstruction. This field is presented to the PLA via the input lines. The PLA translates S2-S0 into a 3-bit micro-operation field which ultimately selects the register file from the OR.

Table 3.3. Position Control Functions

Inputs		Relative Position	Multipurpose Input/Output		
POS1	POS0		PCCOUT/ BMSB	ENCBY2/ AMSB	XWR MSB/LSB
L	H	Least significant position (LSP)	PCCOUT	ENCBY2	XWR LSB
L	L	Intermediate position (IP)	PCCOUT	Hi-Z	Zero
H	L	Most significant position (MSP) Double-signed/double-precision (DS/DP)	BMSB	AMSB	XWR MSB
H	H	Most significant position (MSP) Single-signed/double-precision (SS/DP)	BMSB	AMSB	XWR MSB

Register file source and destination operands are listed in Tables 3.4 and 3.5 respectively. When the register file is used as a destination, the source data is recognized only when a low-level condition exists at the clock input. As shown in Figure 3.8, source data can change during the low-level clock condition as long as the setup time to the low-to-high transition of the clock input is satisfied.

Table 3.4. RF Source Operands

RF → DOB

RF → XWR

RF ALU WR → RF

RF ALU WR → WR

RF plus DIB plus ALUCIN → RF

RF plus DIB plus ALUCIN → WR

RF plus DIB plus ALUCIN → XWR

(RF plus WR plus ALUCIN, XWR) LCIR → WR, XWR

(RF plus WR plus ALUCIN, XWR) RSA → WR, XWR

RF plus WR plus ALUCIN → XWR

RF plus XWR plus ALUCIN → WR

RF plus XWR plus ALUCIN → XWR

Note: When PC PRIORITY is low WR → AOB

Table 3.5. RF Destination Operands

```
DIB → RF
XWR plus ALUCIN → RF
RF ALU WR → RF
RF plus DIB plus ALUCIN → RF
WR ALU RF → RF
```

Figure 3.8 illustrates a typical register file store sequence.

f.   PROGRAM COUNTER REGISTER FILE SEVEN (RF7)

RF7 of the register file features the added flexibility of performing as a program counter. *Independent* of the "present" microinstruction resident in the OR, RF7 may be incremented by a displacement of 1 or 2. Incrementation is accomplished synchronously with the clock and selected, as shown in Table 3.6, via the multifunction $\overline{\text{PCCIN}}$ and ENCBY2 inputs as defined by the relative-position control. For cascading purposes, RF7 overflow is provided via the $\overline{\text{PCCOUT}}$ output.

Furthermore, RF7 has an independent output bus which allows direct access to the AOB via the address multiplexer (ADR MUX). When the PC PRIORITY input is taken to a high-logic level, operation register (OR) control of the ADR MUX is overridden allowing the PC to source the AOB.

Consequently, instruction look-ahead techniques may be employed. While the SBP 0400 is executing the "present" microinstruction, the PC may be independently updated to address/fetch data for the "next" microinstruction. In this manner, when the "next" microinstruction becomes the "present" microinstruction, as evidenced by its residence in the OR, steps will have already been taken to fetch an associated data operand.

Typical configurations for use of the program counter are illustrated in Figures 3.9 and 3.10. The BMSB/$\overline{\text{PCCOUT}}$ multifunction output can be time multiplexed to provide both BMSB and counter overflow for maximum count information. Under control of the POS0 and POS1 inputs (Table 3.3), the BMSB is available anytime POS1 is high, but if POS1 is taken low, $\overline{\text{PCCOUT}}$ is available. This is illustrated in Figure 3.9. After time, t_0, the data contents of the most significant package (MSP) will persist until the next L-to-H clock transition. Thus, BMSB and then the $\overline{\text{PCCOUT}}$ data can both be obtained by changing the POS1 input as shown.

If the program counter can be implemented in a cycle length which is four bits shorter than the processor bit length, the technique illustrated in Figure 3.10 can be used. In this case the counter maximum count is directly available from any package except the MSP.

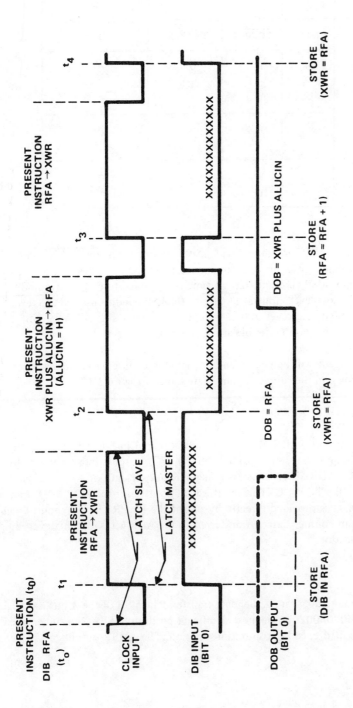

Figure 3.8. Typical Register File Store Sequence

Table 3.6. Program Counter Incrementation

Which PC Is Incremented? Relative Position			Input		PC Is Incremented On Next Clock
LSP	IP	MSP	$\overline{\text{PCCIN}}$	ENCBY2	By
Yes	No	No	H	X	0
			L	L	1
			L	H	2
No	Yes	No	H	X	0
			L	X	1
No	No	Yes	H	X	0
			L	X	1

Also illustrated in Figure 3.10 are count sequences resultant from the $\overline{\text{PCCIN}}$ and ENCBY2 inputs at the LSP. An increment-by-2 instruction is made (prior to the clock transition) causing the counter to advance from 4089 (present state at time H is applied to ENCBY2) to 4091. Note that at maximum count the low-level input at $\overline{\text{PCCIN}}$ to the LSP conditions the $\overline{\text{PCCOUT}}/\overline{\text{PCCIN}}$ carry-enables at the intermediate packages so that the entire counter will cycle to zero on the next clock transition. The alternative (counter disable at max count) is also shown.

A maximum count output will be generated at N-1 if the counter is instructed to count by two at this state. This is shown in the supplementary state table of Figure 3.10.

g.   ADDRESS-OUT MULTIPLEXER (ADR MUX)

The address-out multiplexer (ADR MUX) is a multiport multiplexer which transfers either WR output data, XWR output data, or program counter (PC) output data to the address-out bus (AOB). Control for the ADR MUX transfers either WR output data or XWR output data as provided by the OR, when the PC PRIORITY input is low. Control for the ADR MUX transfer of program counter output data is provided directly by use of the PC PRIORITY input. When this input is taken high, program counter data is transferred to the ADR MUX outputs overriding any OR ADR MUX transfer selection.

h.   A BUS

In addition to 4-bit multifunction parallel data transfers, the MSB of the A bus is available at the AMSB output if the SBP 0400 is in the most significant position (MSP). Remember, the POS1 and POS0 switches are used to encode position information. The AMSB output may be used to

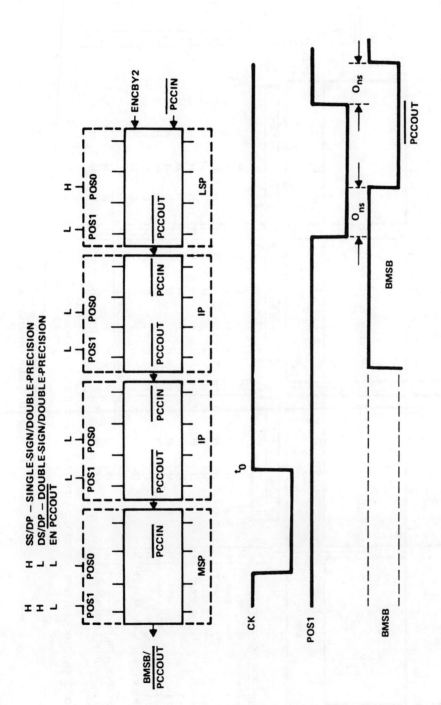

Figure 3.9. 16-Bit Program Counter

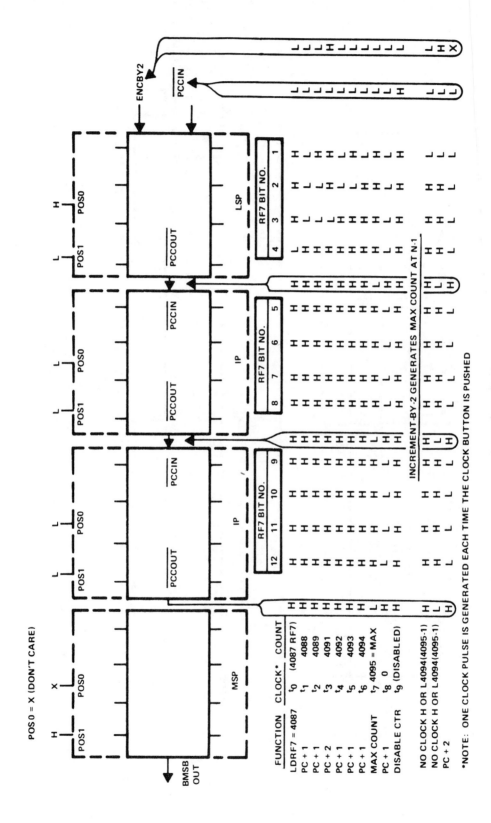

Figure 3.10. 12-Bit Program Counter

monitor the sign-bit of A bus data or, in conjunction with the BMSB output, an impending ALU overflow condition.

i.   B BUS

In addition to 4-bit multifunction, parallel transfers, the MSB of the B bus is available at the BMSB output if the SBP 0400 is in the most significant position (MSP) as defined by POS1 and POS0. When used with subsequent right shifts or circulates, this output can be used to extract B-bus data serially from the selected source. The BMSB output may be used to monitor the sign-bit of the B-bus data, or in conjunction with the AMSB output, an impending ALU overflow condition.

j.   WORKING REGISTER (WR)

The 4-bit working register (WR) is a D-type edge-triggered register which functions as an accumulator for intermediate operands during iterative processing operations. The WR sources the ALU via the B multiplexer and the address-out bus (AOB) via the ADR multiplexer; the WR is a destination, via the WR multiplexer for either the data-out bus (DOB) or data-in bus (DIB).

Working register source and destination operands are listed in Tables 3.7 and 3.8 respectively. When the WR is used as a destination, the source data is recognized only when a low-level condition exists at the clock input. As shown in Figure 3.8, the source data may change during the low-level clock condition as long as the setup time to the low-to-high transition of the clock input is satisfied.

The OR directs the WR to source the AOB via the ADR MUX during 427 of the 0400's standard 459 possible unique operations of the total 512 combinations. In the cases of operation form type Ic and Id, which represent 32 of the 0400's 459 possible unique operations, the OR directs the XWR to source the AOB via the ADR MUX. When the PC PRIORITY input is at a high-logic level, OR direction of the ADR MUX is overridden allowing the PC to source the AOB.

k.   EXTENDED WORKING REGISTER (XWR)

The 4-bit extended working register (XWR) is a D-type edge-triggered register which functions as 1) an accumulator during address derivations, and 2) a WR extension during operations where double-length operands are present/accumulated (iterative nonrestoring divide, double-precision shifts/circulates, iterative multiply, etc.). The XWR sources either 1) the ALU via the B multiplexer, 2) the AOB via the ADR MUX, or 3) itself shifted right or left via the XWR multiplexer. The XWR is a destination via the XWR multiplexer for either the DOB or the XWR, itself, shifted right or left.

Extend working register source and destination operands are listed in Tables 3.9 and 3.10 respectively. When the XWR is used as a destination, the source data is recognized only when a low-level condition exists at the clock input. As shown in Figure 3.8, the source data can change during the low-level clock condition as long as the setup time to the low-to-high transition of the clock input is satisfied.

Table 3.7. Working Register Source Operands

Operation	OP Form	OP-Field OP3 → OP0	D-Field D1 D0	S-Field S2 → S0
*WR ALU DIB → DOB	Ic	LLLL → HHHH	HH	LLL
*WR ALU DIB → WR	Id	LLLL → HHHH	HH	LLH
WR ALU DIB → XWR	If	LLLL → HHHH	HH	HLL
WR ALU RF → RF	Ia	LLLL → HHHH	LL	LLL → HHH
WR ALU RF → WR	Ib	LLLL → HHHH	LH	LLL → HHH
(WR minus DIB minus 1 plus ALUCIN, XWR) LCIR → WR, XWR	IVa	HLLL	HH	LHL
(WR minus DIB minus 1 plus ALUCIN, XWR) RSA → WR, XWR	IVf	LLHL	HH	LHL
(WR minus RF minus 1 plus ALUCIN, XWR) LCIR → WR, XWR	IVc	HLLL	HL	LLL → HHH
(WR minus RF minus 1 plus ALUCIN, XWR) RSA → WR, XWR	IVh	LLHL	HL	LLL → HHH
(WR plus ALUCIN) RSA → WR, XWR	IVe	HLHL	HL	XXX
(WR plus ALUCIN) RSA → WR, XWR	IVe	HLHL	HH	LHL
(WR plus ALUCIN) LCIR → WR	Vd	LLHH	HH	HLH
(WR plus ALUCIN) LCIR → WR	Vd	HLHH	HH	HLH
(WR plus ALUCIN) LSA → WR	Vc	LLHL	HH	HLH
(WR plus ALUCIN) LSL → WR	Vf	HLHL	HH	HLH
(WR plus ALUCIN) RCIR → WR	Vb	LLLH	HH	HLH
(WR plus ALUCIN) RCIR → WR	Vb	HLLH	HH	HLH
(WR plus ALUCIN) RSA → WR	Va	LLLL	HH	HLH
(WR plus ALUCIN) RSL → WR	Ve	HLLL	HH	HLH
(WR plus ALUCIN, XWR) LCIR → (WR, XWR)	VId	HHHH	HH	HLH
(WR plus ALUCIN, XWR) LCIR → (WR, XWR)	VId	LHHH	HH	HLH
(WR plus ALUCIN, XWR) LSA → (WR, XWR)	VIc	LHHL	HH	HLH
(WR plus ALUCIN, XWR) LSL → (WR, XWR)	VIf	HHHL	HH	HLH
(WR plus ALUCIN, XWR) RCIR → (WR, XWR)	VIb	HHLH	HH	HLH
(WR plus ALUCIN, XWR) RCIR → (WR, XWR)	VIb	LHLH	HH	HLH
(WR plus ALUCIN, XWR) RSA → (WR, XWR)	VIa	LHLL	HH	HLH
(WR plus ALUCIN, XWR) RSL → (WR, XWR)	VIe	HHLL	HH	HLH
WR plus DIB plus ALUCIN → DOB	IIi	LHHH	HH	LHL
WR plus DIB plus ALUCIN → XWR	IIb	LLHH	HH	LHL
(WR plus DIB plus ALUCIN) LCIR → WR, XWR	IVb	HLLH	HH	LHL
(WR plus DIB plus ALUCIN) RSA → WR, XWR	IVg	HLHH	HH	LHL
WR plus RF plus ALUCIN → XWR	IIa	LLHH	HL	LLL → HHH
(WR plus RF plus ALUCIN) LCIR → WR, XWR	IVd	HLLH	HL	LLL → HHH
(WR plus RF plus ALUCIN) RSA → WR, XWR	IVi	HLHH	HL	LLL → HHH

Note: When PC PRIORITY is low WR → AOB

*XWR → AOB

Table 3.8. Working Register Destination Operands

Operation	OP Form	OP-Field OP3 → OP0	D-Field D1 D0	S-Field S2 → S0
*WR ALU DIB → DOB	Ic	LLLL → HHHH	HH	LLL
WR ALU RF → RF	Ia	LLLL → HHHH	LL	LLL → HHH
WR ALU RF → RF	Ia	LLLL → HHHH	LL	LLL → HHH
WR ALU RF → WR	Ib	LLLL → HHHH	LH	LLL → HHH
(WR minus DIB minus 1 plus ALUCIN, XWR) LCIR → WR, XWR	IVa	HLLL	HH	LHL
(WR minus DIB minus 1 plus ALUCIN, XWR) RSA → WR, XWR	IVf	LLHL	HH	LHL
(WR minus RF minus 1 plus ALUCIN, XWR) LCIR → WR, XWR	IVc	HLLL	HL	LLL → HHH
(WR minus RF minus 1 plus ALUCIN, XWR) RSA → WR, XWR	IVh	LLHL	HL	LLL → HHH
(WR plus ALUCIN) RSA → WR, XWR	IVe	HLHL	HL	XXX
(WR plus ALUCIN) RSA → WR, XWR	IVe	HLHL	HH	LHL
(WR plus ALUCIN) LCIR → WR	Vd	LLHH	HH	HLH
(WR plus ALUCIN) LCIR → WR	Vd	HLHH	HH	HLH
(WR plus ALUCIN) LSA → WR	Vc	LLHL	HH	HLH
(WR plus ALUCIN) LSL → WR	Vf	HLHL	HH	HLH
(WR plus ALUCIN) RCIR → WR	Vb	LLLH	HH	HLH
(WR plus ALUCIN) RCIR → WR	Vb	HLLH	HH	HLH
(WR plus ALUCIN) RSA → WR	Va	LLLL	HH	HLH
(WR plus ALUCIN) RSL → WR	Ve	HLLL	HH	HLH
(WR plus ALUCIN, XWR) LCIR → (WR, XWR)	VId	HHHH	HH	HLH
(WR plus ALUCIN, XWR) LCIR → (WR, XWR)	VId	LHHH	HH	HLH
(WR plus ALUCIN, XWR) LSA → (WR, XWR)	VIc	LHHL	HH	HLH
(WR plus ALUCIN, XWR) LSL → (WR, XWR)	VIf	HHHL	HH	HLH
(WR plus ALUCIN, XWR) RCIR → (WR, XWR)	VIb	HHLH	HH	HLH
(WR plus ALUCIN, XWR) RCIR → (WR, XWR)	VIb	LHLH	HH	HLH
(WR plus ALUCIN, XWR) RSA → (WR, XWR)	VIa	LHLL	HH	HLH
(WR plus ALUCIN, XWR) RSL → (WR, XWR)	VIe	HHLL	HH	HLH
(WR plus DIB plus ALUCIN) LCIR → WR, XWR	IVb	HLLH	HH	LHL
(WR plus DIB plus ALUCIN) RSA → WR, XWR	IVg	HLHH	HH	LHL
(WR plus RF plus ALUCIN) LCIR → WR, XWR	IVd	HLLH	HL	LLL → HHH
(WR plus RF plus ALUCIN) RSA → WR, XWR	IVi	HLHH	HL	LLL → HHH

Note: When PC PRIORITY is low WR → AOB

*XWR → AOB

Table 3.9. Extended Working Register Source Operands

Operation	OP Form	OP-Field OP3 → OP0	D-Field D1 D0	S-Field S2 → S0
XWR ALU DIB → DOB	Ih	LLLL → HHHH	HH	HHH
XWR ALU DIB → WR	Ie	LLLL → HHHH	HH	LHH
XWR ALU DIB → XWR	Ig	LLLL → HHHH	HH	HHL
XWR plus ALUCIN → DOB	III	HHHL	HH	LHL
XWR plus ALUCIN → RF	IIj	HHHL	HL	LLL → HHH
XWR plus DIB plus ALUCIN → WR	IIk	HHLL	HH	LHL
XWR plus DIB plus ALUCIN → XWR	IIf	HHLH	HH	LHL
XWR plus RF plus ALUCIN → WR	IIe	HHLL	HL	LLL → HHH

Note: When PC PRIORITY is low WR → AOB

Operation form-type Ic and Id represent 32 of the 0400's standard 459 possible unique operations. During these operations, the OR directs the XWR to source the AOB via the ADR MUX. During the remaining 427 of the 0400's 459 possible unique operations, the OR directs the WR to source the AOB via the ADR MUX. When the PC PRIORITY input is at a high-logic level, OR direction of the ADR MUX is overridden allowing the PC to source the AOB.

l.   DATA-OUT MULTIPLEXER (DO MUX)

The data-out multiplexer (DO MUX) is a multiport, special-purpose multiplexer which provides scaled shifting of the ALU output, and direct transfer of the A bus to the data-out bus, bypassing the ALU. The output port of the DO MUX provides, in accordance with Table 3.11, ALU output data not shifted, ALU output data shifted right one place, ALU output data shifted left one place, and A bus data not shifted. Control for the DO MUX is provided by the OR in conjunction with the relative position control. Remember, for a single SBP 0400 providing 4-bit operation, the microprocessor occupies only one position. In this case, the relative position control switches, POS1 and POS0, may be used in simulating an expanded system. (See Table 3.3 for more information on relative position control.)

Special bidirectional-shift accomodations are provided to/from each end of the DO MUX to facilitate intrapackage data shifts when the SBP 0400 is expanded for greater than 4-bit word lengths. The direction of these shift accommodations is selected by the OR. Bit 3 (MSB) of the DO MUX for each 0400 receives intrapackage right-shift data and transmits intrapackage left-shift data via the bidirectional-shift accommodation $\overline{WRLFT}$; bit 0 (LSB) receives intrapackage left-shift data and transmits intrapackage right-shift data via the bidirectional-shift accommodation $\overline{WRRT}$. Both $\overline{WRLFT}$ and $\overline{WRRT}$, low-active signals outside the 0400, become $\overline{WRLFT}$ and $\overline{WRRT}$ respectively, high input signals within the 0400.

Table 3.10. Working Register Destination Operands

Operation	OP Form	OP-Field OP3 → OP0	D-Field D1 D0	S-Field S2 → S0
DIB ALU XWR → XWR	Ig	LLLL → HHHH	HH	HHL
WR ALU DIB → XWR	If	LLLL → HHHH	HH	HLL
(WR minus DIB minus 1 plus ALUCIN, XWR) LCIR → WR, XWR	IVa	HLLL	HH	LHL
(WR minus DIB minus 1 plus ALUCIN, XWR) RSA → WR, XWR	IVf	LLHL	HH	LHL
(WR minus RF minus 1 plus ALUCIN, XWR) LCIR → WR, XWR	IVc	HLLL	HL	LLL → HHH
(WR minus RF minus 1 plus ALUCIN, XWR) RSA → WR, XWR	IVh	LLHL	HL	LLL → HHH
(WR plus ALUCIN) RSA → WR, XWR	IVe	HLHL	HL	XXX
(WR plus ALUCIN) RSA → WR, XWR	IVe	HLHL	HH	LHL
(WR plus ALUCIN, XWR) LCIR → (WR, XWR)	VId	HHHH	HH	HLH
(WR plus ALUCIN, XWR) LCIR → (WR, XWR)	VId	LHHH	HH	HLH
(WR plus ALUCIN, XWR) LSA → (WR, XWR)	VIc	LHHL	HH	HLH
(WR plus ALUCIN, XWR) LSL → (WR, XWR)	VIf	HHHL	HH	HLH
(WR plus ALUCIN, XWR) RCIR → (WR, XWR)	VIb	HHLH	HH	HLH
(WR plus ALUCIN, XWR) RCIR → (WR, XWR)	VIb	LHLH	HH	HLH
(WR plus ALUCIN, XWR) RSA → (WR, XWR)	VIa	LHLL	HH	HLH
(WR plus ALUCIN, XWR) RSL → (WR, XWR)	VIe	HHLL	HH	HLH
WR plus DIB plus ALUCIN → XWR	IIh	LLHH	HH	LHL
(WR plus DIB plus ALUCIN) LCIR → WR, XWR	IVb	HLLH	HH	LHL
(WR plus DIB plus ALUCIN) RSA → WR, XWR	IVg	HLHH	HH	LHL
WR plus RF plus ALUCIN → XWR	IIa	LLHH	HL	LLL → HHH
(WR plus RF plus ALUCIN) LCIR → WR, XWR	IVd	HLLH	HL	LLL → HHH
(WR plus RF plus ALUCIN) RSA → WR, XWR	IVf	HLHH	HL	LLL → HHH
DIB plus XWR plus ALUCIN → XWR	IIk	HHLH	HH	LHL
DIB → XWR	IIIe	LLLH	HH	LHL

Note: When PC PRIORITY is low WR → AOB

m. DATA-OUT I MULTIPLEXER (DO IMUX)

The data-out I multiplexer (DO IMUX) is a special-purpose multiplexer which outputs, in accordance with Table 3.12, appropriate left-shift data via the bidirectional-shift accommodation WRLFT. Control for the DO MUX is provided by the OR in conjunction with the relative position control.

Table 3.11. DO MUX Transfers

Operation Type		DO MUX Output			
		3	2	1	0
Intermediate and Least Significant Positions	Right-shift arithmetic	$\overline{\text{WRLFT}}$	ALU3	ALU2	ALU1
	Right-shift logical	$\overline{\text{WRLFT}}$	ALU3	ALU2	ALU1
	Right circulate	$\overline{\text{WRLFT}}$	ALU3	ALU2	ALU1
	ALU out bus → data-out bus	ALU3	ALU2	ALU1	ALU0
	A bus → data-out bus	ABUS3	ABUS2	ABUS1	ABUS0
	Left-shift arithmetic	ALU2	ALU1	ALU0	$\overline{\text{WRRT}}$
	Left-shift logical	ALU2	ALU1	ALU0	$\overline{\text{WRRT}}$
	Left circulate	ALU2	ALU1	ALU0	$\overline{\text{WRRT}}$
Most Significant Position (MSP)	Right-shift arithmetic	WR3	ALU3	ALU2	ALU1
	Right-shift logical	$\overline{\text{WRLFT}}$	ALU3	ALU2	ALU1
	Right circulate	$\overline{\text{WRLFT}}$	ALU3	ALU2	ALU1
	ALU out bus → data-out bus	ALU3	ALU2	ALU1	ALU0
	A bus → data-out bus	ABUS3	ABUS2	ABUS1	ABUS0
	Left-shift arithmetic	ALU2	ALU1	ALU0	$\overline{\text{WRRT}}$
	Left-shift logical	ALU2	ALU1	ALU0	$\overline{\text{WRRT}}$
	Left circulate	ALU2	ALU1	ALU0	$\overline{\text{WRRT}}$

Table 3.12. DO IMUX Transfers to $\overline{\text{WRLFT}}$

Operation Type		DO IMUX Output to $\overline{\text{WRLFT}}$
Intermediate and Least Significant Positions	Left-shift arithmetic	$\overline{\text{ALU3}}$
	Left-shift logical	$\overline{\text{ALU3}}$
	Left circulate	$\overline{\text{ALU3}}$
Most Significant Position (MSP) Single-Precision (SP)	Left-shift arithmetic	$\overline{\text{ZERO}}$
	Left-shift logical	$\overline{\text{ZERO}}$
	Left circulate	$\overline{\text{ALU3}}$
Most Significant Position (MSP) Single-Signed/Double-Precision (SS/DP)	Left-shift arithmetic	$\overline{\text{XWR3}}$
	Left-shift logical	$\overline{\text{XWR3}}$
	Left circulate	$\overline{\text{XWR3}}$
Most Significant Position (MSP) Double-Signed/Double-Precision (DS/DP)	Left-shift arithmetic	$\overline{\text{XWR2}}$
	Left-shift logical	$\overline{\text{XWR3}}$
	Left circulate	$\overline{\text{XWR3}}$

n. DATA-OUT J MULTIPLEXER (DO JMUX)

The data-out J multiplexer (DO JMUX) is a special-purpose multiplexer which outputs, as per Table 3.13 appropriate right-shift data via the bidirectional-shift accommodation $\overline{\text{WRRT}}$. Control for the DO JMUX is provided by the OR in conjunction with the relative position control (Table 3.3).

Table 3.13. DO JMUX Transfers to $\overline{\text{WRRT}}$

Operation Type		DO JMUX Output to $\overline{\text{WRRT}}$
Most Significant (MSP)	Right-shift arithmetic	$\overline{\text{ALU0}}$
OR Intermediate Positions	Right-shift logical	$\overline{\text{ALU0}}$
(IP)	Right circulate	$\overline{\text{ALU0}}$
Least Significant Position	Right-shift arithmetic	$\overline{\text{ZERO}}$
(LSP)	Right-shift logical	$\overline{\text{ZERO}}$
Single-Precision	Right circulate	$\overline{\text{ALU0}}$
Least Significant Position	Right-shift arithmetic	$\overline{\text{ZERO}}$
(LSP)	Right-shift logical	$\overline{\text{ZERO}}$
Double-Precision	Right circulate	$\overline{\text{XWR0}}$

o. EXTENDED WORKING REGISTER MULTIPLEXER (XWR MUX)

The extended working register multiplexer (XWR MUX) is a multiport, special-purpose multiplexer which provides scaled shifting of the XWR output, and direct transfer of the data-out bus to the XWR input. The output port of the XWR provides, in accordance with Table 3.14, XWR output data shifted left one place, XWR output data shifted right one place, and DOB data not shifted. Control for the XWR MUX is provided by the OR in conjunction with the relative position control (Table 3.3).

Special bidirectional-shift accommodations are provided to/from each end of the XWR MUX to facilitate intrapackage data shifts when the SBP 0400 is expanded for greater than 4-bit word lengths. Bit 3 (MSB) or bit 2 of the XWR MUX for each 0400, selected by the OR in conjunction with the relative position control, receives double-precision intrapackage right-shift data or transmits double-precision intrapackage left-shift data via the bidirectional-shift accommodation $\overline{\text{XWRLFT}}$; bit 0 (LSB) receives double-precision intrapackage left-shift data and transmits intrapackage right-shift data via the bidirectional-shift accommodation $\overline{\text{XWRRT}}$. Both $\overline{\text{XWRLFT}}$ and $\overline{\text{XWRRT}}$, low-active signals outside the 0400, become XWRLFT and XWRRT respectively, high-active signals within the 0400.

Table 3.14. XWR MUX Transfers

Operation Type	XWR MUX Output			
	3	2	1	0
Right-shift arithmetic	$\overline{XWRLFT}$	XWR3	XWR2	XWR1
Right-shift logical	$\overline{XWRLFT}$	XWR3	XWR2	XWR1
Right circulate	$\overline{XWRLFT}$	XWR3	XWR2	XWR1
Data-out bus XWR	DOB3	DOB2	DOB1	DOB0
Left-shift arithmetic	XWR2	XWR1	XWR0	$\overline{XWRRT}$
Left-shift logical	XWR2	XWR1	XWR0	$\overline{XWRRT}$
Left circulate	XWR2	XWR1	XWR0	$\overline{XWRRT}$
Right-shift arithmetic	XWR3	$\overline{XWRLFT}$	XWR2	XWR1
Right-shift logical	$\overline{XWRLFT}$	XWR3	XWR2	XWR1
Right circulate	$\overline{XWRLFT}$	XWR3	XWR2	XWR1
Data-out bus XWR	DOB3	DOB2	DOB1	DOB0
Left-shift arithmetic	ALU2	XWR1	XWR0	$\overline{XWRRT}$
Left-shift logical	XWR2	XWR1	XWR0	$\overline{XWRRT}$
Left circulate	XWR2	XWR1	XWR0	$\overline{XWRRT}$

p. EXTENDED WORKING REGISTER K MULTIPLEXER (XWR KMUX)

The extended working register K multiplexer (XWR KMUX) is a special-purpose multiplexer which outputs, in accordance with Table 3.15, appropriate double-precision left-shift data via the bidirectional-shift accommodation $\overline{XWRLFT}$. Control for the XWR KMUX is provided by the OR in conjunction with the relative position control switches POS1 and POS0. (See Table 3.3 for relative position control information.) The direction of the bidirectional-shift accommodation $\overline{XWRLFT}$ is selected by the OR. As explained previously, this terminal can be used to serially load the XWR.

q. EXTENDED WORKING REGISTER L MULTIPLEXER (XWR LMUX)

The extended working register L multiplexer (XWR LMUX) is a special-purpose multiplexer which outputs, in accordance with Table 3.16, appropriate double-precision right-shift data via the bidirectional-shift accommodation $\overline{XWRRT}$. Control for the XWR LMUX is provided by the OR in conjunction with the relative position control switches (see Table 3.3).

r. WORKING REGISTER MULTIPLEXER (WR MUX)

The working register multiplexer (WR MUX) is a multiport multiplexer which, under control of the OR, selects either data-in bus data or data-out bus data for direct transfer to the WR.

Table 3.15. XWR KMUX Transfers to $\overline{\text{XWRLFT}}$

Operation Type		XWR KMUX Output to $\overline{\text{XWRLFT}}$
Least Significant (LSP) OR Intermediate Positions (IP)	Left-shift arithmetic	$\overline{\text{XWR3}}$
	Left-shift logical	$\overline{\text{XWR3}}$
	Left circulate	$\overline{\text{XWR3}}$
Most Significant Position (MSP)	Left-shift arithmetic	$\overline{\text{ZERO}}$
	Left-shift logical	$\overline{\text{ZERO}}$
	Left circulate	$\overline{\text{ALU3}}$

Table 3.16. XWR LMUX Transfers to $\overline{\text{XWRRT}}$

Operation Type		XWR LMUX Output to $\overline{\text{XWRRT}}$
Most Significant (MSP) OR Intermediate Positions (IP)	Right-shift arithmetic	$\overline{\text{XWR0}}$
	Right-shift logical	$\overline{\text{XWR0}}$
	Right circulate	$\overline{\text{XWR0}}$
Least Significant Position (LSP)	Right-shift arithmetic	$\overline{\text{ALU0}}$
	Right-shift logical	$\overline{\text{ALU0}}$
	Right circulate	$\overline{\text{ALU0}}$

2. Data Handling

The SBP 0400 uses the DO MUX in conjunction with the DO IMUX and DO JMUX to accomplish single-bit WR shift/circulate operations; the 0400 uses the XWR MUX in conjunction with the XWR KMUX and XWR LMUX to accomplish single-bit XWR shift/circulate operations. While single-precision shift/circulate operations involve the WR only, double-precision shift/circulate operations involve the WR in conjunction with the XWR. The 0400's standard operation set does not include single-precision XWR shift/circulate operations.

a. WR SINGLE-PRECISION SHIFTS/CIRCULATES

WR single-precision shift/circulate operations are directed by the OR with expanded word length "end" conditions handled by the relative position controls. These single-precision operations may best be represented by the generalized symbol:

$$(\text{WR plus ALUCIN}) \text{ SHIFTED/CIRCULATED} \rightarrow \text{WR}$$

Within a single cycle (1 clock period), each of six possible WR single-precision shift/circulate operations is capable of:

1) Asynchronously summing the WR with the ALUCIN input

2) Asynchronously shifting/circulating the sum one bit position to the right/left

3) Synchronously storing the shifted/circulated result back into the WR.

The six WR single-precision shift/circulate possibilities, with data flow paths for expanded word lengths, are listed in Table 3.17.

Table 3.17. WR Single-Precision Shifts/Circulates

Shift/Circulate Operation	Shift/Circulate Function	Expanded Word Length Data Flow Paths (Figure No.)	OP Form	OP-Field OP3 → OP0	D-Field D1 → D0	S-Field S2 → S0
(WR plus ALUCIN, XWR) RSL → WR	Right-shift logical (RSL)	3.11	Ve	HLLL	HH	HLH
(WR plus ALUCIN, XWR) LSL → WR	Left-shift logical (LSL)	3.12	Vf	HLHL	HH	HLH
(WR plus ALUCIN, XWR) RSA → WR	Right-shift arithmetic (RSA)	3.13	Va	LLLL	HH	HLH
(WR plus ALUCIN, XWR) LSA → WR	Left-shift arithmetic (LSA)	3.14	Vc	LLHL	HH	HLH
(WR plus ALUCIN, XWR) RCIR → WR	Right circulate (RCIR)	3.15	Vb	LLLH	HH	HLH
(WR plus ALUCIN, XWR) LCIR → WR	Left circulate (LCIR)	3.16	Vd	LLHH	HH	HLH

(WR plus ALUCIN) RSL → WR

The WR single-precision logical right-shift operation (RSL), shown in Figure 3.11 displaces the entire contents of the WR one bit position to the right. In an expanded wordlength system, a logic-level low is automatically right shifted into the WR's most significant bit (MSB) of the most significant package (MSP) as the WR's contents are displaced to the right. This logic-level low, sourced by the least significant package (LSP), exits the LSP via the bidirectional-shift accommodation $\overline{WRRT}$ and enters the MSP via the bidirectional-shift accommodation $\overline{WRLFT}$. During each WR RSL operation, the WR's displaced LSB of the LSP is discarded.

(WR plus ALUCIN) LSL → WR

The WR single-precision logical left-shift operation (LSL), shown in Figure 3.12, displaces the entire contents of the WR one bit position to the left. In an expanded wordlength system, a logic-level low is automatically left shifted into the WR's LSB of the LSP as the WR's contents are

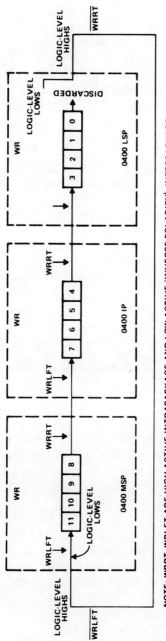

Figure 3.11. Right-Shift Logical — Single-Precision (RSL — SP)

NOTE: WRRT, WRLFT ARE HIGH-ACTIVE INTRAPACKAGE AND LOW-ACTIVE (INVERSE POLARITY) INTERPACKAGE.

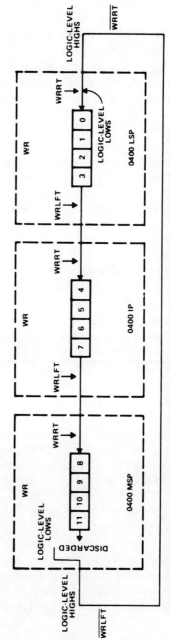

Figure 3.12. Left-Shift Logical — Single-Precision (LSL — SP)

NOTE: WRRT, WRLFT ARE HIGH-ACTIVE INTRAPACKAGE AND LOW-ACTIVE (INVERSE POLARITY) INTERPACKAGE.

displaced to the left. This logic-level low, sourced by the MSP, exits the MSP via the bidirectional-shift accommodation $\overline{WRLFT}$ and enters the LSP via the bidirectional-shift accommodation $\overline{WRRT}$. During each WR LSL operation, the WR's displaced MSB of the MSP is discarded.

(WR plus ALUCIN) RSA → WR

The WR single-precision arithmetic right-shift operation (RSA), shown in Figure 3.13, displaces the entire contents of the WR one bit position to the right. The MSB of the MSP is designated as a sign-bit. As the entire contents of the WR are displaced to the right, the sign-bit does *not* change. Rather the sign-bit is duplicated to the right. The displaced LSB of the LSP exits the LSP via the bidirectional-shift accommodation $\overline{WRRT}$.

(WR plus ALUCIN) LSA → WR

The WR single-precision arithmetic left-shift operation (LSA), shown in Figure 3.14, is functionally identical to the WR single-precision logical left-shift operation of Figure 3.12. The WR's MSB of the MSP, although designated as a sign-bit, is discarded as the entire contents of the WR are displaced one bit position to the left. As each WR LSA operation is performed, the BMSB output may be monitored to detect a WR sign-bit change. Any polarity change at the BMSB output will be indicative that the *previous* WR LSA operation produced a WR sign-bit change.

(WR plus ALUCIN) RCIR → WR

The WR single-precision right-circulate operation (RCIR), shown in Figure 3.15, displaces the entire contents of the WR one bit position to the right. The displaced LSB of the LSP replaces the displaced MSB of the MSP. The displaced LSB of the LSP exits the LSP via the bidirectional-shift accommodation $\overline{WRRT}$ and enters the MSP via the bidirectional-shift accommodation $\overline{WRLFT}$.

(WR plus ALUCIN) LCIR → WR

The WR single-precision left-circulate operation (LCIR), shown in Figure 3.16, displaces the entire contents of the WR one bit position to the left. The displaced MSB of the MSP replaces the displaced LSB of the LSP. The displaced MSB of the MSP exits the MSP via the bidirectional-shift accommodation $\overline{WRLFT}$ and enters the LSP via its bidirectional-shift accommodation $\overline{WRRT}$.

b.   WR, XWR DOUBLE-PRECISION SHIFTS/CIRCULATES

WR, XWR double-precision shift/circulate operations are directed by the OR with expanded word length "end" conditions handled by the relative position controls. The double-precision shift/circulate operations may best be represented by the generalized symbol:

(WR plus ALUCIN, XWR) SHIFTED/CIRCULATED → WR, XWR

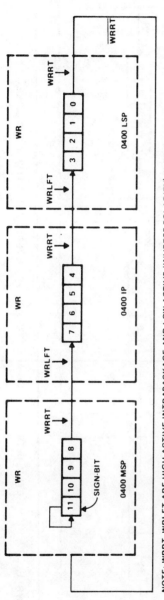

NOTE: WRRT, WRLFT ARE HIGH-ACTIVE INTRAPACKAGE AND LOW-ACTIVE (INVERSE POLARITY) INTERPACKAGE.

Figure 3.13. Right-Shift Arithmetic – Single-Precision (RSA – SP)

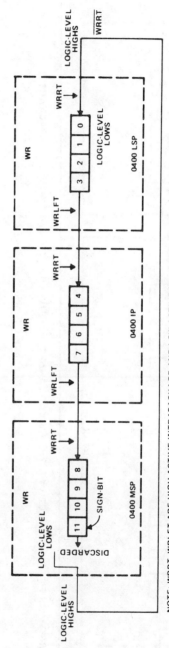

NOTE: WRRT, WRLFT ARE HIGH-ACTIVE INTRAPACKAGE AND LOW-ACTIVE (INVERSE POLARITY) INTERPACKAGE.

Figure 3.14. Left-Shift Arithmetic – Single-Precision (LSA – SP)

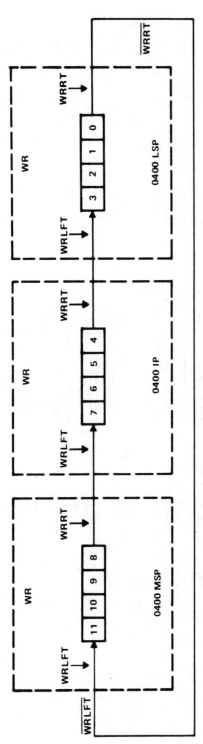

NOTE: WRRT, WRLFT ARE HIGH-ACTIVE INTRAPACKAGE AND LOW-ACTIVE (INVERSE POLARITY) INTERPACKAGE.

Figure 3.15. Right-Circulate – Single-Precision (RCIR – SP)

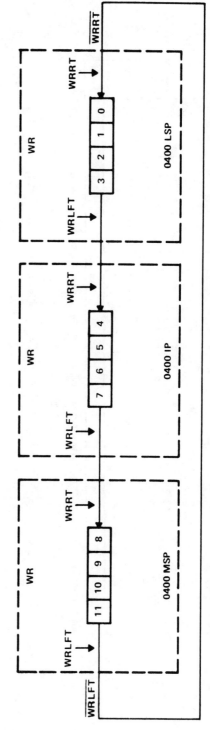

NOTE: WRRT, WRLFT ARE HIGH-ACTIVE INTRAPACKAGE AND LOW-ACTIVE (INVERSE POLARITY) INTERPACKAGE.

Figure 3.16. Left-Circulate – Single-Precision (LCIR – SP)

Within a single cycle, each of eight possible WR, XWR double-precision shift/circulate operations is capable of:

1) Asynchronously summing the WR with the ALUCIN input

2) Asynchronously double-precision shifting/circulating the sum with the WR and XWR considered as one double-length register

3) Synchronously storing the shifted/circulated result into the double-length register formed by WR in conjunction with the XWR. The eight WR, XWR double-precision shift/circulate possibilities, with data flow paths for expanded word lengths, are listed in Table 3.18.

Table 3.18. WR, XWR Double-Precision Shifts/Circulates

Shift/Circulate Operation	Shift/Circulate Function	Expanded Word Length Data Flow Paths (Figure No.)	OP Form	OP-Field OP3 → OP0	D-Field D1 → D0	S-Field S2 → S0
(WR plus ALUCIN, XWR) RSL → WR, XWR	Right-shift logical (RSL)	3.17	VIe	HHLL	HH	HLH
(WR plus ALUCIN, XWR) LSL → WR, XWR	Left-shift logical (LSL)	3.18	VIf	HHHL	HH	HLH
(WR plus ALUCIN, XWR) RSA → WR, XWR	Right-shift arithmetic (RSA)	3.19, .20	VIa	LHLL	HH	HLH
(WR plus ALUCIN, XWR) LSA → WR, XWR	Left-shift arithmetic (LSA)	3.21, .22	VIc	LHHL	HH	HLH
(WR plus ALUCIN, XWR) RCIR → WR, XWR	Right circulate (RCIR)	3.23	VIb	LHLH	HH	HLH
(WR plus ALUCIN, XWR) LCIR → WR, XWR	Left circulate (LCIR)	3.24	VId	LHHH	HH	HLH

(WR plus ALUCIN, XWR) RSL → WR, XWR

The WR, XWR double-precision logical right-shift operation, shown in Figure 3.17 displaces the entire contents of the double-length register, formed by the WR in conjunction with the XWR, one bit position to the right. In an expanded wordlength system, the WR's displaced LSB of the LSP exits the LSP via the bidirectional-shift accommodation $\overline{\text{XWRRT}}$ and enters the XWR's MSB of the MSP via the bidirectional-shift accommodation $\overline{\text{XWRLFT}}$. A logic-level low is automatically right shifted into the WR's MSB of the MSP. This logic-level low, sourced by the LSP, exits the LSP via the bidirectional-shift accommodation $\overline{\text{WRRT}}$ and enters the MSP via the bidirectional-shift accommodation $\overline{\text{WRLFT}}$. During each WR, XWR RSL operation, the XWR's displaced LSB of the LSP is discarded.

(WR plus ALUCIN, XWR) LSL → WR, XWR

The WR, XWR double-precision logical left-shift operation, shown in Figure 3.18, displaces the entire contents of the double-length register, formed by the WR in conjunction with the XWR,

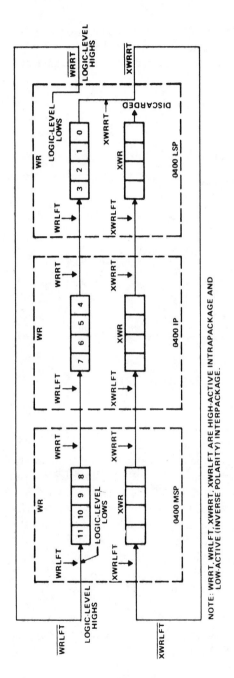

Figure 3.17. Right-Shift Logical — Double-Precision (RSL — DP)

NOTE: WRRT, WRLFT, XWRRT, XWRLFT ARE HIGH-ACTIVE INTRAPACKAGE AND
LOW-ACTIVE (INVERSE POLARITY) INTERPACKAGE.

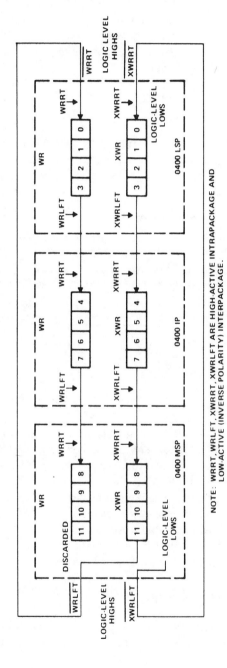

Figure 3.18. Left-Shift Logical — Double-Precision (LSL — DP)

NOTE: WRRT, WRLFT, XWRRT, XWRLFT ARE HIGH-ACTIVE INTRAPACKAGE AND
LOW-ACTIVE (INVERSE POLARITY) INTERPACKAGE.

one bit position to the left. In an expanded wordlength system, the XWR's displaced MSB of the MSP exits the MSP via the bidirectional-shift accommodation WRLFT and enters WR's LSB of the LSP via the bidirectional-shift accommodation WRRT. A logic-level low is automatically left shifted into the XWR's LSB of the LSP. This logic-level low, sourced by the MSP, exits the MSP via the bidirectional-shift accommodation $\overline{\text{XWRLFT}}$ and enters the LSP via the bidirectional-shift accommodation $\overline{\text{XWRRT}}$. During each WR, XWR LSL operation, the WR's displaced MSB is discarded.

(WR plus ALUCIN, XWR) RSA → WR, XWR

The WR, XWR double-precision arithmetic right-shift operations (shown in Figures 3.19 and 3.20) displace the entire contents of the double-length register formed by the WR in conjunction with the XWR, one bit position to the right. In an expanded wordlength system, the WR's displaced LSB of the LSP exits the LSP via the bidirectional-shift accommodation $\overline{\text{XWRRT}}$ and enters either XWR's MSB or MSB minus 1 of the MSP. The polarity of the MSP's relative position control input POS0 selects between single-signed and double-signed double-precision arithmetic right-shift operations.

c.   SINGLE-SIGNED DOUBLE-PRECISION RSA (MSP POS0 = H)

For the single-signed WR, XWR double-precision right-shift operation, shown in Figure 3.19, the WR's MSB of the MSP only is designated as a sign-bit. As the entire contents of the WR, XWR are displaced one bit position to the right, the sign-bit does *not* change. Rather, the sign-bit is duplicated to the right. The WR's displaced LSB of the LSP exits the LSB via the bidirectional-shift accommodation $\overline{\text{XWRRT}}$ and enters the XWR's MSB of the MSP via the bidirectional-shift accommodation $\overline{\text{XWRLFT}}$. The XWR's displaced LSB of the LSP is discarded.

d.   DOUBLE-SIGNED DOUBLE-PRECISION RSA (MSP POS0 = L)

For the double-signed WR, XWR double-precision right-shift operation, shown in Figure 3.20, both the WR's and XWR's MSB of the MSP are designated as sign-bits. The polarity of the XWR's sign-bit is automatically forced to be the same as the polarity of the WR's sign-bit. As the entire content of the WR, XWR is displaced one bit position to the right, the sign-bits do not change. Rather, the WR's sign-bit is duplicated to the right while the XWR's sign-bit is held stationary. The WR's displaced LSB of the LSP exits the LSP via the bidirectional-shift accommodation $\overline{\text{XWRRT}}$ and enters the XWR's MSB minus 1 of the MSP via the bidirectional-shift accommodation $\overline{\text{XWRLFT}}$. The XWR's displaced LSB of the LSP is discarded.

(WR plus ALUCIN, XWR) LSA → WR, XWR

The WR, XWR double-precision arithmetic left-shift operations, shown in Figures 3.21 and 3.22, displace the entire contents of the double-length register, formed by the WR in conjunction with the XWR, one bit position to the left. In an expanded wordlength system, either the XWR's displaced MSB or MSB minus 1 of the MSP exits the MSP via the bidirectional-shift accommodation $\overline{\text{WRLFT}}$ and enters the WR's LSB of the LSP via the bidirectional-shift accommodation $\overline{\text{WRRT}}$. The polarity of the MSP's relative position control input POS0 selects between single-signed and double-signed double-precision arithmetic left-shift operations.

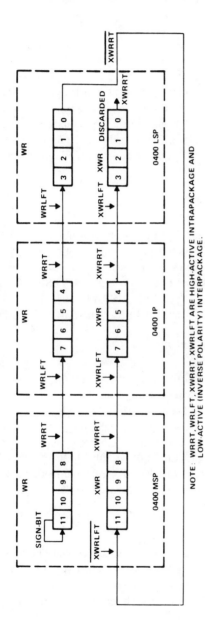

Figure 3.19. Right-Shift Arithmetic — Single-Sign/Double-Precision (RSA — SS/DP)

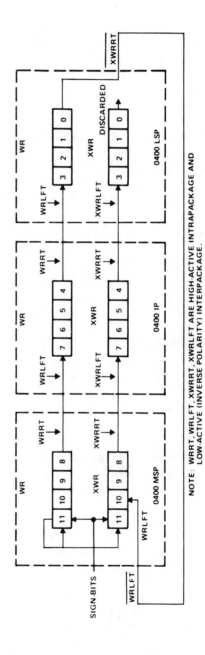

Figure 3.20. Right-Shift Arithmetic — Double-Sign/Double-Precision (RSA — DS/DP)

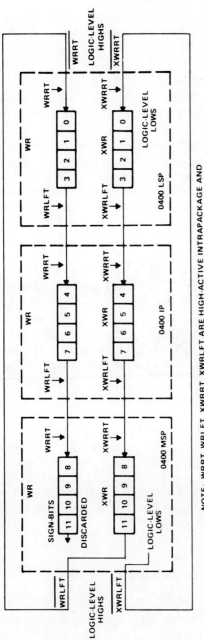

NOTE: WRRT, WRLFT, XWRRT, XWRLFT ARE HIGH-ACTIVE INTRAPACKAGE AND
LOW-ACTIVE (INVERSE POLARITY) INTERPACKAGE.

Figure 3.21. Left-Shift Arithmetic – Single-Sign/Double-Precision (LSA – SS/DP)

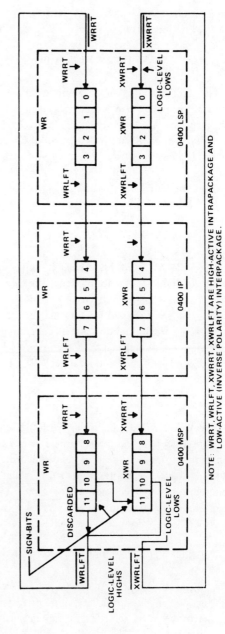

NOTE: WRRT, WRLFT, XWRRT, XWRLFT ARE HIGH-ACTIVE INTRAPACKAGE AND
LOW-ACTIVE (INVERSE POLARITY) INTERPACKAGE.

Figure 3.22. Left-Shift Arithmetic – Double-Sign/Double-Precision (LSA – DS/DP)

E-113

e.   SINGLE-SIGNED DOUBLE-PRECISION LSA (MSP POS0 H)

The single-signed WR, XWR double-precision arithmetic left-shift operation, shown in Figure 3.21, is functionally identical to the WR, XWR double-precision logical left-shift operation of Figure 3.18. The WR's MSB of the MSP, although designated as a sign-bit, is discarded as the entire contents of the double-length WR, XWR register are displaced one bit position to the left. As each WR, XWR LSA operation is performed, the BMSB output may be monitored to detect a WR sign-bit change. Any polarity change at the BMSB output will be indicative that the previous WR, XWR LSA operation produced a WR sign-bit change.

f.   DOUBLE-SIGNED DOUBLE-PRECISION LSA (MSP POS0 = L)

The double-signed WR, XWR double-precision arithmetic left-shift operation shown in Figure 3.22 is, with one exception, functionally identical to the WR, XWR double-precision left-shift operation of Figure 3.18. The exception is, the XWR's sign-bit is automatically forced to the polarity of the MSP WR's displaced MSB minus 1. As each double-signed double-precision LSA operation is performed, the WR's sign-bit is discarded. Consequently, either the XWR MSB or BMSB output may be monitored to detect a sign-bit change. Any polarity change at either of these outputs will be indicative that the *previous* WR, XWR LSA operation produced a sign-bit change in both the WR and XWR.

(WR plus ALUCIN, XWR) RCIR → WR, XWR

The WR, XWR double-precision right-circulate operation, shown in Figure 3.23, displaces the entire contents of the double-length register, formed by the WR in conjunction with the XWR, one bit position to the right. In an expanded wordlength system, the WR's displaced LSB of the LSP exits the LSP via the bidirectional-shift accommodation $\overline{\text{XWRRT}}$ and enters the XWR's MSB of the MSP via the bidirectional-shift accommodation $\overline{\text{XWRLFT}}$. The XWR's LSB of the LSP exits the LSP via the bidirectional-shift accommodation $\overline{\text{WRRT}}$ and enters the WR's MSB of the MSP via the bidirectional-shift accommodation $\overline{\text{WRLFT}}$.

(WR plus ALUCIN, XWR) LCIR → WR, XWR

The WR, XWR double-precision left-circulate operation, shown in Figure 3.24, displaces the entire contents of the double-length register formed by the WR in conjunction with the XWR one bit position to the left. In an expanded wordlength system, the WR's displaced MSB of the MSP exits the MSP via the bidirectional-shift accommodation $\overline{\text{XWRLFT}}$ and enters the XWR's LSB via the bidirectional-shift accommodation $\overline{\text{XWRRT}}$. The XWR's MSB of the MSP exits the MSP via the bidirectional-shift accommodation $\overline{\text{WRLFT}}$ and enters the WR's LSB of the LSP via the bidirectional-shift accommodation $\overline{\text{WRRT}}$.

g.   COMPOUND-FUNCTION WR, XWR DOUBLE-PRECISION SHIFTS/CIRCULATES

Compound-function WR, XWR double-precision shift/circulate operations extend the processing power of the basic double-precision RSA and LCIR operations (Figures 3.19, 3.20, and 3.24) to boost systems-level efficiency in the assembly of iterative macroinstruction such as

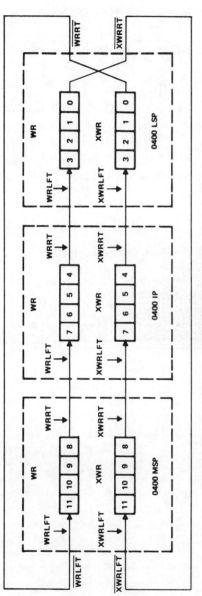

Figure 3.23. Right-Circulate – Double-Precision (RCIR – DP)

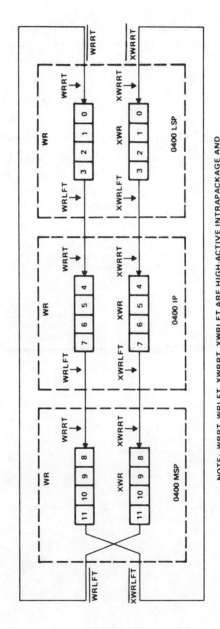

Figure 3.24. Left-Circulate – Double-Precision (LCIR – DP)

multiply and nonrestoring divide. These compound-function shift/circulate operations, directed by the OR with expanded word length "end" conditions handled by the relative position controls, may best be represented by the generalized symbol:

$$\text{(WR plus/MINUS A plus ALUCIN, XWR) RCA/LCIR} \rightarrow \text{WR, XWR}$$

Where A is either DIB or RF(n).

Within a single cycle, each of eight possible compound-function WR, XWR double-precision shift/circulate operations is capable of:

1) Asynchronously summing/subtracting either the RF(n) or the DIB inputs with/from the WR

2) Asynchronously adding the result to the ALUCIN input

3) Asynchronously double-precision shifting/circulating (RSA/LCIR) the result with WR and XWR considered as one double-length register

4) Synchronously storing the shifted/circulated result into the double-length register formed by the WR in conjunction with the XWR. The eight compound-function WR, XWR double-precision shift/circulate possibilities, with data flow paths for expanded word lengths, are listed in Table 3.19.

Table 3.19. Compound-Function WR, XWR Double-Precision Shifts/Circulates

Shift/Circulate Operation	Shift/Circulate Function	Expanded Word Length Data Flow Paths (Figure No.)	OP Form	OP-Field OP3 → OP0	D-Field D1 → D0	S-Field S2 → S0
(WR minus DIB minus 1 plus ALUCIN, XWR) LCIR → WR, XWR	Left circulate (LCIR)	3.24	IVa	HLLL	HH	LHL
(WR minus RF(n) minus 1 plus ALUCIN, XWR) LCIR → WR, XWR	Left circulate (LCIR)	3.24	IVc	HLLL	HL	LLL → HHH
(WR plus DIB plus ALUCIN, XWR) LCIR → WR, XWR	Left circulate (LCIR)	3.24	IVb	HLLH	HH	LHL
(WR plus RF(n) plus ALUCIN, XWR) LCIR → WR, XWR	Left circulate (LCIR)	3.24	IVd	HLLH	HL	LLL → HHH
(WR minus DIB minus 1 plus ALUCIN, XWR) RSA → WR, XWR	Right-shift arithmetic (RSA)	3.21	IVf	LLHL	HH	LHL
(WR minus RF(n) minus 1 plus ALUCIN, XWR) RSA → WR, XWR	Right-shift arithmetic (RSA)	3.21	IVh	LLHL	HL	LLL → HHH
(WR plus DIB plus ALUCIN, XWR) RSA → WR, XWR	Right-shift arithmetic (RSA)	3.21	IVg	HLHH	HH	LHL
(WR plus RF(n) plus ALUCIN, XWR) RSA → WR, XWR	Right-shift arithmetic (RSA)	3.21	IVi	HLHH	HL	LLL → HHH

3. Instructions

Since the standard factory PLA provides the SBP 0400 with 459 unique operations (a nonredundant subset of the 512 available from the 9-bit microinstruction) (Figure 3.25), considerable familiarity with the 0400 unit must exist for programming or a simple organization of the large number of variables must exist. Organization is accomplished by dividing the operations into six operation forms or OP FORMS.

a. OPERATION FORMS

The available transformation logic and the interactivity between the three fields of the microinstruction can best be categorized as follows:

Form	Category of Operation
I	A or B (ALU) C or D → B or C or D or E
II	A or B (plus) B or C or D (plus) ALUCIN → B or C or D or E
III	A or B → B or C or D or E
IV	(WR plus/minus A or B plus ALUCIN) SHIFTED → WR, XWR
V	(WR plus ALUCIN) SHIFTED → WR
VI	(WR plus ALUCIN, XWR) SHIFTED → (WR, XWR)

The 9-bit operation-select word consists of the 4 bit OP, 2-bit D, and 3-bit S-Fields as illustrated:

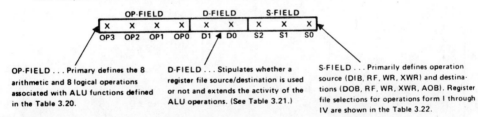

OP-FIELD . . . Primary defines the 8 arithmetic and 8 logical operations associated with ALU functions defined in the Table 3.20.

D-FIELD . . . Stipulates whether a register file source/destination is used or not and extends the activity of the ALU operations. (See Table 3.21.)

S-FIELD . . . Primarily defines operation source (DIB, RF, WR, XWR) and destinations (DOB, RF, WR, XWR, AOB). Register file selections for operations form I through IV are shown in the Table 3.22.

Figure 3.25. Nine-bit Microinstruction (Operation-Select Word)

Note that the letters A, B, C, and D represent operand sources including the data-in bus, the register file, the working register, and the extended working register. Letters B, C, D, or E are used to represent operand destinations including the register file, working register, extended working register, and the data-out bus.

b.   OPERATION FIELD (OP-FIELD)

This 4-bit field programs arithmetic or logical operations, as specified in Table 3.20, for use with combinational sources and the destinations specified under Form I operations below.

Table 3.20. ALU Function-Select Table

ALU OP-Field				Active-High Data	
				ALUCIN = H (With Carry)	ALUCIN = L (No Carry)
OP3	OP2	OP1	OP0		
Arithmetic					
L	L	L	L	$Fn = L$	$Fn = H$
L	L	L	H	$Fn = B$ minus A	$Fn = B$ minus A minus 1
L	L	H	L	$Fn = A$ minus B	$Fn = A$ minus B minus 1
L	L	H	H	$Fn = A$ plus B plus 1	$Fn = A$ plus B
L	H	L	L	$Fn = B$ plus 1	$Fn = B$
L	H	L	H	$Fn = \bar{B}$ plus 1	$Fn = \bar{B}$
L	H	H	L	$Fn = A$ plus 1	$Fn = A$
L	H	H	H	$Fn = \bar{A}$ plus 1	$Fn = \bar{A}$
Logic					
H	L	L	L	$Fn = AnBn$	
H	L	L	H	$Fn = An \oplus Bn$	
H	L	H	L	$Fn = \overline{An \oplus Bn}$	
H	L	H	H	$Fn = \bar{A}nBn$	
H	H	L	L	$Fn = An\bar{B}n$	
H	H	L	H	$Fn = An + \bar{B}n$	
H	H	H	L	$Fn = \bar{A}n + Bn$	
H	H	H	H	$Fn = An + Bn$	

In operation Forms II through VI, this field has fixed values which can be used with a D- and S-Field combination for access to the remaining arithmetic, transfer, and shift operations.

Logic/Arithmetic Form I ALU Operations

The complete versatility of the ALU, including all arithmetic and/or logic functions, can be utilized in Form I operations. Specifically, all Form I operations identify two sources operated on by the ALU, with a single destination. The combinatorial arithmetic functions readily available are:

$$A \text{ plus } B \rightarrow C$$
$$A \text{ minus } B \rightarrow C$$
$$B \text{ minus } A \rightarrow C$$
$$A \text{ plus } B \text{ plus } 1 \rightarrow C$$
$$A \text{ minus } B \text{ minus } 1 \rightarrow C$$
$$B \text{ minus } A \text{ minus } 1 \rightarrow C$$

Included in the dual-source (A, B,) ALU operations are eight combinatorial logic and transfer functions providing:

$A \cdot B \rightarrow C$	$\overline{A} \cdot B \rightarrow C$	$\overline{A} + B \rightarrow C$	$A \oplus B \rightarrow C$
$A + B \rightarrow C$	$A \cdot \overline{B} \rightarrow C$	$A + \overline{B} \rightarrow C$	$\overline{A \oplus B} \rightarrow C$

Four transfer functions offer the capability of routing a single source in its true or complement value to any of four destinations. Arithmetic incrementation and routing of single operands can also be accomplished. The transfer and increment functions provide:

Transfers	Increments
$A \rightarrow C$	$A + 1 \rightarrow C$
$\overline{A} \rightarrow C$	$\overline{A} + 1 \rightarrow C$
$B \rightarrow C$	$B + 1 \rightarrow C$
$\overline{B} \rightarrow C$	$\overline{B} + 1 \rightarrow C$

Direct transfer of the 2's complement of any of the four sources can be accomplished with $\overline{A} + 1 \rightarrow C$ or $\overline{B} + 1 \rightarrow C$.

Two remaining ALU functions can be used to clear (all zero) or preset (all high) any of the four destinations:

Clears	Presets
$0 \rightarrow RF$	$1 \rightarrow RF$
$0 \rightarrow WR$	$1 \rightarrow WR$
$0 \rightarrow XWR$	$1 \rightarrow XWR$
$0 \rightarrow DOB$	$1 \rightarrow DOB$

c. SINGLE-LENGTH ADDITION – FORM II ALU OPERATIONS

The computational capabilities of the ALU are utilized in this operation form to accomplish the addition of two data sources with the result placed in a specified destination. A summary of the basic operations indicates:

$$\text{RF plus} \begin{bmatrix} (\text{WR}) \\ (\text{DIB}) \\ (\text{XWR}) \end{bmatrix} \text{plus ALUCIN} \rightarrow \text{XWR}$$

$$\text{RF plus} \begin{bmatrix} (\text{DIB}) \\ (\text{XWR}) \end{bmatrix} \text{plus ALUCIN} \rightarrow \text{WR}$$

$$\text{RF plus DIB plus ALUCIN} \rightarrow \text{XWR}$$

$$\text{DIB plus} \begin{bmatrix} (\text{WR}) \\ (\text{XWR}) \end{bmatrix} \text{plus ALUCIN} \rightarrow \text{XWR}$$

$$\text{DIB plus XWR plus ALUCIN} \rightarrow \text{WR}$$

$$\text{DIB plus WR plus ALUCIN} \rightarrow \text{DOB}$$

Two additional forms permit the transfer of the XWR to either a RF or the DOB with or without incrementation by the presence or absence of a carry-input signal. Note that the ALU carry-input is active for all Form II operations.

d. TRANSFER – FORM III OPERATIONS

The ALU, including the carry-input, is not involved in the Form III transfer functions. (See operation Form III, Table 3.25.)

e. ADD SUBTRACT WITH DOUBLE-PRECISION SHIFT/CIRCULATE – FORM IV ALU OPERATIONS

This operation form utilizes the full arithmetic capability of the ALU to accomplish additions or subtractions with an active carry in conjunction with a double-precision arithmetic right shift or left circulate. The working register is one operand source and the double precision results are routed to the WR, XWR. The source for the other operand is primarily the data-in bus or a register file.

f. SHIFTS/CIRCULATES WITH ACTIVE CARRY – FORM V AND VI ALU OPERATIONS

Form V and VI operations consist basically of implementing single-precision (Form V) or double-precision (Form VI) shifts or logical circulates in which the working register is the source and WR or WR, XWR is the respective Form V or Form VI destination. The ALU carry-input is active and its external control can be utilized to accomplish shifts and circulates with or without incrementation.

g.   D-FIELD

This 2-bit field defines, in three of four possibilities, those operations which use a particular register file as a source or destination. The fourth possibility (HH) indicates that a register file is not involved, in which case the S-Field value completes the definition for the operation form. The S-Field value of LHL programs an operation in Forms II, III, or IV; and when HLH, a working register shift is programmed in operation Forms V or VI. S-Field values other than LHL or HLH can be used to supplement the source/destination capabilities of the ALU operations provided in Form I.

Table 3.21.   D-Field Register-File Select

D1	D0	S-Field Programming
L	L	Specify RF (LLL → HHH)
L	H	Specify RF (LLL → HHH)
H	L	Specify RF (LLL → HHH)
H	H	See tables for Form I → VI

h.   S-FIELD (REGISTER FILE SELECT FIELD)

This 3-bit field is used primarily to identify the specific register file to be used as a source and/or destination in operation Forms I through IV. Register file selection is shown in Table 3.22. All eight of these registers can be used as general-purpose storage locations. The register selected by an instruction of HHH (RF7) in the S-Field includes the necessary internal logic and external control lines for use as a program counter. This register can be enabled or disabled for counting as follows:

$\overline{\text{PCCIN}}$ = H disables counter

$\overline{\text{PCCIN}}$ = L enables counter

Table 3.22.   Register-File Selection Table

S-Field			Register
S2	S1	S0	Select
L	L	L	RF0
L	L	H	RF1
L	H	L	RF2
L	H	H	RF3
H	L	L	RF4
H	L	H	RF5
H	H	L	RF6
H	H	H	PC

The enabled counter can be incremented by one or two in a single clock pulse as follows:

ENCBY2 = L increments by 1

ENCBY2 = H increments by 2

i.   OPERATION FORM I

Operation Form I (Table 3.23) can be utilized to perform one of 16 ALU functions, selected by the Operation-Select Word (microinstruction) OP-Field, on two of four operand sources, (RF, WR, XWR, DIB). The result is transferred to one of four operand destinations (RF, WR, XWR, DOB).

Table 3.23. Operation Form I

Function	OP3 → OP0	D1	D0	S2	S1	S0
a. RF ALU WR → RF	ALU: LLLL → HHHH	L	L	RF: LLL → HHH		
b. RF ALU WR → WR	ALU: LLLL → HHHH	L	H	RF: LLL → HHH		
c. *DIB ALU WR → DOB	ALU: LLLL → HHHH	H	H	L	L	L
d. *DIB ALU WR → WR	ALU: LLLL → HHHH	H	H	L	L	H
e. DIB ALU XWR → WR	ALU: LLLL → HHHH	H	H	L	H	H
f. DIB ALU WR → XWR	ALU: LLLL → HHHH	H	H	H	L	L
g. DIB ALU XWR → XWR	ALU: LLLL → HHHH	H	H	H	H	L
h. DIB ALU XWR → DOB	ALU: LLLL → HHHH	H	H	H	H	H

Note: When PC PRIORITY is low WR → AOB

*XWR → AOB

j.   OPERATION FORM II

Operation Form II (Table 3.24) can be utilized to arithmetically sum one or two operand sources (RF, WR, XWR, DIB) and a ripple-carry-in (ALUCIN). The result is transferred to one of four operand destinations (RF, WR, XWR, DOB).

k.   OPERATION FORM III

Operation Form III (Table 3.25) can be utilized to transfer one or two operand sources (RF, DIB) to one of four operand destinations (RF, WR, XWR, DOB).

Table 3.24. Operation Form II

Function	OP3 → OP0				D1	D0	S2	S1	S0
a. RF plus WR plus ALUCIN → XWR	L	L	H	H	H	L	RF: LLL → HHH		
b. RF plus DIB plus ALUCIN → WR	L	H	L	L	H	L	RF: LLL → HHH		
c. RF plus DIB plus ALUCIN → XWR	L	H	L	H	H	L	RF: LLL → HHH		
d. RF plus DIB plus ALUCIN → RF	L	H	H	H	H	L	RF: LLL → HHH		
e. RF plus XWR plus ALUCIN → WR	H	H	L	L	H	L	RF: LLL → HHH		
f. RF plus XWR plus ALUCIN → XWR	H	H	L	H	H	L	RF: LLL → HHH		
g. XWR plus ALUCIN → RF	H	H	H	L	H	L	RF: LLL → HHH		
h. DIB plus WR plus ALUCIN → XWR	L	L	H	H	H	H	L	H	L
i. DIB plus WR plus ALUCIN → DOB	L	H	H	H	H	H	L	H	L
j. DIB plus XWR plus ALUCIN → WR	H	H	L	L	H	H	L	H	L
k. DIB plus XWR plus ALUCIN → XWR	H	H	L	H	H	H	L	H	L
l. XWR plus ALUCIN → DOB	H	H	H	L	H	H	L	H	L

Table 3.25. Operation Form III

Function	OP3 → OP0				D1	D0	S2	S1	S0
a. DIB → RF	H	H	H	H	H	L	RF: LLL → HHH		
b. RF → DOB	L	L	L	L	H	L	RF: LLL → HHH		
c. RF → XWR	L	L	L	H	H	L	RF: LLL → HHH		
d. DIB → WR	L	H	H	L	H	L	X	X	X
	L	H	H	L	H	H	L	H	L
e. DIB → XWR	L	L	L	H	H	H	L	H	L
f. DIB → DOB	H	H	H	H	H	H	L	H	L
	L	L	L	L	H	H	L	H	L

1. OPERATION FORM IV

Operation Form IV (Table 3.26) can be utilized to either:

- Arithmetically sum the WR and the ripple carry-in (ALUCIN) with one of two operand sources (RF, DIB), arithmetically double-precision shift the result to the right, and transfer the shifted result to the WR and XWR

- Arithmetically sum the WR and the ripple carry-in (ALUCIN) with one of two operand sources (RF, DIB), double-precision circulate the result to the left, and transfer the circulated result to the WR and XWR

- Arithmetically subtract one of two operand sources (RF, DIB) and minus 1 from the WR, arithmetically add the ripple carry-in (ALUCIN), double-precision circulate the result to the left, and transfer the circulated result to the WR and XWR.

Table 3.26. Operation Form IV

Function	OP3 → OP0				D1	D0	S2	S1	S0
a. (WR minus DIB minus 1 plus ALUCIN) LCIR → WR, XWR	H	L	L	L	H	H	L	H	L
b. (WR plus DIB plus ALUCIN) LCIR → WR, XWR	H	L	L	H	H	H	L	H	L
c. (WR minus RF minus 1 plus ALUCIN) LCIR → WR, XWR	H	L	L	L	H	L	RF: LLL → HHH		
d. (WR plus RF plus ALUCIN) LCIR → WR, XWR	H	L	L	H	H	L	RF: LLL → HHH		
e. (WR plus ALUCIN) RSA → WR, XWR	H	L	H	L	H	L	X	X	X
	H	L	H	L	H	H	L	H	L
f. (WR minus DIB minus 1 plus ALUCIN) RSA → WR, XWR	L	L	H	L	H	H	L	H	L
g. (WR plus DIB plus ALUCIN) RSA → WR, XWR	H	L	H	H	H	H	L	H	L
h. (WR minus RF minus 1 plus ALUCIN) RSA → WR, XWR	L	L	H	L	H	L	RF: LLL → HHH		
i. (WR plus RF plus ALUCIN) RSA → WR, XWR	H	L	H	H	H	L	RF: LLL → HHH		

m.   OPERATION FORM V

Operation Form V (Table 3.27) can be utilized to perform single-precision shifts on the contents of the WR, placing the result in the WR. The WR may be logically shifted left or right (LSL, RSL), arithmetically shifted left or right (LSA, RSA), or circulated left or right (LCIR, RCIR). In operation Form V shifts, the MSB of the ALU is utilized as the sign-bit.

Table 3.27. Operation Form V

Function	OP3 → OP0				D1	D0	S2	S1	S0
a. (WR plus ALUCIN) RSA → WR	L	L	L	L	H	H	H	L	H
b. (WR plus ALUCIN) RCIR → WR	L	L	L	H	H	H	H	L	H
	H	L	L	H	H	H	H	L	H
c. (WR plus ALUCIN) LSA → WR	L	L	H	L	H	H	H	L	H
d. (WR plus ALUCIN) LCIR → WR	L	L	H	H	H	H	H	L	H
	H	L	H	H	H	H	H	L	H
e. (WR plus ALUCIN) RSL → WR	H	L	L	L	H	H	H	L	H
f. (WR plus ALUCIN) LSL → WR	H	L	H	L	H	H	H	L	H

As the WR is passed through the ALU during Forms V and VI, the ALUCIN is active and should be held at a low-logic level for true shifts.

n.   OPERATION FORM VI

Operation Form VI (Table 3.28) can be utilized to perform double-precision shifts on the contents of WR in conjunction with XWR. The WR in conjunction with the XWR may be:

Table 3.28. Operation Form VI

Function	OP3 → OP0				D1	D0	S2	S1	S0
a. (WR plus ALUCIN, XWR) RSA → (WR, XWR)	L	H	L	L	H	H	H	L	H
b. (WR plus ALUCIN, XWR) RCIR → (WR, XWR)	L	H	L	H	H	H	H	L	H
	H	H	L	H	H	H	H	L	H
c. (WR plus ALUCIN, XWR) LSA → (WR, XWR)	L	H	H	L	H	H	H	L	H
d. (WR plus ALUCIN, XWR) LCIR → (WR, XWR)	L	H	H	H	H	H	H	L	H
	H	H	H	H	H	H	H	L	H
e. (WR plus ALUCIN, XWR) RSL → (WR, XWR)	H	H	L	L	H	H	H	L	H
f. (WR plus ALUCIN, XWR) LSL → (WR, XWR)	H	H	H	L	H	H	H	L	H

- Logically shifted left or right (LSL, RSL)
- Arithmetically shifted left or right (LSA, RSA) single- or double-signed
- Circulated left or right (LCIR, RCIR).

In Operation Form VI arithmetic shifts, the MSB of the ALU is utilized as the sign-bit. For single-signed arithmetic shifts, the MSB of the ALU is placed in the MSB of the WR. For double-signed arithmetic shifts, the MSB of the ALU is placed in the MSBs of both the WR and XWR.

Alphabetical listings of all source operands are provided in Tables 3.29, 3.30, 3.31, and 3.32.

Table 3.29. Data-In Bus Source Operands

Operation	OP Form	OP3 → OP0 OP-Field	D1 D0 D-Field	S2 → S0 S-Field
DIB → DOB	IIIf	HHHH	HH	LHL
DIB → DOB	IIIf	LLLL	HH	LHL
DIB → RF	IIIa	HHHH	HL	LLL → HHH
DIB → WR	IIId	LHHL	HL	XXX
DIB → WR	IIId	LHHL	HH	LHL
DIB → XWR	IIIe	LLLH	HH	LHL
*DIB ALU WR → DOB	Ic	LLLL → HHHH	HH	LLL
*DIB ALU WR → WR	Id	LLLL → HHHH	HH	LLH
DIB ALU WR → XWR	If	LLLL → HHHH	HH	HLL
DIB ALU XWR → DOB	Ih	LLLL → HHHH	HH	HHH
DIB ALU XWR → WR	Ie	LLLL → HHHH	HH	LHH
DIB ALU XWR → XWR	Ig	LLLL → HHHH	HH	HHL
(DIB plus WR plus ALUCIN) LCIR → WR, XWR	IVb	HLLH	HH	LHL
(DIB plus WR plus ALUCIN) RSA → WR, XWR	IVq	HLHH	HH	LHL
DIB plus RF plus ALUCIN → RF	IId	LHHH	HL	LLL → HHH
DIB plus RF plus ALUCIN → WR	IIb	LHLL	HL	LLL → HHH
DIB plus RF plus ALUCIN → XWR	IIc	LHLH	HL	LLL → HHH
DIB plus WR plus ALUCIN → DOB	IIi	LHHH	HH	LHL
DIB plus WR plus ALUCIN → XWR	IIh	LLHH	HH	LHL
DIB plus XWR plus ALUCIN → WR	IIj	HHLL	HH	LHL
DIB plus XWR plus ALUCIN → XWR	IIk	HHLH	HH	LHL

*XWR → AOB

Table 3.30. Extended Working Register Source Operands

Operation	OP Form	OP3 → OP0 OP-Field	D1 D0 D-Field	S2 → S0 S-Field
XWR ALU DIB → DOB	Ih	LLLL → HHHH	HH	HHH
XWR ALU DIB → WR	Ie	LLLL → HHHH	HH	LHH
XWR ALU DIB → XWR	Ig	LLLL → HHHH	HH	HHL
XWR plus ALUCIN → DOB	III	HHHL	HH	LHL
XWR plus ALUCIN → RF	IIj	HHHL	HL	LLL → HHH
XWR plus DIB plus ALUCIN → WR	IIk	HHLL	HH	LHL
XWR plus DIB plus ALUCIN → XWR	IIe	HHLH	HH	LHL
XWR plus RF plus ALUCIN → WR	IIf	HHLL	HL	LLL → HHH
XWR plus RF plus ALUCIN → XWR		HHLH	HL	LLL → HHH

Table 3.31. Register File Source Operands

Operation	OP Form	OP3 → OP0 OP-Field	D1 D0 D-Field	S2 → S0 S-Field
RF → DOB	IIIb	LLLL	HL	LLL → HHH
RF → XWR	IIIc	LLLH	HL	LLL → HHH
RF ALU WR → RF	Ia	LLLL → HHHH	LL	LLL → HHH
RF ALU WR → WR	Ib	LLLL → HHHH	LH	LLL → HHH
RF plus DIB plus ALUCIN → RF	IId	LHHH	HL	LLL → HHH
RF plus DIB plus ALUCIN → WR	IIb	LHLL	HL	LLL → HHH
RF plus DIB plus ALUCIN → XWR	IIc	LHLH	HL	LLL → HHH
(RF plus WR plus ALUCIN) LCIR → WR, XWR	IVd	HLLH	HL	LLL → HHH
(RF plus WR plus ALUCIN) RSA → WR, XWR	IVi	HLHH	HL	LLL → HHH
RF plus WR plus ALUCIN → XWR	IIa	LLHH	HL	LLL → HHH
RF plus XWR plus ALUCIN → WR	IIe	HHLL	HL	LLL → HHH
RF plus XWR plus ALUCIN → XWR	IIf	HHLH	HL	LLL → HHH

Table 3.32. Working Register Source Operands

Operation	OP Form	OP3 → OP0 OP-Field	D1 D0 D-Field	S2 → S0 S-Field
*WR ALU DIB → DOB	Ic	LLLL → HHHH	HH	LLL
*WR ALU DIB → WR	Id	LLLL → HHHH	HH	LLH
WR ALU DIB → XWR	If	LLLL → HHHH	HH	HLL
WR ALU RF → RF	Ia	LLLL → HHHH	LL	LLL → HHH
WR ALU RF → WR	Ib	LLLL → HHHH	LH	LLL → HHH
(WR minus DIB minus 1 plus ALUCIN, XWR) LCIR → WR, XWR	IVa	HLLL	HH	LHL
(WR minus DIB minus 1 plus ALUCIN, XWR) RSA → WR, XWR	IVf	LLHL	HH	LHL
(WR minus RF minus 1 plus ALUCIN, XWR) LCIR → WR, XWR	IVc	HLLL	HL	LLL → HHH
(WR minus RF minus 1 plus ALUCIN, XWR) RSA → WR, XWR	IVh	LLHL	HL	LLL → HHH
(WR plus ALUCIN) RSA → WR, XWR	IVe	HLHL	HL	XXX
(WR plus ALUCIN) RSA → WR, XWR	IVe	HLHL	HH	LHL
(WR plus ALUCIN) LCIR → WR	Vd	LLHH	HH	HLH
(WR plus ALUCIN) LCIR → WR	Vd	HLHH	HH	HLH
(WR plus ALUCIN) LSA → WR	Vc	LLHL	HH	HLH
(WR plus ALUCIN) LSL → WR	Vf	HLHL	HH	HLH
(WR plus ALUCIN) RCIR → WR	Vb	LLLH	HH	HLH
(WR plus ALUCIN) RCIR → WR	Vb	HLLH	HH	HLH
(WR plus ALUCIN) RSA → WR	Va	LLLL	HH	HLH
(WR plus ALUCIN) RSL → WR	Ve	HLLL	HH	HLH
(WR plus ALUCIN, XWR) LCIR → (WR, XWR)	VId	HHHH	HH	HLH
(WR plus ALUCIN, XWR) LCIR → (WR, XWR)	VId	LHHH	HH	HLH
(WR plus ALUCIN, XWR) LSA → (WR, XWR)	VIc	LHHL	HH	HLH
(WR plus ALUCIN, XWR) LSL → (WR, XWR)	VIf	HHHL	HH	HLH
(WR plus ALUCIN, XWR) RCIR → (WR, XWR)	VIb	HHLH	HH	HLH
(WR plus ALUCIN, XWR) RCIR → (WR, XWR)	VIb	LHLH	HH	HLH
(WR plus ALUCIN, XWR) RSA → (WR, XWR)	VIa	LHLL	HH	HLH
(WR plus ALUCIN, XWR) RSL → (WR, XWR)	VIe	HHLL	HH	HLH
WR plus DIB plus ALUCIN → DOB	IIi	LHHH	HH	LHL
WR plus DIB plus ALUCIN → XWR	IIh	LLHH	HH	LHL
(WR plus DIB plus ALUCIN) LCIR → WR, XWR	IVb	HLLH	HH	LHL
(WR plus DIB plus ALUCIN) RSA → WR, XWR	IVg	HLHH	HH	LHL
WR plus RF plus ALUCIN → XWR	IIa	LLHH	HL	LLL → HHH
(WR plus RF plus ALUCIN) LCIR → WR, XWR	IVd	HLLH	HL	LLL → HHH
(WR plus RF plus ALUCIN) RSA → WR, XWR	IVi	HLHH	HL	LLL → HHH

*XWR → AOB

MEMORY DEVICES REFERENCE SHEET

RAM

BITS \ WORDS	1	2	4	8
4			74170	
8		74172		
16	7481 7484		54/74S189 54/74S289 7489 10145	
32				TMS4036
64	10140 10148 10142			
128	10147			
256	54/74S201 54/74S301 10144		TMS4039 TMS4042 TMS4043	
512				
1024	54/74S209 TM1103 TMS4033 TMS4034 TMS4035 TMS4062 TMS4063			
2048				
4096	TMS4030 TMS4050 TMS4051 TMS4060			
8192				
16384				

ROM/PROM

BITS \ WORDS	4 R	4 P	8 R	8 P
4				
8				
16				
32			54/7488A	54/74S188 54/74S188A 54/74S288 10139
64				54/74186
128				
256	54/74187	54/74S287 54/74S387	54/74S271 54/74S371	54/74S470 54/74S471
512	54/74S270 54/74S370			
1024			TMS5400	
2048				
4096	TMS4800		TMS4800	
8192				
16384				

GLOSSARY

absolute address

    1.   An address that is permanently assigned by the machine designer to a storage location.

    2.   A pattern of characters that identifies a unique storage location without further modification.

    3.   Synonymous with machine address, specific address.

access time

The time interval between the request for information and the instant this information is available.

accumulator

A device which stores a number and which, on receipt of another number, adds the two and stores the sum.

accuracy

The degree of freedom from error, that is, the degree of conformity to truth or to a rule. Accuracy is contrasted with precision. For example, four-place numerals are less precise than six-place numerals, nevertheless a properly computed four-place numeral might be more accurate than an improperly computed six-place numeral.

ACK

The acknowledge character.

adder

Switching circuit that combines binary bits to generate the Sum and Carry of these bits.

address

An expression, usually numerical, which designates a specific location in a storage or memory device.

address format

    1.   The arrangement of the address parts of an instruction. The expression "plus-one" is frequently used to indicate that one of the addresses specifies the location of the next instruction to be executed, such as one-plus-one, three-plus-one, the next instruction to be executed, such as one-plus-one, two-plus-one, three-plus-one, four-plus-one.

    2.   The arrangement of the parts of a single address, such as those required for identifying channel, module, track, etc., in a disc system.

address register

A register in which an address is stored.

AI

    Address in.

ALGOL

    ALGOrithmic Language. A language primarily used to express computer programs by algorithms.

algorithm

    A term used by mathematicians to describe a set of procedures by which a given result is obtained.

alphanumeric

    Pertaining to a character set that contains letters, digits, and usually other characters such as punctuation marks. Synonymous with alphanumeric.

ALU

    Arithmetic Logic Unit, a computational subsystem which performs the mathematical operations of a digital system.

ALUCIN

    High-active arithmetic logic unit ripple carry-in.

ALUCOUT

    High-active arithmetic logic unit ripple carry-out.

AND

    A logic operator having the property that if P is a statement, Q is a statement, R is a statement . . . . , then the AND of P, Q, R . . . is true if all statements are true, false if any statement is false. P AND Q is often represented by P·Q, PQ, P Q. Synonymous with logical multiply.

AOB

    Address out bus.

arithmetic shift

    1.   A shift that does not affect the sign position.
    2.   A shift that is equivalent to the multiplication of a number by a positive or negative integral power of the radix.

array

    An arrangement of elements in one or more dimensions.

ASCII (American National Standard Code for Information Interchange, 1968)

    The standard code, using a coded character set consisting of 7-bit coded characters (8 bits including parity check), used for information interchange among data processing systems, communication systems, and associated equipment. The ASCII set consists of control characters and graphic characters. Synonymous with USASCII.

assemble

To prepare a machine language program from a symbolic language program by substituting absolute operation codes for symbolic operation codes and absolute or relocatable addresses for symbolic addresses.

assembler

A computer program that assembles.

asynchronous device

A device in which the speed of operation is not related to any frequency in the system to which it is connected.

background processing

The automatic execution of lower priority computer programs when higher priority programs are not using the system resources. Contrast with foreground processing.

base

1.   A reference value.
2.   A number that is multiplied by itself as many times as indicated by an exponent.
3.   Same as radix.
4.   See floating-point base.

base address

A given address from which an absolute address is derived by combination with a relative address.

baud

A unit of signaling speed equal to the number of discrete conditions or signal events per second. For example, one baud equals one-half dot cycle per second in Morse code, one bit per second in a train of binary signals, and one 3-bit value per second in a train of signals each of which can assume one of eight different states.

BCD

Binary-coded decimal notation.

benchmark problem

A problem used to evaluate the performance of hardware or software or both.

binary

1.   Pertaining to a characteristic or property involving a selection, choice, or condition in which there are two possibilities.
2.   Pertaining to the number representation system with a radix of two.

binary coded decimal (BCD)

A binary numbering system for coding decimal numbers in groups of 4 bits. The binary value of these 4-bit groups ranges from 0000 to 1001, and codes the decimal digits "0" through "9". To count to 9 takes 4 bits; to count to 99 takes two groups of 4 bits; to count to 999 takes three groups of 4 bits, etc.

block

1. A set of things, such as words, characters, or digits handled as a unit.
2. A collection of contiguous records recorded as a unit. Blocks are separated by block gaps and each block may contain one or more records.
3. A group of bits, or n-ary digits, transmitted as a unit. An encoding procedure is generally applied to the group of bits or n-ary digits for error-control purposes.
4. A group of contiguous characters recorded as a unit.

block diagram

A diagram of a system, instrument, or computer in which the principal parts are represented by suitable associated geometrical figures to show both the basic functions and the functional relationships among the parts.

block transfer

The process of transmitting one or more blocks of data where the data are organized in such blocks.

bootstrap

A technique or device designed to bring itself into a desired state by means of its own action, e.g., a machine routine whose first few instructions are sufficient to bring the rest of itself into the computer from an input device.

borrow

An arithmetically negative carry.

branch

1. A set of instructions that is executed between two successive decision instructions.
2. To select a branch as in definition 1.
3. A direct path joining two nodes of a network or graph.
4. Loosely, a conditional jump.

branching

A method of selecting, on the basis of results, the next operation to execute while the program is in progress.

breakpoint

A place in a routine specified by an instruction, instruction digit, or other condition, where the routine may be interrupted by external intervention or by a monitor routine.

buffer

An isolating circuit used to avoid reaction of a driven circuit on the corresponding driver circuit. Also, a storage device used to compensate for a difference in the rate of flow of information or the time of occurrence of events when transmitting information from one device to another.

bus

One or more conductors used for transmitting signals or power.

byte

A sequence of adjacent binary digits operated upon as a unit and usually shorter than a computer word.

carriage return

The operation that prepares for the next character to be printed or displayed at the specified first position on the same line.

carriage return character

A format effector that causes the location of the printing or display position to be moved to the first space on the same printing or display line. Contrast with new line character. Abbreviated CR.

carry

1. One or more digits, produced in connection with an arithmetic operation on one digit place of two or more numerals in positional notation, that are forwarded to another digit place for processing there.
2. The number represented by the digit or digits in definition 1 above.
3. Most commonly, a digit as defined in definition 1 above that arises when the sum or product of two or more digits equals or exceeds the radix of the number representation system.
4. Less commonly, a borrow.
5. To forward a carry.
6. The command directing that a carry be forwarded.

carry look-ahead

A type of adder in which the inputs to several stages are examined and the proper carries are produced simultaneously.

cascade connection

Two or more similar component devices arranged in tandem, with the output of one connected to the input of the next.

central processor unit (CPU)

Part of a computer system which contains the main storage, arithmetic unit, and special register groups. It performs arithmetic operations, controls instruction processing, and provides timing signals and other housekeeping operations.

character

A letter, digit, or other symbol that is used as part of the organization, control, or representation of data. A character is often in the form of a spatial arrangement of adjacent or connected strokes.

character check

A check that verifies the observance of rules for the formation of characters.

check bit

A binary check digit, e.g., a parity bit.

check digit

A digit used for purpose of performing a check.

checkpoint

A place in a routine where a check or a recording of data for restart purposes, is performed.

circulating register

A shift register in which data moved out of one end of the register are reentered into the other end as in a closed loop.

clock

1. A device that generates periodic signals used for synchronization.
2. A device that measures and indicates time.
3. A register whose content changes at regular intervals in such a way as to measure time.

COBOL

(COmmon Business Oriented Language) A business data processing language.

code

1. A set of unambiguous rules specifying the way in which data may be represented, e.g., the set of correspondences in the standard code for information interchange. Synonymous with coding scheme.
2. In telecommunications, a system of rules and conventions according to which the signals representing data can be formed, transmitted, received, and processed.
3. In data processing, to represent data or a computer program in a symbolic form that can be accepted by a data processor.

communication control character

A control character intended to control or facilitate transmission of data over communication networks.

communication link

The physical means of connecting one location to another for the purpose of transmitting and receiving data.

compile

To prepare a machine language program from a computer program written in another programming language by making use of the overall logic structure of the program, or generating more than one machine instruction for each symbolic statement, or both, as well as performing the function of an assembler.

compiler

A program that compiles.

complement

A number that can be derived from a specified number by subtracting it from a second specified number. For example, in radix notation, the second specified number may be a given power of the radix or one less than a given power of the radix. The negative of a number is often represented by its complement.

complement notation

A system of notation where positive binary numbers are identical to positive numbers in sign and magnitude notation, but where negative numbers are the exact complement of the magnitude of the corresponding positive value.

computer

A data processor that can perform substantial computation, including numerous arithmetic or logic operations, without intervention by a human operator during the run.

conditional jump

A jump that occurs if specified criteria are met.

control character

A character whose occurrence in a particular context initiates, modifies, or stops a control operation, e.g., a character that controls carriage return, a character that controls transmission of data over communication networks. A control character may be recorded for use in a subsequent action. It may in some circumstances have a graphic representation. Contrast with graphic character.

control hierarchy

Design development used in complex systems to ensure an order of priority to several controls coming from more than one source.

controller

Digital subsystem responsible for implementing "how" a system is to function. Not to be confused with "timing" as timing tells the system "when" to perform its function.

counter

A circuit which counts input pulses and will give an output pulse after receiving a predetermined number of input pulses.

cycle

1.   An interval of space or time in which one set of events or phenomena is completed.
2.   Any set of operations that is repeated regularly in the same sequence. The operations may be subject to variations on each repetition.

data

1.   A representation of facts, concepts, or instructions in a formalized manner suitable for communication, interpretation, or processing by humans or automatic means.
2.   Any representations such as characters or analog quantities to which meaning is or might be assigned.

data bus

One method of input-output for a system where data are moved into or out of the digital system by way of a common bus connected to several subsystems.

data processing

The execution of a systematic sequence of operations performed upon data. Synonymous with information processing.

debug

To detect, locate, and remove mistakes from a routine or malfunctions from a computer. Synonymous with troubleshoot.

decimal

1.   Pertaining to a characteristic or property involving a selection, choice, or condition in which there are ten possibilities.
2.   Pertaining to the number representation system with a radix of ten.

decimal digit

In decimal notation, one of the characters 0 through 9.

decimal point

The radix point in decimal representation.

decoder

A conversion circuit that accepts digital input information − in the memory case, binary address information − that appears as a small number of lines and selects and activates one line of a large number of output lines.

delete character

A character used primarily to obliterate any erroneous or unwanted character. For example, on a punched tape, the delete character consists of perforations in all punching positions. Abbreviated DEL. Synonymous with erase character, rub-out character.

destructive read

A read process that also erases the data from the source.

DIB

Data-in bus.

digit

A symbol that represents one of the non-negative integers smaller than the radix. For example, in decimal notation, a digit is one of the characters from 0 to 9. Synonymous with numeric character.

digital

1. Pertaining to data in the form of digits.
2. Contrast with analog.

direct access

1. Pertaining to the process of obtaining data from, or placing data into, storage where the time required for such access is independent of the location of the data most recently obtained or placed in storage.
2. Pertaining to a storage device in which the access time is effectively independent of the location of the data.
3. Synonymous with random access.

direct addressing

Method of programming that has the address pointing to the location of data or the instruction that is to be used.

direct memory access channel (DMA)

A method of input-output for a system that uses a small processor whose sole task is that of controlling input-output. With DMA, data are moved into or out of the system without program intervention.

DOB

Data-out bus.

double precision

Pertaining to the use of two computer words to represent a number.

DS

Double signed.

dump

1. To copy the contents of all or part of a storage, usually from an internal storage into an external storage.
2. A process as in definition 1 above.
3. The data resulting from the process as in definition 1 above.

duplex

In communications, pertaining to a simultaneous two-way independent transmission in both directions. Contrast with half duplex. Synonymous with full duplex.

edge triggering

Activation of a circuit at the edge of the pulse as it begins its change. Circuits then trigger at the edge of the input pulse rather than sensing a level change.

edit

To modify the form or format of data, e.g., to insert or delete characters such as page numbers or decimal points.

effective address

The address that is derived by applying any specified indexing or indirect addressing rules to the specified address and that is actually used to identify the current operand.

emulate

To imitate one system with another such that the imitating system accepts the same data, executes the same programs, and achieves the same results as the imitated system.

ENCBY2

Enable increment by a displacement of 2.

encode

To apply a set of unambiguous rules specifying the way in which data may be represented such that a subsequent decoding is possible. Synonymous with code.

end-around carry

A carry generated in the most significant digit place and sent directly to the least significant place.

end of text character

A communication control character used to indicate the end of a text. Abbreviated ETX.

end of transmission character

A communication control character used to indicate the conclusion of a transmission which may have included one or more texts and any associated headings. Abbreviated EOT.

ENQ

The enquiry character.

enquiry character

A communication control character intended for use as a request for a response from a remote station. The response may include station identification and, if required, the type of equipment in service and station status. Abbreviated ENQ.

entry point

In a routine, any place to which control can be passed.

EOT

The end of transmission character.

erase

To obliterate information from a storage medium, e.g., to clear, to overwrite.

error

Any discrepancy between a computed, observed, or measured quantity and the true, specified, or theoretically correct value or condition.

ETX

The end of text character.

exclusive-OR function

A modified form of the OR function which has a logic equation equal to the sum output of the half-adder.

execute

That portion of a computer cycle during which a selected control word or instruction is accomplished.

exponent

In a floating-point representation, the numeral, of a pair of numerals representing a number, that indicates the power to which the base is raised.

fetch

That portion of a computer cycle during which the next instruction is retrieved from memory.

field

In a record, a specified area used for a particular category of data, e.g., a group of card columns used to represent a wage rate, a set of bit locations in a computer word used to express the address of the operand.

fixed-point representation

A positional representation in which each number is represented by a single set of digits, the position of the radix point being fixed with respect to one end of the set, according to some convention.

flag

1. Any of various types of indicators used for identification, e.g., a wordmark.
2. A character that signals the occurrence of some condition, such as the end of a word.
3. Synonymous with mark, sentinel, tag.

flip-flop (storage element)

A circuit having two stable states and the capability of changing from one state to another with the application of a control signal and remaining in that state after removal of signals.

flow chart

A graphical representation for the definition, analysis, or solution of a problem, in which symbols are used to represent operations, data, flow, equipment, etc.

format

The arrangement of data.

FORTRAN

(FORmula TRANslating system) A language primarily used to express computer programs by arithmetic formulas.

function

1. A specific purpose of an entity, or its characteristic action.
2. In communications, a machine action such as a carriage return or line feed.

gate

1. A device having one output channel and one or more input channels, such that the output channel state is completely determined by the input channel states, except during switching transients.
2. A combinational logic element having at least one input channel.
3. An AND gate.
4. An OR gate.

general-purpose computer

A computer that is designed to handle a wide variety of problems.

generate

To produce a program by selection of subsets from a set of skeletal coding under the control of parameters.

half duplex

In communications, pertaining to an alternate, one way at a time, independent transmission. Contrast with duplex.

hardware

Physical equipment, as opposed to the computer program or method of use, e.g., mechanical, magnetic, electrical, or electronic devices.

immediate address

Pertaining to an instruction in which an address part contains the value of an operand rather than its address. Synonymous with zero-level address.

indexed address

An address that is modified by the content of an index register prior to or during the execution of a computer instruction.

indexing

In computers, a method of address modification that is implemented by means of index registers.

index register

A register whose content may be added to or subtracted from the operand address prior to or during the execution of a computer instruction. Synonymous with b box.

indirect addressing

Programming method that has the initial address being the storage location of a word that contains another address. This indirect address is then used to obtain the data to be operated upon.

input/output devices (I/O)

Computer hardware by which data is entered into a digital system or by which data are recorded for immediate or future use.

instruction

A statement that specifies an operation and the values or locations of its operands.

instruction counter

A counter that indicates the location of the next computer instruction to be interpreted.

instruction register

A register that stores an instruction for execution.

interface

A shared boundary. An interface might be a hardware component to link two devices or it might be a portion of storage or registers accessed by two or more computer programs.

interrupt

To stop a process in such a way that it can be resumed.

IP

Intermediate package.

jump

A departure from the normal sequence of executing instructions in a computer.

jump conditions

Conditions defined in a transition table that determine the changes of flip-flops from one state to another state.

justify

1. To adjust the printing positions of characters on a page so that the lines have the desired length and that both the left and right-hand margins are regular.
2. By extension, to shift the contents of a register so that the most or the least significant digit is at some specified position in the register. Contrast with normalize.

label

One or more characters used to identify a statement or an item of data in a computer program.

language

A set of representations, conventions, and rules used to convey information.

large scale integration (LSI)

The simultaneous realization of large-area chips and optimum component packing density, resulting in cost reduction by maximizing the number of system connections done at the chip level. Circuit complexity above 100 gates.

LCIR

Left circulate.

level

The degree of subordination in a hierarchy.

line feed character

A format effector that causes the printing or display position to be moved to the next printing or display line. Abbreviated LF.

linkage

In programming, coding that connects two separately coded routines.

load

In programming, to enter data into storage or working registers.

location

Any place in which data may be stored.

logic diagram

A diagram that represents a logic design and sometimes the hardware implementation.

logic shift

A shift that affects all positions.

logic symbol

1. A symbol used to represent a logic element graphically.
2. A symbol used to represent a logic operator.

loop

A sequence of instructions that is executed repeatedly until a terminal condition prevails.

LRC character

The longitudinal redundancy check character.

LSA

Left-shift arithmetic.

LSB

Least significant bit.

LSL

Left-shift logical.

LSP

Least significant package.

machine code

An operation code that a machine is designed to recognize. Usually expressed in ones and zeros.

machine language

A language that is used directly by a machine.

macroinstruction

An instruction in a source language that is equivalent to a specified sequence of machine instructions.

macroprogramming

Programming with macroinstructions.

magnetic disc

A flat circular plate with a magnetic surface on which data can be stored by selective magnetization of portions of the flat surface.

magnetic drum

A right circular cylinder with a magnetic surface on which data can be stored by selective magnetization of portions of the curved surface.

main storage

The general-purpose storage of a computer. Usually, main storage can be accessed directly by the operating registers. Contrast with auxiliary storage.

mask

1.   A pattern of characters that is used to control the retention or elimination of portions of another pattern of characters.
2.   A filter.

microprogramming

Control technique used to implement the stored program control function. Typically the technique is to use a preprogrammed read-only memory chip to contain several control sequences which normally occur together.

mnemonic symbol

A symbol chosen to assist the human memory, e.g., an abbreviation such as "mpy" for "multiply".

modem

(MOdulator – DEModulator) A device that modulates and demodulates signals transmitted over communication facilities.

MSB

Most significant bit.

MSP

Most significant package.

multiplex

To interleave or simultaneously transmit two or more messages on a single channel.

multiprocessing

1. Pertaining to the simultaneous execution of two or more computer programs or sequences of instructions by a computer or computer network.
2. Loosely, parallel processing.

multiprocessor

A computer employing two or more processing units under integrated control.

multiprogramming

Pertaining to the concurrent execution of two or more programs by a computer.

MUX

Multiplexer.

NAK

The Negative AcKnowledge character.

NAND

A logic operator having the property that if P is a statement, Q is a statement, R is a statement, . . . , then the NAND of P, Q, R, . . . is true if at least one statement is false, false if all statements are true. Synonymous with NOT–AND, Sheffer stroke.

negative logic

Logic in which the more-negative voltage represents the "1" state; the less-negative voltage represents the "0" state.

nest

To imbed subroutines or data in other subroutines or data at a different hierarchical level such that the different levels of routines or data can be executed or accessed recursively.

NOR

A logic operator having the property that if P is a statement, Q is a statement, R is a statement, . . . , then the NOR of P, Q, R, . . . is true if all statements are false, false if at least one statement is true. P NOR Q is often represented by a combination of "OR" and "NOT" symbols, such as $\sim$(P Q). P NOR Q is also called "neither P nor Q". Synonymous with NOT—OR.

NOT

A logic operator having the property that if P is a statement, then the NOT of P is true if P is false, false if P is true. The NOT of P is often represented by P, $\sim$P, P, P$'$.

object code

Output from a compiler or assembler which is itself executable machine code or is suitable for processing to produce executable machine code.

object language

The language to which a statement is translated.

operand

That which is operated upon. An operand is usually identified by an address part of an instruction.

operating system

Software which controls the execution of computer programs and which may provide scheduling, debugging, input/output control, accounting, compilation, storage assignment, data management, and related services.

operation

1. A defined action, namely, the act of obtaining a result from one or more operands in accordance with a rule that completely specifies the result for any permissible combination of operands.
2. The set of such acts specified by such a rule, or the rule itself.
3. The act specified by a single computer instruction.
4. A program step undertaken or executed by a computer, e.g., addition, multiplication, extraction, comparison, shift, transfer. The operation is usually specified by the operator part of an instruction.
5. The even or specific action performed by a logic element.

operation code

A code that represents specific operations. Synonymous with instruction code.

OR

Operation register.

pack

To compress data in a storage medium by taking advantage of known characteristics of the data, in such a way that the original data can be recovered, e.g., to compress data in a storage medium by making use of bit or byte locations that would otherwise go unused.

parallel operation

The organization of data manipulating within circuitry wherein all the digits of a word are transmitted simultaneously on separate lines in order to speed up operation.

parity check

A check that tests whether the number of ones (or zeros) in an array of binary digits is odd or even. Synonymous with odd-even check.

PC

Program counter.

$\overline{\text{PCCIN}}$

Low-active program counter carry-in.

$\overline{\text{PCCOUT}}$

Low-active program counter carry-out.

peripheral equipment

Units which work in conjunction with a computer but are not part of it.

PLA (programmable logic array)

An integrated circuit that employs ROM matrices to combine sum and product terms of logic networks.

positional notation

A numeration system in which a number is represented by means of an ordered set of digits, such that the value contributed by each digit depends upon its position as well as upon its value. Synonymous with positional representation.

positive logic

Logic in which the more-positive voltage represents the "1" state; the less-positive voltage represents the "0" state.

POS0

Position pin 0.

POS1

Position pin 1.

priority interrupt

Designation given to method of providing some commands to have precedence over others thus giving one condition of operation priority over another.

problem oriented language

A programming language designed for the convenient expression of a given class of problems.

processor

1. In hardware, a data processor.
2. In software, a computer program that includes the compiling, assembling, translating, and related functions for a specific programming language, COBOL processor, or FORTRAN processor.

program

1. A series of actions proposed in order to achieve a certain result.
2. Loosely, a routine.
3. To design, write, and test a program as in definition 1 above.
4. Loosely, to write a routine.

programmable read only memory (PROM)

A fixed program, read only, semiconductor memory storage element that can be programmed after packaging.

PROM

See programmable read only memory.

propagation delay

The time required for a change in logic level to be transmitted through an element or a chain of elements.

pushdown list

A list that is constructed and maintained so that the item to be retrieved is the most recently stored item in the list, i.e., last in, first out.

pushdown stack

A register which implements a pushdown list.

radix

In positional representation, that integer, if it exists, by which the significance of the digit place must be multiplied to give the significance of the next higher digit place. For example, in decimal notation, the radix of each place is ten; in a biquinary code, the radix of the fives place is two.

RAM

See random access memory.

random access memory (RAM)

A memory from which all information can be obtained at the output with approximately the same time delay by choosing an address randomly and without first searching through a vast amount of irrelevant data.

RCIR

Right circulate.

read only memory(ROM)

A fixed program semiconductor storage element that has been preprogrammed at the factory with a permanent program.

real time

1. Pertaining to the actual time during which a physical process transpires.
2. Pertaining to the performance of a computation during the actual time that the related physical process transpires, in order that results of the computation can be used in guiding the physical process.

refresh

Method which restores charge on capacitance which deteriorates because of leakage.

register

Temporary storage for digital data.

relative address

The number that specifies the difference between the absolute address and the base address.

relocate

In computer programming, to move a routine from one portion of storage to another and to adjust the necessary address references so that the routine, in its new location, can be executed.

RF

Register file.

right-justify

1. To adjust the printing positions of characters on a page so that the right margin of the page is regular.
2. To shift the contents of a register so that the least significant digit is at some specified position of the register. Contrast with normalize.

ROM

See read only memory.

routine

An ordered set of instructions that may have some general or frequent use.

RSA

Right-shift arithmetic.

RSL

Right-shift logical.

sequencing

Control method used to cause a set of steps to occur in a particular order.

sequential logic systems

Digital system utilizing memory elements.

serial

1. Pertaining to the sequential or consecutive occurrence of two or more related activities in a single device or channel.
2. Pertaining to the sequencing of two or more processes.
3. Pertaining to the sequential processing of the individual parts of a whole, such as the bits of a character or the characters of a word, using the same facilities for successive parts.
4. Contrast with parallel.

serial access

1. Pertaining to the sequential or consecutive transmission of data to or from storage.
2. Pertaining to the process of obtaining data from or placing data into storage, where the access time is dependent upon the location of the data most recently obtained or placed in storage. Contrast with direct access.

serial operation

The organization of data manipulation within circuitry wherein the digits of a word are transmitted one at a time along a single line. The serial mode of operation is slower than parallel operation, but utilizes less complex circuitry.

set-up time

The minimum amount of time that data must be present at an input to ensure data acceptance when the device is clocked.

shift

A movement of data to the right or left.

shift register

A register in which the stored data can be moved to the right or left.

sign and magnitude notation

A system of notation where binary numbers are represented by a sign-bit and one or more number bits.

significant digit

A digit that is needed for a certain purpose, particularly one that must be kept to preserve a specific accuracy or precision.

sign position

A position, normally located at one end of a numeral, that contains an indication of the algebraic sign of the number.

simulate

1. To represent certain features of the behavior of a physical or abstract system by the behavior of another system.

2. To represent the functioning of a device, system, or computer program by another, e.g., to represent the functioning of one computer by another, to represent the behavior of a physical system by the execution of a computer program, to represent a biological system by a mathematical model.

simulator

A device, system, or computer program that represents certain features of the behavior of a physical or abstract system.

skip

To ignore one or more instructions in a sequence of instructions.

software

A set of computer programs, procedures, and possibly associated documentation concerned with the operation of a data processing system, e.g., compilers, library routines, manuals, circuit diagrams.

source language

The language from which a statement is translated.

source program

A computer program written in a source language.

state

The condition of an input or output of a circuit as to whether it is a logic "1" or a logic "0". The state of a circuit (gate or flip-flop) refers to its output. A flip-flop is said to be in the "1" state when its Q output is "1". A gate is in the "1" state when its output is "1".

static storage elements

Storage elements which contain storage cells that retain their information as long as power is applied unless the information is altered by external excitation.

stored program

A set of instructions in memory specifying the operation to be performed.

stored program computer

A computer controlled by internally stored instructions that can synthesize, store, and in some cases alter instructions as though they were data and that can subsequently execute these instructions.

subroutine

A routine that can be part of another routine.

system

1. An assembly of methods, procedures, or techniques united by regulated interaction to form an organized whole.
2. An organized collection of men, machines, and methods required to accomplish a set of specific functions.

temporary storage

In programming, storage locations reserved for intermediate results. Synonymous with working storage.

terminal

A point in a system or communication network at which data can either enter or leave.

transfer

1. Same as jump.
2. Same as transmit.

transmit

To send data from one location and to receive the data at another location. Synonymous with transfer definition 2, move.

truth table

A chart that tabulates and summarizes all the combinations of possible states of the inputs and outputs of a circuit. It tabulates what will happen at the output for a given input combination.

TTL

Bipolar semiconductor transistor-transistor coupled logic circuits.

2's complement notation

A system of notation where positive binary numbers are identical to positive numbers in sign and magnitude notation, but where 1 must be added to 1's complement notation to obtain negative numbers.

USASCII

United States of America Standard Code for Information Interchange. The standard code used by the United States for transmission of data. Sometimes simply referred to as the "as'ki" code.

variable

A quantity that can assume any of a given set of values.

volatile storage

A storage device in which stored data are lost when the applied power is removed.

word

A character string or a bit string considered as an entity.

working storage

Same as temporary storage.

WR

Working register.

write

To record data in a storage device or a data medium. The recording need not be permanent, such as the writing on a cathode ray tube display device.

$\overline{\text{WRLFT}}$

Low-active, working register left bidirectional-shift accommodation.

$\overline{\text{WRRT}}$

Low-active, working register right bidirectional-shift accommodation.

$\overline{\text{XWR}}$

Extended working register.

$\overline{\text{XWRLFT}}$

Low-active extended working register left bidirectional-shift accommodation.

$\overline{\text{XWRRT}}$

Low-active extended working register right bidirectional-shift accommodation.